IMMANUEL KANT

Lectures and Drafts on Political Philosophy

The purpose of the Cambridge Edition is to offer translations of the best modern German editions of Kant's work in a uniform format suitable for Kant scholars. The edition includes all of Kant's published works and a generous selection of his unpublished writings, such as the *Opus postumum*, *Handschriftlicher Nachlaß*, lectures, and correspondence.

This book is the first translation into English of the *Reflections* which Kant wrote whilst formulating his ideas in political philosophy: the preparatory drafts for *Theory and Practice*, *Towards Perpetual Peace*, the *Doctrine of Right*, and *Conflict of the Faculties*; and the only surviving student transcription of his course on Natural Right. Through these texts one can trace the development of his political thought, from his first exposure to Rousseau in the mid-1760s through to his last musings in the late 1790s after his final system of right was published. The material covers such topics as the central role of freedom, the social contract, the nature of sovereignty, the means for achieving international peace, property rights in relation to the very possibility of human agency, the general prohibition of rebellion, and Kant's philosophical defense of the French Revolution.

Frederick Rauscher is Professor of Philosophy at Michigan State University. He is the author of *Naturalism and Realism in Kant's Ethics* (2015), co-translator with Curtis Bowman and Paul Guyer of Kant's *Notes and Fragments* edited by Paul Guyer (2005), and editor with Daniel Omar Perez of *Kant in Brazil* (2012).

Kenneth R. Westphal is Professor of Philosophy at the Boğaziçi Üniversitesi, İstanbul. He has published widely on German philosophy, and on Kant's philosophy in particular. His publications include *Kant's Transcendental Proof of Realism* (2004) and *How Hume and Kant Reconstruct Natural Law* (2016).

THE CAMBRIDGE EDITION OF THE WORKS OF IMMANUEL KANT IN TRANSLATION

General editors: Paul Guyer and Allen W. Wood

Advisory board: Henry Allison
Reinhard Brandt
Ralf Meerbote
Charles D. Parsons
Hoke Robinson
J. B. Schneewind

IMMANUEL KANT

Lectures and Drafts on Political Philosophy

EDITED BY

FREDERICK RAUSCHER

TRANSLATED BY

FREDERICK RAUSCHER

AND

KENNETH R. WESTPHAL

CAMBRIDGE
UNIVERSITY PRESS

CAMBRIDGE
UNIVERSITY PRESS

University Printing House, Cambridge CB2 8BS, United Kingdom

Cambridge University Press is part of the University of Cambridge.

It furthers the University's mission by disseminating knowledge in the pursuit of education, learning and research at the highest international levels of excellence.

www.cambridge.org
Information on this title: www.cambridge.org/9780521843089

© Cambridge University Press 2016

First published 2016

Printed in the United Kingdom by Clays, St Ives plc

A catalogue record for this publication is available from the British Library

ISBN 978-0-521-84308-9 Hardback

Contents

General editors' preface

Within a few years of the publication of his *Critique of Pure Reason* in 1781, Immanuel Kant (1724–1804) was recognized by his contemporaries as one of the seminal philosophers of modern times – indeed as one of the great philosophers of all time. This renown soon spread beyond German-speaking lands, and translations of Kant's work into English were published even before 1800. Since then, interpretations of Kant's views have come and gone and loyalty to his positions has waxed and waned, but his importance has not diminished. Generations of scholars have devoted their efforts to producing reliable translations of Kant into English as well as into other languages.

There are four main reasons for the present edition of Kant's writings:

1. *Completeness*. Although most of the works published in Kant's lifetime have been translated before, the most important ones more than once, only fragments of Kant's many important unpublished works have ever been translated. These include the *Opus postumum*, Kant's unfinished *magnum opus* on the transition from philosophy to physics; transcriptions of his classroom lectures; his correspondence; and his marginalia and other notes. One aim of this edition is to make a comprehensive sampling of these materials available in English for the first time.

2. *Availability*. Many English translations of Kant's works, especially those that have not individually played a large role in the subsequent development of philosophy, have long been inaccessible or out of print. Many of them, however, are crucial for the understanding of Kant's philosophical development, and the absence of some from English-language bibliographies may be responsible for erroneous or blinkered traditional interpretations of his doctrines by English-speaking philosophers.

3. *Organization*. Another aim of the present edition is to make all Kant's published work, both major and minor, available in comprehensive volumes organized both chronologically and topically

so as to facilitate the serious study of his philosophy by English-speaking readers.

4. *Consistency of translation.* Although many of Kant's major works have been translated by the most distinguished scholars of their day, some of these translations are now dated, and there is considerable terminological disparity among them. Our aim has been to enlist some of the most accomplished Kant scholars and translators to produce new translations, freeing readers from both the philosophical and literary preconceptions of previous generations and allowing them to approach texts, as far as possible, with the same directness as present-day readers of the German or Latin originals.

In pursuit of these goals, our editors and translators attempt to follow several fundamental principles:

1. As far as seems advisable, the edition employs a single general glossary, especially for Kant's technical terms. Although we have not attempted to restrict the prerogative of editors and translators in choice of terminology, we have maximized consistency by putting a single editor or editorial team in charge of each of the main groupings of Kant's writings, such as his work in practical philosophy, philosophy of religion, or natural science, so that there will be a high degree of terminological consistency, at least in dealing with the same subject matter.

2. Our translators try to avoid sacrificing literalness to readability. We hope to produce translations that approximate the originals in the sense that they leave as much of the interpretive work as possible to the reader.

3. The paragraph, and even more the sentence, is often Kant's unit of argument, and one can easily transform what Kant intends as a continuous argument into a mere series of assertions by breaking up a sentence so as to make it more readable. Therefore, we try to preserve Kant's own divisions of sentences and paragraphs wherever possible.

4. Earlier editions often attempted to improve Kant's texts on the basis of controversial conceptions about their proper interpretation. In our translations, emendation or improvement of the original edition is kept to the minimum necessary to correct obvious typographical errors.

5. Our editors and translators try to minimize interpretation in other ways as well, for example, by rigorously segregating Kant's own footnotes, the editors' purely linguistic notes, and their more explanatory or informational notes; notes in this last category are treated as endnotes rather than footnotes.

We have not attempted to standardize completely the format of individual volumes. Each, however, includes information about the context in which Kant wrote the translated works, a German–English glossary, an English–German glossary, an index, and other aids to comprehension. The general introduction to each volume includes an explanation of specific principles of translation and, where necessary, principles of selection of works included in that volume. The pagination of the standard German edition of Kant's works, *Kants gesammelte Schriften*, edited by the Royal Prussian (later German) Academy of Sciences (Berlin: Georg Reimer, later Walter de Gruyter & Co., 1900–), is indicated throughout by means of marginal numbers.

Our aim is to produce a comprehensive edition of Kant's writings, embodying and displaying the high standards attained by Kant scholarship in the English-speaking world during the second half of the twentieth century, and serving as both an instrument and a stimulus for the further development of Kant studies by English-speaking readers in the century to come. Because of our emphasis on literalness of translation and on information rather than interpretation in editorial practices, we hope our edition will continue to be usable despite the inevitable evolution and occasional revolutions in Kant scholarship.

PAUL GUYER
ALLEN W. WOOD

Acknowledgments

This translation could not have been completed without the generous contributions of many individuals and institutions over more than a decade.

Above all I would like to thank Ken Westphal for his contributions to this volume. He agreed to tackle the thorniest of the texts for this volume, the unpunctuated and sometimes nearly inscrutable preparatory drafts for the *Doctrine of Right*. His informed perspective on terminology shaped the translation choices we made for this volume. His patience and understanding in reviewing my editorial decisions balanced cooperation with firm insistence on principle.

Werner Stark kindly not only provided access to a copy of the hand-written Naturrecht Feyerabend notes at the Marburg Kant Archive but also helped to decipher some of the most difficult passages as we compared that manuscript to the published version in *Kants gesammelte Schriften*. He answered many queries about the process used by Kant from earliest jottings to published work and the status of various other material included here. He provided me workspace and encouragement during a research visit to the Kant Archive. I also have to acknowledge the influence his published assessments of the available editions of Kant have had on my work with these texts.

Steven Naragon answered questions about Kant's lectures in person and through the work he did in creating his comprehensive website *Kant in the Classroom*. Emily Katz, Daniel Sutherland, and Alessandro Pinzani provided help in understanding Kant's references to Aristotle, mathematics, and the French Revolution, respectively. Christian Lotz puzzled over complicated passages with me. Paul Guyer and Allen Wood offered editorial and terminological suggestions that improved the work.

The translation of the Feyerabend lecture on Natural Right in particular resulted from the assistance of many individuals. Jeppe von Platz and Fernando Costa Mattos both saved me from many errors with their thorough review of my drafts. I am very grateful to Lars Vinx for making his own unpublished translation of the Feyerabend lectures available. His renderings of the original are generally more felicitous and less

are subdivided into two halves, with some halves further subdivided into two parts, were published in 1900; the final half of the final volume has yet to appear.[6] The four sections composing the Academy edition are: (1) published works, (2) correspondence, (3) the *Handschriftlicher Nachlaß* or unpublished writings of various kinds left at Kant's death, and (4) course lectures. Translations in this volume are drawn from seven different volumes of the Academy edition (15, 16, 19, 20, 21, 23, and 27) from the last two sections. Of these only Volume 27 consists of course lectures; detailed discussion of the editorial issues of that volume will be given in the editor's introduction to the Feyerabend Natural Right course lecture. The remaining volumes are all part of the third, and unfortunately also most problematic, section.

When this four-part structure was proposed to the Royal Prussian Academy of Sciences in 1895 by Wilhelm Dilthey (1833–1911)[7] for the most extensive collection of Kant's writings up to that time (and since),[8] the third section was assigned to Erich Adickes (1866–1928), a

---

[6] Volume 26.2 consisting of Lectures on Physical Geography is in preparation. Volume 29 is incomplete on paper but not in practice: its two published books are the first part of the first half, consisting of "lesser lectures" on philosophical encyclopedia, mathematics, and physics, plus a fragment of a lecture on ethics, and the second part of the first half, consisting of miscellaneous lectures on metaphysics, logic, and religion discovered after the publication of their corresponding volumes. Their editor Gerhard Lehmann appears to have left room for a second half of Volume 29 for any other lectures that might be found. Detailed information about the content and structure of the Academy edition is available in Steve Naragon, *Kant in the Classroom* (www.manchester.edu/kant/Home/index.htm).

[7] The most detailed history of the origin and production of the Academy edition, focusing on the second and third sections, is in Werner Stark, *Nachforschungen*. Paul Guyer drew mainly on Stark when providing a detailed summary in the Introduction to *Notes and Fragments* in the Cambridge Edition. Information from these sources is the basis of much of the material presented here.

[8] Earlier in the nineteenth century several collections appeared, none of which had the range and depth of the proposed Academy edition. *Immanuel Kant's Werke* edited by Gustav Hartenstein (Leipzig: Modes und Baumann, 1838–39) appeared in ten volumes and arranged Kant's published works by topic; a few decades later an edition entitled *Sämmtliche Werke* also edited by Hartenstein, this time in chronological order, was published in eight volumes (Leipzig: Voss, 1867–68). At the same time as Hartenstein's first collection Friedrich Wilhelm Schubert and Karl Rosenkranz published their own similarly titled *Sämmtliche Werke* in twelve volumes (Leipzig: Voss, 1838–42) which consisted mainly of Kant's published works but added a biography and Rosenkranz's "History of the Kantian Philosophy" as the twelfth volume. An eight-volume edition appearing in 57 parts (!) edited by Julius Hermann von Kirchmann was published in Berlin, Leipzig, and Heidelberg as *Kant: Sämmtliche Werke* over many years as part of the series *Philosophischen Bibliothek* that he began, one that evolved into the most respected series of philosophical texts in Germany and for the past century published by Felix Meiner Verlag. (Some information from Erich Adickes, *German Kantian Bibliography* (Boston: Ginn & Company, 1896), the reprint of Adickes's original bibliography in *Philosophical Review* 2 (1893) number 3 and for the following nine numbers as well.)

very young and detail-oriented Kant scholar, because of his work habits already displayed in, among other things, a 622-page annotated bibliography of primary and secondary works on Kant published in Germany up through the time of Kant's death.[9] "He exhibited the greatest precision in the use of sources, complete acquaintance with the contemporary literature, penetrative acumen" according to Paul Menzer (1873–1960), at the time working under Dilthey, making Adickes the ideal person for the job.[10] Adickes was faced with the task of editing and annotating the collection of Kant's loose sheets and marginal notes that had already been published in separate editions by Rudolf Reicke (1825–1905) and Benno Erdmann (1851–1921)[11] as well as any other material he could collect together.

Adickes dedicated the remaining years of his life to sorting through several different types of material on various loose sheets and books left by Kant. The first type is the notes Kant wrote in the margins and other spaces of his textbooks to use for his course lectures and to work out his ideas on subjects related to those books. Second is the loose sheets of paper (*Löse Blätter*) on which Kant wrote longer arguments and outlines of material. Third is material identifiable as drafts or preparatory work (*Vorarbeiten*) for a published book or essay, a few of which are fragments of surviving copies of the final or near final versions of his books and essays prepared for the printer.[12] A fourth type is complete or nearly complete works that Kant did not publish in his lifetime.[13] Fifth is the

---

[9] Guyer, *Notes*, xix–xx.   [10] Stark, *Nachforschungen*, p. 80.

[11] Rudolf Reicke, *Lose Blätter aus Kants Nachlaß*, 3 vols. (Königsberg: F. Beyer, 1889, 1895, and 1898) and Benno Erdmann, *Reflexionen Kants zur kritischen Philosophie*, 2 vols. (Leipzig: Fues's Verlag, 1882 and 1884). Reicke's material was, as the title suggests, material Kant had written on loose sheets of paper. Erdmann included material Kant had written in his copy of Alexander Baumgarten's *Metaphysica*, which Kant used for his lectures on metaphysics and for part of his lectures on anthropology concerning empirical psychology, and in the margins of his copy of his own *Observations on the Feeling of the Beautiful and the Sublime*.

[12] This volume includes all of the first three types; two other volumes in the Cambridge Edition include some of this material as well. The material in *Notes and Fragments* in the Cambridge Edition includes generous selections from the Academy edition volumes of Reflections on Anthropology, Logic, Metaphysics, and Ethics (Academy edition volumes 15–19). The *Opus Postumum* volume in the Cambridge Edition includes selections of the material on loose sheets identified as preparatory work for a book on the transition from metaphysical philosophy of nature to empirical physics, a project which as it evolved came to center on the very nature of transcendental philosophy itself (Academy edition volumes 21–22).

[13] The three are the "First Introduction" to the *Critique of the Power of Judgment*, included in the Cambridge Edition of the third *Critique*, his essay for the prize competition on progress in metaphysics, and an essay in response to Eberhard's objections, both included in *Theoretical Philosophy after 1781* in the Cambridge Edition.

notes Kant wrote in the margins of two of his personal copies of his own works.[14]

Adickes decided to arrange the material into two distinct, though unlabeled and unnumbered, parts. He planned to include both marginal notes in Kant's textbooks and loose sheets that he saw as either preparatory for Kant's lectures or as notes not directly related to any published work in six volumes arranged by topic in accordance with Kant's various courses: 14: Mathematics, Physics and Chemistry, and Physical Geography; 15: Anthropology; 16: Logic; 17 & 18: Metaphysics; and 19: Ethics, Political Philosophy, and Philosophy of Religion. These fragments he numbered continuously from number one in Volume 14 – a small sketch of relations among angles in a figure (14:3) – to number 8112 in Volume 19 – Kant's few marginal notations in his own copy of the Bible (19:651–54); these numbers are used today with the prefix "R" for "reflection" universally by Kant scholars. The second part would be drafts for books and essays, to be arranged chronologically rather than by topic, and some material of publishable quality that Kant, for various reasons, did not publish during his lifetime, arranged in a separate chronological order (14:xxvi–xxviii). Adickes did not assign any numbering or other identification system to this material. No space was set aside for the notes and drafts for Kant's incomplete project known as the *Opus postumum* because at the time it appeared that the right to publish it would not be given by its owners.[15]

This division rested on an assumption that even Adickes himself acknowledged as questionable, namely that there was a sure way to identify which notes were written as drafts for particular books or essays and which were not. In many cases it is not clear whether Kant had in mind a particular completed work when he wrote the material on the *Löse Blätter*. Even material in Kant's textbook margins could be related to the drafts. For example R8055 bears a striking resemblance to an argument in the *Doctrine of Right*; did Kant write that reflection in anticipation of

---

[14] The few short marginal notes to Kant's copy of the first "A" edition of the *Critique of Pure Reason* are included in annotations to that volume in the Cambridge Edition. The lengthier remarks written in *Observations on the Feeling of the Beautiful and the Sublime* are included in full in Kant, *Observations on the Feeling of the Beautiful and the Sublime and Other Writings*, ed. Patrick Frierson and Paul Guyer (Cambridge University Press, 2011) and in part in *Notes and Fragments* in the Cambridge Edition.

[15] Guyer, *Notes*, xx. Eventually the *Opus Postumum* rights were obtained and the material published as Volumes 21 and 22 of the Academy edition, before the publication of Adickes's originally planned Volumes 20 and 21, forcing the renumbering of the originally-planned volumes of preparatory notes and supplements to 20 and 23. Gerhard Lehmann, final editor of all four volumes, considered all of them to fall under the "Preparatory Drafts and Supplements" label (23:v), although that name appears only on the title page of volume 23. The title page of volumes 21 and 22 has "Opus Postumum" and the title page of Volume 20 has no title.

the book, or did he happen to find and use an old marginal note when writing the book? In addition the majority of the notes on metaphysics contained in Volumes 17 and 18 of the Academy edition are seen now as preparatory work for the two editions of the *Critique of Pure Reason*, and were likely seen as such by Kant as well, although many are written in Kant's textbook for his course on metaphysics and some bear only a tangential relation to the actual language and specific arguments used in the published *Critique*.

Adickes listed several criteria for labeling a given manuscript as a draft rather than a reflection (14:xxvi–xxvii):

1. The relation to a projected or an actually published work is "fairly certain."
2. If part of a sheet was identified as a draft, then all the material on that sheet related to the topic of that work would be included even if other particular portions were not themselves clearly drafts for that work.
3. If the material could be a draft for any of several different works, it would be included among the Reflections, not the drafts, but would be noted as such.
4. The one exception to the above rules was the material clearly intended for the *Critique of Pure Reason*, which would be included in the earlier volumes as Reflections rather than the later volumes as drafts. Adickes made two exceptions to this exception (!) and included two loose sheets as drafts for the *Critique* in Volume 23 (23:17–20) because he thought that they related to the final form of the *Critique*.

Adickes specifically notes that he would include the loose sheets on ethics and political philosophy among the drafts only if "no doubt" remained that they were related to published works, in particular the *Metaphysics of Morals*. Adickes's susceptibility to doubt has since been questioned in several cases, e.g. R8077, whose content Adickes notes in his annotation "recalls" the second part of *Conflict of the Faculties* (19:603), has been clearly identified as a draft and is included among the drafts for that work in this volume. The distinction between mere reflection and draft, then, is not hard and fast. In this volume of translations I follow the identification of drafts by Werner Stark of the Kant Archive in Marburg. Everything that Adickes identified as a draft remains in that category, but a few Reflections are also included among the translated drafts.

Adickes also faced the task of discerning which of the mass of lines on a book page or loose sheet belonged together as distinct Reflections. Some of this work had been done by Erdmann in his earlier collection of Reflections taken from Kant's textbooks, but Reicke had published the loose sheets in his collection in the order they were found regardless of topic. The divisions between Reflections were based on factors such as placement on a page, the different sizes of Kant's handwriting, different tints of the inks used, and the like. Of course more substantive clues such as the topic could play a part in distinguishing Reflections as well, but this method played a larger role in the assessment of the contents of the loose sheets. Loose sheets were often folded in half before use, making for four pages of material. Sometimes the loose sheets were devoted to a single topic or the writing flowed as a single sustained treatment of a series of related topics, in which case their contents could be reprinted as a whole either as one Reflection or, if a draft, simply as a unit. In other cases material covering many different topics appeared on the same sheet. Adickes then divided the loose sheet's contents into several parts and placed these among the appropriate sets of Reflections or drafts. He planned to devote the last half of the last volume to a comprehensive explanation of the origin of each Reflection on the various textbook pages and loose sheets, explaining their relation on the page and the justification of their specific place in the Academy edition, both topically and chronologically (14:xliv).

As mentioned, the drafts were to be arranged chronologically in accordance with their corresponding book or essay. The draft material is relatively easy to date as within a few years of the publication of its corresponding work, some work was apparently done to distinguish earlier from later drafts within these narrow time periods. For the volumes of Reflections, while their large-scale arrangement is by lecture topic for Kant's courses, Adickes wanted to arrange the material chronologically as well. He would place reflections from the same time period into chapters, and within each chapter arrange the notes in accordance with the table of contents of Kant's various textbooks (when possible). Identifying the date for particular note was difficult. Adickes decided to use some obvious means to provide an absolute date for a few: for example, notes on the back of a letter or that mention a specific event could not possibly pre-date that letter or event. He could assign a relative date using visual clues such as the placement of one note in a more distant marginal spot on a textbook page rather than immediately adjacent to the relevant text, as an obviously earlier note is. But these did not satisfy Adickes. For even more precision, he turned to the tint of the ink Kant used in scratching out the notes, sometimes "black," sometimes "red-brown," sometimes "black-brown to black" (14:xxxvii). This method also helped to distinguish one reflection from another. In the end Adickes used a combination of all these clues to identify thirty-three different periods, which he called "strata" in geological fashion, some overlapping others, some quite narrow and specific and others lengthier or approximate. He was able to assign Kant's notes in some cases to particular strata; in many cases he suggests that a note might be from any of several periods. When he identified more than one period he generally considered some more likely than others and marked the notes accordingly; he then placed the Reflection in the chapter for the most likely period. More specifics about how these notes are presented are given in the editor's introduction to the Reflections. Adickes's achievement in bringing such a detailed chronological and topic order out of the bundles of loose sheets and marginal notations ranks as the greatest contribution to Kant studies made by any one individual and has formed the basis of countless studies of Kant's philosophical development.

Adickes set to work and in 1911 published the first of his assigned volumes. By 1928, the year of his death, he had published Volumes 14–18 and also second editions of Volumes 14–16. The first volume is quite unlike the others since most of the space is taken up by Adickes's own annotations. Given his interest in Kant's natural sciences he had much to share, often comparing Kant's notes to other contemporary works that Kant knew. R42 is an extreme example: the four-page loose sheet and Adickes's commentary extend from 14:174 through 14:233. The later volumes have fewer substantive annotations. They also reprint some of the textbooks that Kant used in full, allowing users to find the page or section in the book where Kant wrote each note.

Adickes's death in 1928 meant that others would have to complete the third section of the Academy edition. Volume 19, which contains Kant's Reflections on the Philosophy of Right, was well along at the time, and Adickes's assistant Friedrich Berger (1901–1975) was appointed to complete Volume 19 and "if possible" Volume 20.[16] Berger himself wrote that the Reflections were by and large already transcribed and chronologically ordered by Adickes when he was assigned the volume (19:vi). Still, it took six years before publication, and Berger's work was apparently further edited by de Gruyter house editors Arthur Buchenau (1879–1946) and Gerhard Lehmann (1900–1987). The final work, although excellent, fell a little short of Adickes's high standards.[17] Since nearly all of the Reflections translated here stem from this volume, one must have just a little less faith in the details than one would had Adickes seen it to press. Disputes between Berger and Buchenau

---

[16] Stark, *Nachforschungen*, pp. 152–58, provides information about Berger's tenure as editor.

[17] Berger did not, for example, compare the Reflections on ethics with student transcriptions of Kant's lectures on ethics. In R6624 (19:116) this led to a likely error where Kant had left a blank space obviously intended for a philosopher's name. Based on the context Berger suggested one name, while a look at the student lecture notes suggests another. See *Notes and Fragments*, pp. 426 and 604–05 note, and Stark, *Nachforschungen*, p. 157.

and Lehmann team also led to the remaining volumes of the third part (the *Handschriftlicher Nachlaß*) being assigned to Lehmann.

Lehmann, then, edited Volumes 20–23, including the material translated in this volume as drafts.[18] Lehmann first edited and published the two volumes (Academy edition 21–22) of the *Opus postumum*, pushing the volume of drafts to a new Volume 23, separated from its companion Volume 20. When editing the *Opus postumum* Lehmann relegated Adickes's careful chronological ordering of the material to a small chart and instead arranged the material in the order it was found, a series of fascicles or bundles of loose sheets created by folding another sheet over several loose sheets as a wrapper. This method makes the text difficult to use, and other problems in the transcription also harm the edition.[19] Lehmann then turned to Volume 20, which contains Kant's draft reply to a review of the *Doctrine of Right* translated in this volume, and Volume 23, the most problematic of the material in this translation.

As with the *Opus postumum*, Lehmann's presentation of the material identified as drafts for the published books and essays is problematic. He follows Adickes's plan to place the material in chronological order by publication date of book or essay, but he abandons any attempt to put the material within each work into chronological order. Further, some material identified as drafts by Adickes were overlooked and excluded from the Academy edition; this material has been identified and later printed in other venues. Along with more recently discovered fragments, that missing material was examined for inclusion in this volume of translations. Lehmann did produce a very workable volume despite these lapses, providing material ranging from fragments related to a prize essay competition in 1754 to a draft of Kant's preface to an 1800 work by his friend Jachmann on Kant's philosophy of religion.

Werner Stark notes that Lehmann also did not fulfill Adickes's original plan to include a comprehensive explanation of the relation of each particular manuscript (the loose sheets and textbook pages) with its various appearances in the Academy edition and to provide its provenance and dating. Stark, who must be acknowledged as equal to Adickes in his dedication, knowledge, and thoroughness, himself undertook part of that effort, producing two different tables: one arranging the loose sheets by identification letter or name and showing each place in the Academy edition or elsewhere where its parts are printed (and including the text for those that were not printed anywhere else), and one arranging the loose

---

[18] Details about Lehmann and the production of these volumes are given in Stark, *Nachforschungen*, pp. 158–205.
[19] For information about the *Opus Postumum*, see the editor's introduction to the Cambridge Edition of the *Opus Postumum*, edited by Eckart Förster.

sheets appearing in Volumes 20 and 23 by the published or planned work for which they are drafts.[20]

A few more details regarding particular material will be given in separate editor's introductions to each part of this translation. Here it must be noted that I have traced the history of the publication of the Reflections and drafts but not the lecture, the third of the major divisions in this translation. A few brief words about the Academy edition of the Feyerabend Natural Right lecture are appropriate here; much more detail is given in the particular editor's introduction later in this volume. The same Gerhard Lehmann edited the volume of lectures in which Feyerabend appeared in 1979. His edition was deliberately included as an appendix to the lectures on ethics without annotations of any kind. The problematic nature of the edition has been long acknowledged. As I and others began to work on translations into English, Italian, Portuguese, and Spanish, the need for a revised edition increased. Over the past decade a team has produced what is now to be considered the standard edition. Heinrich P. Delfosse, Norbert Hinske, and Gianluca Sadun Bordoni have published an annotated edition in the series *Kant Index* based on a fresh reading of the manuscript with all the appropriate editorial apparatuses.[21] The translation here is based on this new edition, with reference both to the manuscript and to the Academy edition.

III. THE TRANSLATIONS IN THIS VOLUME

The material translated in this volume is arranged into three parts, in very rough chronological order, followed by an English–German and German–English glossary of important terminology, a Concordance to aid in comparing the Reflections with the course lecture, the endnotes, and a comprehensive index.

The first part consists of a generous selection of Reflections that range in date from 1764 through 1799, although the vast majority are from the 1770s and 1780s and only a handful date from the 1790s. These Reflections are arranged in the order they appear in the Academy edition: they are first grouped in accordance with Volume number by broad topic (Anthropology, Logic, Ethics, Political Philosophy), and then within each major group in chronological order as determined by Adickes's strata. Adickes further arranged the Reflections from one stratum into

---

[20] Stark, *Nachforschungen*, pp. 186–87, 279–319.

[21] Heinrich P. Delfosse, Norbert Hinske, and Gianluca Sadun Bordoni, *Stellenindex und Konkordanz zum 'Naturrecht Feyerabend'*, three parts. Forschungen und Materialien zur deutschen Aufklärung. Abteilung III: Indices. Kant-Index. Section 2: Indices zum Kantschen Ethikcorpus. Bände 30.1, 30.2, 30.3 (Stuttgart-Bad Cannstatt: frommann-holzboog, 2010 and 2014).

topics in accordance with their place in the Achenwall textbook, or for loose sheets the corresponding topic. The Concordance at the end of this volume lists all the topics from Achenwall's book and orders the Reflections by number into those topics. The Concordance also distinguishes these Reflections very roughly by date so that one can see which topics were of most concern to Kant at which period of his development. In these Reflections one can see Kant attempting to resolve such difficulties as whether sovereignty is embodied in the people or a ruler; whether individuals have any right of disobedience to the state; whether a social contract is pragmatic or moral and how the idea of a social contract functions; whether and how punishment is justified; the legal relations between husband and wife, and between them and children and servants; and what rights people have in the state of nature. Kant also provides a detailed argument in the last series of these notes that the early French Revolution was perfectly in accord with right (an important passage given his stringent opposition to revolution in general but support for radical republican principles). Rauscher is responsible for these translations.

The second part of the book consists of the 1784 Feyerabend Natural Right course transcript. Since Kant used the Achenwall text for this course lecture, Feyerabend's transcript itself is divided into books, sections, and titles matching those in Achenwall. The Concordance shows which of Achenwall's section corresponds to which pages in the lecture, thus also allowing a comparison of the Reflections with that segment of the lecture. The Reflection dating in the Concordance makes it easy to see which Reflections are probably before and which are certainly after the course was given. The first quarter of the lecture provides one of Kant's clearest summaries of the foundations of his practical philosophy in general and the relation between right (*Jus, Recht*) and ethics proper (*Ethic, Tugend*), showing how Kant thought that the *Groundwork of the Metaphysics of Morals*, which he was completing at the time, ranged over both; this introductory material also explains the principle of right and the innate right of freedom. The middle portion of the lecture adheres more closely to Achenwall's text and provides detailed evaluation of property and contract. The last quarter turns to family right, public right, and international right, featuring discussions of marriage, the state of nature, sovereignty, punishment, rebellion, and the principles for just war. Rauscher is responsible for the translation of this lecture material.

The third part of the book provides extensive selections from Kant's drafts for four works: *Theory and Practice* (1793), *Perpetual Peace* (1795), the *Metaphysics of Morals*, mainly from the *Doctrine of Right* (1797), and the second essay in *Conflict of the Faculties* on progress in history (1798). These drafts date after nearly every Reflection, mainly because Kant stopped lecturing on Natural Right in 1788 (or possibly 1790[22]) and so did not use the Achenwall text any more. The vast majority of the drafts are for the *Doctrine of Right*, and the bulk of those concern the nature of and justification for property. This material is not included in the Concordance because Kant's *Doctrine of Right* does not mirror the arrangement of Achenwall's *Jus Naturae* in any but the broadest fashion.[23] Perhaps most telling about the importance of these drafts is that his surviving loose sheets reveal that the three projects which seem to have demanded the most effort from him, as measured by the quantity of surviving draft arguments for material destined for books, are the *Critique of Pure Reason*, the unfinished *Opus postumum* project, and the *Doctrine of Right* of the *Metaphysics of Morals*. In the drafts for that work Kant struggles with his conception of property, formulating drafts of a deduction, searching for the proper relation between empirical fact and transcendental basis for right acquisition, and trying to fit his property theory onto marriage and family relations. He also provides different versions of the distinction between right and virtue and discusses the nature of a constitution and the importance of freedom. In the drafts of the other works Kant is more explicit about the French Revolution and the nature of a republican government than he is in their published versions. Rauscher translated the shorter drafts of *Theory and Practice*, *Towards Perpetual Peace*, and *Conflict of the Faculties*, while Westphal translated the much longer set of drafts for the *Metaphysics of Morals*, most of which are related to the *Doctrine of Right*.

The German–English, English–German Glossary follows standard Cambridge Edition format. No Latin–English Glossary is provided because the Latin terms, used extensively in the Feyerabend lecture, are retained and translated within the text itself. Much time was devoted to the index so that individuals can find the material related to a subject of interest despite the scattered occurrences throughout the various types of material. Each part and, for the drafts, also each work, is given its own specific introduction to provide useful information unique to the given material. The translators' remarks range over all material in the book.

Parts of this volume were originally slated to be included in *Notes and Fragments*, originally conceived as the only Cambridge Edition collection of Kant's *Nachlaß* outside the *Opus postumum*. When it became apparent that not all the material would fit in one volume it was decided

---

[22] See the editor's introduction to the Feyerabend lecture below, note 3.

[23] A recent study does provide some correspondence between the Feyerabend lecture and the published *Doctrine of Right*. Philipp-Alexander Hirsch shows that most of the material in Kant's Introduction to the *Doctrine of Right* is also found in the early sections of the Feyerabend lecture as well as the contemporaneous Mrongovius lecture notes on ethics. Hirsch, *Kants Einleitung in die Rechtslehre von 1784* (Universitätsverlag Göttingen, 2012).

that the material from the *Nachlaß* on political philosophy would be spun off from *Notes and Fragments* and placed in a new volume alongside the Feyerabend course lecture. This arrangement also allowed for a much more extensive selection from the drafts for the *Doctrine of Right* and the inclusion of other drafts as well. This volume is both an extension of the Cambridge Edition version of the *Nachlaß* and an addition to the Cambridge Edition set of Kant's lectures.

Translators' remarks

One principle lying behind the Cambridge Edition of the Works of Immanuel Kant is consistency of translation across volumes. The particular relation between some of the materials in this volume – the drafts of *Theory and Practice, Towards Perpetual Peace*, the *Metaphysics of Morals*, and *Conflict of the Faculties* – and the translations of their published versions in the Cambridge volume *Practical Philosophy* by Mary Gregor made consistency particularly important for this volume. We have tried to retain as much of Gregor's terminology as possible while still allowing for occasional differences when context or clarity warranted a different term. Gregor's translations are a model of elegance and accuracy; she captures Kant's style extremely well while conveying the philosophical content accurately. Our rendering of the drafts in the stages nearest to publication attempt to reflect this combination but cannot match the level of excellence she was able to achieve. Our focus on consistency of terminology and clarity of philosophical content should enable the reader to discern the most important similarities and differences between these drafts and the published works in Gregor's volume.

The other material in this volume is less directly related to Gregor's translations. The Reflections themselves were written in a direct tone given that Kant generally intended them as notes for his lectures or as sketches of arguments; in this material our policy naturally favored a more literal rather than ornate style. The other material translated in this volume was not even penned by Kant but by a student reproducing Kant's course lecture; the style of the translations follows suit, with very direct discussions of specific points and few rhetorical flourishes. We of course maintained consistency of terminology across all these different types of material.

The key term *Naturrecht* rarely appears in the material Gregor translated but figures prominently both in the lecture and in Kant's notes for it. We translate it as "natural right" in part to link it to the term *Recht*, which is itself best rendered as "right" as Gregor notes in her remarks on the terminology she used in her translation.[1] *Recht* contains elements of the English terms "law," "justice," and "right." "Right" best captures the normative element involved while alone fitting all of Kant's uses of the term *Recht*. The term *Naturrecht* must be understood in the same vein as "natural right." The reader should keep in mind, however, that *Naturrecht* is the German term used for the tradition known in English as "natural law." German legal theory in the time Kant was writing was dominated by the natural law tradition. The textbook Kant used for his course on right was *Jus Naturae*, traditionally rendered as "natural law." Kant's *Rechtslehre* certainly contains his philosophy of law, and some secondary sources on Kant's *Rechtslehre* translate *Naturrecht* as "natural law."[2] Nonetheless "natural right" is preferable to "natural law" in order to maintain connection to the core term *Recht*. If "natural law" were used for *Naturrecht*, then there would be two equally unacceptable options for Kant's other uses of *Recht*. On the one hand the translation could follow suit by using "law" and related terms such as "legal" to avoid the confusion of a plurality of English terms for the variations of *Recht* and *Naturrecht*. This option would result in a near-total loss of connection with Gregor's translation and to important terms such as "a right." Further, German has the distinct word *Gesetz* for law as a particular rule; using the English "law" for both *Gesetz* and *Recht* would entail frequent confusing passages and arguments. If on the other hand only the terms directly related to *Naturrecht* were translated as "natural law" and "right" were retained for all other uses of *Recht*, then readers would get confused when these terms are used by Kant in ways that exploit the connection between them (see R7084 for a particularly complex case). In this volume, *Naturrecht* is always "natural right" and *Recht* almost always "right." The only exceptions made were either in rendering *Römischer Recht* as "Roman law" or in the extremely rare case when *Recht* clearly refers to a set of actual laws in practice (e.g. "inheritance law" for *Erbrecht* at 27:1349); these instances are all footnoted. The Latin equivalent *jus* is rendered as "right" except in similar circumstances.

Another important set of terms relates to the gendered nouns, pronouns, and possessives in German. We have used "a human being" or "the human being" for Kant's *der Mensch* and sometimes use "human being" or "a human being's" for the corresponding German pronoun *er* (he) or possessive *sein* (his). A similar issue arises for the German *die Person*, for which we unproblematically use "a person" as in "most of a person's actions." While this noun is feminine, the German pronoun

---

[1] Mary Gregor, "Translator's note on the text of *The Metaphysics of Morals*," in the Cambridge Edition *Practical Philosophy*, pp. 357–59.

[2] See, for example, Sharon Bryd and Joachim Hruschka, *Kant's Doctrine of Right: A Commentary* (New York: Cambridge University Press, 2010), p. 17.

sie (she) and possessive *ihr* (hers) are made gender-neutral with "a person" or "a person's" unless exceedingly awkward; since it is clear that women are not Kant's paradigm cases in his discussion, "she" and "hers" are avoided. The exceptions to these gender-neutral uses come in Kant's discussion of issues of gender and sex. In those discussions we tend to use the gendered pronouns and possessives for *Mensch* and *Person* to show that Kant's intention, at least on the abstract level of right, is that marriage right is applied equally to both sexes. Kant himself of course also suggests that it is natural for the husband to rule over the wife, so actual relations between spouses are not equal in every respect. In his broader political philosophy, where Kant almost exclusively uses the pronoun *er* (he) and masculine gendered nouns (e.g. *der Eigentümer*), we have used the masculine "he" or "his" in most cases to avoid imposing on Kant a comprehensive view of gender equality he did not have. Regarding property in the Germanized version of the Latin *meum et tuum* (mine and yours), Kant sometimes uses *Sein* (his) along with *Mein* and *Dein*. We render *Sein* as "one's" or less frequently "one's property" in parallel with our treatment of "mine and yours" unless the term is used in reference to a previous pronoun *er* (he).

Because Kant's views of property over the decades covered in this volume changed, most dramatically in the introduction of a deduction and an antinomy for property in the drafts to the *Doctrine of Right*, no consistent equation of the Latin stemming from Gottfried Achenwall's text *Jus Naturae* to Kant's German terms is possible. One example is that in the Feyerabend lecture Kant never uses the term *Besitznehmung*, which he later equates with the Latin *apprehensio* in the *Doctrine of Right* (e.g. 6:264). He does at one point say that an explorer who plants a flag on a newly discovered land and "takes possession" {*Besitz nimmt*} (27:1342) does not have a right to it, but if the person works the land and applies his power to it, then he *apprehendirt* (the Germanized verb form of *apprehensio*) it. Elsewhere in the lecture Kant uses a distinction between *apprehensio* and *occupatio* as between merely taking an object on the one hand and doing something further to it on the other; we have translated these terms as "taking" and "taking control" and not equated either with "taking possession." The Latin *acquisitio* completes this triad as "acquiring." Kant uses the Latin *appropriatio* only once in Feyerabend but identifies it in the drafts for the *Metaphysics of Morals* as equivalent to *Zueignung*, which we translate as "appropriation." Kant's uses of the Latin terms do not consistently match his final version in the published *Metaphysics of Morals*, where *Besitznehmung* ("taking possession") is associated with *apprehensio*, so our translation refrains from imposing the crucial meaning "taking possession" on any particular Latin term; the context of Kant's uses of the term can be used to track his evolving position on this point.

Kant was not consistent in his use of terms that denote political power (see R7977 for an example of his hesitancy). We retain *souverain* in French and translate its German derivative *Souverän* as well as the Latin *imperans* as "sovereign." When translated as "sovereign" or "sovereignty," *Herrschergewalt, Oberherrschaft*, and other terms are always footnoted. *Gewalt* is used in different ways in different contexts. Given the importance of political legitimacy, we have used "authority" as often as "power" when referring to the political powers of the ruler over subjects or citizens or the roles of executive, legislative, and other aspects of sovereignty. "Control," "force," and even "violence" are appropriate in certain contexts as well. In most cases *Gewalt* is footnoted for clarity. The words with similar meanings tend to be footnoted as well: *Kraft* more directly indicates physical force; *Obrigkeit*, used rarely, is rendered as "authority"; *Macht* indicates power irrespective of normative force.

Volk and the related *Völkerrecht* are translated as "people" and "right of nations." Rarely is *Volk* translated as "nation" because most of Kant's uses of the term concern the relation of the people to the state as citizens or subjects or to the people as the bearer of sovereign authority. But clearly the sense of *Volk* at work in *Völkerrecht* is that of "nation," or even "state" as Kant laments in the published *Metaphysics of Morals* (6:343). Regarding *Volk*, we have followed English in using a plural verb form when Kant is referring to the collection of people; when he is clearly indicating a single people, as opposed to the people constituting another nation, we use the singular verb form or on occasion "nation."

Most other terms worth noting are easier to explain. Kant uses the terms *Sache* and *Ding* almost interchangeably; we have used "thing" for both. *Grundsatz* and *Princip* both become "principle"; likewise *Beziehung* and *Verhältnis* are both "relation." We sometimes footnote these terms to highlight possible differences in use. In many of Kant's works the terms *Object* and *Gegenstand* overlap as "object" but with the latter term connoting a physical object and the former the more abstract sense of the term; we have generally footnoted these terms for clarity.

The term *Tat* like the Latin *factum* is "deed" in the sense of act. To avoid confusion with the sense of the English "deed" as title to property, the German equivalent *Titel* is always translated as "title." It is important to note this (and it is footnoted) in Kant's occasional discussions of the need for a deed to legitimize property; he means that only a person's act (deed) of working with an object or otherwise declaring ownership of it in a juridical manner can make it property, not that a piece of paper as title itself constitutes legitimate acquisition of property. "Act" is reserved for *Akt* (Latin *actus*). *Handlung* is generally given as "action."

Latin terms play an extensive role in the Feyerabend course lecture and Kant's corresponding Reflections. The central part of the course lecture on property, contract, and other matters he will later call "private right" utilizes Achenwall's Latin terminology in a close and detailed discussion of the philosophical aspects of fine legal points. Here Latin terms are retained in Latin in their original position in Kant's sentences and a translation is provided in braces immediately following the term or phrase *unless* the term or a form of that term or phrase has been translated already within the immediate past sentences or paragraphs. We lean on the side of repetition rather than failing to provide frequent enough translations so that those who start to read a particular paragraph or section will not have to search upward in the text too far to find the translations. When quoting from this translation, users should feel free to delete, shift, or transfer the English material in brackets from passages in order to obtain maximal clarity for the particular passage being quoted; some might also wish to provide the English translation in the sentence and relegate the corresponding Latin to the braces. Latin terms, unless embedded in a phrase or sentence, are given in the nominative case. We have silently replaced the German "ß" with "ss" when used in the Latin terms. When the text used a Latin term with a German ending, we have treated the term as incorporated into German and translated it directly into English. We have footnoted the term only if the English is not cognate to the Latin. In some cases the English equivalent of a Latin term is itself an obscure legal term.

When Kant wanted to emphasize a word in his script he underlined it. Published works used spaced type (*Sperrdruck*) for this emphasis. We use **bold** rather than either of the other options for Kant's emphasis. *Italic* type is reserved for Latin and other non-German words, except that the rare Greek is given in Greek letters. Braces {} contain translations from the non-German words. Editor's remarks are printed in italics in brackets []. The pagination in the margins refers to the Academy edition in nearly every case. A few loose sheets included here did not make it into the Academy edition and were published in later journals or books; in these cases the pagination is explained in editor's remarks and included in the margin.

There are three types of notes. Kant's own footnotes within his Reflections and drafts are indicated by symbols such as "*," and because in most cases these marks reflect Kant's links to later additions, his notes are given in a subsequent paragraph in the main text. Editor's footnotes directly concerned with the translation are indicated by letters and provided at the bottom of each page. Finally editor's explanatory endnotes are numbered and provided at the end of the book. The distinction among these three types of notes should be evident.

The diffuse Reflections, lecture notes, and drafts included in this volume, though demanding to read, exhibit Kant's struggles (in two languages!) to develop his own critical political philosophy. Every effort has been made to translate Kant's drafts and notes faithfully, accurately, and clearly, and to avoid rewriting Kant's sentences or revising his thoughts or expressions. The additional materials provided to help the reader both within the text and in the notes and glossary are intended to provide background for understanding the text itself with a minimal amount of interpretive interference.

Reflections on the philosophy of right

Editor's introduction

Kant typically entered his classroom armed with very few notes. One student recounted that "In many classes he did not even once use a notebook, instead he had a few things marked in the margins of his textbooks to serve as an outline."[1] Kant was known for an engaging teaching style, one that aimed at getting students to think for themselves. He was required in most classes to use a textbook as the basis for his lectures, but he usually used the textbook as a sounding board and even when presenting the author's views evaluated them from his own perspective. In his lectures on ethics he was said to move his students to tears with his exhortations to duty. We don't know whether students shed any tears in Kant's course on Natural Right, but we do know that he wrote his notes for this course in a textbook. His personal note-filled copy of the second volume of Gottfried Achenwall's *Jus Naturae* survived into the twentieth century and served as the core for the section of the Academy edition for Kant's Reflections on the Philosophy of Right. It was lost after the Second World War. Kant wrote in the margins of this text but did not go the lengths that he did for other textbooks which he had bound with interleaved blank pages so that he would have a full blank space opposite every page of text. The number of pages of Reflections gleaned from Kant's copy of Achenwall is further reduced by the fact that Kant's copy of the other half of Achenwall's text, which Kant must have owned given the extensive use of that volume in the Feyerabend course transcript, has been unaccounted for since Kant's death.[2]

The basic history of the production of the Academy edition of the Reflections is explained in the General introduction to this volume of translations. Erich Adickes, the editor of part three of the Academy edition dedicated to Kant's handwritten but unpublished writings left after his death, had created an elaborate system for dividing the writings into distinct Reflections and dating each (14:xxxv–xliii). For his full identification of the time periods for all of Kant's Reflections he used the twenty-four letter Greek alphabet; unfortunately he had identified thirty-three distinct time periods and had to resort to using the same letter more than once using superscripted numbers in order to label all the time periods,

3

some thus appear as sub-periods in his system. For the Reflections on Metaphysics, Ethics, and Philosophy of Right he presented the material itself in rough chronological order by arranging the Reflections in chapters corresponding to the twenty-four lettered time periods. Within each chapter the notes are arranged topically and no further division into the sub-periods is given. Each Reflection is presented with a full list of the possible time periods (or sub-periods) into which it could fall. Adickes rarely felt confident enough in his dating system, based on imprecise factors such as relative page position and ink color as it was, to assign only one time period to a Reflection. Usually he offered a series of possible time periods, using parentheses and question marks to indicate levels of likelihood. He used the most plausible, and when tied the earliest, time period to assign the Reflections to the chapters.

He quite plausibly dated the earliest Reflections found in Kant's copy of Achenwall not to the publication date of the book (1763) but to Kant's first course offerings using it (1766–68) (14:xxxvii). He assigned all the Reflections on the Philosophy of Right to nine different chapters corresponding to time periods in reference to the initial starting dates (given here without using Adickes's Greek lettering system):[3]

(a) around 1766–68
(b) 1769
(c) around 1772 but certainly between (b) and (d)
(d) certainly later than (c) but before (e)
(e) around 1773–75
(f) approximately 1775–1777
(g) around 1776–78
(h) 1780–89
(i) 1790–1804

The latter two time periods are subdivided into shorter sub-periods when assigning dates to particular Reflections but they are not given separate chapters or sub-chapters. In each chapter the notes are arranged in accordance with their location in Achenwall's text using Achenwall's headings for books, sections, and titles. Adickes assigns the rare case of a loose sheet to a topic "general" at the start of each chapter; others in the "general" category are Kant's notes in the very earliest or very last pages of the book.

In arranging the Reflections translated below I simply present them in numerical order. Doing so retains, in the broadest division, the separate volumes from which they stem, so that, e.g., relevant Reflections from Kant's reflections on Anthropology, Logic, Ethics, and Philosophy of Right are presented together. Within each of those broad subjects the numerical system then roughly tracks chronological order using the nine periods listed above corresponding to the chapters; in the material in the phase 1780–89, where the sub-periods do not constitute chapter parts but are simply given with each Reflection, one must find the particular sub-period in the identifying information for each Reflection. I do not present the headings for Achenwall's divisions. For each individual Reflection I use the Reflection number (in all of these cases using four digits), followed by the years of likely composition (in which I join together time periods of the same likelihood), followed by the location (for Reflections) or identification name (for loose sheets, labeled using the German *loses Blatt*). I do not include information that Adickes provided identifying relation to earlier German editions of some of the material. Most of these Reflections are drawn from Kant's notes in his edition of Achenwall's book *Jus Naturae*. The location indicator "J. x" means that that Reflection is on page x of Achenwall. "Pr." indicates Baumgarten's text on practical philosophy. "M" indicates Baumgarten's text on metaphysics, part of which Kant used in his Anthropology course. Section numbers indicate sections of the corresponding text. These texts are reprinted in the Academy edition, enabling one to see precisely the topic that (likely) prompted Kant to write the Reflection.

A concordance that correlates the Reflections to the Achenwall text and the Feyerabend lecture is provided at the end of this book. This concordance in the first column reprints the table of contents from Achenwall, showing section numbers for the entire work and "J" pagination for the second volume to which the Reflections correspond. One can use this to find the topics of particular Reflections as used by Adickes. The second column reprints the headings used in the Feyerabend course lecture transcript; some are inaccurately headed or numbered and in several cases Feyerabend skips entire sections of Achenwall. The Academy edition pagination corresponding to each of these sections of the lecture is given. One can use this to find particular sections of the course that correspond to particular Reflections and vice versa. The third column arranges the Reflections on the Philosophy of Right in accordance with the topics in the previous columns as assigned in the Academy edition; the fourth column similarly arranges the Reflections from other sources to these topics as assigned by me. In both cases the actual content of the Reflection might also cover other topics to a lesser extent because the boundaries between topics are not always exact. The Reflection numbers themselves are printed in a way to identify their rough chronology so that one can see the approximate temporal emphasis on different topics.

Some of Kant's notes are simply reminders or summaries of others' positions clearly intended as a guide for his lectures. These reflections are not translated here. Others are paragraph-length evaluations of issues that might not have even arisen in the course lecture, as with R8055 discussing the French Revolution, which occurred after the last confirmed offering of Kant's course on Natural Right; these types of Reflections might be preparatory for Kant's planned publications. The majority of the notes, however, relate directly to the topics in Achenwall's book and provide Kant's own criticism of Achenwall or simply his own alternative views on the matter.

I. FRAGMENTS FROM NOTES ON ANTHROPOLOGY

At the end of Kant's lectures on anthropology he turned to the topic "The Character of the Species." While most of this material covers issues about history and human nature, a few reflections provide some insight into Kant's political philosophy because he considers human beings destined to live in a society with others under a civil constitution as a condition for the moral perfection of the individual and the species. Kant wrote these notes in his copy of Alexander Baumgarten's *Metaphysica*, a textbook he used for his lectures on metaphysics as well as on anthropology, using the empirical psychology portions in the latter course. None of the content of Baumgarten's book directly matches Kant's topic "The Character of the Species," although some does discuss human beings understood as rational beings. Kant's notes for this topic appear in various places in the book, including the margins of the index. Here the page of Baumgarten's book on which each note was written is indicated by "M"; a page number with an apostrophe indicates that the note was written on a blank page opposite the numbered page. The text of the Baumgarten volume is reprinted in two pieces in the Academy edition. The selections from Baumgarten's text in volume 15 containing Kant's reflections on anthropology (15:5–54) ironically do not include any of the pages on which Kant wrote the notes presented here. Those pages are instead included in the material in volume 17 on metaphysics (17:5–226).

1399. 1772–73. M 301.   15:610

The vicar of God on earth is always the ~~community~~ universal human being (*maximus homo* {greatest human being}). Only the state is absolute lord; the *souverain* is its representative, and since, because of his attunement with the will of the state he is not and must not be answerable to any human beings, he must be answerable to the one absolute lord of the whole of nature. A *souverain* must thus, in his function as the highest representative, instruct and be inspired by a religious disposition.

1401. 1772–75. M 306'.   15:611

Every individual shuns death; but the commonwealth, which wants to preserve itself, has reasons for wishing the death of individuals. Everyone wants to be rich, but the commonwealth wants the poor. Everyone wants to be content, but the *publicus* {public as a whole} demands inequality of the estates. Everyone wants great talent, but the *publicus* requires little. Indeed, the *publicus* wishes for there to be no evil inclinations, but they make the existence of a *publicus* possible in the first place. Thus a particular evil becomes a good in the whole. If one would want to further pursue this wish so that we would ascribe completely different laws of generation, completely different inclinations and spiritual powers to human beings, this wish would be absurd, for one would give up one's own person and put another in its place.

15:626   **1432. 1776–78. M 321.**

In unlimited government freedom of the press in that which refers to the general arrangement can be allowed (as in good military subordination). They are representations that cannot restrict power at all. To regard this as insurrection is a figment of the mind.

That in England no one kills another in order to defend one's honor.[4] This ill is strongest in Prussia, perhaps because charlatanism is greater here at this point. To speak of one's honor is even to be compared with damning someone and is externally more evil.

15:626   **1434. 1776–78. M 322.**

There is a particular inclination in human beings for uniting in a society, not always for the unity of their dispositions but to create a united will whose power is stronger, and from a love of system, i.e. of a whole in accordance with laws. But when the society becomes large there is also a propensity to division and to sects, leading to even smaller ones which *socius* {the members} can better relate to and in which unity would be
15:627   more intimate. In this situation the motivating ground is, then, not so much power but more the order and interconnection.

Thus the division of great states, *esprit de corps*.

15:628   **1438. 1776–78? (1773–75?). M 325'.**

The history of the state must be written so that one sees what use the world has had of a[a] government. The revolutions of Switzerland, Holland, England are the most important in recent times.[5] Russia's transformation contributes nothing to the well-being of the world except in a distant way. History must itself contain the plan for the improvement of the world, and indeed not from the parts to the whole but vice versa. What is the use of philosophy if it does not direct the means of instruction of humanity to its true interest? Protect citizens from one another not only through laws but also through human-made institutions where everyone is safe from everyone else through laws. Be subordinated in no other way but according to the law. No advantage except when one has right on one's side. Easy access to administration of justice. Insight into legislation and wisdom in directing the administration.

History can still separately [be written] as biography or for public ends.

---

[a] *einer*. alternate reading: *einerlei*, for "one type of government"

1443. 1776–78. M 325. 15:630
For the plan of a universal history: 1. The nature of the civil- and the state-constitution; the idea, even if it never becomes fully actual, and indeed the idea of right, not of happiness.

1444. 1776–78. M 325. 15:630
In the history of England in the present time, its subjection of America leads cosmopolitan reflection on England back to the past. The English want the Americans to become subjects of subjects and the English want to pass the burden off to others.[6]
  Good government is not crucial, but good form of government.

1449. 1776–78. M 407. 15:633
Despotism is coercion that deprives the subjects of all of their choice[a] and judgment. A despot who makes his subjects happy does this merely according to his own taste without taking in the advice of the others.

1464. 1783–88. *Loses Blatt* G 8. 15:644
[*second page*] The great difficulty in the problem of establishing a civil constitution is: that the human being is an animal that demands rights and yet does not willingly concede his right to anyone else, who thus has need of a master who in turn can always only be a human being. From such crooked timber no Mercury[7] can be cut.[b]

1465. 1783–89. *Loses Blatt* Ha 39. 15:644
[*second page*]
  In the eyes of a reflective man the worldly business of people loses its importance by and by, for the world is still too unripe for great progress. Freedom in religion and civil relations are still the only thing of interest; for otherwise a state can do nothing for the betterment of the world but only for itself.

1468. 1785–89. *Loses Blatt* Ha 10. 15:647

Continuation of the history of the human species

On what rests the generation of all this perfection in which the philosophical chiliast believes and furthers in accordance with his abilities?
  On the perfection of the civil constitution (which would be able to maintain itself perpetually). In this alone are all talents developed,

---

[a] *Wahl*
[b] *Aus so krummem Holtze laßt sich kein Mercur schnitzen*

the greatest unity to common ends through outer laws and the greatest durability of this condition through the best personal disposition.

Freedom, law, and power.[a]

The citizen must stand under laws that he himself has given (freedom, equality), and these laws must receive reinforcement and durability through irresistible power.

[*added 1790s:* The human being is an animal that requires instruction and discipline. 2. that in the species progresses to his vocation. 3. requires a lord in society]

1. Law and freedom without power: anarchy
2. Law and power without freedom: despotism
    a. Freedom without law and power is the condition of savages
    b. Power without freedom and law: barbaric regime.
    _____ [*Kant's line*]

What are the inclinations that serve nature for producing civil society? Jealousy, mistrust, violence,[b] which necessitate human beings to subject themselves to laws and to give up savage freedom. The development of all good natural predispositions comes this way.

[*added 1790s:* One can consider the history of every people as a striving of nature toward establishment of a perfect civil constitution. The history of states as attempts toward the right of peoples.]

[*second page*]

Civil society, externally as state, is until now still in the state of savage nature: freedom and power without law.

15:648 Even here nature is effective in pushing for a union of peoples. Only through universal peace (cemetery) can the core[c] of the civil constitution achieve its perfection.

[*remainder of Reflection omitted*]

---

[a] *Gewalt* [b] *Gewaltthätigkeiten*
[c] *das innere*

II. FRAGMENTS FROM NOTES ON LOGIC

A few Reflections pertaining to political philosophy are found among Kant's notes in his copy of the text he used in his Logic course, George Friedrich Meier's *Auszug aus der Vernunftlehre*, although no corresponding discussion is found in Meier's text and only a brief example is given in Kant's lectures. These Reflections, 3345–3358 (16:789–98), do in part bear some connection to questions of method. The Reflections translated here discuss contract theory and property acquisition, topics that correspond to material in the missing first volume of Achenwall's *Jus Naturae* and thus topics for which we have no other Reflections by Kant. One additional Reflection from this group on positive law and concepts of right, R3345, has already been included in *Notes and Fragments* (pp. 412–13). The page of Meier's book on which each note was written is indicated by "L". The text of the Meier volume is reprinted in the Academy edition 16:3–872, interspersed with all of Kant's reflections on logic.

3346. 1772? 1773–78?? L 115. 16:792

The law is either necessary (*stricte*) or contingent, the latter is called a statute and has the general welfare as its aim. The law (*legis stricte tales* {narrow laws as such}) must not be derived from principles of the unity of a system but of the will.

3350. 1776–89. L 115. 16:793

To every right there is a corresponding obligation of another not to hinder that right in practice. But because all human beings have a right (like 16:794 the owner) to acquire *per occupationem* or *translationem* {through taking control or transfer}, so corresponding to the right there is for the owner an obligation to mark out his property openly and precisely,[a] but there is not an obligation on the part of another to investigate this differentiation or the *titulus* {title} of possession of a third.

The *dominus* {owner} thus has no right against the *primus laedentem* {primary wrongdoer} [in a case of a non-owner selling property]; the others *juste* {justly} disregard the *titulus possessionis* {title to possession} of the latter. Either it is the fault of the *dominus* {owner} or bad luck for him if after an interrupted possession the thing is transferred in a rightful manner.

It is to be proven that everyone in the *permutatio jurium* {exchange of right} has a natural right to ignore the *titulus possessionis* of another, and more so that he is not competent to research it before he makes it his

---

[a] *Sein Eigenthum kenntlich und sicher zu unterscheiden*

own. Otherwise it would follow that everyone who wants to transfer his right would first have to prove that he has one.

16:794 **3351. 1776–89. L 115.**
The right that someone acquires from another rests solely on the *modus translationis* {mode of transfer} of the thing and not on the right the other has to the thing. Otherwise we could not acquire anything *originarie* because there would not yet be any right in the thing. Thus no one can give to another any more (things) than he has, but yet a right is constituted that he does not have, since the other acquires by means of his acceptance and does no one any wrong, although the first does a wrong.

16:795   He has a right to transfer a thing even if it remains undetermined how he obtained it. I can sell something that someone else gave to me to sell as if it were mine.

16:795 **3355. 1776–89. L 116.**
There are three parts to the sale of a thing: 1. The seller, 2. The thing, 3.
16:796 The buyer. No wrong lies in the contract between them, the seller does no wrong in this matter.

    The buyer has no obligation, otherwise the seller could coerce the buyer to transfer the thing to another. The seller does not wrong the buyer, and vice versa. This is an *actus originarius* and not *derivatives* (except when the buyer knows that the seller is *non dominus* {not the owner}). To be clear: that the buyer must derive his right from the right of the seller would transform the problem into an infinite regress, if one takes the right of the seller in a way that he must not act contrary to obligation toward anyone else and harms no one in the process. But what is important for the *actus translatorium* {act of transfer} is that he has the thing in hand and no one is permitted to take it from him except the owner. But the owner is not involved here. Thus among these three the seller really transfers his right, which is secure. If, however, the thing relies for its existence on particular land from which it cannot be moved without being destroyed the buyer must first inquire about the right. For it is clear that the land cannot really be possessed and thus cannot have a genuine *dominus* {owner}, but can only be used; it can belong only to the one who can do no wrong in his possession and original taking possession of it, i.e. society, which has the power to hold the right for itself.

    With regard to things no one does any wrong, they may belong to whoever wants them, but this is still a wrong toward the owner. The owner also has just such a right to the thing, but the priority in obligation for all others is to avoid harming his right.

From my point of view the thief has a right to possess the thing that he is offering for sale to me. I would wrong him if I took it away from him by force. He renounces this right for my benefit and I acquire it. That he may have wronged another is someone else's concern, not mine. My *actus* is in accord with right. I have traded with the person and do not know of any other.

III. FRAGMENTS FROM NOTES ON ETHICS

For his frequently taught course on moral philosophy, Kant used Alexander Baumgarten's *Initia Philosophiae Practicae*. Some of the topics in that book, for example, law, legislator, and punishment, straddle the line between morality and political philosophy, while others define the precise difference between right and virtue. Thus the reader will find material related to political philosophy in Kant's lectures on Ethics[8] and in the notes Kant wrote in his copy of Baumgarten's text. The bulk of Kant's Reflections written in that text already appear in translation in *Notes and Fragments*, and the reader is directed to them for their political aspects. The few fragments that bore more relevance for political matters than for ethics were not included in *Notes and Fragments* but appear here. The page of Baumgarten's book on which each note was written is indicated by "Pr."; a page number with an apostrophe indicates that the note was written on a blank page opposite the numbered page. The text of the Baumgarten volume is reprinted in the Academy edition, 19:7–91.

19:94   **6583**. 1764–68. Pr. II.
The best condition of human beings in accordance with the rule of right is society, and the best condition of the human being in society regarding his security is irresistible power[a] that necessitates him to act in accordance with this rule of right. The arts and sciences cause him to resist even less.[9] He is not made better in this way, but tamer. One can easily get him to do something through a little bit of pleasure or through honor. He actually becomes weaker, because every requirement of a group is such that it obligates him to the laws even if these laws are arbitrary.

[*remainder of Reflection on Greek conceptions of the highest good omitted*]

19:100   **6594**. 1764–68. Pr. XVII'.
Right is not determined by utility but rather by the will of all individuals. But since in accordance with the rule of freedom each must determine utility in accordance with his own thoughts, the other has no authorization to judge of the utility but only of the will of another.

The many can form a political body in accordance with rules of prudence even though it will not have arisen in accordance with rules of right.

No one can convey to another all power to execute his own judgments of right without reserving for himself an equal power to necessitate the other to fulfill his obligation for then he would give the other a right to do whatever he wants (*licentia* {license}); yet if the other can do nothing

---

[a] *Gewalt*

that is not right through his action, then his actions rest only on his power and not on his right.

6666. 1769–70? 1772? Pr. 25.   19:127
How one can acquire a right through *injuria alterius* {injury of another} must be explained. Every free action is right except insofar as the will of another resists [it] and makes the action impossible in accordance with the rule of the common will.[a] It follows that I have no right to alter   19:128 another's condition except with his consent, *pacto* {by contract}, or *facto injusto previo* {by a previous unjust deed} for in the latter case he surrenders his right, his resistance ceases, and the other can determine his will without a positive ground of right.

6667. 1769–70? (1772?) Pr. 25, 24.   19:128
[Pr. 25:] Right between two is whatever is possible through their common will.[*,b] (Whatever is necessary through this will is called obligation.) One has a right with respect to another (*affirmative*) if one's private will can be seen as identical with the common will. The necessity of an action on account of the rule of right is called formal obligation, on account of the right of another, however, material obligation. The rule, which depends necessarily upon this common will in general, is found by seeking the condition of the will which is necessary, so that it will be universally valid. One can compare the relations of right with those of body. Every body is in a state of rest towards all others except insofar as each is moved by others, and likewise everyone has duties of omission towards others except insofar as others either create a concordant will with him or transform his condition against his will. *Actio est aequalis reactio* {action is equal to reaction}. As much as a larger body has an effect on a smaller one, so much does the smaller one have on the larger one in return. The common center of gravity,[c] i.e. the common will, is identical before and after the action.

[Kant's footnote on Pr. 24:] *The same action, which is possible under a rightful condition in conformity with right, is conditionally right. E.g. to punish someone under the condition that his actions contradict the law of the common will.

6670. 1769–70? 1771? 1764–68? Pr. 26. Next to §57 conclusion and §58.   19:129
The ethical rule says this: do what seems to you to be good for another; that of right says: do what conforms to the universal rule of actions, insofar as each does what seems to him to be good.

[a] *gemeinschaftlichen Willens*   [b] *gemeinschaftlichen Willen*
[c] *der gemeinschaftliche Schwerpunkt*

19:132   **6681.** 1764–68? 1769? Pr. 74.
pragmatic punishments are warnings and have to do with the external aspect of action,
> **moral** with evil disposition.
> Authorities punish pragmatically.

19:144   **6733.** 1772–73? 1773–75? 1776–78? Pr. 27.
What cannot possibly be an object of a common power of choice[a] is unjust;[b] that which, were it an object of that power of choice, would yet be impossible to carry out in conformity with laws of the power of choice, is wrong.[c]

19:145   **6738.** 1772? 1773–75? Pr. 30.
An action is right in general insofar as one is free with respect to it. However, a right is the freedom through which the freedom of another is restricted: *jus quaesitum* {acquired right}. *A natura* {by nature} everyone is free, and only those actions are right which do not restrict the freedom of anyone.

19:147   **6746.** 1772. Pr. 33. Next to the conclusion of §68 and between §§68 and 69
Whoever has equity on his side cannot coerce another who has right for his side and also cannot avoid the other's rightful coercion.
    A right that lacks the necessary conditions of an external law is a right of equity.
    Whatever is not possible through the tacit universal will but is still allowed through the necessary conditions of external law is inequity.

19:155   **6767.** 1772? 1769? 1764–68? Pr. 49.
Morality (objective) is freedom in accordance with (under) laws.
    Freedom under inner laws is ethical obligation.
    Freedom under outer laws is juridical obligation.
    Law is the restriction of freedom through universal conditions of the consensus of freedom with itself.
    Freedom which is good without law is original.
    The agreement rests either on the unity of the end or the unity of [*breaks off*]

> 1. Act in accordance with law without coercion.
> 2. Exercise coercion, but in accordance with laws.
> 3. Subject freedom to the coercion of the laws.

[a] *einer gemeinschaftlichen Willkür*   [b] *ungerecht*
[c] *Unrecht*

    a. Create security for each with regard to what is his (through sub-jection to coercion).

    b. Create security for each with regard to everyone else (through the execution of lawful coercion).

6855. 1776–78? 1780–89? Pr. 128.   19:180
State prudence is grounded solely on empirical principles, state right on rational. One blends the conditions of the former with those of the latter   19:181 in the concept of a state constitution in general.

6896. 1776–79? Pr. X'.   19:199
A case of necessity[a] is when I myself am necessitated to use my [*later addition*: own] power[b] in defense of my right. Otherwise the authorization to exercise coercion on behalf of my rights means: that there are certain criteria of judgment in accordance with which a third person who is a competent judge can judge[c] and in general coerce. This rule determines the conditions of a legitimate coercion. But this authorization does not extend to what is *jus controversum* {disputed right}. The rules of right toward another are reciprocal. I must also procure the other his right. Thus I must subject myself to coercion in accordance with which the other's right is secured. That I will conduct myself toward the other legitimately is the condition of obligation to the other. I first determine what is right. Then the question remains whether I am obligated to allow myself to be restricted in regard to the other through his right alone. This is valid only when exactly the same right secures me and the other reciprocally, so that I do not need to rely on my own power.

(Sufficient) coercion is legitimate, when it secures my right for me from the other side, and this makes it possible for all actions to be directed solely through the rule of right in a universally valid way.

A case of necessity is when I take the law into my own hands and am my own judge.

Nature rules in lieu of right when there is no valid administration of right,[d] e.g. saving one's life.

There is never any case of necessity which justifies lying, yet speaking an untruth is in accord with right.

7075. 1776–78. Pr. 54, 55. In and to §92   19:242
[Pr. 54:] Make it so each is secure in what belongs to him[e] relative to what is yours. [Pr. 55:] This is the duty of civil society, the universal condition of all right and property of human beings.

---

[a] *Notfall*   [b] *Gewalt*, in this Reflection
[c] *Richter ist, urtheilen . . . kann*   [d] *Rechtspflege*
[e] *Das Seine*

19:243   [Pr. 54:] Make each secure relative to you for the sake of his right (*suus cuique* {to each his own}); because only then can he say that something is his, and indeed *facto* {by deed} not merely *jure* {by right}, if he is secure in his possessions. This is the single affirmative outer natural duty: *exeundum e statu naturali* {one must leave the state of nature}.

19:243   **7078.** 1776–78. Pr. 55. Next to and in §§93–94
The human species cannot exist without right, hence also without duty and therefore without coercion.

     Subject yourself to the conditions under which each may determine what is his. This is coercion. The principle *honeste vive* {live uprightly} is the ethical *principium* and demands *rectitudino actionum internam* {rectitude in internal actions}, uprightness (of disposition). The principle *neminem laede* {wrong no one} is the principle of *rectitudino externam* {rectitude in external [actions]} and *justitia negativa* {negative justice}. The principle *suum cuique tribue* {give to each what is his} is the principle of *justitia positiva*, i.e. "make each secure in his right" (*justitia distributiva* {distributive justice}); the *principium status civilis* is "enter into the civil condition[a] or subject yourself to the conditions[b] of a civil constitution." *Suum cuique* can only be created insofar as there are positive outer laws to which each subjects himself.* Subject yourself to authority[c] in accordance with laws.

19:244   [Pr. 54, inside §92]

     [Kant's footnote:] **Naturaliter* {by nature} I do not have to give anything to anyone or to pay him tribute; for each must concern himself with his own property. But I am still bound to lend a hand to that condition in which each can acquire what is his own with security. This is the *principium juris publici* {principle of public right}, just as *neminem laede* is the *principium juris privati* {principle of private right}. I should therefore afford each security in his possession with respect to mine. Whether *justitia distributiva* {distributive justice} can be partial, i.e. pardon one, punish another?

     Ethics is not concerned with the actions that I should do, but with the *principium* from which I should do them. Maxims.

19:245   **7084.** 1776–78. Pr. 56. In §94
Without civil order, the entire right of nature[d] is merely a doctrine of virtue, and bears the name of a right solely as a plan for possible outer coercive laws, hence of civil order.

---

[a]   *Zustand eines Bürgers*   [b]   *Bedingungen*
[c]   *Gewalt*   [d]   *Recht der Natur*

Since the phrase "right by nature"[a] is used ambiguously, we must make use of a subtlety in order to eliminate this ambiguity. We distinguish natural right from the naturally right.[b] The former is opposed both to the universal and to that dependent on choice; the latter is also grounded on nature, but is either the naturally private right or public right.

7192. 1776–78? 1779? Pr. 135. To §198?   19:268
The jurists are correct when they claim that one could kill another in order to save his own life. More particularly one cannot be coerced to refrain from doing so, because the punishment which one is supposed to want to avoid cannot be greater than that which one tries to escape through one's action, and the latter is closer. Also, the condition for *casu necessitatis* {a case of necessity} is only saving one's life, for the great force of the penal law rests in punishment by death. And yet such a human being, because he saved a life for which he is not worthy, should as such be treated with all contempt.

7193. 1776–78? Pr. 134.   19:268
But one still has a right to coerce others to at least barely maintain our lives[c] while maintaining their own. For property is only a share in the common provisions of nature.

7271. 1780s? 1776–78?? Pr. 57.   19:299
For external commands duty is not the motivating ground. The ought is here coercion. We are not asked to do out of inner motives what we are commanded to do by coercion.[d] The *imperativus juridicus* {juridical imperative} is *externe tantum obligans* {obligating only externally} and not at all moral. It is the *imperativus* of power[e] that is in conformity with right and its necessitating force[f] is also only in proportion to this power. Still the judgment of this legislator regarding the *vis obligatoria* {obligatory force} is based on his will.

Juridical *principium* is: freely do what lawful power requires (or can require).

Ethical: Act in accordance with motivating grounds of an inner universally valid will, i.e. so that you would be tolerated, loved, and honored.

7275. 1780s. Pr. 63.   19:300
Obligation is toward a human legislator, for otherwise we would make the rights of others insecure, and thus power[g] gives him a right toward the unjust and he can only be wrong in relation to another legislator.

---

[a] *natürlich Recht*
[b] *das Naturrecht vom natürlichen Recht*
[c] *das unsrige Nothdürtigst erhalten*
[d] *zwangsmäßig*
[e] *Gewalt*
[f] *Kraft*
[g] *Gewalt*

19:303 **7287.** 1780s? 1778–79? Pr. 78, in the bottom margin:
If I am in debt to someone[a] that is a "–" in a practical sense; if I pay him
that is a "+," i.e. with both together it = o. But if I am at fault toward
someone[b] then it is not enough to compensate him for the harm; the
wrong must still be made good, and then the juridical "–" with the ethical
"+" is = o, i.e. debt free.

19:303 **7289.** 1780s. Pr. 78.
The *principium* of retributive punishments[c] (regarding crime against
another) rests on each always being aware that whatever he does to
another he authorizes to be done to himself in conformity with the rule
of justice. Though it is a duty of love, it can also be a duty of obligation
to the whole in *status civilis* for public justice to make all punishments
corrective or exemplary [*later addition:* pragmatic]. But if they were not
already retributive punishments they would not be able to be used as a
warning to others. One cannot harm anyone who is not at fault for the
benefit of others.

19:308 **7309.** 1780s. Pr. 119, 118. To §178:
The doctrine of right (as right of human beings) is the content of laws
without which freedom cannot subsist externally together with the freedom of everyone. The doctrine of virtue is the content of all duties
or laws insofar as their idea alone contains sufficient determination to
action. The former is the duty of actions, the latter of dispositions. [Pr.
118:] Both could also be grasped under the division between perfect and
imperfect duties. The former rest merely on the form of actions, namely
freedom which, considered in its outer and inner universality, can exist
with itself. The latter consists of the relation of freedom to ends: 1. ends
in themselves, 2. Ends of humanity.

[a] *ich jemand schuldig bin* [b] *an jemand verschuldet habe*
[c] *rächenden Strafen*

IV. FRAGMENTS FROM NOTES ON
NATURAL RIGHT

For his course on Natural Right, as discussed in the editor's introduction, Kant used the two-volume *Juris Naturalis* by Gottfried Achenwall. The reflections below are drawn only from the second volume, the first having been lost before the preparation of the Academy edition. Some fragments on loose sheets are also included. The page of Achenwall's book on which the note was written is indicated by "J". The text of the Achenwall volume is reprinted in the Academy edition, 19:325–442.

7373. 1775–77. J 29. In §40   19:346
All laws of the *summus imperans* {supreme sovereign} must arise *quasi ex consensu communi* {as if by common consent}, namely not **necessarily** contradict them. This makes the *imperium* into *patriotico.* If some laws are possible only *ex arbitrio privato (unus adversum omnes)* {from private choice (one against all)}, then they are thuggish,[a] hence despotic.

7430. 1775–77? 1773–75?? on J 85:   19:372
The well-being of a state is completely different than that of the people. The former has to do with the whole in regard to its subordination under laws and the administration of justice, the latter with the private happiness of each; to have concern for this last is meritorious for a ruler.

7432. 1773–75? 1772? J 85.   19:373
Someone can be wronged by the process of administration. Specifically subjects must know what obligates them in accordance with a certain rule. This is law. Whoever applies the law can also do wrong. Thus there must be a higher one by whom he[b] can seek his right.

7439. 1773–75? 1772? 1769?? J 89. To §107, "libertas civilis"   19:376
Civil freedom consists in equality of support from public justice.
    Private freedom in the authorization to freely decide over everything that does not concern the *publicum.*
    The freedom to do what one wants without being restricted by another as delineated by the universal coercion of the laws.

7529. 1766–68? 1769? J 17. To §26   19:447
Society can decide by means of the majority of votes only about universal matters; it can be concerned only with the universal, therefore there are laws.

---

[a] *gewaltthätig*
[b] *er*, likely refers to the person wronged in the first sentence, but the direct antecedent is the one who applies the law.

The whole decides for the whole; yet the whole less a part is not the whole.

Everyone must decide for all exactly the same thing that all decide for him, i.e. it is a law.

In voting, society is considered to be one person and the members to be particular wills and inclinations of that one person.

In society one can either view the *socius* {association} as *accidens* {accident}, that subsists *intro* {internally}, or society and a *socius* that only subsists in *socio* {combination}.

19:448 **7531.** 1766–68? 1776–78?? J 19. To §28
Whether freedom is more limited when the *unanimitas* or *pluralitas* decides; the former secures independence,[a] i.e. negative freedom, the latter power, positive free power.

19:448 **7536.** 1766–69. J 77. To §94
The public person that is created in the *pactum civilis* {civil contract}
19:449 is called the political body, republic. In this all members considered together as vested with the supreme authority,[b] called *souverain*, as ruled through the will of the *souverain* is called the state. Every member of the republic as a part of the *souverain* is called citizen, as a part of the state is called subject. The members of the state in relation to one another insofar as they are the subjects of this association are called the people.

19:450 **7540.** 1766–69. J 88.
Bona {goods} belong to all understood *disjunctive* {disjunctively} and are *privata*, not to all taken *collective* (*copulative*) {collectively (in connection)}, and are not *publica*. The *sovereign* is an ideal person and has no property. The laws of the republic are laws *juris non ethicae* {of right not of ethics}; the particular rights of each against one another and not the greatest happiness of society should be protected.

19:451 **7542.** 1769. J 7.
The lord of the land[c] is not authorized to necessitate the citizen to actions which are in accord with the *bonum commune* {good of the community}, but only to apply the common power so that the *finis privatus* {private end} of each is not hindered.

19:452 **7548.** 1769–70? 1773–75? J 15.
Societas aequalis est, in qua non sunt obligationes (affirmativae) nisi arbitrio contractae et media juris utrinque aequalia. {A society is equal in which there

---

[a] *Unabhängigkeit*   [b] *der obersten Gewalt*
[c] *Landesherr*

22

are no (affirmative) obligations except those contracted by choice and in which the means of law are equal on all sides.}

All *societas* is *aequalis*. For all parts of a whole are coordinated with each other (that is *reciproce actio* {reciprocal action}). For a *unione voluntatum* {free union} requires that every will be a part of the collective will,[a] and so that everyone wills to be ruled only by the whole[b] insofar as each has combined his own will with those of others. There is no society between *imperante* {sovereign} and *subdito* {subject}.

7563. 1769–70? 1772–73? 1776–78? J 27. In the upper margin   19:455
Power[c] restricted to the condition of the stability of the state and the permanence of the rules of government is unlimited because power first becomes legitimate this way. (The exception to that, which would be wrong in itself, i.e., a moral non-entity, is not a limitation but only an establishment of a rule.)

7568. 1769–70. J 31.   19:457
One cannot acquire a right in a person of the opposite sex from the consent to use one's reproductive organs unless one constitutes a right to give the other enduring proprietorship[d] in the use of one's own reproductive organs. [J 30:] Here *jura utendi* {rights of use} are derived *a jure in re propria* (*societatis*) {from proprietary right in a thing (society)}. For since, in accordance with the first end of nature the *functiones sexuales* aim at propagation and education, so it is the highest law that paternity be certain; thus one and the same wife cannot be common to several; thus the right of intercourse is a proprietary right of the husband.

7571. 1769? 1770–72? J 30.   19:458
Regarding the sexual attributes neither *mas* {the man} nor *femina* {the woman} has *jus utendi re sua* {the right of use of their own} but only *jus alteri usum fructum concedendi* {the right to concede use and benefits to another}. The reason is because the essence [*added:* condition] of these members rests on the preservation of the species and he must not act against that. One wrongs humanity when one acts against the means of humanity's essential ends but not when one does not promote these ends. For in the latter case they are allowed to be based on one's desires and they make use only of instinct but not of duty. One cannot dispose over oneself *per vagam libidinem* {through wanton lust}.

[*added 1773–75 within §41:*] This is the single disposition over another's person, otherwise it is only a *jus reale* {right to a thing} in things. The *dominium reciprocum personae* {reciprocal ownership of a person} is

---

[a] *gesamten Willen*   [b] *den Gantzen*
[c] *Gewalt*   [d] *Eigenthumlichkeit*

possible so that no one can dispose over those of another without *consensu alterius* {the other's consent}. *Unio perfecta* {a perfect union}.

19:458 **7572.** 1769–70? 1773–75? J 30.
On the *pactum* {contract} in which someone disposes over his person for the use of the other. They are all null and void except *matrimonium*; for no one is his own property because otherwise he is a thing insofar as he is disposed and insofar as he disposes is a person. If [someone], however, can dispose over him, he can have no *jura* {rights}. [J 31:] For if he disposes over himself (not merely over his *pertinens non adhaerens* {belongings that do not inhere in him}), he has renounced his personality. But the renunciation cannot be an *actus juridicus* {rightful act}, because it
19:459 belongs to a person, thus etc. etc. That which one can dispose of can also be disposed of by another *ad satisfaciendum juri suo* {to satisfy his right}, consequently something a person can take as payment.

Commercium sexuale {sexual union} is allowed under no other condition but *matrimonium*. Whoever rejects this condition in a relation with another has, so to speak, acted against the *conditio tacitus* {tacit condition} of this *actus*, and the victim can coerce the other into marriage because one must repair all harm resulting from an action forbidden by nature and everything must again be arranged in conformity with nature.

19:460 **7580.** 1769–70? 1773–75?? J 32, 33.
All parts of the human being have according to their natural organization[a] an absolute use for that person with the exception of the sexual organs and powers. They belong to that person as part of the body, but insofar as they should be used there must be a right to them constituted for another. Now *dominus utilis* {ownership of what is used} is completely necessary,* if *usus* {use} to someone is to be *licitus* {allowed}. That person is not *dominus utilis*, thus a *dominium utile* for a single other person must be constituted. Now this *usus* can be yielded to no one without the other yielding the *usum vicissim* {use reciprocally}, and this also cannot be yielded without the *dominium utile*. Thus the husband and **wife** have **reciprocal** *dominium utile* regarding the sexual organs, yet so that it does not contradict the *dominio directo*, that is the health and ease of the other which only the other party can judge. This *dominium utile* cannot be separated from *jus utendi* {right to use}. It is not **divisible** and also not **alienable**. It is *jus in re* {right in a thing}. For it is *jus in membra non praestationem operae* {right in the organ not to performance of service}. Despite this there is no *jus in re ad alterius personam pertinente*

[a] *Natureinrichtung*

{right in a thing extended to another person}. [*later addition:*] If it were *jus personale ad praestandam operam* {right in the person to the performance of service}, then this right could not exclude *ab eadem opera praestanda* {the same service performed for} another.

From this it follows:

1. That prostitution would be forbidden *jure naturae* {in natural right} not because one thereby injures another but because according to the rule of right the use of sexual properties can be gained by another only *sub conditione dominii* {under the condition of ownership}; this is thus *tacite* given, and it is a contradiction of right that nothing further should be bound to the other.   19:461
2. that this *dominium utile* would be indivisible; thus polygamy and polyandry are forbidden.
3. that the *dominus utilis* could not alienate his right in parts.
4. that this *pactum* could not be dissolved otherwise than as *delictum partis alterius* {an offense on the part of another}.
5. that celibacy is allowed, consequently that *connubium* {marriage} could also be entered into as *sterile*.
6. that, because no one else except the *paciscentem* {party to the contract} has a right to judge the use of the sexual properties of the other; that *spadones* {the impotent} and *unuchi* {eunuchs} could be married even if it is *civiliter vetitum* {prohibited in civil law}.
7. that the validity of the *pacti matrimonialis* rests not on the *spe propagandae sobolis* {hope for propagation of offspring}, because otherwise it would be valid only as long as this hope lasted, and because we have no instinct which is aimed immediately at propagation but only one which is aimed immediately at sex and from which nature produces children unintended by human beings. But whoever follows natural instincts according to this law does not act against the law of nature if he simultaneously does not intend this distant end and also knows that he will not attain it. This is *malum defectum non vitium* {evil from defect not from vice}.

[32:] *coelibatum* {celibacy}
to whom does the child resulting from prostitution belong
[33: Kant's footnote to the first paragraph:] *It is peculiar that regarding the procreative parts no human being would have *dominium utile* over his own, and thus one would have no right to use them alone: *jus utendi, fruendi re sua* {right of use and enjoyment of one's own}, since I could say of this that it does not injure anyone else; firstly, here is *peccatum internum* {an internal sin}, 2. *Actio, qua utile non solum privatur usu sed etiam utilitate*

externa, est laesio potentialis {An act that is useful not only for private use but is also useful for others is a potential wrong}.

19:463 **7587.** 1769–70? 1776–78?? J 33.
The husband has *potestatem rectoriam rei domesticae* {the power of governing the household} but cannot the wife direct[a] it?; thus he has priority in disposing over it.[b]

19:463 **7591.** 1769? 1773–75?? J 34.
If *matrimonium temporarium* {temporary marriage} were possible, then a *momentaneum* {momentary} one would be possible, but this is a *stuprum* {fornication}.

19:466 **7599.** 1769? 1773–75? J 37.
God gave us an appetite for sex which is not always love but is an aim often entirely at odds with the happiness of the other sex. God thus based the most urgent end, one that allows for no respite, namely the maintenance of the species, on an insatiable drive.

19:467 **7602.** 1769–70? 1766–68? J 38.
The *mutuus adiutorium* {mutual support} is a natural consequence of the *pactum matrimoniale* {marriage contract}.

Whether marriage is naturally *societas aequalis* oder *inequalis* {a society of equals or of unequals}, whether the husband is *imperans* {sovereign}?

Whether marriage without *delictum alterutrius* {either being at fault} (from aversion[c]) could be dissolved with the agreement of both sides?

19:468 **7608.** 1769–71? 1773–75? 1766–68?? J 40.
Parental right regarding a child would not extend to disposition over the child's substance or health or limbs; a parent cannot abandon the child and the child is not to be left alone, nor can the parent alienate the child.

19:474 **7633.** 1769? 1773–75? J 54, outer margin. To §72
No one can alienate his freedom and create for another a personal right to himself without reserving for himself the authority to coerce the other to perform his duty. One can entrust no one with *jus illimitatum* {unlimited right} to his person; but if it is *restrictum* {restricted}, then one must reserve to himself the power to coerce the other to perform what is stipulated. Whoever places this in the will of another has placed the other in the position of doing no wrong to him. One can indeed sacrifice one's life but not one's freedom.

[a] *befehlen* [b] *ein Vorzug der disposition*
[c] *aus Ekel*

7638. 1769? 1773–75? J 56.   19:475
Bondsmanship can be nothing other than punishment for an affront for
it is a positive evil. One cannot offer oneself for bondsmanship, nor can
the other accept it, just as when one were to offer to let another cut
out part of his own flesh the offer cannot be accepted. But punishment
does not extend to descendants. Yet it must be possible to free oneself
from punishment through good behavior. So if bondsmanship were also
hereditary, there would have to be a specific means to release oneself
through service to the state or reconciliation with the lord.

7644. 1769? 1770–72? 1773?? J 72.   19:476
Civil society
    In inner relations, the commonwealth (citizens, subjects)
    In outer relations, the state

    1. authority[a] internally
    2. power[b] externally

7646. 1769? 1770–72? 1773?? J 73.   19:476
In the peaceful condition I am secure through my right. In the state of
nature I am secure through nothing but my power;[c] I must always be
prepared for war, I am always threatened by others; thus this is a state of
war *juridice* {juridically}.

7647. 1769? 1770–72? 1773?? J 73.   19:476
I am *laesus per statum* {wronged through the condition} by other human
beings who are in the state of nature. For I have no security and property   19:477
is always endangered. I am not obligated to endure this fear.

7651. 1769? 1770–72? 1773?? J 73.   19:477
In *statu naturali*, a valid basis of right[d] can indeed be found that allows
a right, externally valid in conformity with public laws, to be constituted. But it is still not an external right, for no externally valid rule is
determined.
    On the obligation to enter into *status civilis* {civil condition}.

7653. 1769. J 97.   19:477
1. The legislator must **not** be **judge**, for the judge must **stand under the
laws** in order for his judgment to agree with the laws, thus he himself
cannot be the legislator; moreover the *souverain* is always the whole and
the judge a part.

---

[a] *Gewalt*   [b] *Macht*
[c] *Gewalt*   [d] *Rechtsgrund*

19:478   2. The *souverain* is the ground of rights of the **state toward the subjects** (of the subjects toward the state) and the subjects against the subjects. It follows that his laws must refer **not merely to the whole** but **to all**. Thus equality of rights is necessary. All *praestationes subditorum* {performances for the subjects} occur for all and with regard for everyone's benefit. Yet so that all *bona privata* {private goods} remain.

19:478   **7654**. 1769. J 97.
It is a main duty of the *souverain* to relate everything to the equality of the subjects in both degree and aim. For this equality obtains before the social contract. The social contract is also possible only by means of this equality, it follows that the social contract is the condition of legislative power.[a] The contract can thus indeed introduce a **difference in power** in the administration of public commands, but can concede no superiority of anyone over anyone else in private life. Also the distribution of **burdens must** be **equal**. No one must[b] have authority **to make another happy**. Each makes himself as happy as he can, and has in this no obligation toward others.

19:479   **7658**. 1769–70. J 119.
In matters of religion and of opinions generally speaking no one is *judex competens* {competent judge} other than the human being's own reason or God.
    The external judge can exist only to restrict the freedom that each has to the degree that he does not impair the freedom of another.

19:481   **7663**. 1772? 1773–77? J 71.
Because one cannot have an exclusionary right to anything unless the right to land is previously determined, no one can wield sovereignty[c] over a people without being the owner of the land, for otherwise he would be only tolerated.[d] Thus ownership of the land is the condition of all his other rights. A foreigner merely stands under his laws because he is on his land. The *jus reale* {right to a thing} is the *fundamentum* of *personalis* {basis of personhood}. Children are subject to
19:482   the law not because they are connected to their parents' obligations but because they grow up on the same land over which the lord is *souverain*. Thus he is ruler because he is **lord of the land**.[e] From this the determination of the rights of jurisdiction. They must not consist in that which is brought forth from the land by culture but which the land *origetinus*

---

[a] *Gewalt*
[c] *Oberherrschaft*
[e] *Beherrscher weil er Landesherr ist*

[b] *Muß* with capital letter
[d] *wird er nur Geduldet*

{originally} contains in itself and belongs to its substance. Metals, lake and springs, to name some, must be available for general use because the substance has a general usefulness.

7664. 1772? 1775–77? J 71.   19:482

The *potestas legislatoria* {legislative power} must rest on the condition that it can do no wrong. Therefore the *originarie potestas legislatoria* {original legislative power} is only in the people. This is *illimitata* {unlimited}, for one can do no wrong to oneself; all the rest is restricted. This *potestas originaria* refers to the idea of a *pactum originari* {original contract}, for, if all conclude something in agreement, it is a *pactum*.

7665. 1772? 1773–77? J 72.   19:482

There is no right or property without law. But exactly the same laws which forbid me from encroaching on something which another possesses in certain form and quality must also provide me security that I will also be protected in what I am entitled to. I can only be ~~coerced~~ subjected to coercion as far as I am able to coerce others. Accordingly there is no right without an irresistible power.[a] But there is indeed ground for this right and these laws before this power is attained, and on this the laws must also be grounded. These grounds of right are, however, the common[b] will *in potentia* {potentially} and for the state laws the common will *actu* {actually}.

Thus all property right begins only in civil society. Whatever precedes it is the *jus necessitatis*, i.e. the right of necessity;[c] i.e. the right of self-subsistence which animals have and on which rests the security which one cannot disturb without placing oneself in danger, and where each follows his own inclination.

Therefore the first property belongs to the state. Everything else is derived. Not the property of the state[d] through voluntary contract of all.

The power of the state consists of property and the industry of hard-   19:483
working citizens for acquiring property. The idle citizen is a o in this regard.

The state cannot alienate its original property to the citizen. Because then this citizen would be independent. The state can only entitle this citizen to hereditary use and disposition of the property. For all power of the state is grounded upon this common property as the first *actus* of the constitution[e] of the rights of citizens.

---

[a] *Gewalt*, in this Reflection
[c] *Nothülfe*
[e] *der constitution*

[b] *Gemeinschaftliche*
[d] *des Staats seines*

19:483 **7667.** 1772? 1773–77? J 73.
Hobbes considered all laws, even moral laws, as despotic, i.e. laws which do not require our consent at all, at least our rational consent or concurrence. For he believed that wherever power[a] may reach, it would constitute[b] what is right. Likewise he did not differentiate the wrong which the *usurpator* {usurper} commits from that which he does to the subjects.[10]

19:485 **7673.** 1772. J 131.
The *souverain* must judge[c] what a constitution is and how it conforms with the **will** of the whole. The regent must judge what conforms with the particular **ends** of all, hence judge what is subsumable under a universal will in conformity with ends, and he must himself have a power to judge and not in turn be instructed how to judge. Finally the judge[d] must judge whether or not the subsumption of an individual's end under the law of the freedom of all would be right. There is thus: 1. Power[e] and freedom 2. Capacity and end 3. End under the law of freedom.

19:485 **7674.** 1772? 1773–77? J 136.
Whether something is a public or a private good is not determined through the application and use of the good but through the will of the one who disposes;

> over the *bona privata singulorum* {private goods of each} each disposes *exclusive* {exclusively}.
> over the *bona privata universorum* {private goods of all} each disposes without exclusion of the other.
> over the *bona privata universitatis* {private goods of the whole} only the collective will[f] disposes.

All *bona privata* belong to the *suum universitas sed non sunt communia* {property of the whole but are not communal}. These *bona universitatis* [*breaks off*]

19:486 **7680.** 1772–73? 1775–77?? J 185, 184. To §203
The *summus imperans* {supreme sovereign} does something wrong
19:487 and could be coerced with power.[g] The subjects* are right but do not have any authorized power and avail themselves of what they have, in this case they do not wrong the *imperans* but it is *formaliter* wrong. They act against the form of both the commonwealth and its

---

[a] *Gewalt*	[b] *mache*
[c] *Urteilen*	[d] *der Richter*
[e] *Macht*	[f] *gesammte Wille*
[g] *Gewalt* in this Reflection	

contract.[a] The resistance of the subjects contradicts itself as well as the constant call of their happiness, the former decides.

[Kant's footnote added 1773–75 or 1778–79:] *they can never oppose but only resist, i.e. refuse to do what is in itself morally impossible and endure the consequences.[b] The reason for this is because a human being is an animal that is good only under coercion, and he who is to coerce him is himself a human being. No wrong is done in this way to the one who wants to sever the bonds of right.

7681. 1772–73? 1773–75? 1769?? J 66. To §85   19:488
The establishment of society is voluntary if the human beings in the state of nature are not in a community. Here they could be moved to constitute a right with each other only if they benefit.[c]

If they are in a community, then everyone already has a right against the others, and the constituting has to do only with the means to enforce this right.

All constituting has to do either **with a benefit** which would not be attained without society (be it protection of a benefit already existing in the state of nature or the expectation of another), or **with defense of right;**[d] the former constitutes a **political** body, the latter a **moral** body.

7683. 1772–73? 1774–75? 1776–78? J 66: in §85, conclusion. J 67: over   19:489
and next to §87, beginning
[J 66:] Right and justice must exist in the world. If human beings are good by nature, then the condition of **public justice** is *status naturalis* {a state of nature}, if they are evil, i.e. because of them rights are insecure, then it is a condition of **public coercion** to justice.[e] To coerce private right is not a condition of justice. Creatures who are without coercion are without security. Were there a third fully [J67:] good and considerate being, who would proceed with irresistible strength, then it would be the head of the civil constitution. How is a civil condition ~~necessary~~ possible for corrupt human beings alone. Whoever ought to command and coerce must be without blame and, if not, could be coerced. The central law[f] is not *salus publica* {for public well-being} but *justitia publica* {for public justice}, but in order to attain it a certain public power[g] must be established. The object of right is not private welfare, i.e. that of the citizen, but the welfare of the state, yet without being detrimental to the private right of the citizens to attend to their own happiness.

---

[a] *Vertrag*
[c] *durch ihren Nutzen*
[e] *einer öffentlichen Zwangsgerechtigkeit*
[g] *Macht*

[b] *darüber alles erdulden*
[d] *Bevestigung des Rechts*
[f] *Das Hauptgesetze*

19:489   **7684.** 1772–73? 1772? 1769?

The *summum imperans* {supreme sovereign} also has *potestatem legisla-toriam* {legislative power} regarding religion, namely negatively, namely that no one has power to coerce outer religion, i.e. that there be no outer religion. He does not hereby hinder the public teaching of religion, but he blocks all means of coercion of *cultus externi* {outer worship}. One

19:490   can assume that a sound-thinking *summum imperium* would never set up obstacles to inner religion. It is, however, perverse that in addition to the *summo imperio in civilibus* {supreme sovereign in civil matters} there should also be an *independentes* one in *ecclesiasticis* {ecclesiastical matters}, who makes judgments that cannot be appealed on outer matters and pur-ports to control the administration of *souverain* power,[a] *status in statu* {a state within a state}. It is even more irksome if the lord of the land exer-cises this churchly power and constitutes a *forum externum* {outer court} concerning that which belongs solely before the *forum internum* {inner court}.

The lord of the land can make any sin that does not contradict the *pactum civile* {civil contract} (of citizens with one another) permissible in civil law and thus can permit all irreligion. **But first** he must provide all opportunity for the *forum internum* and its enlargement.

Whether in addition to the *pactum civile* there is another way that the *summum imperium* is constituted.

19:490   **7686.** 1772–73? 1769? 1774–75?? J 93.

A despotic monarch treats the state as his inheritance (*patrimonium*), a patriotic one as his fatherland. The country itself is a fraternity stemming from a communal[b] father. It is the dominion of the oldest. Consequently subjects also have a fatherland in the state. Because they know what they have received from fathers and can bequeath as fathers.

19:490   **7687.** 1772–73? 1769? 1774–75?? J 93.

The proposition that the government of a despot, if he is wise, i.e. clever and at the same time good, would be the best, contains a contradiction because if he were so, then he would lead such an inequitable[c] dominion only until he had transformed it into a lawful one in which the state rules itself. But this type of government or state constitution is certainly bad simply because the soundness of the government depends on whether or not the will of an individual is good.

19:491   The will of all is always good. The will of an individual may yet be evil. Yet the evil will has in it something peculiar, that it is not in confor-mity with the will of all together and yet can restrain itself in a way that

---

[a] *der souverainen Gewalt*   [b] *gemeinschaftlichen*
[c] *unbillige*

produces no results other than those in conformity with the rule of the good will.

7691. 1772–73? 1769? 1774–75?? J 93.   19:491
The monarch is one who has sole right to legislate.

The nobility are those who each have an inherited right to legislate.

The people are those who have a right to legislate only together not individually.

The nobility make the ground for a standing rule through which the state becomes something permanent, thus they are the pillars of the state. The people each see to their own right and constitute a people. The monarch constitutes the strength[a] of the state, i.e. the unity and that he is a power.[b]

7695. 1772–73? 1770–71? 1773–75? J 178.   19:492
A criminal court exercises *justitia punitiva* {penal justice} not *distributiva*; it must take the *factum* {deed} not in accordance with the letter of the law but in accordance with that which is advantageous to the one under investigation;[c] but in *civilactionibus* {civil actions} he must take it in accordance with the letter so that what belongs to each is precisely determined through the law. But punishment concerns the commonwealth not the *privatus*, thus punishments must seek to preserve its citizens.

7701. 1773–75? 1769? J I.   19:495
The whole doctrine of *jus reale* {right in a thing} is grounded on a philosophical fiction that pretends to the obligation[d] of things toward human beings. And this is the means of the (commonly valid) acquisition of right; however, the concepts of the obligation to the person and to *jus personale* {personal right} are the ground of a merely speculative judgment of right. In legislation one sees the former, one sees the doctrine of conscience in the latter. The thing is free by nature, it becomes obligated through the will of another and exclusively, namely it refuses others by means of signs of the coercion which one has over it. If he did not have it wholly in his power,[e] then he could not coerce it and it would remain *eatenus* {to that extent} free, e.g. *territorium* that I cannot discover or cultivate.

To whom befalls the misfortune: the one who has a thing stolen or the one who has purchased it *bona fide* {in good faith}? Because the latter is neither hindered by the power of the buyer nor is he bound to the sale, it is misfortunate for the owner not for the buyer if the thing is stolen.

---

[a] *Stärke*
[b] *Macht*
[c] *inquisiten*
[d] *Verbindlichkeit*
[e] *Gewalt*

19:495 **7702.** 1773–75? 1769? J 39.
The coercive duties of parents toward children are derived solely from the natural principles[a] of civil right. For the state must exist in perpetuity, at least the natural increase that occurs must not be destroyed. In themselves children have no coercive rights against parents; they could thus be thrown out by them, and although in accordance with the divine order this greatest duty falls upon the parents, they are nonetheless not obligated to the children.

19:496 **7704.** 1773–75? 1776–78? J 43.
Children do have a coercive right regarding their parents but no further than to their nutrition, maintenance, conservation, care, and defense. But they have no authorization to prescribe how this is done. They cannot demand anything except what is required for the most extreme natural needs. Accordingly no authorization about whether force can be used as the manner in which they are to be educated,[b] and if so what can be compelled by force unless it could result in death; they could be considered *opera parentum* {the work of their parents} as *gratuitam* {free} and are obligated to obedience, indeed from a *quasi contractu*.

19:497 **7708.** 1773–75? 1769? J 66.
The *quaestio juris* {question of right} is this: how to create a condition beneficial for every human being that can subsist in conformity with a rule that also works for the benefit of others and thus is just? **Is the establishment of a state merely arbitrary**, or is an establishment of a state [*added by Kant: juridice* {juridically}]] necessary; correspondingly what constitution[c] of the state alone conforms to right. Thus it is a ground of right that makes the **establishment of a state** necessary and is a ground of right which makes only one single **state constitution** in conformity with right. [*remainder of note added:*] Is the *status naturalis* {state of nature} a *status juridicus* {rightful condition} or a condition of injustice, a condition with no standing.[d] The *status naturalis* {state of nature} is a condition[e] of freedom without law, and so freedom to do wrong.

19:497 **7710.** 1773–75? 1769? 1770–71?? J 66.
If human beings were perfectly ~~knowledgeable~~ in agreement in will then no law would be necessary. If they were in agreement in judgment about a case, no judge would be necessary. If they were happily to do what is good for all, no coercion would be necessary.

---

[a] *principien*
[b] *erzogen*
[c] *Verfassung*
[d] *Zustand aber kein Stand.*
[e] *Zustand*

7712. 1773–75? 1769? J 66. To §85   19:498
The idea of the condition of external right.

7713. 1773–75? 1769? J 67.   19:498
There must be an unlimited supreme power: sovereignty.[a] Only the common[b] will can have this supreme power. It can do no wrong. But the execution is not by the common will. Here there can be wrong.

7719. 1773–75? 1780–89? J 68.   19:499
The civil condition is subjection under the laws as a subject. The one who is supreme, to whom everyone else is subject, is not a subject, hence is outside the civil condition. Hence free of his rightful obligation and observation. Here it is as hard to conceive of the first as it is in ontology.

7721. 1773–75? 1778–79? J 69.   19:499
Woe to the one who distorts the law or the idea of perfection that serves as a model, who passes them off as chimera, and who even accommodates his rule to the evil he finds before him.

Human beings could become better and better under a just govern-   19:500
ment, thus they could become ever smaller hindrances to the execution of a good rule; but if the rule is idiotically made or is falsified, then it stamps out the seed of the good.

7723. 1773–75? 1769? J 69.   19:500
That we do not have a right to ask to be ruled in accordance with the idea of perfect justice, for we ourselves must always be coerced.

7725. 1773–75? 1769?? J 69.   19:500
Majesty befits the one who is not subordinated; supreme power[c] the one who is supreme among all subordinates. The government is under the laws and thus has no majesty. It is not holy for it can rightly be held responsible.[d] The *souverain* cannot govern, for the regent stands under the laws, is obligated to rule in conformity to them, and can be held responsible. In contrast the law (*ex voluntate communi* {proceeding from the common will}) is beyond reproach[e] and is holy. The *dignitas legislatoria* {dignity of a legislator} is thus *majestas* and the legislator is beyond reproach. He lowers himself when he governs. He only inspires the regent. (The people cannot govern themselves.) The regent and to a

---

[a] *uneingeschränkte oberste Gewalt: souverainität*   [b] *gemeinschaftliche*
[c] *Hoheit*   [d] *getadelt werden*
[e] *untadelhaft*

35

lesser extent the *souverain* can judge.[a] Yet in addition the judge can judge[b] the government, but not *valide* {validly}, and the *souverain* has *potestatem inspectoriam* {oversight powers} over both.

19:502 **7733.** 1773–77? 1790–1804?? J 74. In §89, 2
Jus naturae {natural right} consists in universal happiness insofar as it is
19:503 possible through the universal agreement of private choice, *jus publicum* {public right} in the means to actualize this condition.

19:503 **7734.** 1773–77? 1790–1804?? J 76.
The social contract is the rule and not the source of the state constitution.

    The social contract is not the *principium* for the establishment of the state but for the administration of the state and contains the ideal of legislating, governing, and public justice.

    If one were to ask what is the *principium objectivum* {objective principle} for the establishment of the state, then I would answer: in a union of freely acting beings who should still all be considered as subject to coercive law, **coercive power**[c] **is necessarily independent of them** and no *principium objectivum* for the establishment of the state is possible. Power precedes each coercive law. If this power is not ascribed by nature to him who also has the right to legislate then it cannot be rightfully established at all. For since his power is tied to the condition that his will be right and that it acts in conformity to these rules, **whoever coerces him to act in conformity with rules of right** ought also share such a will. Further, whoever has a contingent right to do this must be capable of being obligated in conformity with coercive laws so that he has his power only through right and not through choice. Only then is there is no other power that could coerce him.

    The right to legislate is *originarie* in the people but *derivative* in the monarch. The right to govern can only be a derivation since its execution presupposes two opposing persons, where neither has *jus originarium* with respect to the other.

19:503 **7735.** 1773–77? 1790s?? J 76.
The proposition *exeundum est a statu naturali* {one must leave the state of nature} means that one can force everyone to enter *in status civilis* {a civil condition} with us or our republic. Hence in this respect alone is war just.

19:503 **7736.** 1773–77? 1790s?? J 76. To the conclusion of §91
Justitia publica est finis republicae. {Public justice is the end of a republic.}

---

[a] *richten*   [b] *Der Richter kann auch urtheilen*
[c] *Gewalt* in this paragraph

finis constitutionis est 1. conservatio totius, 2. suus cuiusque. {The end of 19:504
the constitution is 1. the preservation of the whole, 2. of the property of
each.}

7737. 1773–75? 1769?? 1770–71?? J 76. 19:504
The idea of the social contract is only the guideline for judgment about
right and for instruction for the ruler regarding a possible perfect establishment of the state,[a] but this idea does not allow the people any actual
rights.
    Nothing seems more natural than that if the people have rights, they
also have power;[b] however, even in this regard the people have no strict
right but only an ideal because the people cannot establish rightful
power.

7738. 1773–75? 1769? 1770–71?? J 77. 19:504
Contractus originarius {The original contract} as the guideline, *principium,
exemplar* of the right of a state. It must be derived from ideas, not from
factis {deeds}, also not from the grounds of the *flores* {prosperity} of the
state, i.e. from well-being.

7742. 1773–75? 1776–78? 1769?? 1770–71?? J 78. 19:505
In every *civitas* {body politic} there must be a *summum imperium*
{supreme sovereign}. *Imperans universitatis* {commanding universally},
the *summus imperans* must have an unlimited right and all the power.[c]
Summus imperans thus cannot be distinguished from the people. For then
the people would have no right at all. For if there were such a situation,
then there would be no commonly valid pronouncement[d] and no power,
both of which can necessitate.

7744. 1773–75? 1769? J 79. 19:505
(*Imperium summum est plenum et illimitatum* {the supreme sovereign is
complete and unlimited}, it does not have only the highest power but all
power.)

7747. 1773–75? 1776–78? 1769?? J 79. 19:506
If the right of the king is derived from an act[e] (*facto*) of the people then
the people would be able to grant no greater power[f] than they themselves
had. They must, therefore, have had sovereignty in order to transfer it
to another. Now the people cannot rule or govern themselves, thus also

---

[a] *Staatserrichtung*. Could also be *Staatseinrichtung*, "direction of the state"
[b] *Gewalt* in this paragraph   [c] *Gewalt*
[d] *Ausspruch*   [e] *Thathandlung*
[f] *Macht*

they cannot transfer this authority[a] to the other. Human beings could renounce only their natural freedom for the benefit of another, but then they cannot reserve any of it.

19:506 **7748.** 1773–77? 1778–79? 1770–71? J 78.
Were the subjects to have transferred *summmum imperium* {supreme sovereignty} through an actual *pactum* {contract}, would they have been able to *valide* {validly} reserve for themselves the right to judge the observance of the *pacti* on the side of the *imperantis*? One can see that such a *pactum* in which one reserves rights for oneself but not an authority to coerce the other would be a juridical nullity.

19:507 **7752.** 1773–77? 1772? J 79.
The will of the *summus imperans* {supreme sovereign} is universal, but it ought to be applied to every individual, either insofar as each is a member of the state, in order to go from the particular to the universal, or insofar as each one stands in relation to what is private (in private relations). The regent actualizes[b] the general will in the particular. But the judge must judge in a controversial case whether it is in accordance with the universal. The regent can do wrong.

19:508 **7754.** 1773–75? 1772? 1769?? J 78.
The *souverain etc.* cannot be alienated.[c]
In the state the *souverain* is the united power.[d]

19:508 **7756.** 1773–75? 1772? J 78.
The will of the *summus imperans* {supreme sovereign} must always be right (i.e. inculpable) because his will is to determine what right and the supreme *primcipium justitiae publicae* {principle of public justice} should be. His power (regarding justice in the land) must be irresistible because only in this way can the *imperans* secure to each his right as they stand under his laws. It must be united. It must be *voluntas communis* {the common will}.

19:508 **7758.** 1773–77? 1772? J 80.
Does the *souverain* have a right to the person by means of the land or to the land by means of the person, for both rights are connected. The first is true, for only the land remains, the persons change and an ancestor can place no obligation on a descendant except by means of a third thing, a right to which the ancestor wants to bequeath to the descendant. Now if this is true, then the *souverain* is *dominus directus* {direct owner} of the

---

[a] *Gewalt* [b] *actuirt*
[c] *alienirt* [d] *einige Macht*

land, the subject is only *dominus utilis* (*dominium publicum*) {owner of the use (public ownership)}; from here, however, *privatum* {private [owner-ship]} is derived, which must then be restricted under the condition that 19:509 civil society as well as its substratum endures. That is air, water, earth, and fire.

Therefore he does not permit the woods to be completely cleared.

7765. 1773–75? 1772? 1776–78?? J 89. 19:510
One does not lose any rightful freedom but only the lawlessness of the *status naturalis* since the coercive law restricts freedom to conditions of universal security. Human beings must stand under coercive laws; this is a proof that they are evil by nature. The good in them in the civilized condition is itself an effect of coercion, which imperceptibly removes savagery and develops moral motives through the restraint of self-love.

7769. 1773–75? 1772? 1769? J 91. To §109 19:511
The *actus* {act} through which a multitude becomes a people through its unification already constitutes a *souverain* power which they transfer to someone else through a law. For *pacta* {contracts} are laws and already suppose a legislative power.

If the people hand sovereignty over to someone they cannot limit it for otherwise it is not sovereignty. All limitation presupposes that the people retain supreme power.

7771. 1773–75? 1772?? J 92. 19:511
Without the patriotism of the government no patriotism of the subjects is possible (for the latter consists in the subject being viewed as a member of the state and not as its property). Under the rights of a subject of a patriotic state belongs his standing under equality of merit which he can himself raise up; he can also attain the same dignity as every other. So he must not himself belong to another's *patrimonium* {patrimony} and not be a hereditary subject of a private man. As means for this the freedom of the pen.

7777. 1773–75? 1772?? J 94. 19:513
The ruler is either lord of the land[a] or not. In the first case the vassals obtain the land as a fief from him and are its natural defend-ers and are thus born leaders. The one who has inheritance rights for succession of the fief is an actual noble and is a born officer under the barons. Those with the 'von' title are titular nobles, and are thereby qual-ified to hold offices and are able to purchase fiefs. The English *cadets* and

[a] *Landesherr*

their male descendants are true nobility, for the remainder is allowed to them, although not *exclusive* {exclusively}.[11] The lord who is *dominus utilis* {owner of use} of the entire land to whatever extent he wills is a despot. The citizen is absolutely never *dominus*. The noble is *dominus eventualis* {indirect owner}.

Aristocracy is the sovereignty[a] of the *collegium* {council} of lords, i.e. of the proprietors of the land. The rest are the people: citizens,[12] farmers, servants, and workers, and of these the last three are called the rabble.[b] Democracy is when all of them together are like the head of a family, are all citizens.

The ruler who can do nothing without the consent of the nobility and the people obtains the government as a fief but does not have *dominium* {ownership} of it.

19:515 **7781**. 1773–75? 1772?? J 98.

The *souverain* gives laws, governs (not administers), and oversees justice. He must not administer because that is an **actus singularis**, which stands **under the law**, which **can be wrong**, and against which a safeguard must exist in the state. His will does not refer to an *actus singularis*, where a case is subsumed under the law (thus a **wrong** can occur in this subsumption but **not in the sanction** of the laws, because they alone determine right); such things the directors, the government, and magistrate do; the *souverain* makes his will known to them through the minister. Although he does not **administer, he does indeed govern**, in that he appoints, removes, etc., the government.[c] He is chief judge (overseer). He **issues no judgments** in particular cases but appoints other judges or also directs a special court, because this is again a general action, for he takes assistance for their right from the people themselves and thus the people themselves rightly issue judgments. To him no blame

19:516 is attributed, he is holy and irreprehensible. If he however lays his hand on the rights of an individual, then he has a *jus controversum* {disputed right} not *sanctum* {a sacred right}.

All judging[d] must be public. The members of courts must be named by the *magistratus*, which represents the *publicum*.

19:519 **7794**. 1773–77. J 119.

All teachers of religion have a right to examine their religion, also to objections and doubts and alterations of it. Even those who serve a church, because they or their predecessors are still the ones who gave form to the religion and thus they must be able to improve it.

---

[a] *Oberherrschaft*
[c] *gouvernement*

[b] *der Pöbel*
[d] *Alles Richten*

7795. 1773–75? 1772? J 119.   19:519
Even the people themselves cannot force a consensus on religion by
positive coercive laws. For one cannot be coerced by human beings
to that which only concerns God, and they cannot pledge themselves
to anything which, as soon as their opinion changes, would require
all to change. Even less can this occur through the judgment of the
majority.

To believe in a God, at least to swear by him, can be coerced because
the conscience of the one who does not believe in God can be against
it.

7796. 1773–75? 1772? 1776–78?? J 119.   19:519
The people have a strict right to look after their own welfare uncon-
cerned about the well-being of later descendants, who may also care
for their own welfare. But nevertheless in religious matters it is a duty
of equity not to make restrictions on freedom which make progress
toward perfection impossible for the human species, e.g. that pastors
must swear to certain articles and that government positions be conferred only under special and arbitrary religious conditions.

7810. 1773–75. J 186.   19:523
Self-defense in the *statu naturali* is the single *casus necessitates ad agendum
(permissionis)* {a case of necessity to act (permissive)}, but in *status civilis*
it is never anything but *ad patiendum* {to suffer}. The highest obligation
is toward the *corpus civilis* {civil body}. If the monarch no longer represents the *corpus civilis* in his actions, then the people has a right against
him, if the people constitute a *corpus civilis* without him. Since this never
occurs in a *souverain* government, the *multitudo* has no right at all and
each individual would wrong the people in challenging the basis of the
unio civilis. That is why while the *souverain* as an individual has no right
to be a tyrant, the subjects in turn have no coercive right against him
and are to be punished by him in the event of a rebellion or a conspiracy
because of his rights as head of state or as regent.

The *souverain* is presumed always to act in *bona fide* {good faith}.
The presumption is against one who opposes him when the opportunity arises.

7812. 1773–75? 1776–79? 1780–89?? J 187.   19:523
If every one of the people must fear for his own destruction, then this
is a *casus necessitatis* {case of necessity} and has *favorem necessitatis* {pre-
sumption in favor of necessity} before the judgment of reason;* but it
still wrongs the *imperans* who can with right resist. This right cannot be
established by law.

19:524   [Kant's footnote:] *The reason is that this resistance cannot be forbidden because individuals can be threatened only up to an equivalent ill.

19:524   **7814.** 1773–75? 1776–79? 1780–89?? J 187.
Merely passive obedience consists of enduring not of acting.

In this regard, not everything is allowed to the monarch himself, but only *externo jure* {external rights}.

19:524   **7815.** 1773–75? 1776–79? 1780–89?? J 186.
The question is whether the people can make a contract with the *souverain* such that they reserve for themselves the right to resist him. Then they must also reserve for themselves an authorization to judge him as well as to direct executive power.[a]

19:525   **7818.** 1773–75? (1776–78?) 1769?? 1770–71?? J 236.
The right of nations rests on this single touchstone: If my undertaking is so constituted that its maxim can be publicly known without contradiction, then it is right. In contrast that action is [wrong] whose maxim, were it publicly known, must normally bring about general resistance.

Universal power[b] is regarded as irresistible. Because, however, everyone who is bound to right must also be able to rely upon his right, it follows that there is an obligation in the right of nations to render assistance to each who is subject to open force.[c]

Thus if someone simply chooses to suppress another state given an advantageous opportunity, then he must imagine that this maxim were publicly known; here anyone could judge that the same could be done to him.

It is appropriate that I can publicly express the maxim that I will use open force in any matter that I consider to be just. By contrast attacks without a declaration of war, poisoning, assassination, incitement to treason, bribing another's servant, counterfeiting (but not privateering) are all founded on maxims that one could not express. The loss is in vain. If the disadvantage that accrues to me from making my maxim public were greater than the loss can be to my purpose, then to accept its being known is impossible. All malicious actions are of this type.

19:526   Actions whose maxims must necessarily be dissimulated are wrong. Maxims of all rightful actions must be public and such that they can at least be accepted by everyone.

---

[a] *Gewalt*   [b] *Gewalt*
[c] *eine offenbare Gewalt*

7819. 1773–75? (1776–78?) 1769?? 1770–71?? J 236.   19:526
One must have maxims for actions that are possible when declared publicly. One must waive the advantage of being secretive and behave and
act before everyone's eyes. Ethical maxims, if they are to be publicly
known, cannot be unloving because they would rob us of all love, and also
cannot be unnatural because we would thereby separate ourselves from
humanity.

7824. 1773–75? 1776–79?? J 238.   19:527
War is merely a use of power in the face of a problematic administration of right *in statu naturali*. The enemy is thus not an offender but a
counterpart in the assertion of a right that is subject to doubt. Thus neither hate nor revenge must have a place here. The evil of war can refer
only to the use of weapons and the right of human beings must be left
untouched.

7826. 1773–75? (1776–78?) 1769?? J 239.   19:527
I do not require consent to an action that I can coerce someone into
performing. And in the case of consent when I have used coercion, my   19:528
right is not based on the consent but instead on the legitimacy of my
demand.

7832. 1773–75? (1776–78?) 1772?? J 249. To §278   19:529
All final and supreme means for maintaining the right of human beings
are holy. Thus another's good, promising, what I do for a fellow citizen,
are not holy, but contracts among nations, peace treaties, above all the
supreme power of the *souverain*, but even above that the divine will, are
holy, for there is nothing at all above this that serves as means to determine and to secure right.

7837. 1773–75? 1776–79? 1780–89? J 252.   19:530
Peace must always be understood as grounds that actually exist for a perpetual overcoming of all conflicts of right; for otherwise the suspension
of hostilities is only an *armistitium* in which one nonetheless willfully
reserves reasons for future hostilities. Thus every peace presupposes that
all claims that one state could have had against the other up to that point
in time and that could result in hostilities are given up and declared null.
Hence peace opens a new chapter between two states after which no old
claims could be raised that would be considered as unsettled.

7847. 1775–77? 1778?? J67.   19:533
The civil constitution is not arbitrary but necessary in conformity with
grounds of right regarding the security of others. Society is not the

cause of this condition but the effect. The practical *souverain* ground of right makes a society, but because this ground is derived from the will of all[a] toward one another and not from the will of each yielding in submission, the laws are regarded as given by all. An already established commonwealth can indeed be improved but not destroyed, and awareness of general injustice does not suffice for any right even against

19:534 a tyrant because one provides him with no security if one reserves for oneself the right to punish him.

19:535 **7853.** 1775–79. J 83.
There is a simple state constitution in which each would give laws in community with others and each would in this way rule himself. But beyond legislation there should exist a power to coerce each to act in accordance with the laws and simultaneously a power for the preservation of the state, so the arrangement cannot be simple, one may make a single human being or a senate or the whole people into the head. Sole authority does not befit one individual. ~~Thus the power to enact laws must itself~~ There must always be three estates. Authority,[b] dignity, majesty, which have equal weight. 1. A head. 2. The people, which has the largest property. 3. A body of nobility, which is the greatest *corps* {body} of rich people, that is united and acts as a counterweight to the two others. The nobility rule through honor and the people through advantage.

19:535 **7854.** 1775–77? 1772? J 87.
Every human being seeks his happiness and also enters into the civil union with the intention of promoting his happiness. But he does not intend for the state to determine in what he should place his happiness; rather he will take care of this himself. The state should only secure him against people who could hinder him in his own concern for his happiness.

19:538 **7862.** 1776–78? 1780–89? J 28.
The binding force of all right does not really lie in what is inherent in a person but more so in the right of humanity. Therefore all human beings have the obligation to protect the right of each individual. This right of humanity also obligates each one toward himself. He was conceived in humanity, acquired its rights, but with the duty to preserve its dignity. Therefore all duties towards oneself.

One must distinguish what belongs to the person of the human being and what to his possession, to the last organ, faculty, and everything over which freedom has power. All possession is contingent. Thus the

---

[a] *von aller Wille*   [b] *das Ansehen*

right regarding possession is not *originarium* {original} but *acquisitum* {acquired}. I acquire all of this only *conformiter* with the idea of humanity (because this is the ground of the possibility of human beings); thus acquisition is possible under the condition of the conformity of freedom with the idea of humanity; thus a *status originarie* is *obligatorius* {original status is obligating} and my *jura* {rights} [*breaks off*] 19:539

7880. 1776–79? 1769? 1780–89? J 37. 19:543
Because no one can acquire a right to the use of another's sexual organs[a] without at the same time acquiring an unlimited right to the whole person,* and because this also holds reciprocally from the other party; then** this must be limited to the extent that a common will must emerge that is valid for all actions and the concerns of each one, so this is marriage as a *communio voluntatis ac jurium* {community of wills and also of rights}; whether *commercium sexuale* [*breaks off*]

We can of course acquire the *usus* {use} of things but not of persons. In light of this only *usus operae* {the use of a service} can happen because if the will of another from it no actus of the nothing can be required except free actions in which they themselves cannot dispose of themselves as things and so would be able to concede their use. 19:544

[Kant's footnotes added 1780s:] *A *jus reale* {real right} in the person of another cannot relate to a part for the person is an indivisible whole. One moral person arises from two.

**There ought to be a *jus in re* {right in a thing} and yet at the same time a *jus personale* {right in a person}, i.e. to the person alone and depending on her will. There must therefore be a right that extends not merely to a person regarding a particular use but to the entire will of the person, i.e. the person herself must be acquired.

7881. 1776–78? 1778–79? 1780–89? J 39. 19:544
A three-fold relation[b] arises from the nature of humanity: 1. that a human being has need of another sex. 2. That he requires parents. 3. That he finally has need of a lord.* All three are for his subsistence. In all three there is the juridical dignity[c] of humanity, which sets limits to this relation of subordination. This *dignitas juridica* {juridical dignity} is the *personalitas* {personality}. In this way society and not mere subjection is necessary, i.e. not *jus reale* {right in a thing} in a human being but *jus personale*.

Complete deprivation of freedom negates the person.

---

[a] *des Geschlechts des andern*   [b] *Verbindung*
[c] *juridische würde*

[Kant's footnote:] *A human being requires subjection under another human being as supreme, for without command the human will does not agree universally.

19:547 **7895.** 1776–79? 1780–89?? J 57. Over and in §74
If the human being is placed in the condition where another's will[a] has complete disposition over him, then he can never be obligated; for he cannot choose between an action and its opposite. He can therefore do no wrong, and hence he is allowed to resist coercion. Power[b] that corresponds to an authorization to resist is unjust; consequently power over a bondsman is unjust. Each and every *pactum subjectionis servilis* {contract for slavery} is in itself null and void. It can be arranged only *operam* {for work}; but how far does this go? That is the difficulty. So far as the mandatory duty toward his life and health, likewise his human vocation for the species, can still be fulfilled. A human being who recognizes no further obligation (such as a murderer, because he must be considered as one who eliminates *obligantes*) must be killed. He can cease to exist, but not live and cease to be a human being, because without obligation, he would have no right, and without right, he would not be a human being, but still free, hence a general obstacle to freedom in conformity to rules. Still less can he speak for his children's *operas* {works}. Where no *pactum* for application of power is possible, there no right is possible; consequently either this power is wrong or the human being who is incapable of all *pacti* wrongly lives.

19:548   Absolute subjection (or bondsmanship) takes place only under a completely good will that can never be wrong, thus one to which our wills would be subjugated entirely passively (the will of all others is restricted); but we must also consider whether the will is also a completely just will, hence obligation is never a blind subjugation which is entirely passive.

19:548 **7897.** 1776–79? J 58. To the conclusion of §74
A human being can be neither absolute lord nor absolute subject relative to one another, for the first does no wrong at all, the second has no rights at all. Every right presupposes obligation from the other side. Obligation is, however, only a restriction of the right of a person, but only under the conditions of another's right. The right of a human being relative to another is restricted in this way at all times.

19:551 **7912.** 1776–79? 1775? J 181. To §197
Laesus {the victim} has *adversus laedentem jus infinitum* {infinite right against the perpetrator}. Thus also the people against one who threatens their lives. The murderer is thus punished by death, not as if he were

     [a] *fremder Wille*   [b] *Gewalt*

himself to have agreed to it and were thus obligated to permit the punishment. For no one can be said to be obligated to permit coercion, for coercion concerns only one who does not want to fulfill his obligation. Instead the offended party has a right to exercise *jus talionis* {the right of retaliation} without consent.

[Kant's footnote:] *Summus imperans* {the supreme sovereign} has the obligation to secure for everyone their indispensable possessions and those whose loss is irreparable. This is possible only through the elimination of the criminal.

7913. 1776–79? 1780–89? J 180.   19:551
Because the murderer himself is a danger to the existence of other human beings, he completely loses the right of a human being and is an outcast.

7914. 1776–79? 1780–89? J 180.   19:551
The citizens have not, as Beccaria[13] believes, given the right to dispose of their lives to the *souverain*, and nor have they made an impermissible   19:552
and void contract in which he cannot dispose of their lives; instead it has nothing at all to do with his preference whether or not a citizen wants to be punished, he instead loses the *status civilis* {civil condition} and is an outcast.

7915. 1776–78? 1780–89? J 180. To §197, "*vocatur jus necis*"   19:552
What someone perpetrates against another he gives to the other a right to perpetrate against him unless they have agreed to the contrary. Therefore there does not first need to be a *pactum* {contract} for the commonwealth to have the right to punish the murderer by taking his life; that right befits *lege* {by law} all on whom the defense of all rights of the offended party is incumbent. He cannot complain about wrong at all. It is also not a violation of humanity in general (like some lies) but an action through which that which dishonors humanity is negated. Also, the punishment must be specifically identical with what the perpetrator[a] has done to which the injured party did not consent: insult with insult, robbery with robbery. The *publicum* requires still something more for its security. Blows do not insult if one reciprocates, but indeed they would if one were to put up with them for love or money. A fine works as if the offended party had allowed his right to sue[b] to be bought.

7916. 1776–79? 1780–89? J 183.   19:552
Capital punishment cannot be seen as voluntarily imposed on each person himself (likewise everyone else) through a *pactum*, because it is

[a] *Täter*   [b] *klagen*

self-evident that if another were to do to him what he has done to someone he could not complain about a wrong. He has himself forfeited the right of preservation. It is ridiculous to demand that by means of a law one who has done something like that should be spared from the right of retaliation. It is also absurd that someone should make himself obligated to be punished. Each can have a basis for a right only to the extent that he can claim to keep himself above suspicion about all future violation of others. He always agrees with the punishment of others, and thus is it done in his case, so he is subjected to punishment through the right of others without his consent. Otherwise one must say that he is obligated to voluntarily accept being coerced. In that case the evil that befalls him would be no coercion and thus also no punishment, as some repentant sinners want to pay for their faults and offer themselves to the judge.

19:553

19:554 **7919**. 1788–89 (after October 13, 1788) *Loses Blatt* D 7.
[*R7919 is on a fragment of a letter to Kant with the date October 13, 1788. This sheet also contains R5654 (18:312–313; titled "Against Idealism"). The text of R7919 is printed twice in the Academy edition: the second occurrence is 23:255 in the section "Drafts for Introduction to the Rechtslehre"; the translation appears only here. The differences between the two versions resulting from transcriptions by different editors will be noted in brackets.*]

The difficulty of determinately giving not the rule for right but more the rule for the securing of one's rights in a state is nearly insuperable. Were one certain about justice being reciprocated then everything would be determinate. But this uncertainty, which is yet in conformity with contract,[a] has the result that in such a condition of injustice the only rule that would remain is to direct one's practices so that a reciprocal trust could arise from them as well as a general mental obligation[b] to maintain it, just as if it were [*only in 23*: a *status* {condition} in contrast to] a *status civilis* {civil condition}.

The right of necessity arises not from physical need [*only here*: in contrast to duty] but from the moral necessity that must take second place to a greater one, e.g. to allow one's parents to die in order to sustain one's children.

The state can coerce no one to be happy or to make another happy but must secure everyone's freedom. From this it follows that because all state constitution is nothing but the condition of a reciprocal lawful coercion of the citizens that only the *souverain* exercises, the principle of state constitution is not the happiness of the citizens, but happiness could be at best only a means for the proper end.

[a] *vertragsmäßig*　　　　[b] *eine allgemeine Mentalverbindung*

Qualification of [*only here:* maxims for universal; *only in 23:* the opinions of all in the] law whose form without matter becomes a determining ground through reason. 19:555

7920. 1780–89. J conclusion. 19:555
Despotism appears to be the type of government where the *collegia* {corporations[a]} do not have the right to remonstrate, hence to represent the welfare of the state to the lord of the land,[b] or also when the ruler himself rules.

The right of the state is metaphysical when everything is derived from the mere concept of the state without the intermixture of anything contingent in human nature and of the empirical nature of the course of the world.

7930. 1780–89. J 59. In §75 19:558
No human being can be born into a condition in which he must serve another. Thus if he does not make himself obligated to service through contract[c] or crime, he is free. Many lords of the manor[d] believe that they are able to care for the happiness of their subjects better than the subjects themselves; thus that their subjects should obtain their welfare from their lord's benevolence, not from that which they could demand as their right, namely to care for their happiness themselves.

7932. 1780–89? 1778–79? J 68. 19:559
If *servitus personae* {enslavement of a person} were possible in accordance with natural right, then the *souverain* would relate to his subjects as owner to a slave. For there is nothing limiting his will. Only democracy would be allowed where each simultaneously acquires[e] himself while he has *condominium* {co-ownership} over all others.

7937. 1780–88. J 64. 19:560
A natura {by nature} everyone is indeed free and no one is obligated to enter into a *pactum unionis civilis* {contract for a civil union} with anyone as long as one is certain that he will not be harmed, i.e. as long as I am safe for him. But where this is not the case, everyone is obligated, as long as various individuals[f] stand in *commercio* {interaction}, to either leave the *commercio* or leave the *statu naturali* {state of nature}. *Primum principium juris publici et justitiae externae constitutivum status civilis* {The

---

[a] Corporations include guilds and other trade organizations, but Kant might more narrowly have in mind the specific corporation, or college, of university faculty members or more broadly the reading public, as in the 1784 essay "What is Enlightenment?"
[b] *Landesherrn*   [c] *contract*
[d] *Gutsherren*   [e] *acquirirt*
[f] *verschiedene*

first principle of public right and external justice is to establish a civil condition}.

19:560 **7938.** 1785–88. J 64.
In the right of a state, the principle[a] of the constitution is constituted[b] not by the happiness of citizens (for they may look after that themselves) but their right. The prosperity of the whole is only the means to secure their right and to place them in a condition to make themselves happy in every way. Thus they must themselves care for the poor, maintain schools, and educate their children, but also have the freedom to do that, to determine their religion themselves, but to alter it only through agreement.

19:562 **7950.** 1780–89? 1778–79? 1773–75?? J 74.
Every society[c] is voluntary,[d] the *totum civile* {civil whole} is necessary, cannot be dissolved.

19:563 **7953.** 1780–89? 1776–79? J 78. Over and in §95
Despotism (power[e] of a single individual unrestricted by law) is wrong in that, if it is accepted, then no right any longer restricts the will of the supreme lord, for everything is right that he wills to do to others. What someone wills regarding himself, hence the state in regard to its members, is right. Thus it is absurd that an authorization that allows one to be incapable of doing wrong is assigned to someone, or that it would have rightful force if human beings waived their rights in general. Here is the whole difficulty in a nutshell: as in the metaphysics of absolute *necessario*, how a supreme will that would determine what is right is possible, and yet itself be an irresistible power conforming to right, although it is not restricted by anything external nor by the right of others, for in that case a still higher power would be required.

19:564 **7955.** 1780–84. J 74. In and to §89
Not the principle of general happiness but freedom according to universal laws constitutes the principle of the establishment of the state and its idea.

19:565 **7960.** 1785–89. J 75. In §90
Because *unio civilis* {a civil union} is necessary, the idea of a *pactum* {contract} as *originarie* {original} must come first, but one whose content has to do only with the *institutiones externas* {external institutions} that secure

---

[a] *princip*
[c] *societät*
[e] *Gewalt*, in this Reflection

[b] *der Verfassung ausmacht*
[d] *willkührlich*

Reflections on the philosophy of right

salutem publicam {the public safety}, regarding everything else each may care for his own well-being.

7961. 1785–89. J 75. In §90   19:565
Whether the constitution[a] requires *unanimia*. In the idea of good human beings, yes. But as they are, it requires enough so that others can be coerced. According to the *principio exeundum e statu naturali* {the principle that one must leave the state of nature}.

7966. 1785–89. J 77.   19:566
The *pactum originarium* {original contract} is concluded in order to constitute 1. a commonwealth in itself, 2. a state, i.e. a condition among other commonwealths, 3. a power[b] in order to constitute a unity with other commonwealths.

7969. 1785–89. J 79. In and to §97   19:567
Originario {originally} the *imperium* {sovereign power} is in the people and also remains in them in the idea. *Regimen summum* {the supreme governing power} is also in them but not the magistrature.

7970. 1785–89. J 81. To §98   19:567
The question of who would have a right to *summum imperium* {supreme sovereignty} is a legitimate question only when the people do not yet have a *summus imperans* {supreme sovereign}. If the people do have one then it is already a *status civilis* {civil condition} and only through power[c] can it be determined who the *summus imperans* {supreme sovereign} would be, and the people can only speak out, thus the *summus imperans* cannot abrogate sovereignty[d] without falling back into the *status naturalis* {state of nature}.

7971. 1785–89. J 82, 83.   19:567
The supreme head of state represents a three-fold person: as legislator he is *souverain*, has no one over him and everything is under him. As ruler[e] who should distribute repose and happiness in accordance with laws, he stands under the laws, must be able to be coerced, and can thus not be one and the same person as the *souverain*. As judge he stands under the laws and the government[f] for the sake of the distribution of happiness in accordance with the laws of the *souverain* and the will of the ruler, and sees that everyone has a part of welfare. He should determine goods only in proportion to the holiness of the law, thus he is as before a distinct

---

[a] *constitution*   [b] *Macht*
[c] *kraft*   [d] *sich selbst nicht aufheben*
[e] *Regirer*   [f] *Regiment*

person and certainly not one with the regent because he would limit his good. These three persons can only be united in the deity because the deity contains all these perfections at the same time. Provision is for the whole but also for individuals. The law requires performances (burdens); how should they be distributed? and also sacrifices, on whom should they befall?

19:569   **7975.** 1785–89? 1778–79? J 88, 89.
NB. Nothing is open to the *summus imperans* (ruler, supreme lord[a]) which the private will *arbitrium* {choice} cannot itself dispose over, e.g. morality. To choose religion. To sell oneself (*contra* Hobbes[14]). But it is open to the ruler in matters where each can decide over his own right, e.g. taxes, criminal laws, war, peace.

Princeps {first and foremost}, the supreme head of state[b] is not subject to the state. The *souverain* has no private goods, domains, but the ruler does, and is in their regard subjected to the law. The goods are isolated from the person. In this way the person of the ruler cannot be violated.

NB. In regard to which condition should one avoid being passive, because one cannot be subjected to the law, e.g. religious judgments and doctrine. Consequently the supreme power[c] cannot have control over the freedom of religious opinion* and its public declaration.

When, however, the *summus imperans* transgresses all the limits, no opposition is allowed. But in moral matters nevertheless to refuse one's obedience and to passively suffer everything. For there one can decide for oneself.

[Kant's footnote:] *The subject can require only protection against power; however, the opinions of others are not power but rather the single condition for correcting one's own opinions. The clergy cannot ask that others' opinions and objections be forbidden. They can ask for no exclusive privileges to expound their own. There can be no power through which they justify themselves, rather they must defend themselves through the supremacy of their reasons. The *summus imperans* is restricted only through the nature of a law in general and is bound not through law but to laws, all of its *actus* are *publici* not *privati*.

19:570   The legislation, government, and administration[d] or state administration[e]. The last proceeds from the right of the subject against the *souverain* and the representations which he as subject has to make against the law or government.

---

[a] *Beherrscher, Oberherr*   [b] *Staatsoberhaupt*
[c] *Gewalt* in this Reflection   [d] *administration*
[e] *Staatsverwaltung*

7976. 1780–89? 1776–79? J 88.   19:570
The *territorium* (but only *universorum* {of all} not *singulorum* {of each})
belongs to the *souverain*. For it belongs to the whole people. But just as
the whole people cannot dispose over the *territorium* of an individual
what it does not impose on itself, so also the monarch cannot dispose
over the *territorium* of an individual without at the same time incorpo-
rating it back into the whole. The question arises whether all of the *souverain's jura in rem* {rights in things} must be derived from the *jus territorii*
{right to territory}. No, for the *territorium* cannot originally be occupied by the society but only by individuals. Thus property was prior
to society and thus also prior to the *imperium civilis* {civil state}. Even
more do the *coloni* {colonists} as *subdita* {subjects} (or vice versa) base
their rights against the *souverain* on this basis. Only abroad it cannot be
sold.

7977. 1785–89? J 93.   19:570
The *souverain* is the ~~supreme lord, self-ruler~~ ruler, who is not a subject
[*added:* sovereignty, sovereignty[a]]
  The monarch is the supreme lord.
  The monarch as *souverain* is self-ruler, autocrat.

7980. 1785–89. J 94, 95.   19:571
Decrees in the despotic government.
  The difference between despotism and patriotic government is not
found in the type of government but in the actual rule. One cannot say of
any kingdom "it is a despotic kingdom" but "it is despotically governed."
Except that Russia would be one since the monarch is allowed to name
his successor.
  Military government is a meaningless term,[b] for when the military governs there is no genuine state constitution; instead the military
constitutes the supreme power which appoints and dismisses magistrates
not lawfully but through turmoil. It is a *status belli* {state of war}. But
where the entire constitution is applied to war, as in Sparta, that is not a
military government.

7981. 1785–89. J 96.   19:571
The *souverain* will is one that decides in accordance with a principle[c] that
can also be valid for the state under every successor. Thus despotism

---

[a] Kant here works on finding German equivalents for the French derived *Souverain* and
  Latin derived *Monarch*. The first sentence is *Souverain ist der* ~~Oberherr, Selbstherrscher~~
  Beherrscher, der nicht Untertan ist; (Souverainetät, Oberherrschaft)
[b] *ein Wort ohne Begriff*   [c] *Grundsatz* in this Reflection

is a will that does not lower itself. E.g. imposing a particular religious opinion, because the successors can have other opinions.

The *souverain* is limited only through that which is beneath his dignity, for nothing is higher. So not through the right of the people against him but because he counts himself among the people. The will of the *souverain* must also be unalterable in the future regarding principles, for otherwise it would be blameworthy on account of this alone.

19:572   **7983.** 1785–89. J 99.
What a people cannot do, neither can any *souverain*. He cannot administer and judge, for a part would be reaching conclusions over another part and thus could do something wrong, but there can be no one superior to the one who secures the right of each. He can legislate and no more. The rest is beneath his majesty.

But the people can name individual persons to offices under the condition that they can also take the offices away if they prefer, yet the people cannot punish and judge. For in the first case the civil servant himself can give his assent, but in the second case not.

19:574   **7989.** 1785–89. J 102, 103.
In the state there must be a single *potestas legislatoria* {legislative power}; this must at the same time have the highest, irresistible power.[a] Now it can indeed consist of several persons or members who all have a share in the legislation and power, but not of members who are indeed legislative but have no power,* because otherwise they can obligate no one through the law since they cannot at the same time protect them with the law. It can be, however, that the one who has the highest power has done wrong in that he seized it for himself, but because he is now the overseer[b] of justice, everyone who uses power against him would do wrong. Thus as head of state he is always right, although as human being wrong.

[Kant's footnote, J 103:] *The state must have a single *souverain* (ruler, ~~self-ruler~~, ruler[c] – he is the sole self-ruler), who is alone legislative and also alone in possession of power. Now no one [can[d]] restrict the *souverain* with regard to the laws, thus there must be a part of the *souverain* which limits the other part and thus also has full power.[e] For if that were not so, then this part would indeed have legislative standing[f] but not a corresponding power. The *souverain* whose legislation is restricted, however, does not have complete legislative standing, and since

---

[a] *Gewalt*   [b] *Oberhaupt*
[c] *Beherrscher ~~Selbstherrscher~~ Herrscher*   [d] Added by KS editor
[e] *Gewalt* in this Reflection   [f] *Ansehen*

without it and without right there can be no power, then lawfully also not all power would be due to him, i.e. he would not be the *souverain*. If he is in such a situation yet under a *pactum constitutionalibus* {constitutional pact} that restricts him to the agreement of others among the people, then his *privilegium* {privilege} has no legislative standing; rather he has only the right of remonstration, which is not a right to oppose but to implore, which is not a strict right, and can also be taken from the *souverain*.

The subjects themselves do harm to their security through resistance   19:575
to the *souverain*, for this is the ground of their *pacti civilis* and in the case of this change in its power, and by the fact that it is resistible, they are not secure. Even a *usurpateur*, once he has all power, indeed wrongs the claimants to the crown, but the people have no right to resist, ~~because they either thereupon themselves~~ for either they would have received all power required for that but without abdication of the *souverain*, in which case there would be two *souverains* at once, or they would not have this power, in which case there would be no complete legislator because power precedes the law. [end of footnote]

7991. 1785–89. J 102.   19:575
What must the *souverain* really do if he actually wants to give the people an influence on legislation, thus also grant them power,[a] hence wants to transform himself from a *souverain* into a monarch: he must call up the whole people and let them advise him about it; for otherwise the security of the many with regard to their rights could suffer under a divided supreme power.

7992. 1785–89. J 103.   19:575
It is impossible to conceive of a constitution in which the people lawfully receive a right to judge[b] the *souverain*, to sit in judgment[c] over him and to remove him, indeed even to limit him in the slightest. For then they must also have a power for that, and since there can be only one *souverain*, then the first would not be *souverain*.

7995. 1785–89. J 104.   19:576
Punishment must itself be determined in the law and absolutely not by the criminal but instead by the *publici* and, because of their freedom regarding the power of choice, by the judge. Otherwise no wrong can be done to the criminal.

---

[a] *Gewalt* in this Reflection   [b] *beurtheilen*
[c] *richten*

19:576   **7997. 1785–89. J 105.**
No one has a realizable[a] share in the legislative power[b] except one who is also granted through constitutional law a sufficient power and authority[c] to use it in order to secure rights to those who obey the law. Someone can have a non-realizable share in it, namely to remonstrate through *votum consultativum*. Now if the constitutional law promises that the agreement (to refuse negative share) of everyone is required for a law applied to
19:577   them but does not grant any authority to use any kind of power against the legislator or his instruments, then the people, insofar as it obeys the one who can legislate, cannot hope for protection, and this court[d] does wrong in that it moves them to opposition, namely it wrongs the people. But also a wrong to the *souverain* because the *votum* of the court is only consultative.

19:577   **7999. 1788–89? 1790–1804? J 108.**
Under the state system there is 1. the administrative system (governing and magistrate, *gouvernement*), 2. the treasury system[e] (*quaestura* {office of public funds}), 3. the police system. In all three the type of government is the ground of the state administration and of the difference between the subject of the state and the citizen of the state or citizen of the city. State administration is to be differentiated from state economy. The last in accordance with the physiocratic system, in accordance with which only the first merchant is protected with regard to the basic means of life and can set the price, or in accordance with the physiopathic system,
19:578   in accordance with which the principle[f] of free commerce lies at the basis of all valuing.[g] The *souverain* must **never set the price** not only not in the administration of the state but also not when he himself is the buyer. He must **not trade**, not **participate in agriculture**, not neglect **the arts.** – Taxes must be laid on real property[h] and commerce but never ~~on persons~~ as poll tax,[i] because this is contrary to the population, whose number is the measure of good administration.[15]

19:578   **8000. 1785–89. J 117.**
Institutes for the poor. Helpless poor must be fed and, if they are children, cared for. Why? Because we are human beings and not beasts. This stems not from the right of the poor as citizens but from their needs as human beings. Not the innocent; for then there would be few. Who should feed them? The question is not whether it is the state or the

---

[a] *wirksamen*   [b] *Macht*
[c] *Gewalt und Befugnis* in remainder of Reflection
[d] *Hof*, here the consultative legislative body   [e] *Beschatzungssystem*
[f] *Princip*   [g] *Schätzung*
[h] *Grundbesitz*   [i] *auf den Kopf*

citizens, for if the state feeds them then the citizens are also feeding them, but only whether it should depend on the free will of the citizens or on coercion – as gift or as contribution (tax). The latter requires the concurrence of the candidates for their care: it is a *modus acquirendi* {means of acquisition} and also a *titulus* {title} to claims. But who should determine the helplessness? The magistrate, who knows his citizens? And the contribution occurs by collections by the ones who are themselves the most generous. Encouragement and reproving in general by clergy. All private beneficence can remain, but it is ignored by the magistrate and the clergy. It is *opera supererogationis* {supererogatory work}.

8001. 1785–89. J 117.   19:578
The question is whether through a fund or through a contribution for each case. Every age must feed its poor, for otherwise in the end the ones who are fed live more comfortably than the age is in a condition to provide. Poverty often arises from lack of diligence or of frugality, and so distributions to the poor must occur. But from a fund a disproportion in the level of poverty and of the well-to-do would arise. It is like   19:579
drinks which are given out cheaply. Just as many would be consumed as otherwise.

8003. 1780–89? 1778–79? J 119.   19:579
The *summus imperans* {supreme sovereign} cannot command or forbid any religion, because he cannot dispose over the private will of the *subditi* {subjects}. Nor can he make a certain religion a condition for public servants (except when he has an *imperans* that departs from the *summo imperio*), for the subjects have a right to serve the state as long as they are not criminals. One sees that he must see to it that there is an opportunity to acquire religious cognitions. Teachers and supporters of universal peace and the subjects themselves, or the sciences, must be entrusted to determine religion. Otherwise the *souverain* gets involved with matters that are beneath him.

8006. 1785–89. J 120–21.   19:580
Everything in which the *souverain* can do wrong to the people, and thus where he is subject to reason in the judgment of the people, is beneath his dignity. Now he can do wrong in religious determinations, consequently he must leave them to the people (to the *publicum*). It is even further beneath his dignity to strengthen the *placita* {decisions} of his subjects through his legislative standing, for then he is just a tool of the legislative power[a] of the clergy (whose membership he is not permitted to determine).

[a] *Macht*

19:580 **8008.** 1780–89? 1778–79? J 124.
The state can set up a restriction so that no one teaches anything but what they are assigned to teach, but cannot make a prohibition that some cannot make public their own recommendations for the general improvement.

19:582 **8014.** 1785–89? 1778–79?? J 143.
There can be only one in a state who does not stand under the laws, namely the one who has surpreme executive power.[a] For if there were many, then ~~there would have to be a still higher executive power~~ they both would have to have supreme executive power, ~~consequently two equal~~ which is impossible for the supreme power is that of the whole people. The monarch as regent appoints the magistrate and the *forum* but cannot remove the latter except insofar as they are condemned by another judge. He has ministers, but they stand under the laws, and for that reason he must act through them. He himself cannot do wrong.

19:582 **8018.** 1788–95. J 144.
The people can indeed make a contract[b] with the ruler[c] through which they obligate him and in turn obligate themselves to him, but only insofar as the people themselves have and hold sovereignty. For whoever invokes his right from a contract must at the same time have the authorization and power[d] to coerce. Thus if the people do not have
19:583 sovereignty, then they cannot coerce and also cannot obligate themselves to anything, just as if the people were to have a free will, for the people are coerced to everything by the *souverain*. But for this reason the *souverain*, if he is separated from the people, also has his privileges not from a contract[e] but merely *facto* {by an act}, because no contract for passive obedience is possible: instead the highest power at the same time presides over rights. Thus if a king summons the people together through their representatives in order to reform the state, then no obligation prevents them from changing the state to an entirely different form, and they can take sovereignty upon themselves immediately.

19:583 **8019.** 1785–89. J 148–49.
Whatever instructions a monarch wants to command would be a matter for the people to judge against the *souverain*, which is impossible; but

---

[a] *Gewalt* in this Reflection [b] *contract*
[c] *Fürsten* [d] *Macht*
[e] *Vertrage*

whatever he will distribute to them is the matter of a part of the people against the other, and there the monarch can do wrong if he makes the distribution for the benefit of one and the detriment of another. Thus the people do have a right to judge in this regard.

Through a well-disciplined army sovereignty has the advantage that from it can come the greatest good for the world, because then everyone is freely permitted to write about religion as well as legislation, which free states perhaps grant but cannot risk complying with, for to the state everything new threatens rebellion or loss of freedom. Gradually such a government becomes patriotic. World patriotism inspires the philosopher to wish for that. In time the *souverain* will not be divided from his people by so infinite a chasm in which not he but only the people are subject to his laws. Instead he will have *collegia* {councils}, who will also possess power[a] and who as magistrates are inviolable but still stand under the laws, through this good government will become better and better and could be transmitted to posterity. But to restrict power[b] comes to this, that officers are [not[c]] at the same time magistrates.

8023. 1780–89. J 176.   19:585
Whether a state could be an inheritance for another state. No. For the state has its natural freedom and independent interests and in this case it would be dependent on the interests of another state. In this way it would lose its self-standing. It can be inherited from one who alone ought to possess the state, for then the state always remains on the whole *sui juris* {independent} and does not become a *pertinens* {extension} of another state. The new lord does not so much acquire the state as he succeeds the previous lord so that the state alters only the name of the ruler.[d] Except for this there has been no transformation, just as when a generation of citizens follows another.

Whether one part of a state could be added to another state by means of a *pactum pacis* {peace treaty}. Here it first had a common interest with another state, then it begins another. At a minimum its interest is changed without its consent, it is not independent as a state. For this term encompasses people and *souverain*.

8026. 1780–89. J 177.   19:585
Punishment is the coercive means to obtain respect for the **law**. Wrongs to a person are resisted but not punished in *status naturalis* {state of nature} because in it there is no outer law.

---

[a] *Macht*   [b] *Gewalt*
[c] The Academy edition editor suggests adding this *nicht*
[d] *Oberhaupt*

19:586   **8027.** 1780–89. J 177.

When someone robs another citizen of something which he should enjoy in accordance with the *pacto civili* {civil contract}, then the robber also robs himself of a share of the *pacto*.

19:586   **8028.** 1780–89? 1776–79?? J 179. To beginning of §194

Whether the right to punish implies an obligation to suffer punishment? Yes, insofar as the obligation is taken juridically but not insofar as it is taken morally, i.e. so far that an additional special punishment can be imposed for resistance to what the penal judge rightly exercises. Thus the judge must consider for this addition only inflicting punishment as *poena correctiva* {corrective punishment}, which is applied out of concern for the criminal; for he expects even from him still further actions to be done out of obligation. But for *poena vindicativa* {vindictive punishment}, capital punishments it is otherwise.

19:586   **8031.** 1788–95. J 176.

Contra Beccariam. No one can will that he be punished. For punishment is something which is done to him against his wish and will,[a] otherwise it would not be a punishment. He can, however, will it insofar as he represents himself in an imaginary person, namely as others could in any case judge him, that for example he could also be a murderer. On this imag-
19:587   inary person, thus on someone morally other than himself, he imposes the punishment. – Someone who is aware that he could indeed at some time become a murderer or a thief or a swindler cannot to that extent legislate. Everyone legislates for everyone insofar as no one knows how he will be disposed, although everyone believes his own person to be upright.

19:587   **8033.** 1785–89. J 178–79.

A *delictum publicum* {public offense} cannot be pardoned because the right or the security of the people cannot be given away. A *delictum privatum* {private offense} can be pardoned. For in the latter case it is, for the victim, all the same how the *laedens* {the one doing the harm} would satisfy him and he can ignore it, because it is a matter between him and other private persons, but not if the *laesio* {harm} was a *delictum publicum*; for the whole state is harmed by these, so the state must not put the *laedentem* {the one doing the harm} in a state of need through a similar *delictum* in order to compensate the first.

19:587   **8035.** 1788–95. J 178–79.

Justitia punitiva {punitive justice} has as its aim: 1. to transform a subject from a bad to a better citizen; 2. to deter others through examples

[a] *wieder Wunsch und Willen*

60

as warnings; 3. to eliminate those who cannot be improved from the   19:588
commonwealth, be it through deportation, *exilium*, or death (or through
prison). But all this is only political prudence. – The essential thing is
the exercise of justice itself so that the constitution would be preserved.[a]

Whether experiments with the prisoners for medical reasons are
permitted.

8036. 1780–89. J 181.   19:588
The right to punish is not based on a *pactum* but immediately on law.
For all laws are penal laws. The type of punishment is all the same, as
punishment what matters is only the degree, and that is exactly the same
as the evil that can be seen in the deed. If the penal law were to presuppose a special *pactum*, then if someone were to evade the punishment
one would again have to make a *pactum* in order to punish him.

8037. 1780–89? 1778–79? J 180.   19:588
If a society were assembled for the sake of a discretionary end, then it
cannot obligate anyone to punishment of death. But if it were assembled
for the necessary end prescribed by nature, to found a civil society, then
all are necessarily obligated to include death among the punishments.

8041. 1785–89. J 182.   19:589
All punishments and rewards are either **precautionary**[b] or **retributive**
(*praemunientes vel rependentes*). The precautionary ones are either **punishments of example** or **chastisement**. The retributive punishments
declare that the criminal would himself feel[c] the ill that he brings about,
and are possible in accordance with all rules of wisdom. But this is
not advisable in the constitution of the state, which does not look to
morality. Yet even as precautionary punishments they must first of all
be just. They are indeed allowed as mere means but are just only as
retributions.

Also precautionary rewards must not incentivize actions beyond their
merits.

8042. 1788–89? 1790s? J 182.   19:589
Punishments that threaten (prevention of crime) must be all the greater
as the temptation thereto is greater; however, they are commonly on
that account all the more unjust to the individual, only appropriate for
the rights of the citizens. Conversely they could be smaller when the
temptation thereto is smaller. In both cases the punishment is considered
only as a means. But if one considers them morally in accordance with   19:590

---

[a] *aufgehoben*   [b] *vorkehrende*
[c] *ihn selbst fühlen lassen*

the absolute absence of worth[a] of a human being in this action, then they must be all the greater as that is smaller. There was temptation, but it must as such not be threatened. There is thus a contradiction here between the threat and the moral worthiness of punishment or even the sentencing.

19:590 **8043. 1785–89. J 184.**

If the *summus imperans* {supreme sovereign} has broken the *pactum fundamentalis*, then the people cannot vindicate their freedom through rebellion (*seditione*) but only through the right given to them in the constitution[b] and then not through a new suitable power but by means of that power which they have always had according to the *pactum fundamentale* in accordance with a law which has determined this power together with its limits, so that the *summus imperans* remains at all times uninterrupted in accordance with the form of the constitution, and the *status naturalis* would not intrude in the meantime, for in this latter situation they would cease to be a people, there would be no law, no higher authority toward [*which*[c]] obedience is a duty. He who rebels,[d] insofar as he infringes on the right of the supreme lord,[e] is a rebel.[f] Not everyone who rebels is a rebel, namely not one who withdraws obedience to a ruler who himself has infringed upon the fundamental contract. For he does not do him a wrong, nevertheless he can still do wrong with regard to the right of nations in general (*scandalum juris gentium*, in that he weakens or annuls the respect for the civil law on which the health[g] of a commonwealth depends). If, however, one assumes a universal rebellion of the people, then he grounds a claim that his duty to obey ceases because, since there is now no one entitled to the place of the deposed ruler for legislating and governing, no one can require obedience and so a *status naturalis* would arise; so whoever would defend the rights of the people in accordance with the constitution must always already have restricted the regent partly in legislation and partly in administration. In that case, however, he must also have possessed a power[h] because he must be able to protect those from whom he would require obedience. In that case, however, it is not a rebellion because the opposition is lawful. Wherever

19:591 that is not in the constitution, the people have yielded to the good will of their sovereign power[i] and any rebellion can be judged as wrong, not against the rulers but against the right of the people in general, and can be punished in the name of the people because this situation, in which

---

[a] *absoluten Unwerth*
[b] *constitution* – in this Reflection, Kant uses *constitution* throughout
[c] *welche* added by Academy edition editor   [d] *ein Aufrührer*
[e] *Oberherrn*   [f] *Rebell*
[g] *Heil*   [h] *eine Gewalt*
[i] *Oberherrschaft*

no one except the ruler is authorized to command, is changed *in status naturalis* by the rebellion. – Everything that takes place by mob rule[a] (*per turbas* {by the mob}) is against the right of the state.

8044. 1785–89. J 184.   19:591
The question who should judge[b] whether a *pacto* is broken, can easily be answered. But who should sit in judgment,[c] that is, judge[d] with rightful power, so that it will be obeyed? In England that can be the parliament because it already has power,[e] but not the people *per turbas* {by the mob}.

8046. 1785–89. J 185, 174.   19:591
[J 185:] The people must be thoroughly represented and as such have not only a right to resistance but also power[f] to recover their freedom without rebellion and deny obedience to the regent.

Properly it should be said: the people must not cease at any moment to constitute a whole, for otherwise everything occurs *per turbas* {by the mob}, i.e. through usurped power, which cannot justly be transferred to anybody. Thus the people must be represented if they can lawfully separate and resist.

It can happen that if a state would alter its type of government it would immediately become too weak for its neighbors. The greatest mob[g] here has no voice, for to them it is the same whoever they belong to, but the state wants to and must preserve itself. *vid. p.* 174.[h]

[174:] *vid. p.* 184. Dominion[i] is the subjection of the will of one person   19:592
or several under the absolute power of choice of a single will (whether that be of a single person or of unity of several). All dominion is *facto* usurped, *jure* it ought to be constitutional.[j] For a right is usurped if it is acquired without a *pactum* or *delictum alterius* {through offense to another}. Dominion over human beings is a thing which as *res jacens* {a thing in abeyance} needs a possessor, because human beings can rightfully exist only in a society under laws (this is the *status* of human beings) and it is taken control of as *res nullius* {an unowned thing} by the first to take control. With time the *imperium* becomes constitutional; yet even at that time when it is only usurped, it must still be respected. The *imperium* of the lord over the servant or bondsman is not constitutional by nature, but taking control either *occupatione bellica* {by taking control by war} or

---

[a] *durch Rottirung*   [b] *Urtheilen*
[c] *richten*   [d] *Urtheilen*
[e] *Gewalt*   [f] *Gewalt* in this Reflection
[g] *Haufe*
[h] Kant's "*see p.* 174" and corresponding marks clearly unite the two halves of this Reflection in Kant's mind
[i] *Herrschaft*
[j] "constitutional" in this Reflection is *constitutional*

63

usucapione {by uninterrupted possession} must one day become constitutional. There is no constitution if only one gives laws and the other is passively subject to them. But since unification into one body must precede all discussion about the form of the constitution, yet this unification must already be arranged by a few according to a certain plan which unites all the discussants, then all regeneration of a former and now annulled constitution[a] is again only usurpation (*per turbas agitur* {by mob action}), and the attaining of supreme authority through sedition is always usurpation.

In accordance with its concept supreme power is unrestricted. It can, however, arise from the reciprocal restriction of the wills of those who ought to obey the law that they at the same time also give. Then it is an *imperium patrioticum*. If, however, a will that is not the will of the whole is unrestricted, then it is despotism, whether of the nobility or the common people or the ruler. – Of the servitude of the Tartars and the Arabs, whose freedom became dangerous to the intermediaries, by the Mongolian people.[b]

19:592 **8047. 1785–89. J 174.**
If, because the supreme lord has broken his promise (through which
19:593 he has certainly forfeited his right), the civil union is dissolved, the rebels do not immediately have a new one. Old authorities have lost their standing, which was based on a commission of the head of state. A new authority must now arise, or there must even more so already be one in order to bring about the form of equality that is necessary for free establishment.[c] But here the greater power[d] makes the establishment.

19:593 **8048. 1785–89. J 174.**
Finally the question arises whether, if a sovereign calls together the whole nation[e] and it is completely represented, he nonetheless retains the rights of a *souverain* during this time? He was not more than a placeholder, a steward, with whom the people did not make a contract but instead one to whom they have merely transferred the right to act as their representative. As long as he does this, he can hinder any movement in the people through which they are planning to constitute themselves as such. But if even once he calls them together and constitutes them as such, then not only is his authority suspended but it can also be broken

---

[a] *Verfassung*
[b] This sentence is unclear in itself and in its connection to the rest of the Reflection
[c] *Einrichtung*   [d] *Gewalt*
[e] *Nation*

off entirely, like the standing of every representative when the one who gave him that power is himself present.

8049. 1785–89. J 174.   19:593

Between the *souverain* and the people there is no *pactum* that contains a condition which if unfulfilled would justify its suspension. For in the concession of all power the renunciation of all authorization for resistance is already contained. There is therefore no contract but a *pactum gratuitum* {free agreement} [*added:* no contract] and even as *expressum* {express} it would be *illicitum*. It is therefore *tacitum* {tacit}, since the people feels itself to be incapable of ruling itself. – But if the monarch as *souverain* feels himself to be incapable of preserving the state and calls upon the people, through its representatives, to preserve itself, then that is likewise no contract but rather, since he was only the representative of the people, a surrender of his dignity.

8050. 1780–84? 1778–79?? J 188.   19:593

The *souverain* acts as a tyrant unjustly and no injustice is done to him; if he is driven out, he also loses all claims, yet the people does not have   19:594
the right to drive him out. In such a case both sides commit injustice, although neither does an injustice to the other.

8051. 1780–84? 1778–79?? J 188, 189.   19:594

188. Everything* is permitted where there is no external law against it, and there is no outer law without a competent judge being constituted, who judges in accordance with it, and a power to coerce everyone in accord with it. Now no judicial power and no rightful coercion can be above the *souverain*, for otherwise not he but this power would be *souverain*. Thus no external law valid *coram foro humano* {before the court of humanity} restricting the *souverain* can be found.

The people have no right except where there is an outer law, and secret rights which could not be declared in outer laws are usurpations. Thus power against the *souverain* is always contrary to the principles of all civil constitution. But all subjects can still be bound to obey the laws that restrict the power of the monarch, and there can be a court which judges and adjudicates the actions that they perform on the command of the *souverain*. In such a way complete obedience can be withdrawn from him. But it is a question whether he then ceases to be the head of state. Indeed he returns to the *status naturalis*, but because the state needs a head, he will be compelled either to live as a subject or to leave the country.

189. [Kant's footnote likely 1785–88:] *(Where the people do not have such a right it is not permitted to use force against the monarch. For

19:595 suppose the people stood upon its natural right, then this too must still be capable of becoming a civil law, indeed it ought to become one, since the civil constitution must ~~determine~~ contain all rights of the people and of the *souverain*. The people have therefore surrendered and neglected their right and have no right. But since the power of the people can retain its right to do this, it appears as if it also has a right to power. But power for which there is no antecedent judgment with the force of right is not rightful, consequently the people cannot resist except in those cases which cannot fall at all under the terms of the *unionis civilis*, e.g. religious coercion, coercion to unnatural sins: assassination, etc.)

19:595 **8054.** 1785–89. J 190.
A despotic regime is one in which the *souverain* treats the people as his property. Even democracy can be despotic if its constitution is without insight, e.g. like the Athenian democracy, which allowed people to be condemned solely through the majority of votes without rightful cause in accordance with prescribed laws. The people cannot even regard themselves as property. – There can be despotic regimes, but there is no despotic constitution of the state, i.e. constitution through the universal will of the people and clearly in accordance with a formal law.

A patriotic regime is when the *souverain* considers ~~the people~~ his land as a fatherland and its organization as that of his own person. Only in a patriotic constitution can there be constitutive, i.e. proper organization.

19:595 **8055.** 1789–95? J 190–91.
[190:] In France* the National Assembly was able to alter the constitution though it was, to be sure, called together only to bring order to the nation's credit system. For once the king had allowed it to make decrees in accordance with indeterminate authority,[a] they were the representatives of the whole people. The king otherwise represented the peo-
19:596 ple; here he was negated because the people themselves were present. In Great Britain one cannot say that the king represents the people but that he taken together with the estates first constitutes the people and is in this regard *primus inter pares* {first among equals}. Thus the misfortune of the king comes directly from his own sovereignty, after he had once allowed all the people's deputies to assemble, then he was nothing; for his legislative power was founded only on his representing the whole people; this also illuminates [191:] the injustice of a single person as *souverain*. He cannot concede that the one whom he represents would present itself.[b] Because he represents the whole, he becomes nothing when he himself allows this whole, of which he is no part but whose substitute he is, to

[a] *unbestimmten Vollmachten*
[b] *daß der, welchen er repreaesentirt, sich selbst darstelle*

represent itself. Were he a part, then the whole could do nothing without his assent and a common will would arise which is the supreme legislation. Can, however, a *souverain* not also call the estates together? Yes, but only to deliberate over the rights that one estate has against another in view of the universal will of the king, where the king has the third vote. Thus the estates forming a coalition was directly something which raised power against the king.

[191:] [Kant's footnote:] *The national assembly was called in order to save the state by covering with their guarantee all the debts imposed upon the state by the extravagance of the regime (not merely to make plans). Thus they had to voluntarily guarantee it with their property [*added:* they must therefore have put themselves in a condition where they alone could dispose of their property, hence in the condition of freedom under laws but such laws as they themselves would give, i.e. a republican or free civil[a] condition] and the court had itself yielded the right to encumber them. But so that they could achieve this state of citizenry,[b] they had to establish a constitution that could exercise no acts of authority over them.

8056. 1785–89. J 200.   19:596
The league of nations[c] is not a universal monarchy. For if it were the *civis* {citizens} would not be nations, which is, however, what is required   19:597
here. Such a league would, however, be possible only with difficulty if each of the states was not itself a free state.

8057. 1785–89. J 200.   19:597
We consider the right of nations in the *status naturalis* of nations only as a paragon[d] of laws in order to approach the *status pacis*, and in the meantime in its absence to obtain its rights.

8060. 1785–89. J 216. To §233   19:597
Because every peace that has no restrictions annexed to it is perpetual, it is arranged so that no one has claims on anything that the other party possesses at that time. Otherwise it would be a *pacificatio dolosa* {deceitful peacemaking}. Thus all claims on that which a state already possesses prior to the peace with another state are canceled if they are not mentioned in the peace treaty.

8061. 1783–88. 1778–79?? J 234–35.   19:598
The right of nations is a right in the state (*juridice* {juridically}) of war, i.e. the absence of public justice, and there is thus no other principle[e]

---

[a] *einen freybürgerlichen*   [b] *Bürgschaft*
[c] *Völkerbund*   [d] *Inbegriff*
[e] *Princip*

for it than that all actions of nations toward other nations stand under the conditions under which alone the foundation of public justice, i.e. a league of nations,[a] is possible. The right to war and the rights in war are based on this. The first has as its basis the attribution of motives to the enemy ~~which are hindrances to the possibility of a universal league of nations~~ that would necessarily be forbidden in a universal league of nations, the second the kind of conditions under which alone a universal league of nations is possible. For even if there is no public justice, nations are still bound to that through which it is at least possible.

In war, poisoning and assassination are not allowed, because they would negate security in a universal league of nations since these actions are completely contrary[b] to public justice.

Status[c] signifies a place that someone holds in relation[d] to others, from which the laws of his relations are derived; situation[e] signifies real modification in this condition. The *positus* {place} or the station[f] must in itself involve principles[g] which are valid for every situation. Natural right *in statu hominis vel civis* {in the human or civil condition}. There he is thought of merely as a human being among other human beings without obligation (yet there is *potentia obligatio* {potential obligation}), namely without voluntary obligation, and has neither judge nor legislator. The rightful condition is either that of the right of war or of the right of peace.

19:599   **8063**. 1780–89. J 235.
In a legitimate war only subsumption under a good maxim must be in dispute. The good maxim is one which contains within itself compliance with all rules of right. The outcome of evil maxims, e.g. to act merely to increase one's superiority, is that there is no disposition for peace and that war is unending and both constant and all against one. Thus war, which necessarily destroys the general will, is unjust. Thus the maxims of a state which wages war must... to the [*breaks off*]

19:599   **8065**. 1780–89. J 240.
The power[h] of a state grows 1. through inner improvement of its well-being. 2. Through increase in its ability to wage war (e.g. building fleets, creating new corps). 3. Through cultivation of newly acquired *territorium* as *res vacua* {an unpossessed thing}. 4. Through inheritance, purchase, exchange. 5. Through *occupatio bellica* {taking control through war}. The first growth provides no cause for war, because it contains no

---

[a] *Völkerbund*   [b] *gänzlich ... entziehen*
[c] *Stand*   [d] *Relation*
[e] *Zustand*   [f] *station*
[g] *Principien*   [h] *Macht*

preparations for war. All others have no other basis than the augmentation of external power, consequently increase in danger for others.

Individual human beings *in statu naturali* can be coerced to enter *in statum civilem* with others. So can peoples[a] who do not have a genuine civil constitution, so that a neighboring civilized nation[b] would find justice in relation to them through power over individual persons. But nations[c] cannot coerce another into the *status civilis* to recognize a common lord for or with the other, for in this case its infringement would make peace in vain from then on, for this declaration can occur only with the agreement of the other.

Because an individual human being can obtain no other security for   19:600
his future preferences, he is juridically only *accidens* {an accident}, which[d] can exist only *inhaerendo* {inherently}. A civil whole is substance.

The question is whether transformation of substance into *accidentia* or this into substance would itself be the end of humanity and the duty of the state to itself, to preserve itself as a particular state, and this duty cannot be abandoned. In the last case unity of *commercium* (league of nations) remains the single thing which constitutes the end of humanity, not the unity of inherence, not the unity of dependence on a supreme arbitrator,[e] but the freedom of each individual state under universal laws. Autonomy.

8068. 1780–89. J 241.   19:600
The *principium* is: every war must be begun or waged on grounds whose end could be compatible with entering into a universal league of nations and a condition of external justice among nations.

8076. 1796–1804. (1799) *Loses Blatt Reicke* 10 b 14.   19:603
[*first page*]
Just as one says that besides the visible church there lies at its basis an invisible church (as its model) with the prescript: there is no salvation[f] outside the church; so one now rightly says of the political condition[g] of states and nations: there is no salvation outside the republic, instead everlasting war, not always with everlasting combat but with everlasting threats to fight were anyone to let up in armaments and taxes on the citizens as preparations for war: so it is right to say **"there is no salvation outside the republic."** – A world republic would in any case be one where no individual state would have enough forces[h] to fight the great republic if necessary, such a state is the same position as the

---

[a] *Völker*	[b] *Volk*
[c] *Völker*	[d] The referent of *welches* is unclear
[e] *Schiedsrichter*	[f] *Heil*
[g] *Zustande*, in this Reflection	[h] *Kräfte*

barbarians who threaten it with attack, since it would fight the republic or care for itself alone. – The condition outside the republic is thus a condition lacking salvation from which we never emerge.

[**8077**, a long draft for *Conflict of the Faculties* is included with the drafts for that work.]

19:612   **8078**. 1790–95. J 97.
The definition of **"freedom"** in the "Declaration and Determination of the Rights of Man" from the national assembly in Paris is: to be free is to be able to do everything which does **not harm** another. – Further the
19:613   law permits society to prohibit **only harmful actions**.[16] Both propositions are false. For perhaps I could prove that the other benefits from my action – but he is still not thereby free.

V. FRAGMENTS FROM OTHER SOURCES

Opus Postumum: Kant did not stop reflecting on political philosophy after he published the *Doctrine of Right*. Some issues related to natural right appear in the *Conflict of the Faculties* of 1798, the drafts for which are elsewhere in this volume. But a few scattered notes related to right are included in the material for Kant's uncompleted book project known as the *Opus Postumum*. Kant began this project as an attempt to provide a bridge between the *Metaphysical Foundations of Natural Science* and empirical physics. In the *Metaphysical Foundations of Natural Science* (*Metaphysische Anfangsgründe der Naturwissenschaft*) of 1786 Kant attempted to apply the *a priori* categories from the *Critique of Pure Reason* that are valid for nature in general to one specific kind of nature, namely corporeal nature (4:469–70). The two parts of the *Metaphysics of Morals* parallel this project in the practical sphere by applying the *a priori* moral law, valid for rational beings in general, to the particular circumstances of human beings living together in a finite space. The titles of the two parts reveal this parallelism in their full titles: the *Metaphysical Foundations of the Doctrine of Right* (*Metaphysische Anfangsgründe der Rechtslehre*) and the *Metaphysical Foundations of the Doctrine of Virtue*.

From second Convolute, third Bogen, page 3. August–September 1798   21:178

Pure and statutory doctrine of right are differentiated from each other as rational from empirical. But because the latter without the former would be simply a mechanical collection[a] that is really not an objective (derived from laws of reason) but a merely subjective one (proceeding from the choices of the supreme power[b]) and hence in itself containing no right, so it is necessary to insert a special part of the **doctrine of right in general** between the two connecting them together as a transition from the pure doctrine of right **to a statutory doctrine of right in general**. Such a discipline, which would be presented at best simply episodically by the law professors, would be very useful for instructing a future administrator of the law about domestic need as a transition from the rational to the empirical and for judging the latter in conformity with reason, indeed it would be necessary for this (but admittedly only for the philosopher as theoretician); however, the practitioner whom he would advise to close this gap, without seeking the principles themselves in accordance with which to determine whether the statutory laws themselves would be right or at least should be right, stubbornly denies them, but also sees them as necessary as they constantly patch and transform their legislation.

---

[a] *ein blos mechanisches Machwerk*   [b] *Macht*

[*Loses Blatt Stuttgart:* The activity of the Marburg Kant Archiv has unearthed several previously unknown student lecture notes, additional loose sheets with Kant's reflections, and even Kant's personal and earliest copy of the third edition of Alexander Baumgarten's *Metaphysica* (Halle, 1750). None of this material was available for inclusion in the Academy edition. The following fragment was published as Marie Rischmüller and Werner Stark, "Ein weiteres Loses Blatt aus Kants Nachlaß," in *Neue Autographen und Dokumente zu Kants Leben, Schriften und Vorlesungen.* Kant Forschungen Band 1, hrsg. Reinhard Brandt und Werner Stark (Hamburg: Felix Meiner Verlag, 1987). The pagination below is to this Brandt/Stark volume. Stark (1993) lists it as a preparatory note for the *Doctrine of Right,* but I place it here simply as a Reflection, given that it could alternatively be a preparatory note for *Theory and Practice* since some of that material also discusses property.]

[*Brandt:*116]   *Loses Blatt Stuttgart.* Summer 1792.

[*first page*] Possession is connection with an object for possible use – the ability to possess is to have something in one's power[a] but also to have in one's power the connection to all relations of use. Whoever alters the thing that is in someone's possession also alters the possessing subject and does it through his own power,[b] so wrongs him. Possession of a thing makes an object[c] into property.

[*material on synthetic propositions not included*]

[*Brandt:*117]   [*second page*] Every initial taking possession of land is based upon the original common[d] possession of the earth's surface but does not have as an effect any appropriation through one's own power. If it is not based on a common[e] will that constitutes what is mine and yours, i.e. to each his share in relation to others and in agreement with their power of choice.

Possession precedes all that is mine or yours and is also the basis for the right to the use of an object[f] even when it belongs to no one. – *ad* 1^{mum} {regarding the first point} without possession of an object no one can be harmed by the use another wants to make of it. *ad* 2^{dum} {regarding the second point}.

<hr>

[a] *Gewalt*   [b] *eigenmächtig*
[c] *Gegenstand*   [d] *gemeinsamen*
[e] *gemeinsamer*   [f] *Object*

Natural right course lecture notes by Feyerabend

Editor's introduction

Around 8:00 a.m. on Thursday April 29, 1784, Kant stood in a lecture hall in a house near the Albertina University in Königsberg for the first session of his course on Natural Right.[1] Since the renovations in his recently purchased house were not yet complete, and professors held their lectures in private rooms in their dwellings, he probably held the lecture in a room in the house near the Ochsenmarkt where he had lived for the previous six years. He had just completed his hour-long lecture for his Logic course, which had started the previous Monday and had met for the third time with a group of one hundred students. The day before, Kant had begun his Physical Geography course for sixty-three students at 8:00 a.m.; from this day until Saturday, September 25, he would teach every day but Sundays and university holidays. He was scheduled to lecture Mondays, Tuesdays, Thursdays, and Fridays on Logic and Natural Right for one hour each and Wednesdays and Saturdays on Physical Geography for two hours. Before beginning this third course of the summer semester, Kant referred to the few notes he had written in his own copy of the course textbook, Gottfried Achenwall's *Jus Naturae*, and perhaps others on loose scraps of paper. He began to lecture to the twenty-three registered students in the course, "The whole of nature is subject to the will of a human being as far as his power can reach excepting other human beings and rational beings."

Among those twenty-three students who wrote those words down was Gottfried Feyerabend. He had matriculated at the university almost one year beforehand. Feyerabend was determined that day to write down as much as possible of what his professor was saying and continued to record Kant's lectures throughout the semester. If he worked like other student note-takers, he wrote quickly using many abbreviations and later worked through those notes to create a polished, full transcript. When the semester ended Feyerabend hired a copyist to produce clean copies of his transcript to be bound and sold to other students. Some copying must have been done months afterward since in the manuscript at hand the copyist mistakenly identified the semester as Winter Semester 1784. Nothing else is known about Feyerabend or his original notes. Only one copy of a bound clean version has survived the two centuries since, providing the only record of any of Kant's course lectures on Natural Right.

Kant lectured on Natural Right a dozen times between 1767 and 1788 and announced but did not end up offering it eight other semesters.[2] Among the dozens or hundreds of other students taking his course during that time only one other student is thought to have produced a set of notes, but those notes were not available for the Academy edition and are considered lost.[3] Our only source for Kant's lectures on Natural Right, then, is the Feyerabend manuscript.[4] The manuscript was located in the Danzig library when Paul Natorp examined it as part of his preparation of the *Metaphysics of Morals* for publication in the Academy edition. Natorp concluded that the Feyerabend manuscript shed little light on the *Doctrine of Right*,[5] but he was interested only in explanations of specific points in that book and not interested in the broader issue of the development of Kant's political philosophy. The manuscript remained in the same library as it became the Academic Library of Gdansk in Poland after 1945.

The manuscript itself is 132 pages of text plus a title page sheet (blank on the reverse).[6] The pages are bound using quarto leaves. The copyist had clear handwriting and used both German and Latin lettering, sometimes in the same word when using a German ending for a Latin root word. A different hand on occasion entered some words in the margin and within the text, likely someone correcting the copy and perhaps Feyerabend himself. Other marginal material is clearly the original copyist adding some initially overlooked sentence or phrase. Occasional smudges are luckily not dark enough to obliterate the letters. Paragraphs are not indented, leading to at least one ambiguous transition, but sections are separated by the underlined numbering and titles adopted – sometimes inaccurately – from Achenwall's text. Underlining is also used for emphasis within the text. There are two distinct pagination systems, neither of which provides an accurate count of the pages of text.[7]

In the 1970s Gerhard Lehmann undertook the task of preparing volume 27 of the Academy edition devoted to Kant's lectures on moral philosophy. He was nearly finished preparing the material and would have considered the volume complete when the Feyerabend manuscript, along with a rich set of course lecture notes from Mrongovius, "surfaced" at the Gdansk library.[8] Recognizing their value he included the Feyerabend lecture along with the Moral Mrongovius lecture in the third and final book of volume 27 devoted to the variant readings and editorial notes for the previous books in that volume. Apparently wanting to avoid further delays he did not include any editorial apparatus for either Feyerabend or Mrongovius. This choice made the material available as an aid to the other lecture notes in volume 27 but did not accord them the same treatment to bring them up to the editorial standards of the other notes. Lehmann certainly did not take sufficient time to thoroughly examine and transcribe the Feyerabend manuscript. The lecture on Natural Right is presented with no indication of any gaps in the manuscript, material inserted into the margins, words crossed out and replaced, or unclear or ambiguous words. Nor is any indication given when Lehmann added a word to fill in a gap in the manuscript that an uncertain copyist presumably left for Feyerabend to fill in. The text has numerous errors such as missing words (including "not" on more than one occasion) and misreadings of particular words in the manuscript. Worse, in two places Lehmann leaves out entire sentences. The state of the manuscript in the Academy edition is simply unreliable.

In the past decade an international team consisting of Heinrich P. Delfosse, Norbert Hinske, and Gianluca Sadun Bordoni prepared a new edition of Feyerabend based on a close examination of the original manuscript (Delfosse 2010, 2014). Published in the series *Kant Index* this edition corrects misreadings and omissions from the Academy edition and also provides suggestions for corrections to the manuscript that differ from Lehmann's. The *Kant Index* edition includes the Academy edition pagination and identifies every instance in which it differs from Lehmann's edition in reading the manuscript as well as identifying nearly every instance in which both agree in correcting some obvious error in the manuscript. As part of the *Kant Index* series, it also offers extensive indexes of terms and word usage. This edition should now be considered the standard German edition. It is available in one volume with an accompanying Italian translation but without the standard *Kant Index* concordances of terms.[9]

* *
*

The content of the manuscript is a hybrid of Kant's considered views on right on the one hand and a detailed presentation and analysis of legal issues on the other. The first quarter of the course consists of Kant's own introduction to the material. Kant was also working on the *Groundwork of the Metaphysics of Morals* at this time and his introduction reflects the concern with the place of right in practical philosophy. He identifies the core value in right as freedom, discusses the nature of practical laws, provides examples of treating others as ends-in-themselves in right, and contrasts right with virtue. He turns to the text but continues to provide his own discussion of the initial material on motivation and obligation, the principle of right, equity, innate rights, and more on right in relation to ethics.

The middle part of the course is the longest. Here Kant adheres more or less closely to the text, depending on the topic, in his discussions of property and contract. His look at property right is not at the depth he will later present in the *Doctrine of Right* but focuses on the rightful manner of taking possession of a thing and the basis of ownership in the relation among persons. He has a detailed analysis of rightful use of property and the transfer of ownership through use and by means of various types of contracts. His discussion of contract centers on the role of the wills of the parties but also enters into detail on legal responsibilities of the parties, negligence, alterations, deposits, loans, employment contracts, guarantees, inheritance, lawsuits, and the like. One example of a distinctly Kantian commentary is when he asks how a transfer of ownership is possible given that in any instant of time the ownership is determinate, comparing the issue to paradoxes about motion and rest (27:1348). This material is somewhat over half the manuscript.

The final part of the course turns to social, state, and international right. Here he presents his account of the nature of non-state society, marriage, parenthood, and household right. He turns to public right and in a concise but substantial account he assesses the state of nature and the social contract, the nature of sovereignty and representation, the powers of a state, the requirement of obedience to law, freedom of religion and enlightenment, the right of necessity, the role of monarchy, punishment, and rebellion. It appears that Kant, like professors today, was rushed toward the end of the semester because he very quickly presents his views on the right of nations without detailed argument and refers his students to another book as the best to read on the topic (27:1392). The course ends with a warning that an insufficient peace settlement always serves as a new source of war.

Through the lecture, then, but most prominently in the sections on property and contract, Kant uses the textbook as a springboard for his own views. Professors at the Albertina University were required to use a textbook for their courses. Kant chose Gottfried Achenwall's *Jus Naturae* for his course on Natural Right. In this lecture Kant used the fifth edition of 1763.[10] This book was originally published in 1750 as *Elementa Juris Naturae* co-written by Achenwall and Johann Stephan Pütter, both professors at the University of Göttingen, the former in the philosophy faculty and the latter in the law faculty.[11] Achenwall was chiefly responsible for the material on natural right in general, property, and contract, and the law of nations, while Pütter bore responsibility for the rights of a state and of citizens against the state, although both substantially agreed with each other (27:1054). After a second edition Achenwall revised and published his own *Jus Naturae* without Pütter in two parts (1755 and 1756).[12] Others considered this to be a continuation of the earlier work and it became known as a third edition of that work. Kant used the fifth edition published in 1763 in two parts. Achenwall's shorter *Prolegomena*, also an edition from 1763, is referred to in Kant's lecture but not used extensively. As noted in the Editor's general introduction to this volume, not all copies of these books that Kant used have survived. Only the second half of *Jus Naturae* survived long enough for Kant's marginal notes to be included in volume 19 of *Kants gesammelte Schriften* as the "Reflexionen zur Rechtsphilosophie." The text of the second half of *Jus Naturae* is also provided in that volume. This surviving volume overlaps only the final 15 percent of the Feyerabend notes so that the course lecture expands upon rather than repeats the content of the Reflections. A concordance showing the precise relationship of topics among the Achenwall texts, the Feyerabend lecture, and the Reflections is included at the end of this volume of English translations. The *Kant Index* edition cites and quotes from Achenwall's textbooks extensively in Latin. Those interested in these detailed comparisons between the Feyerabend lecture and Achenwall's books are urged to use the *Kant Index* apparatus.

* *
*

In preparing this translation I consulted the Academy edition version, the *Kant Index* version, and an electronic copy of the original manuscript made for the Kant Archive in Marburg. I do not footnote every variation or correction made by the *Kant Index* to the Academy edition version but only those that affect the translation, leaving out grammatical improvements or alternate words that do not affect the meaning of the sentence. Where both published versions agree on an obvious improvement to the manuscript of this kind I silently adopt the improvement. I generally follow the *Kant Index* edition, marking changes from the *Kants Schriften* edition, while a few other changes are based directly on the manuscript and in some cases agree with *Kants Schriften* over the *Kant Index*, or with neither. In a handful of cases I make a change not reflected in either the *Kant Index*, Academy edition, or the manuscript to capture what I take to be the apparent meaning of the text; I always footnote these and include the alternative versions. When the *Kant Index* openly disagrees with the manuscript, I include a reference to the manuscript in the footnote; otherwise the *Kant Index* reading follows the manuscript and the Academy edition. I have silently altered some of the punctuation but have retained sentences in their entirety. In the footnotes I use the following abbreviations: MS = manuscript, KI = *Kant Index*, KS = *Kants Schriften* (Academy edition).

The lecture contains numerous paraphrases or quotations from the Latin textbooks by Achenwall that Kant used and just as often a mention of a specific point made by "the author." I have not provided references to the Achenwall text in these instances. The exception is that I have provided the correct titles of sections from Achenwall in footnotes to give an accurate indication of the topics at hand. I have retained all Latin words and phrases (using the nominative case unless embedded in a phrase) and provided translations in braces unless the term is obvious or the translation already appeared in a recent sentence or paragraph. The few French terms remain untranslated.

For detailed discussion of the translation policy from German, please see the translators' introduction.

Natural right course lecture notes by Feyerabend

TRANSLATED BY FREDERICK RAUSCHER

Kant's Natural Right 27:1317
  Read
  in
  Winter Semester[a] of the year 1784
  Gottfr. Feyerabend

INTRODUCTION 27:1319

The whole of nature is subject to the will of a human being as far as his power can reach excepting other human beings and rational beings. Considered rationally, things in nature can be viewed only as means to ends but a human being alone can be viewed as himself an end.[b] I can think of no value in other things unless I consider them as means to other ends, e.g. the moon has a value for us insofar as it lights the earth, causes the tides, etc. The existence of non-rational beings has no value if there is nothing there that can serve rational beings, i.e. if no rational being uses it as a means. Animals also have no value in themselves because they are not conscious of their existence – the human being is thus the end of creation; he can, however, also be used as a means for another rational being, but a rational being[c] is never a mere means, instead at the same time an end, e.g. if the mason serves me as a means for building a house, so I serve him back as a means to obtain money.[13] Pope in his *Essay on Man*[14] had the goose say, "A human being also serves me for he gives me my food." In the world as a system of ends there simply must ultimately be one end[d] and that is the rational being. Were there no end then the means would also be in vain and would have no value. – A human being is

---

[a] In fact the course was given in the Summer Semester 1784. The phrase *Im Winterhalben* was written over and replaces some other words that might have read *von Herrn Pr.*
[b] *als Zweck selbst angesehen werden*   [c] KI: *es.* KS: *er,* for *"a human being."*
[d] *ein Zweck*

81

an end so it is contradictory to say that a human being should be a mere means. – If I make a contract with my servant then he must also be an end just as I am and not a mere means. He must also will it. – The human will is thus limited by the condition of the universal consent of the will of others. – Should there be a system of ends then the end and the will of a rational being must agree with that of every other. The will of a human being is not limited by even the whole of nature except by means of the wills of other human beings. – For every human being is himself an end[a] and thus he cannot be a mere means. I cannot take something from another's field in order that it serve[b] my own, for then the other would be a mere means. This limitation is based on the condition of universal consent with the will of others as far as possible.[c] There is nothing except a human being that can be posited as more worthy of respect[d] than the right of human beings. – To be precise a human being is an end in itself, from this a human being can have only an inner value, i.e. have dignity in whose place no equivalent can be set. Other things have outer value, i.e. price, for which each and every thing that is fitting for the same end can be set as an equivalent. The inner value of a human being is based on his freedom, that he has a will of his own. Because he should be the final end his will must be dependent on nothing else. – An animal has a will but it does not have a will of its own but the will of nature. The freedom of a human being is the condition under which a human being can himself be an end. Other things have no will but they must be determined by another will and be usable as a means. If a human being is thus an end in itself,[e] then he must have a will of his own for he is not permitted to be used as a means. Right is a limitation of freedom according to which freedom can exist[f] with the freedom of all others in accordance with a universal rule. Suppose someone wants a seat that someone else occupies and he wants to take the other's place. I can sit where I want and he also where he wants. If, however, he is sitting there, then I cannot at the same time sit there: there must be a universal rule under which the freedom of both can exist. So I promise him something and then he is indeed a means but also an end. Is a limitation of freedom necessary, and can freedom limit nothing but itself by itself in accordance with universal rules under which it can exist with itself? If human beings were not free then their wills would be arranged in accordance with universal law. Nothing worse could be thought than that each would be free without law. For each would do with the other what he wants and so no one would be

27:1320

[a] *ist selber Zweck*
[b] KI: *um meinem damit zu dienen.* KS: *um meinen damit zu düngen:*"fertilize"
[c] *der möglichsten allgemeinen Einstimmung*
[d] KI: *achtungswerther.* KS: *achtungswerthes,* for "as worthy of respect other than"
[e] KI: *an sich selbstsein.* KS: *sein,* for "is thus an end"
[f] *bestehen*

free. The wildest animal is not as frightening as a lawless human being. This is why Robinson Crusoe, after being on his desert island for many years, was frightened when he saw the footprint of a human being so much that he was restless from that moment on and could not sleep at night.[15] – This is also why sailors don't think twice of shooting a savage to death on an unknown island because they do not know what to expect from him.[a] – One can also consider the death of the Chevalier Marion in New Zealand who lived for a month with the savages in the best of friendship and did no harm to them but subsequently they devoured him along with twenty-two sailors merely because they wanted to eat him.[16] –

An animal is determined by its instinct, which has rules, but from such a human being[b] I do not know in the least what to expect. Sparrman explains in his *Journey to the Cape of Good Hope*[17] that the lion does not hunt its prey but sneaks up to it and then when it believes it is close enough springs at once and if it misses its prize steps back as if it wants to see where it went wrong and then sneaks there. Human beings know that and can judge accordingly. Thus once a Hotentot was going home and a lion snuck after him at a distance. Now he knew that he would not be able to get home before evening and that the lion would then suddenly tear him to pieces. He took off his clothing and put them on a stick so that it seemed that he was standing there. But he made himself a hole in a hill and hid there. The lion came slowly closer and sprang and, because the stick immediately gave way, tumbled down the hill with the clothes and stick and then slunk away. However, a lion will hunt its prey when it is very hungry.

Freedom must thus be limited but this cannot be done through natural laws, for otherwise the human being would not be free, thus he must limit himself. Right thus depends upon the limitation of freedom. It is easier to explain than duty. – Happiness does not come into consideration at all with regard to right for each can try to attain happiness however he wants.

27:1321

One does not as yet know how to determine from principles the place for *jus naturae* {natural right} in practical philosophy or to show the border between *jus naturae* and morals. For that various propositions from both sciences must be run through and compared.[c] – In order to settle these matters one must try to develop the concepts of right. In the previous hour we wanted to present things somewhat unsystematically but now seek to make it more methodical.

[a] KS: *von ihm*. KI: *zu ihm*, for "what to provide to him"
[b] *einem solchen* might mean such a human being with instinct (earlier in this sentence) or such a human being without (previous paragraph)
[c] *laufen . . . in einander.*

That something must exist as an end in itself and that not everything can exist merely as means is as necessary in the system of ends as *ens a se* {a being in itself} is in the series of efficient causes. A thing that is an end in itself is *bonum a se* {a good in itself}. What can be considered merely as a means has value merely as a means when it is used as such. Now for this there must be a being that is an end in itself. One thing in nature is a means for another; that continues on and on and it is necessary in the end to think of a thing that is itself an end, otherwise the series would have no end.[a]

In the series of efficient causes there is *ens ab alio* {a being dependent on another} but finally I must come upon *ens a se*. The end is a basis in volition for the existence of the means. One thing is means for another, hence finally there must be a thing which is not another means but instead is an end in itself. But how a being can be in itself just an end and never a means is as hard to conceive as how in the series of causes there would have to be a necessary being. And yet we must accept both because of the needs of our reason to have everything complete. It lies in the nature of human reason that it can never have insight into something except as conditioned, never have insight into something without a ground, and there is no ground for *ens* {being} and *bonum a se* {good in themselves}. I say a human being exists in order to be happy. But why does being happy have value? It has only a conditioned value namely because[b] the existence of a human being has value. But why does that existence have value? Because it pleased God. Then it has no value in itself. I can now also ask why does the existence of a God have value?

A human being is an end in itself and never merely a means; that is against his nature. If someone deposits something with me and he wants to have it back but I do not give it back to him and I say "I can use it for the general good[c] better than he can" then I use his money and him merely as a means. Should he be an end, then his will must also be the end that I have.

If rational beings alone are capable of being ends in themselves it cannot be because they have reason but because they have freedom. Reason is merely a means. – A human being could through reason and without freedom produce in accordance with universal laws of nature what an animal produces through instinct. – Without reason a being cannot be an end in itself for it cannot be conscious of its own existence, cannot reflect on it. But reason still does not constitute the ground[d] since a

27:1322

---

[a] KI, KS: new paragraph. MS: uncertain.

[b] KI, KS: *Werth, nemlich weil das Daseyn.* MS: *Werth, nehmlich das Dasein,* leaving out the "because." KI notes possible *Werth, sofern nemlich das Daseyn,* for "value, namely insofar as the existence"

[c] *zum Weltbesten nützen* [d] KI: comma. KS: period

human being is an end in itself, he has dignity which cannot be replaced by any equivalent. Reason does not give us dignity. For we can see that nature produces through instinct in animals what reason first discovers[a] only through a long process. Now nature could have directed our reason entirely in accordance with natural laws[b] by devising all kinds of artifices so that every human being would learn to read by themselves and all of this in accordance with certain rules. In this way we would be no better than the animals. But freedom and freedom alone makes us an end in itself. Here we have an ability to act in accordance with our own will. If our reason were directed according to universal laws then my will would not be my own but the will of nature. – If the actions of a human being lie in the mechanism of nature then their grounds would not be in him but outside him. – I must presuppose the freedom of a being if it is supposed to be an end for itself. Such a being must thus have freedom of the will. I do not know how to understand[c] freedom; it is nonetheless a necessary hypothesis if I am to think of a rational being as an end in itself. If he is not free then he is in the hand of **another**, thus always for the end of another, thus mere means. Freedom is thus not only the supreme but also the sufficient condition. A freely acting being must have reason, for if I were affected only by the senses then I would be ruled by them. Under what condition can a free being be an end in itself? That freedom be a law to itself. He must in each case be considered as an end and never as a means. Laws are either laws of nature or laws of freedom. If freedom is to be under laws it must give the laws to itself.

If freedom took laws from nature then it would not be freedom. – How can freedom itself be a law itself? Without laws no cause, hence no will, is thinkable for the cause is that from which something follows in accordance with a constant rule. If freedom is subject to a law of nature then it is not freedom. It must thus itself be a law. Comprehending this appears to be difficult and on this point all the teachers of natural right have erred, they simply never noticed it. All laws of the will are practical and express necessity either objectively or subjectively. Thus objective and subjective laws of the will. The first are rules of a will good in itself, how it would act, the latter rules[d] in accordance with which a given will really does act. – The subjective rules of the will are very different from the objective. A human being knows that he should not eat something because it would be harmful to him. That is an objective rule. But he lets himself be led by his sensibility and eats; in this case he is acting in accordance with subjective rules of the will. – If the will of a being is   27:1323

[a] KI: *ausfindet*. KS: *aussucht*, for "selects"
[b] KI: *Naturgesetzen*. KS: *Naturgesetz*, for "natural law"
[c] *begreifen*   [d] KI: *Regeln*. KS, MS: *Regel*, for "a rule"

good in itself then the objective laws of his will are no different from the subjective. – The human will is not the kind in which the subjective rules of volition correspond with the objective. Now the objective rule of volition applied to a will whose subjective rules do not correspond with the objective is called an **imperative**. No rule serves[a] as an imperative for a being whose will is already good in itself. An imperative is a law insofar as it necessitates a will that is not good in itself through the idea of a will good in itself, it presupposes a will that does not want to do the act but must be necessitated. This is necessitation, where the contingent must be made necessary. A human being can choose good and evil, thus in human beings the good will is a contingent will. As for God his good will is not contingent; thus also for God there are no imperatives that would necessitate him to a good will. For that would be superfluous. Necessitation of an action that is in itself contingent through objective grounds is practical necessitation, which is different from practical necessity. There are also laws for God but they have practical necessity. – Practical necessitation is an imperative, a command. If a will is good in itself then it does not need to be commanded.[b] Thus there are no commands for God. Objective practical necessity is for God also subjective practical necessity. Constraint is necessitation[c] to an unwanted action. Accordingly I must have an incentive to the contrary. – Practical laws can thus also be constraint, also if a human being does something he does not like, he must simply do it. "I **ought to do that**" means an action that is necessary through me would be good. It does not follow that I will do it, for I also have subjective opposing grounds. I represent the action as necessary. Laws are thus for an imperfect will. Practical laws as necessitating[d] grounds of actions[e] are called imperatives. No virtue can be found in human beings where no degree of temptation can be found which they can overcome. Thus the supplication "lead us not into temptation" is a glorious thought. We have three imperatives: technical, pragmatic, and moral, rules of skill, prudence, and wisdom. [1][f] Imperatives that command something under the condition of a possible volition merely as a means for a merely possible and discretionary end are imperatives of skill. They are practical sciences, e.g. you ought to make a cut across a line. That is not an imperative for everyone except under the condition that one wants to obtain a merely possible end (the division of a line into two equal parts). It is good as a means to a merely possible end. These are imperatives of art, of skill. We learn skills and

[a] *gilt*
[b] *darf ihm gar nicht gebothen werden.*
[c] *Zwang ist Nöthigung*
[d] *necessitirende*
[e] KI: plural *Handlungen*. KS: singular *Handlung*
[f] Adding a "1" to match the "2)" and "3)" below

means to ends without knowing or expecting that we[a] will need to have the ends. Thus parents often do not ask whether their child has become moral[b] but whether he has learned a lot. Nature has given an impulse in order to preserve human beings. For I do not know whether I will encounter a situation where I can use it. Imperatives of skill are merely conditioned and commanded under the condition of a merely contingent and possible end. 2) Imperatives of prudence are those that prescribe the means to a universal end to which all subjective grounds of volition in human beings relate, i.e. happiness, which all creatures require. Here the imperative commands under the condition of an actual end. 3) The imperative of wisdom commands the action as itself an end. The rule "You shall not lie" can be skill and a means to deceive another. It can be prudence because I can attain all my aims using it. I will be taken to be honest, others will trust me, speak highly of me, etc. But I can also see this rule as wisdom. Here I do not consider it as a means to my end. – Things will go for me as they will, good or bad, that does not concern me. The law still remains as always. Even if I cannot follow it the law still remains something honorable for me. – This unconditioned good we consider to be much higher than anything that we would be able to attain through actions were we to use it as a means. – A beneficent act[c] is much more valuable in itself than the good which the beneficent agent attains by it, e.g. that someone loves him, etc. Good consequences do not determine value. Virtue has dignity in itself even if it cannot be practiced, the good consequences have values which could be replaced by an equivalent. All imperatives are conditioned or unconditioned, the conditioned are either problematic, an imperative of skill, or assertoric, an imperative of prudence. The unconditioned imperative of wisdom is apodictic, all imperatives are thus hypothetical or categorical. One must speak the truth, that is completely unconditioned. How is such a categorical imperative possible? Categorical imperatives command without empirical conditions. They can still have conditions, but *a priori*, and the condition itself is categorical. All discretionary ends refer eventually to happiness. This is the sum total of achieving all ends. Happiness, however, is an empirical condition for I cannot know whether something will contribute to my happiness and how I will be happy; instead I first have to experience it. – Imperatives of prudence are pragmatic. One calls laws 'pragmatic sanctions'[d] which aim at well-being for the common good.[e] Pragmatic history is that which makes one prudent. Pragmatic is that which serves to further happiness. Pragmatic imperatives

27:1324

[a] Reading *wir ... werden.* KI, MS, and KS: *er ... werde,* for "he"
[b] *moralisirt*
[c] *Wohltat*
[d] *Sankzionen*
[e] *das Wohl des gemeinen Besten*

27:1325 are to be distinguished from the moral. Pragmatic imperatives lie at the basis of imperatives of skill for I learn about them because I believe that sometime it will contribute to my happiness if I can think using them. Happiness is thus not a moral principle. Can I not give rules for happiness *a priori?* No, I can surely think about the happiness of a thing but I cannot think *a priori* about what constitutes that happiness. For agreeableness is not a concept but a sensation, how I am affected by things. Thus I also cannot have any rule for happiness *a priori*, I know[a] nothing *in concreto* {definite} in such a rule. Thus a pragmatic imperative is based on empirical conditions alone. Shaftesbury says that happiness can give no value to morals.[18] In order to give value to morality this way we would have to presuppose that a human being has an immediate satisfaction and dissatisfaction in the action. He calls that the moral feeling. Actions have no value if I experience enjoyment only from the consequences, for the actions would have value only as a means; Hutcheson agrees.[19] Despite this the moral imperative is not categorical for it presupposes at least that a being has a value, which this feeling has imparted in his moral actions, and[b] one cannot indicate this feeling *a priori* but from experience. What experience teaches us is contingent; we cannot have any *a priori* insight into the necessity of this feeling. The value of moral actions is thus just in relation to the one who has a moral feeling and it depends on the will of the highest being to give us such a feeling, and moral actions are in themselves neither good nor evil. Indeed there is such a moral feeling in human beings, however it does not precede knowledge[c] of the moral rule and make it possible but first follows upon it. If the moral feeling is the cause in a human being for his recognizing actions either as good or as evil then this feeling could exist in various degrees. And since the moral feeling is not stronger than the other feelings and since it cannot be proven then it is the same as all physical feelings and a human being will thus choose from among the feelings what to him appears to be the most satisfactory. Where the feeling comes from does not matter at all. They all stimulate us. Feelings are differentiated only according to degree and are all one according to type. Moral laws, however, command in a way such that no instinct or feeling is allowed to outweigh them. Now for this the moral feeling would have to be the strongest[d] feeling but it is clearly not. A human being would be a fool if he wanted to follow a weaker[e] feeling to the detriment of a stronger one. If the moral feeling were the strongest then everyone would be virtuous. Virtue pleases

---

[a] *kenne*
[b] KI: *ist, und,* for "and." KS: *ist. Denn,* for new sentence starting with "For"
[c] *Kenntniß*   [d] *größte*
[e] *kleineren*

above all, if I represent it to myself *a priori* then I wish most dearly to have a feeling that would pull me toward virtue in the strongest possible way,[a] the pleasure is based on the approval of reason:[b] If I want virtue to be above all enjoyments for me then I want to be always virtuous. Moral laws are always categorical and have obligation, i.e. moral necessitation to an action. The action to which I am necessitated through moral laws is a **duty**. A moral law comes first. If the will is in itself good then the moral law needs no obligation. If the will is not then it must be necessitated. Morals must not be derived from inclination; even the most common sense knows that. All human beings have an inclination to live. If one is sick he seeks all possible assistance; he does that from inclination. If a human being is unhappy in his life and yet cares for his life when sick, he certainly does not do this from inclination but from duty. In the latter there is a moral content. If a man marries a beautiful woman then he will love her from inclination. If, however, through the years she becomes wrinkled and he still loves her then he does it from duty. A moral action has value not when it arises from inclination but from duty.[c] An action can be in accordance with duty but not take place[d] from duty. We must perform moral actions without the least incentive merely from duty and respect for the moral law. The law must on its own accord determine the will. If the actions are done from duty then they have a moral value. Universal lawfulness alone places me under an obligation. If everyone did not heed his promises and this were a universal rule then it absolutely could not serve as a universal law for then no one would promise because he would know that he would not keep it and the other would also know it.

27:1326

Obligation is moral necessitation of action, i.e. the dependence of a will that is not[e] good in itself on the principle[f] of autonomy or objectively necessary practical laws. Duty is the objective necessity of an action itself[g] out of obligation. Respect is esteem[h] for a value insofar as it limits all inclination. We respect someone when we so esteem[i] him that we limit our self-love, etc. We esteem him higher than ourselves. Actions must not be done from necessity of inclination. If an action is done from fear then it is not really duty. The value must lie in the duty itself. All laws can necessitate the will through their lawfulness or through their accompanying incentives or through coercion and fear. The law does

---

[a] *am stärksten*
[b] KI: *Vernunft*. KS: *Lehre*, for "the doctrine"
[c] MS: *sondern aus*. KI, KS: *sondern wenn sie aus*, for "but when it arises out of"
[d] *geschehen*   [e] KI: *nicht*. KS, MS omit *nicht*
[f] *Princip*   [g] KS omits *selbst*
[h] *Schätzung*   [i] *schätzen*

not necessitate through inclination and fear in itself but conditionally; the law that necessitates in itself must necessitate from respect. With regard to respect I place my inclinations aside, I place an absolute value in the action. Our author[20] and others talk about *obligatio per poenas* {obligation stemming from punishment}, Baumgarten[21] does too. But to oblige someone through *poenae* {punishments} and *praemia* {rewards} is *contradictio in adjecto* {a contradiction in terms} because in this case I move him to action which he does not out of obligation but out of fear and inclination. Through them I can also constrain him to things[a] which are not obligatory for him. But how can a law have respect for itself and also necessitate through respect? God does not have respect for the law for he has no inclination that should be limited by respect. Respect is something necessitating; for God, however, nothing is allowed to be necessitating. A rational being as an end in itself must have his own will and thus this will must be free. As free the human will cannot be determined through[b] incentives for then it[c] would not be free but like the animals. It would be determined through nature. Thus no incentives determine it and yet it cannot be without law so the law must determine it already as law. The form of law must determine the will, he must thus have respect for the law. I can ask whether I am supposed to return a *depositum* {deposit} which was entrusted to me alone to another. If his inclination were to determine him then he would keep it. But he is free so he must have a law. The law is that[d] you must return a *depositum*. Can I use it to benefit myself? No. Must I fear that it will be made public? Then suppose that the other person is already dead and I can deny everything. If I make it a universal rule that everyone can and will keep a *depositum* whenever it pleased them then that could never be a universal law for in this situation no one would ever deposit[e] anything. So if my will ought not to be unrestrained but should have laws then they must be of this kind. Respect for the law rests on this, that this is the possibility for how the action can hold under universal laws. – To settle one's debts is a duty. The obligation is the relation to law, here to contract. Legality[f] is agreement of an action with duty without considering whether or not duty is the determining ground of the action. Morality is the agreement of an action with duty insofar as duty is the determining ground of the action. In all juridical actions their legality is conformity with duty, but

27:1327

---

[a] KI, KS: *Dingen*. MS: *thun*, possibly as "actions"
[b] KI: *durch*. KS: *von*, for "by"
[c] *er* could refer to a human being (he) or to a human will (it) here and in the next few
sentences.
[d] KI: *das*. KS, MS: *da*, for "is there"   [e] *deponiren*
[f] Here and in the remainder of this paragraph Kant uses the latinate *Legalitaet* and *Moralitaet*.

not their morality, they are not done from duty. Legality is only concerned with whether I act in conformity with duty, beyond that it is all the same whether I act out of respect or inclination and fear. But if I do observe[a] the law but not out of respect for it then the actions are not moral. Most actions by human beings in conformity with duty are legal most of the time, especially the ones which can be coerced with force.[b] It is legal if I discharge my debts at the proper time. If I know that the creditor is a punctual man then I do it out of fear. If he were indulgent then I would probably still be hesitant. *Ethic* {ethics} is the science of judging and determining an action in accordance with its morality. *Jus* {right} is the science of judging an action in accordance with its legality. *Ethic* is also called the doctrine of virtue. *Jus* can also concern actions that can be coerced. For it is all the same whether the actions are done out of respect, fear, coercion, or inclination. *Ethic* is not concerned with actions that can be coerced; *ethic* is the practical philosophy of action regarding dispositions. *Jus* is the practical philosophy of actions regardless of dispositions. Everything obligatory belongs to *ethic*, thus all duties. *Jus* is concerned with duties and actions that are in accord with the law and can be coerced. Actions are called right if they agree with the law, virtuous if they originate out of respect for the law. Thus there can be an action that is right and yet not virtuous. The disposition to act from duty, out of respect for the law is virtue. *Ethic* consists of the doctrine of virtue and *jus* the doctrine of right. If the action is also coercible[c] then it can be lawful. One says that right is a doctrine of the duties that can and should be coerced through force, but this is based on what was already said. Duty is necessitating, for that reason should it be necessary without respect for the law then it must be done through coercion. Besides coercion and respect nothing necessitates [us] to an action. Coercion is a limitation of freedom. An action is right if it agrees with the law, **just**[d] if it agrees with the laws of coercion, i.e. agrees with the doctrines of right. In general one calls something right that agrees with a rule. This is why *linea recta* {a straight line} has that name; if it runs parallel to the straight edge then the line is called a rule.[22] Right is thus either virtuous or just. When is an action enforceable? An action that is directed in accordance with a universal rule of freedom is right, if it contradicts freedom in accordance with a universal rule then it is unjust. The aim may be whatever it will. My action is allowed[e] to be constituted only in a way that accords with universal freedom. I may not take anything from anyone but also give nothing. In this way I do not act unjustly if I

27:1328

---

[a] KI: *Beachte.* KS, MS: *Betrachte*, for "consider"
[b] KI: *mit Gewalt.* KS: *ohne Gewalt*, for "without force." MS unclear
[c] *zwangsmäßig*   [d] *gerecht*
[e] KI: *darf.* KS, MS: *dürfe*, for "would be allowed"

see someone being killed by another without helping him. That is *actio justa* {a just action}. The action is externally right although not inwardly. I simply do not want to rob another of his happiness, I am indifferent to everything else, he may try to be happy however he wants. An action that opposes any action that itself opposes universal freedom is right. Opposition to a wrong action is a hindrance to the action that opposes universal freedom thus it is an advancement of freedom and of the agreement of private freedom with universal freedom. Opposition to an action reflecting the freedom of another is called coercion. The agreement of private freedom with universal freedom is the supreme principle[a] of right, it is a law of coercion.[b]

Our author and others define right without a science of the laws which one can be coerced to observe when this coercion does not contradict duty. Coercion is rightful if it advances universal freedom. A law of actions to which one can be coerced is a **coercive law** and the corresponding right is a coercive right. A right that is not a coercive right is equity. The latter is *jus late dictum* {a right in a wide sense}. The former is *jus stricte dictum* {a right in a narrow sense}. Equity is a right without coercion.[c] The responsibility which one has to observe a law that one cannot be coerced to observe is coercion-free responsibility. I can be coerced to anything that is necessary for the preservation of universal freedom. Equity is an ethical right. If I can require something of someone in a strong right then I can coerce him to it if he refuses, but if I can require something due to equity then it is his responsibility but I cannot coerce him. An action that conforms to the universal law in accordance with expressed attitudes[d] but not in accordance with inner attitudes is inequitable.[e] That is an imperfect right and not a perfect right or strong right which is one in regard to which I can be coerced. It is imperfect but it is certainly still a right. My freedom agrees with that of another if he agrees with it. If I arrange with my servant to give him 20 reichsthalers per year but it later turns out to be more expensive to live so that he cannot make do with that money I do him no wrong if I continue to give him no more than the 20 reichsthalers even though he asks for more for I act in accordance with his [earlier] expressed attitudes. I have nonetheless not acted equitably because he had thought that he would be satisfied with the 20 reichsthalers only[f] as long as the relatively inexpensive times would allow it. I would be able to assume his intention.

27:1329

---

[a] *Princip* [b] *Zwangsgesetz*
[c] *zwangslose Recht*
[d] Here and in the remainder of the paragraph, *Gesinnungen*
[e] *unbillig*
[f] KI: *nur*. KS: *werde*, for unnecessary extra "would"

He thus had an actual right but not a coercive right for attitudes cannot be the basis of a coercive law[a] because they are inner. "Equitable" can also be called "ethically just."

We will not be concerned with equity but only with strict right. Jurists are often wrong about this because they often coerce for equity. *Ethic* contains duties of strong right and of equity. Right concerns freedom, equity the intention. If I do not contribute to another's happiness I do not infringe upon his freedom but I allow him to do what he wants. Freedom must agree with the universal; when this does not happen then one can coerce him for he hinders freedom. Here neither happiness nor a command of duty but freedom is the cause of right. The author has grounded it in his *Prolegomena* by saying that it is a divine law and that we would be made happy through it but that is not needed here at all. His *Prolegomena* appears to have belonged to the preparation for a particular *collegium* {lecture course}.

Treatise[b]

Titulus I

De norma actionum liberalium et in genere[c]

{Of the rule for free actions and in general}

The author has defined "obligation" through necessitation by the greatest good. He thus puts emphasis on the amount of the greatest consequences[d] and by means of it determines the true good. *Necessitatio* is necessitation to an action toward a true good. What is that? This one sees from the author's following sentences. *Nulla obligatio datur nisi per praemia et poenas* {no obligation exists except by means of rewards and punishments} he next says. *Praemia* {rewards} are those through which happiness is increased.[e] *Poenae* {punishments} through which it is decreased. Happiness determines the true good for him and he has a

---

[a] KI: *Zwangsgesetzen*. KS: *Zwangsrecht*, for "coercive right"

[b] *Abhandlung* signifies the point in the course which Kant moves to direct discussion of Achenwall's text.

[c] Achenwall has "De norma actionum liberarum et obligatione in genere." "Of the rule for free actions and obligation in general." *Titulus I* is part of the Introduction and is followed in Achenwall by further parts that Kant skips: *Titulus II: De legibus naturalibus* {Of natural laws}, *Titulus III: De legibus perfectis* {Of perfect laws}, and *Titulus IV: De legibus perfectis qua legibus externis* {Of perfect laws as external laws}, and an addition to the Introduction, *Historia litteraria juris naturalis* {literary history of natural right}. Kant nonetheless discusses some of these issues under *Titulus I*.

[d] KI: *Folgen*. KS: *Folge*, for "consequence"

[e] KS, MS: *vermehrt wird*. KI: *vermehrt*, for "happiness increases"

pragmatic principle. Reason need only attend to the consequences and their agreement with happiness. We can never will something without having an interest in it. An interest is satisfaction in the existence of a thing. I must thus also take an interest in moral actions. Interest can either be immediate in the action, that is *directe* {immediately} practical. Or mediately to the action, merely through that in the consequences which I hope to take an interest, then it is *indirecte* {mediately} practical. Here nothing in the existence of the action really pleases me except the consequences. If I could attain happiness another way then I would take no interest at all in the action. Here the actions have no other value except as mere means to blessedness.[a] An action whose necessitation is determined only from the consequences is of only as much value as the consequences are or even less. But the actions that are moral are of more value than the consequences.[b] The action of a human being who rescues someone from the water has more value than the consequence that the one rescued is still alive for many will still drown and even the one rescued must die eventually. Actions have a completely separate[c] value that is to be differentiated from the value of the consequences. If actions were to have value merely as means to happiness then I would always be able to take other means and the action would not be necessary. Nature would not have given us reason to discover that means but instead a shorter way, instinct, as in animals. Obligation is based on the principle of the lawfulness of an action in general; if I have promised something to some little nobody and I want to make a present out of it for someone powerful so that he would become my patron then according to Achenwall I must choose the latter, for the little nobody would not sue me out of fear. But I must stick to my word for I cannot think that the opposite would be possible as a universal law. My action must be made into a universal law; however, immoral actions are not possible as universal law. To decline to give alms to a beggar is possible as a universal law for if we are separated from one another then one[d] does not require the alms, thus the action is right but not yet[e] equitable for in equity I want others not merely to do nothing that impairs[f] my happiness but also to contribute to it. *Obligatio ethica est practica simpliciter talis* {ethical obligation is simply such a practical obligation[g]}. *Secundum quid* {after which} come the consequences, thus *indirecte*. Cicero says *si quaero, quid sit utile, obscurum est, si quaero quid*

---

[a] *Seligkeit*
[b] This entire sentence is missing in KS.
[c] *separaten*
[d] KI: *einer*. KS: *er*, for "he"
[e] KI: *noch nicht billig*. KS: *nicht billig*, for "not equitable"
[f] KI: *keinen Abbruch thue*. KS, MS: *Abbruch thue*, leaving out a negative
[g] KI: *ethica est practica*. KS, MS: *ethica et practica*, for "ethical and practical obligation [is] simply such a kind"

sit honestum [perspicuum] est {if I ask what is useful it is obscure, if I ask what is honorable it is [obvious[a]]}.[23] Regarding what is useful one must calculate a long time and still one will not know what is the most useful. But I immediately recognize that I must comply with the moral rule.[b] Hume says that if a human being acts virtuously on prudential grounds then he will usually act that way but he will still reserve the right to make an exception in each case.[24] For he will observe the rule only when he sees that the action is useful to him. But the virtuous will comply with the rules whether or not they are useful or disadvantageous to him. How can I have absolute satisfaction in mere legality? I have no *a priori* insight into this. I simply cannot prove *a priori* that something will provide satis-faction because this belongs to feeling. From reason I cannot derive any feeling; that there is feeling, however, I can prove. Our actions as free must stand under laws.[c] Free will is an efficient cause and cause already leads to the concept of law. Freedom is independence of the will from sensible impulses as determining grounds. It can thus be determined not through the effect of the law[d] but through its form because it must still determine the will.[e]

All actions stand under the principle[f] of lawfulness. Respect is the immediate estimation of the value or the lawfulness of the actions. – In the *Prolegomena* the author says that *Necessitatio per motiva* is *moralis.*   27:1331 *Motiva sunt elateres ei, qui distincte repraesentantur. Obligatio est necessita-tio per motiva potiora* {Necessitation by a motive is moral necessitation. Motives are those incentives which are represented distinctly. Obliga-tion is necessitation by the stronger motive}. He alludes here to degree. Where there are the most grounds, whether they are intellectual or sen-sible, that is what one must choose and it would be[g] the true good. *Ergo* he says that *sine spe vel metu proposito non datur obligatio* {if there is no con-sideration of hope or fear there is no obligation}. It is just the reverse. An action to which I have an obligation must be done entirely without hope and fear. I cannot say, "I am obligated to serve a man because he loves me." A tyrant necessitates his subjects[h] out of hope and fear to actions to which we have no obligation. I have an obligation to my action when I must do it regardless of advantage. If a human being does not let himself

---

[a] Adding *perspicuum* to follow Cicero's original and complete the sentence. Not in KI, MS, or KS.
[b] KI: *die moralische Regel.* KS: *die moralische,* for "what is moral"
[c] KI: *unter Gesetzen.* KS: *unter Gesetz,* for "the law"
[d] KI: *durch den Effekt des Gesetzes.* KS: *durch den Affekt des Gesetzes,* for "through the feeling accompanying the law"
[e] KI, KS, MS have colon instead of period   [f] *Princip*
[g] KI: *da sey.* KS, MS: *da seyn,* for "they are"   [h] *Unterthanen*

be constrained to an action through obligation[a] then fear and hope will do it. But this use of fear and hope is not essential to obligation because the obligation precedes it and it is *vehicel* {a means} for obtaining more access to the law because the will is not perfect and cannot determine itself through the law alone. Fear and hope are opposed only to the inclinations which are contrary to the law and its observance. The teachers of natural right have never thought of lawfulness and have never brought up the law because it appears to them incomprehensible. But that does not matter as long as it is there. The author further says that *ultra posse nemo obligatur* {no one is obligated to that which is beyond his ability}. Actions that are physically impossible could never be necessary, morally impossible I cannot say[b] for I assume the human being to be free, so I assume in him also the practical capacity to control all his inclinations for otherwise no laws are possible. I can be obligated to nothing beyond my physical powers. But if I am free then it is not impossible for me in a practical sense to comply with a law though it still may be difficult. If one wants to say that there are cases in which it is impossible and others in which it is possible to surmount our inclinations then[c] no rule can be universal. For in this case I could not know whether an inclination that is surmountable by me is in another insurmountable. Whether we are free or can at least assume freedom is for metaphysics to decide; through[d] freedom we are also enlightened with[e] an explanation of why we are already obligated out of respect for the law alone. *Obligatio est activa i.e. obligantis* {Obligation is active, i.e. for the one obligating} and *passiva i.e. obligati* {passive, i.e. for the one obligated} the one obligates, the other has an obligation, e.g. creditor and debtor. *Obligatio affirmativa ad committendum, negativa ad omittendum* {affirmative obligation to perform, negative to omit}. In the state of nature one has merely negative obligations to refrain from anything that can hinder the freedom of another. A positive obligation is related to a formally promulgated law and so differs from an affirmative one. Many things appear to be *actio committenda* {an action to be performed} but are actually *omittenda* {to be omitted}. The affirmative laws are *praeceptiva mandata* {mandated maxims}. The *negativae* laws are *prohibitivae* or *vetitae* {prohibited or forbidden}, e.g. the proposition that you should pay what you are responsible for appears to be an affirmative obligation and yet is only negative for it stands under the law *neminem laede* {wrong no one}. One obligation can have greater

[a] MS has extra *nicht* in this sentence
[b] KI: *kann ich nicht sagen.* KS: *kann auch nicht sein,* for "also cannot be"
[c] KI: *dann.* KS: *denn,* for "because"   [d] KI: *durch.* KS: *ohne,* for "without"
[e] KI: *bekommen wir auch Licht.* KS: *bekommen wir auch Lust,* for "we also gain the desire for"

motivating grounds than the other, but this is impossible according to his [the author's] principles because for him obligation is the greatest sum of motivating grounds and there cannot be anything greater than the greatest and more necessary than the necessary.[a] No obligations can be greater than another but their *motivae* can be *fortiores* {stronger}. A law can hold only under conditions. It is thus a ground for obligation but it is still not sufficient; only if an unconditioned law is added to it is it *fortior*.

Lex perfectiva {the law of perfection} is *bonorum sibi oppositorum praesta melius* {of opposed goods, pursue the better one}. Actions are neutral if they are neither good nor evil and thus do not belong to morality. They are *adiaphora* {indifferent things} since they are neither determined through moral grounds nor hindered by them.[b] Actions are forbidden if they contradict obligation. They are *officium* {duty} if they are necessary in accordance with universal laws of the will.

Imperative. *Causa per libertatem auctor, effectus auctoris qua talis, factum* {an agent is a cause through freedom, a deed is the effect of the agent as such}; I agree with this. Because here I think only[c] of freedom, I think a law that as such binds freedom. In each *factum* {deed} there is its relation to law and of the law to the *auctor* {performer} of the *factum*. The author says that *consectaria legis* {the legal consequences} that connect a law with an action are *praemia* {rewards} and[d] *poenae* {punishment}, sensations of pleasure or pain in the acting *Subject*. According to the author *bonum* {good} and *malum* {evil} do not fit because the other terms have more significance. Now the author says that all laws obligate merely *per praemia* and *poenas*; that is false. God is not benevolent if God rewards those actions that human beings would not[e] be obligated to perform[f] were God not to have connected the reward to those actions, for then the reward would be God's obligation:[g] instead God is benevolent because God also provides rewards for actions which we already must do in themselves. A transgression of a law in which one acts contrary to his duty is *reatus*, fault. An action in which we do something more than we are obligated[h] to do is *meritum* {meritorious}, the first makes us deserving of *poenae* the other of *praemia*. If I act entirely in accordance with the law then I am deserving of neither reward nor punishment. Here one sees the correct concept of *poena* and *praemium*.

---

[a] KI: *als die*. KS: *als sie*, for "more necessary than they are necessary"
[b] KI: period. KS: comma
[c] KI: *nur* possible copying error for *nun*, for "now." KS, MS: *nur*
[d] KI: *und*. KS: *oder*, for "or"   [e] KS omits *nicht*
[f] *schuldig zu tun*   [g] *Schuldigkeit*
[h] *verbindlich*

In *jus* something can be *meritum* that is *debitum* {required} in morals. In his *Prolegomena* the author takes for a principle[a] of right the agreement of the laws with the divine will. But then I must still know what duty would be and how the divine will would be constituted. – – For us the principle[b] is that if an action can exist together with the freedom of all in accordance with a universal law this action is allowed and we have authorization. I have a right when I have a ground to necessitate the wills of others. That is right considered *materialiter* {materially}, what I can compel another to do. Right *formaliter* {formally} is what is not wrong. I cannot act wrongly without being subject to coercion, in the latter case right is considered *adjective* and can be taken only *singulariter* {in the singular} in the former it is *substantive* and is taken *pluraliter* {in the plural}. So I have a right when I can coerce someone. An action is

27:1333   right if it can be made into a universal law without doing harm to universal freedom, that is *adjective*. For that a human being needs only avoid doing wrong to another, but if I have a right then I can compel him to something that really, directly limits the freedom of another. A wrong is that which contradicts universal freedom, thus hinders freedom, and the opposite must increase freedom. I have a right if I were to limit the freedom of another. That is coercion. A right is thus authorization to coerce another. We see here that the principle[c] of right cannot concern happiness at all and we must not mix it in here at all. Everyone may care for his own happiness as he will. Neither the greatest happiness nor unhappiness contradicts universal freedom; if someone happens to be happy he is not allowed to transfer any to his unhappy neighbor. The whole world can operate in accordance with self-interest. It does no harm to another's freedom. If only all human beings observed the laws under which freedom can exist and acted in accordance with self-interest the rest of the time. But because they always need each other each would contribute to the happiness of others out of self-interest. An action is right if it agrees with a rule. A lack of agreement with a rule is *defectus rectitudinis* {lack of rectitude}. *Defectus rectitudinis* that can be punished is *reatus* {fault}. All punishment is coercion but not all coercion is punishment. Punishment is coercion which is under the *auctoritas* {authority} of a law. Every wrong is deserving of punishment. Punishment is a cessation of someone's freedom. I put him in a condition he has not willed to be in, for to resist actions that contradict universal freedom is to promote universal freedom. Thus it is necessary and every law of freedom is a penal law. *Factum est actio libera* {a deed is a free action} that stands under law. *Factum* is *culpabile* {culpable} if it is not in accordance with the law, or *inculpabile*. The *culpabile* {culpable deed} is also *dolosum* {malicious} or

[a] *Princip*   [b] *Princip*
[c] *Princip*

culposum {negligent}. The *defectus rectitudinis* {lack of rectitude} is *dolus* {malice} if it is done with awareness, or *culpa* {negligence} if without awareness. The first is intentional, the second unintentional transgression. Only the awareness and not the aim belongs to the first; there is more reason to impute *dolosum* {the malicious act} because I publicly scorn the law and universal freedom is more at risk. Divine laws are the origin of all obligation.

In order to know by means of reason what God wants I must conceive of the most perfect will. The idea of that will contains in itself all practical laws.[a] The laws of duty are thus already divine commands. If I did not obtain the laws by means of reason then I could not know without revelation whether or not they are proper to God. What all this amounts to: If I posit God prior to duty then I consider him as a being acting according to mere choice and need.

All obligations stand under laws and are either *perfectae* {perfect} or *imperfectae* {imperfect}. I can be coerced to the former, not to the latter. Coercion is limitation of my freedom. If I do not limit the freedom of another then neither can anyone limit mine. Thus all *obligationes per-* 27:1334 *fectae* {perfect obligations} are part of *jus naturae* {natural right} but the imperfect ones part of morals. – It should be called *obligatio perfecta externa* {perfect external obligation}. Right is either a coercive right or a non-coercive right.[b] This latter is equity. *Obligatio externa*, what stands under outer laws. Equity is agreement of the will also with the inner state of mind[c] of another human being, the strong right however with the expressed state of mind. I can be coerced only in accordance with the literal meaning of what I said even if I can guess the intention. But we cannot know the thoughts of a human being, otherwise equity would also be a strong right. Equity is, however, also a right and not a good. Outer laws can refer only to outer actions and so also to outer coercion.

Right is **the limitation of the particular freedom of each by the conditions under which universal freedom can exist.** Right properly consists in *negativen*, in omission. The supreme law *neminem laede* {wrong no one} is of course[d] *negative*. The author says that I am bound by my nature to preserve my life; this would be the principle[e] of right. But that does not belong to right at all for in right I can do with my life whatever I will. It is solely a duty of virtue. Each is obligated as far as he is able to refrain from anything that interferes with the self-preservation of others, *scil. moraliter* {namely morally}, says the author. This is

---

[a] KI, KS: *praktische Gesetze.* MS: *praktische*, with no blank space, for "all that is practical"
[b] *Zwangsfreies Recht* [c] *Gesinnung*
[d] KI: *ist doch negative.* KS: *ist negative*, for "is *negative*"
[e] *Prinzip*

indeterminate from the start for I do not know how far it goes. – How do I know that something belongs to my own self-preservation?[a] One may figure upon a lot, another a little, for his self-preservation. If someone is[b] indebted to me but has nothing at all I cannot take what is owed me. – That is certainly not a juridical proposition. How does his self-preservation concern me? I am required only not to resist his freedom. – So I can also infringe upon his self-preservation. In right I must direct everything in accordance with laws of freedom, otherwise everything would be chaotic. If states give laws for the preservation of citizens they must see whether they do not thereby suppress the freedom of others. All paternalistic laws are useless. Where there are only laws of freedom the greatest welfare is promoted. Each one can seek his happiness however he will as long as he does not violate universal freedom. – If in order to spare *banqueroteur* {a person with excessive debt} a law were given that *creditores* {the creditors} ought to have patience; that would be a great harm. For then little *credit* would be available and it would forestall the welfare of many more than now when without that law only the welfare of one is hampered. *Justitia pereat mundus* {justice, though the world be destroyed[c]} i.e. I am not concerned with happiness at all. But the world would not cease for this reason but would rather be preserved. – The rules must be universal, otherwise they are not law.[d] The author bases himself on the claim that obligation rests on divine command. But we have already refuted that by claiming that it would be useless to refer here to God.

27:1335   *Actio*[e] *minus recta* {an act lacking right}, that which is opposed to duty, *injusta* {unjust} if it is opposed to duties of right, if opposed to inner states of mind,[f] inequitable, if to the expressed state of mind, *injusta* in the strict sense. We talk of *actiones injustae et justae stricte sic dictae* {just and unjust actions strictly speaking}. An action can be *minus recta* {lacking right} out of ignorance but *injuria* {a wrong action} is *factum culpabile* {a culpable deed}. **Concept of *sui* and *alienum in generale* {one's own and another's in general}.** That which someone can make use of to the exclusion of others is his own[g] according to the author. That with regard to which someone can limit the wills of everyone else according to laws of universal freedom is my own. The use of my freedom

---

[a] KI, KS, MS: period instead of question mark
[b] KI: *Ist jemand*. KS: *Ist also jemand*, for "Thus if someone is"
[c] The full saying is "Fiat justitia pereat mundus," i.e. Let justice be done though the world be destroyed.
[d] There is no immediate referent for the neuter *es*. The nearest is *das Gesetz*.
[e] KI, MS: new paragraph. KS: continuous text
[f] KI: *denen innren Gesinnungen*. KS: *innren Bestimmungen*, for "to inner determination"
[g] *das seinige*. Next sentence: *das meinige*

over things is not opposed to universal freedom. I can do with them what I will. The land that no one has used so far and that I am the first to use is my own. My use of it is consistent with universal freedom. Thus it is right. Right is that in regard to which I can limit the freedom of others if they should act against this right. Now this is what the author's definition amounts to. *Res* {a thing} is that in regard to which another's freedom can in no way be limited if he needs it. The thing[a] has no freedom, thus it can certainly not act wrongly, thus it cannot limit my freedom. But *persona*, a free being, limits my freedom. The Romans also considered slaves[b] as things. But it is still pleasing to note that their right hung together so well. They considered the slaves as things and so a slave could never do wrong. *Res propria* {private property} is where I would limit the freedom of another. *Res communis* {common property} limits the freedom of others outside the society but they have a share in it and are not limited with regard to the use of their freedom.

A freedom[c] is limited through itself. Things[d] that have no freedom could thus not be limited in their freedom. In relation to beings who themselves do have freedom the freedom of everyone else is limited. The latter is a person, the former a thing.[e] – Right is nothing other than the law of the equality of action and reaction[f] regarding freedom through which my freedom agrees with universal freedom. If someone acts against this universal freedom and the other resists him then this resistor acts in conformity with universal freedom and thus right. So I have a right to coerce others to comply with right. All of the authors have failed to explain this. They have already included it in the definition but it is derived from it. – They said right is authorization to coerce, but they could not explain how right stands freely in relation to me. All principles of right are laws of the equality of action and reaction regarding freedom. *Meum* {mine} and *tuum* {yours} are to be taken only in regard to things. The human being is not a thing. But cannot a human being belong to himself? The principle[g] of right is that through which the outer use of freedom can hold. There is, however, also an inner use of freedom and corresponding laws. If e.g. a human being prostitutes herself to earn a living. Can I coerce her to keep her word? No, for she was

---

[a] *Sache*
[b] *Knechte*. Otherwise *Sklaven* throughout
[c] *Eine Freiheit*
[d] *Dinge*
[e] *Sache*
[f] Reading *das Gesetz der Gleichheit der Wirkung und Gegenwirkung*. KI, MS, and KS: *das Gesetz der Gleichheit, der Wirkung und Gegenwirkung*, for "the law of equality, [the law] of action and reaction." Kant alludes here to Newton's "law of the equality of action and reaction." Six sentences later the phrase is written with no comma in KI, MS, or KS.
[g] *Prinzip*

27:1336 not authorized to dispose of herself. She was *persona* not *res* {a thing}. Thus also if a human being sells himself into bondsmanship his *pactum* {contract} is not valid. I am free, for that reason[a] I cannot throw my freedom away. In relation to marriage etc. more will be said. *Laesus* {a victim} is that whose right one infringes upon and *laedens* {wrongdoer} the one who does it. *Damnum* is damage[b] which results from it. There can be something wrong yet with no *damnum*. *Res* {a thing} cannot wrong and also cannot add to *damnum* but merely to disadvantage. – An action which is wrong and which is done inadvertently is *inculpabilis* but if it is done knowingly[c] is *culpabilis*. – *Culpa* {negligence} is if he does not know the law although he has the obligation to know it.[d] *Dolus* {malice} if he does it with knowledge. *Reatus est actio minus recta, quatenus imputabilis* {a fault is an action lacking right insofar as it can be imputed}. *Minus recta* is wrong *materialiter* {materially}, *injusta formaliter* {an unjust action formally}.

The principles[e] of a free will [determined] through thoroughgoing agreement according to laws concern either ourselves or others. Principles of the outer use and the inner use of freedom. We cannot be coerced[f] to the first for they do not contradict the freedom of another. Duties to oneself belong with these. Thus these belong to ethics. The last ones are principles of agreement with the freedom and the interest of another's will. The first is strict right. To the last belong benevolence and kindness, for interest is happiness. That also belongs to ethics. I can comply with the first principles without these last principles. *Jus* thus contains merely the rules[g] of freedom through which one limits another, thus action and reaction. Right is based solely on freedom.

Honeste vive {live uprightly}, *neminem laede* {wrong no one}, and *suum cuique tribue* {give to each what is his} are the three main propositions of practical philosophy which divide it into three parts. Ulpian, the famous teacher of right,[h] presumably took them from the Greeks.[25] *Honeste vive* is virtuous, indicating morality, *Honestas* is called honorableness. Honor is not profit namely inner honor. Virtue is the ruling maxim of actions solely from duty. There can be actions in conformity with duty not done from duty. Virtuous actions must be done not out of fear or coercion but from duty. They cannot be coerced for they are based on the

---

[a] *darum*   [b] *Schade*
[c] *mit Wissen* here and in the sentence after next
[d] *es zu wissen*   [e] *Grundsätze* in this paragraph
[f] KI: *wir nicht gezwungen werden*, referencing "the first" to duties concerning ourselves. KS: *wir gezwungen werden*, for "we can be coerced," referencing "the first" to principles for the outer use of freedom
[g] KI: *Regeln*. KS: *Angabe*, for "account"   [h] *Rechtsgelahrter*

disposition. *Neminem laede* do no wrong. Under ethics belong all duties including those of *jus* {right} but only considered in accordance with their morality. Right refers to the principle[a] *neminem laede*. Do the action in accordance with the law so that it is in conformity with the right of humanity. The cause of your doing the action is irrelevant. Actions to which someone is coerced have just as much legal value as those that are not coerced. If they are actions done from duty they belong to ethics. One divides duties into *officia necessitatis* {duties of necessity} and *caritatis* {of charity}, the former belong to *jus*, the latter to *ethic* and are meritorious just as the former are obligatory duties. But this division is incomplete for duties to oneself are not *officia caritatis*. Duties to oneself are sometimes *officia necessaria*. *Leges strictae* {narrow laws}, those which have no exceptions, *latae* {wide}, which allow for exceptions. Those who always want to make exceptions are *latitudinarii* {latitudinarians}. Duties can better be divided into inner and outer. The outer are *necessitatis* or *caritatis*. In the *Princip juris neminem laede* {principle of right "wrong no one"} I see that I am merely to refrain from doing things, it appears to be *lex vetita* {a law of prohibition}. But yet it appears to be *jus mandata* {a right of mandate}, e.g. that I should hold to the contract which I have made.[b] But *materialiter* it is negative for the other considers it as already his own. In contrast in beneficence I give to another what is my own. The rule of right cannot be to give to another what is his own. For he already has that, but take from him nothing of his own.[c] Right thus has nothing but *leges omissivae* {laws of omission}. The right of another consists in his freedom being sacrosanct as long as it does not infringe upon universal freedom. All actions are right insofar as they refrain from obstructing the freedom of others in accordance with universal law or when they contradict an obstruction of freedom. *Suum cuique tribue* {give to each what is his} is the same as the preceding. If two are in conflict with one another then a third can decide how the right of one affects the right of the other. For they [the first two] do not act in accordance with the other's judgment but only in accordance with their own. *Justitia commutativa* {commutative justice} is the right in which each cognizes himself through his own understanding, *distributiva* {distributive} where also the judgment of a third must confirm the right for me. *Neminem laede* is *principium justitiae commutativae* {a principle of commutative justice} but not *distributivae*. Outer laws that are universally valid for everyone belong to *justitia distributiva* and each determines what is right or wrong. *Justitia commutativa* has no *effectus* without *distributiva* {distributive justice}.

27:1337

[a] *Princip*
[b] KI, KS: *gemacht habe halten soll*. MS: *gemacht haben soll*, missing the "hold to"
[c] Period missing in KS

It is *principium dijudicationis* {a principle of dijudication} not *executionis* {of execution}. For I judge what is right, others could judge otherwise, and they do not act in accordance with my judgment. Through *justitia distributiva* I am secure in my property. That is *status civilis* {the civil condition} and there is outer legislation and authority.[a] *Principium* of *justitia distributiva* is said to be *suum cuique tribue* {give to each what is his}. Enter into the condition of *justitia distributiva*.[b] If one does not do that when one can, then one wrongs the other. For then one does not give any security to the other [in exchange] for my right. To enter into *status civilis* is thus one of the first duties. The proposition *neminem laede* means you should deprive no one of his right and his security for right. – That entry into the civil society is one of the first duties no one has yet properly seen. Of course Hobbes and Rousseau have a few thoughts about that.[26]

To be strict it should be divided as follows: All duties belong to *ethic* {ethics} or to *jus* {right}. All those belonging to *jus* either to *jus privatum* {private right} or *publicum*. Natural right contains *principia* of dijudication not of execution. Law must have authority and the authority of those whose will is at the same time a law is legitimate authority. If I e.g. shoot a wild animal and it runs to another's land and dies there, then I believe I have the right to get it from there. The other, however, can say, "What I find on my land is mine." Now I cannot will that the other should judge in accordance with my will. Now therefore outer laws must be established with the will of society. The will which thus produces the law is itself a law for everyone. Natural right alone is not sufficient for execution. I do wrong to others if I will to make my will into their law, for this I am obligated to subject myself to an outer law which is valid for everyone. The will which is law can give authority to it. If someone who was in a civil society encountered someone who was not in it then I would want to say to him, "We are not safe from you because you do not stand under law so join us or be off or else you will be murdered." But we cannot make use of authority.[c] For in the state of nature my judgment is different from yours. Because of this my will is not a law for him and I cannot coerce him. – Ethics encompasses all duties but right not all. Right considers duties as coercive duties and in accordance with their legality and not in accordance with their morality. *Jus* relates merely to the matter of the action, ethics also to the form, the way in which they are done.[27] In this way it has less than ethics. But on the other side it has more than ethics, namely coercion. This can be applied only to outer actions but not to dispositions as in ethics. The author now includes the

27:1338

---

[a] *Gesetzgebung und Gewalt.*
[b] KI: period. KS: exclamation point, emphasizing the command
[c] *Gewalt*

history of *jus naturae*. It is better, however, to leave that for the end of the science because I must know the science if I want to understand its history correctly.

Libr: I.

Jus naturae strictius sic dictum[a]

{Natural right in the narrower sense of the term}

Sect: I.

Jus naturale originarium[b]

{Original natural right}

The author explains the *jus naturae strictissime* {narrowest sense of natural right[c]} as that in *status naturalis* {the state of nature} and places it in opposition to the *socialis* {social condition}. But it is opposed to the *civilis* {civil condition}. For there could also be societies in *status naturalis* such as marriage. It is the right of a human being insofar as it rests merely on inner laws. The content of all principles[d] of dijudication of that which is right. *Status naturalis* can exist as[e] *originarius* {original} or *adventitius* {adventitious}. – A deed from which right is created by someone is *factum juridicum* {the juridical deed}. *Status originalis* {the original condition} is that which precedes any *factum juridicum*. *Status adventitius* is the right which originates out of *factum juridicum*. Do human beings have rights *originarie* {originally}? Yes. But I can still obtain rights[f] through *factum juridicum*. But I have no right in another[g] except through *factum juridicum*. My rights against others are negative; they are *original*, namely *jura connata* {innate rights}. [The first innate right is[h]] Everyone has *jus connatum* with his person. No one does wrong to another if he performs actions that concern himself alone. – I can thus resist another

[a] Achenwall has "Jus naturale strictissime dictum," "Natural right in the most narrow sense of the term"
[b] Achenwall has "Jus naturale absolutum," "Unconditional natural right." In Achenwall this section is divided into six titles that Kant does not list but does discuss: *Titulus I: De jure cuiusvis respectu sui ipsius* {Of right of anyone regarding himself}, *Titulus II: De aequalitate naturali* {Of natural equality}, *Titulus III: De libertate naturali* {Of natural freedom}, *Titulus IV: De jure circa declarationem mentis* {Of right concerning declaration of one's mind}, *Titulus V: De jure circa existimationem* {Of right concerning reputation}, *Titulus VI: De jure circa res* {Of right concerning things}.
[c] KI: *jus naturae strictissime*. KS: *jus strictissime*, for "narrowest sense of right"
[d] *principien*
[e] KS: *kann sein als*. KI, MS: *kann als*, for "possible as"
[f] KI: *noch Rechte*. KS: *noch mehr Rechte*, for "still more rights"
[g] *am andern habe ich kein Recht*
[h] Kant does not identify the first by number

27:1339

if he wants to resist my use of my freedom. – The second *connatum* right is: all are equal to each other, not in understanding, powers, but in right. Inequality of rights must originate through *factum juridicum*, i.e. when I have a right toward another which he does not have toward me. If I lend something to someone then I have a right toward him that he does not have toward me, that is clearly through *factum juridicum*. – 3) *Libertas*. Before *factum juridicum* I infringe on no one and thus also no one can limit my freedom. 4) The right to a good reputation. A juridically good reputation is the judgment of others on agreement with the laws. If I have done nothing then I have not acted contrary to the law. 5) A *jus connatum* to acquire things. *A natura* {by nature} everyone is *sui juris* {his own master}, but not also things for they are not innate[a] to him. Before *factum juridicum* I do not have any positive right to a thing.[b] He does have a negative right of nature because he cannot do wrong to a thing. If he cuts down a tree then he already has an affirmative right that has first occurred by means of *factum juridicum*.

Jura connata {innate rights} are *ante factum juridicum* {prior to a juridical deed}. They are all negative, are not rights to coerce another but to resist him if he wrongs me.[c] – Others are *jura acquisita* {acquired rights} and *contracta obligationis* {contractual obligations}. It is important that we know the innate rights by means of which we resist others.

The first right is that of unlimited freedom concerning one's person. **Quilibet est sui juris** {each one is his own master}. If his actions are not related to other persons then they are not wrong. 2) The **jus aequalitatis** {right of equality}. *Ante omnia facta juridica* {prior to any juridical deeds} I have no rights greater than anyone else.[d] For all privileges[e] originate from *factum juridicum* {a juridical deed}. Here everyone has equal rights because no one actually has any affirmative right against the other. If someone in the civil state claims something from someone else and will not allow him a defense then the defendant relies on the natural right of equality, that he has just as much a right to defend himself as the other to accuse him. Physically and ethically there is a great difference among human beings but juridically human beings are equal. The concept of right is simply the concept of equal action and reaction – *quod tibi non vis fieri, alteri ne facias* {do not do to others what you do not want done to yourself}. What you would consider as a right for yourself you must also consider as a right for all others. – For that is right

---

[a] *angebohren*
[b] *Sache* here and in the next sentences. In the previous two sentences Kant used the word *Dinge*.
[c] KI: *er mir Unrecht tut.* KI, MS: *sie ihm Unrecht tun,* for "they wrong him"
[d] *kein Recht vor dem andern*   [e] *Vorrechte*

by which universal freedom can hold. 3) *Jus libertatis* {the right of freedom}. Practical not physical freedom is to be understood here and it means everyone can do whatever he wills as long as he does not limit the freedom of another. He is free who stands under no affirmative obligation. Coercion is not allowed toward other human beings insofar as he has not exercised any *factum juridicum* {juridical deed}; thus he is also free of all coercion. I can coerce another if he offends me or even just has the intent to offend me. If I claim that someone else is guilty and he denies it then the first must prove it. For the latter denies the *factum* and locates[a] himself *in jure naturali libertatis* {in the natural right of freedom}. So that[b] he is free *a natura* {by nature} from all obligation. 4) The right to a good reputation is *jus existimationis* {right of reputation}. *Ante omne factum juridicum* {prior to any juridical deed} while no one has done anything wrong each must be considered good, and that is *a natura* {by nature}; also I cannot hold him responsible for it. For this reason I must also not consider him good positively but merely negatively. I do not have an ethically good reputation *a natura* but a juridical one. Suppose a rogue is accused and he denies it. Who has the burden of proof? The accuser, for the rogue, even if he has actually stolen something, grounds[c] himself on the natural right to a good reputation, that he has not done anything wrong. Since the time of his evil tricks he can have already improved himself. *Quilibet praesumendus est justus, donec probetur contrarium* {each is presumed to be just until it is proved to the contrary} is here the principle of right. *Quilibet praesumendus sit malus, donec probetur contrarium* {let each be presumed evil until it is proved to the contrary} is the principle of morals. 5) *A natura res omnes sunt res nullius* {by nature all things belong to no one}. *Res nullius* {an unowned thing} that which belongs to no one, *res vacua* {an unpossessed[d] thing} which no one has made use of. *A natura non datur propria nec aliena* {by nature neither I nor another has property}, no difference between mine and yours regarding things. For *ante omne factum juridicum* {prior to every juridical deed} the thing can serve anyone for he does not infringe upon my freedom. It does not belong to his property; it is *res omnibus communes* {a thing held in common by all}. – 6) *Jus de declaratione mentis* {right of declaring one's mind}. *Declarare mentem suam, si significamus se velle, alteri mentem suam significare* {To declare one's mind, if we mean that one wills it, means one's mind in relation to another}. If I get someone to

27:1340

---

[a] *befindet sich*
[b] KS: *libertatis. Sodaß.* MS: *libertatis. Daß*, for "freedom. That." KI: *libertatis, so daß*, for "freedom, so that."
[c] *fundirt*
[d] Literally "vacant" or "empty" when applied to land

understand me about something one way but I understand it another way then it is *falsiloquium* {falsehood}. *Falsiloquium dolosum* {malicious falsehood} intentionally is *mendacium* {deceit}. The jurists say that *mendacium* would be *falsiloquium in praejudicium*[a] *alterius* {a falsehood to another's disadvantage}. *Falsiloquium* in regard to a thing to which I have an obligation. But every untruth even about unimportant matters is *mendacium* and he wrongs me through it. If someone tells me a story that is completely harmless then he wrongs me. I am then allowed to tell the whole world that he has lied. Through this telling he loses *credit* and that would be a wrong to the other if he had not already himself done a wrong. All *mendacia* {deceits} are also *directe*[b] {immediately} wrong. Whoever says it to me is the cause of my believing it and telling it to another and of me losing my good reputation among others when they find out it is false. That is thus a wrong to me. If, however, I do not have the right to demand *declaratio*[c] *mentis* {a declaration of the mind} from him then it cannot be imputed to him *coram foro externo* {in the public realm}.

Jus naturae hypotheticum[d]

{Conditional natural law}

That consists of the rights which are derived for one in accordance with[e] a *factum juridicum* {juridical deed} either for me through *factum justum* {a just deed} or for another through *factum injustum* {an unjust deed} or a wrong. – I obtain my rights this way or contract[f] a *pacta* {contract}. *Factum* {the deed} out of which right or obligation arises is *factum juridicum* {a juridical deed}. Now we will talk first about *facta justa* {just deeds}.

27:1341

Cap: I[g]

De occupatione

{Of taking control}

We have a right in regard to all things that are *res vacuae* {unpossessed things} for I can never directly wrong it. This right is merely negative. – *A natura res omnes sunt res nullius* {by nature all things are unowned}.

---

[a] KI: *praejudizium*. KS: *praepositione*, for "falsehood preferred by another"
[b] KI: *Auch directe*. KS: *Durch decrete*, for "by *decrete* {decree}"
[c] KI: *declarationem*. KS, MS: *delatationem*, which should be *delationem*, for "a denunciation of the mind"
[d] Achenwall has *Sect II* before the title *Jus naturale hypotheticum*
[e] KI: *nach*. KS: *aus*, for "from"
[f] *kontrahire*   [g] Achenwall has *Tit: I*

Vacua res is that which is not being used by the freedom of another. Now how does *res vacua* become *res propria* {a privately owned thing}? We are talking here thus of the origin of mine and yours. We belong to ourselves by birth, thus our mine and yours of ourselves has no beginning. Can one say that *statu originali res* {things in the original state} would be *nullius* {belong to no one} and thereby would be *communes* {in common}?[a] The author denies *communio primaeva* {primitive holding in common}. *Communio negativa* {holding in common in the negative sense} is when everyone has a right to exclude others from use. He really does thereby have a right to use the thing. The right is conferred here. *Res nullius* {unowned things} are *res communes negativae* {things in common in the negative sense}. – *Communio affirmativa* {holding in common in the positive sense} is assumed to be *proprietas plurium simul sumtorum* {the property of many taken together} to exclude all who are outside the community. It is property of this society. *Originarie* human beings were not in society so there must first be a *factum juridicum*. It is the property of the community. *Res omnes sunt originarie communes* {all things are originally in common}. Each can make use of the thing but still not exclude others. – If I make use of a thing then that does not have to exclude others – for he can make use of it later. The author and his opponents have not understood this correctly. The author says that Caius[b] helps himself first to *res vacuae* {unpossessed things} and in that wrongs no one. He excludes everyone else during his use because his use is rightful. Everyone who would hinder him in his use wrongs him. He declares to Titius that he wants to keep the thing, i.e. even if he does not use it everyone is still excluded from the use of the thing. On what basis does this usurpation become rightful? Give me the right to first use and to exclude all others from future use even if I do not need it? Is it possible that there could be *res nullius communes* {unowned communal things} and indeed without an owner? Yes. There are things which are consumed in use. We will talk about that in what follows. The mere declaration to Titius that I want to keep it does not give me any right. The other can will the opposite with the same right. The will alone cannot limit the freedom of another but my free actions. My will can limit another in use of his freedom because I already have a right to the action. There my will can make his action right or wrong; if that were so then others would be absolutely subjected to my will. – I have worked the land and harvested the fruit from it. If I declare that I will also use the land in the future then that is wrong. – If the other had hindered me in the use of the thing I would have considered it wrong. But now I hinder the other in his use in that I am excluding him. – What kind of *factum* {deed} is that through which I

---

[a] KI, KS, MS have period. The word order (*Kann man sagen*) implies a question.
[b] "Caius" and "Titius" are names Achenwall uses in an example in the textbook.

27:1342 can first subject a thing to my will and through which my declaration is rightful? That is 1) *Apprehensio* {taking}, 2) *Declaratio, me velle rem apprehensam, mihi permanere* {declaration, [is when] I will that the thing I have taken remain with me}. *Apprehensio cum*[a] *animo, illud pro meo acquirere* {taking with the intention that I acquire it for my own} is *occupatio* {taking control}. If my will is powerful enough to exclude[b] others after use then it also can be and is powerful enough to do this before use, for use is mere ceremony for that. Things are products of nature and of freedom. A product of freedom belongs to my freedom and is dependent on it, thus someone attacks my freedom if he attacks me. A product of freedom is a product of nature which has been modified through my freedom with regard to its form, e.g. a tree which I have cut down. Whoever makes use of this thing acts against my freedom because he hinders the product of my freedom and the actions of my freedom and the intention I have in mind. Taking[c] is not every use of a thing but that in which the form of the thing is modified through freedom. *Apprehensio physica* {physical taking} is *redactio in potestatem* {bringing under one's power} but *apprehensio juridica* {juridical taking} is if my freedom gives the thing a form. Even if someone is the first to discover a land and plants a flag there and takes possession, he still does not have a right to it. But if he works the land, applies his powers to the land, then he takes[d] it. When a Greenlander finds some driftwood he pulls it to the beach and lays a stone on it, when another comes and sees it he lets it lie – for the first one has exerted his powers in recovering the wood from the control of the seas and the stone serves as a sign that a human being has done it.[28] The wood has received a form different from its previous form with regard to its location.[e]

The author says that *apprehensio* {taking} is enough for through it *tacita declaratio* {a tacit declaration} that I will keep it has already occurred – for in rightful actions, he says, others must be content with my advantage. But he presupposes here that it would be right. If, however, the other believed that it is wrong then it is not valid. My will that I have to keep something must be declared through the *effectus* {effect} of freedom and thus no outer declaration is necessary. In *jus gentium* {the right of nations} the taking[f] of lands can be sustained only in cultivation. If I have built on a part then this part alone belongs to me and the remainder which is unbuilt does not. I have no right in regard to things but in regard to human beings. I cannot limit the freedom of another[g] if he does not hinder my freedom. If, however, my freedom has done no *actum* through

[a] KI: *cum animo*. KS, MS: *animo*, for implied "with"
[b] KI: *auszuschließen*. KS, MS: *einzuschließen*, for "include"
[c] *apprehension*
[d] *apprehendirt*
[e] *Lage*
[f] *apprehension*
[g] KI, KS, MS: period after the word "another"

which the thing is altered then he can always also make use of the thing and it is still *nullius* {unowned}. Otherwise he resists my freedom. The author talks at great length about whether *communio primaeva* {primitive holding in common} occurs or not, which Pufendorf and Grotius have stressed.[29] *Communio negativa* {holding in common in the negative sense} not *affirmativa* – for *communio affirmativa* {holding in common in the positive sense} presupposes a juridical *factum*, the founding of society, and it is the property of the community. *Communio negativa* shows that human beings can make use of things prior to all property. It is still this way for many savage peoples. *Communio negativa* is that each can make use of all things without exclusion of others. The Bedouins and Mongols have no property. There is no declaration; instead one can will that the things should be communal. The Arabs have made *communio primaeva* {primitive holding in common} into law through a *pactum* {compact} and for property. The beginning of property is hard to comprehend. In all acquisition the raising of *jus adventitium* {an adventitious right} or *quaesitum* {a right being claimed} is the *actus juridicus* {juridical act} through which right is either obtained or lost; in the one case it is *modus acquirendi* {a way of acquiring} in the other it is *medium acquisitionis* {a means of acquisition} which is *apprehensio* {taking}. Further *titulus acquisitionis* {title to the acquisition}, the rectitude of the action, is that it previously belonged to no one and is *effectus* of my freedom. *Titulus* is the rectitude of an[a] action. *Occupatio, titulus est jus occupandi ipsi connatum* {[Regarding] taking control, title is the innate right of taking control for oneself}. *Factum validum* {a valid deed} has rightful force[b] *quod facientis fini consentit, –quod effectum legibus consentaneum profert* {because it is consistent with the limitation on agency, since it produces an effect consistent with the laws}. *Modus acquirendi rem alienam est derivativus, rem nullius, originaria occupatio est modus* {The way of acquiring a thing owned by another is derivative, the way of acquiring an unowned thing is original taking control} _____.[c] I acquire *derivatione* {by derivation} when I derive my right from the right of another. – *Prior tempore potior jure* {The earlier in time has a stronger right}. – *Occupans* is the one who takes[d] so he must be the first. If someone has already taken[e] it previously then his *acquisitio* is merely *derivativa*. – *Possessio physica* {physical possession} if I have control of a thing for use to the exclusion of others, *juridical* possession whoever possesses a thing with the will that it should be his – regarding whoever makes use of a thing we must believe that he would

27:1343

---

[a] KI: *einer*. KS: *meiner*, for "my"   [b] *rechtskräftig*

[c] KS, MS: blank space between *modus* and the period. Likely the copyist could not read the word and left the space for Feyerabend to fill in. KI, following Achenwall, suggests *adquirendi rem nullius*, for "way of acquiring an unowned thing" but ignores the period and runs this sentence into the next.

[d] *apprehendirt*   [e] *apprehendirt*

will that the thing would be his insofar as he has not stated the contrary. Because someone has a right to a thing[a] to the exclusion of another he possesses it *juridice. Appprehensio* {taking} and *possessio* {possessing} are distinct like beginning and duration. It is conservation of taking.[b] No one must be disturbed in his possession because he rightfully continues to possess it. – Taking[c] is not *possessio*. I have *rem in potestate* {a thing in my power} without being able to will rightfully to keep it. When I find something I keep or hold[d] it. I can also possess something while absent.[e] I have something in my control *virtualiter* as far as I have a right to make use of such a thing and to bring it under my control. We possess not only things but also rights. I possess a right if I am not hindered in the use of the right. So I can have it yet not possess it because I can be hindered in it. Even if possession of a right or a thing is interrupted ownership does not cease.

Someone possesses something *physice* if he has it under his control. *Juridice* if we have the will to keep it. If we are hindered by another in the use of a right we cannot say that he possesses it but that he has it. If I do not have the thing under my control I am still in possession of it for I could always exercise *actus possessorius* {an act of possession} through another. For many possessions an *actus possessorius* must take place. – If in the purchase of a horse I settle how long it should remain in the hands of the previous owner[f] then I exercise an *actus possessorium*. Property begins with taking control[g] of things. In this way *obligationes* {obligations}

27:1344 become[h] *negativae*, that they should avoid everything that someone has taken control[i] of. – What is necessary for that? To show that one has taken[j] it. For then one must presume that he also wants to appropriate it. I see that something is under another's control[k] so I cannot take[l] it from him because I do not know whether I would not wrong him. The will of the other alone cannot limit me with regard to the things belonging to him but only the things which are a product of freedom in which case I act contrary to the freedom of the other. I can make a thing into a product of freedom by taking it from one place to another, altering the form, etc. – In general either through alteration of the inner form or the relation. Núñez Balboa staked a flag in the South Seas and proclaimed that the land belongs to the king of Spain.[30] I cannot use a thing which is the product of freedom for I would thereby do offense to his freedom.

---

[a] *Recht zu einer Sache*   [b] *apprehension*

[c] *apprehension*

[d] KI: *zurückhalte*. KS: *zurückbehalte*, for "retain"

[e] *abwesend*   [f] *Herr*

[g] *occupation*   [h] KI: *werden*. KS: *würden*, for "would be"

[i] *occupirt*   [j] *apprehendirt*

[k] *Gewalt*   [l] *apprehendirt*

If I put a fence around some land the other can tear down the fence and climb over. *Res* {things} are *animatae* {animate} and *inanimatae*[a] {inanimate}. The latter are *mobiles quae salva substantia, immobiles, quae non salva substantia moveri possunt* {movable things, which can be moved with their substance intact, and immovable things, which cannot be moved with their substance intact}. Things can be taken control[b] of. If I touch a tree and also make a sign that I have done it that is still not enough for taking.[c] In such a way I[d] can take more than he possesses. If he has once slept in the woods under a tree he cannot will that if he had not slept there no one else should sleep there either. Persons cannot be taken control of,[e] not even through a *pactum* {contract}. But through *delictum* {an offense} they could be made into things. Hunting is a type of taking control.[f] If the location is not dependent on my will, as [when I have] an animal tucked into my scarf,[g] then the animal does not belong to me and not any earlier than when I have shot it. – If an animal gets away from me then it is free and another does not do any wrong to me if he takes control of it. If an animal is shot but runs to another place which does not depend on my will then it is not mine either unless it was mine already.

De occupatione putativa[h]

{Of putative taking control}

Whoever acts on an opinion held *bona fide* {in good faith} as if it is right but without fault because he does not know it, and he acquires things, then that is *occupatio putativa*. His action is then *inculpabilis* {inculpable} because he neither can know the wrong nor is he linked to it but is still *iniusta* {wrong}. If e.g. I shoot a hawk which has flown out of a cage. – This case belongs either to *ignoratio invincibilis* {overpowering ignorance} or *inculpabilis*. Under *ignoratio* one means *error* here. This is not quite

---

[a] KI: *inanimatae*, following Achenwall. KS, MS: *exanimatae* with a connotation of "having been animate"

[b] *occupirt werden*   [c] *apprehension*

[d] KS, MS: *ich*. KI: *jemand*, for "someone"   [e] *occupirt*

[f] *occupation*

[g] KI: *als in einem Tuche eingeschloßnen Wilde*, presumably a way hunters would carry small animals. KS: *als in einer Tiefe eingeschloßen wird*, for (roughly) "as when enclosed in the deep," perhaps suggesting a place in the deep woods that is not owned by anyone. The KI reading is closer to the MS than the KS reading although the KS reading fits the earlier part of the sentence better. MS: *als in einem Buche* [unclear] *eingeschlossnen Willen*, which by invoking "a will included in a beech tree" or "in a book" (both ungrammatical) makes even less sense.

[h] Achenwall has *Tit: II* before this title.

logically precise, but if a human being were to know something more then he would not err. Such a human being acts with a good intention and with the opinion that he has acquired something although it is not really true. Only *dolosae* and *actiones culposae* {malicious and culpable acts} are to be imputed. He does not act rightly *materialiter*, i.e. wrongly, but *formaliter* {formally} he does, that is, he is not unjust.[a] *Bona fide possessor* is someone who possesses[b] something without guilt. – *Mala fide possessor* {possessor in bad faith} is if I possess another's thing even though I now know or at least should have known that it belongs to another. *Bona fide possessor* can consume the thing. He is therefore not required to render it *infacta* {undone}, i.e. to offer compensation, for it cannot be imputed to him. But as soon as he hears that the thing belongs to another he must immediately give up what remains, if he keeps it any longer then he is to be considered as *possessor dolosus* {malicious possessor}. *Modus acquirendi putativus* {the putative way of acquiring} is wrong but when someone does not know that it is wrong it is clearly not his fault. Everything that I possess *titulo putative* {through a putative title} and all of my *actus possessorii* {acts of possession} are based on that. To find something *sensu juridico* {in a juridical sense} is to take[c] a thing that had previously been hidden, this is taking control[d] if I have the intention of keeping the thing found. It can be *putativa* if it concerns *res alienae* {others' things}. *Occupatio putativa* has its *titulus, i.e. ratio legalis* {title, i.e. a legal basis}, and also *actus possessorii* have their *titulum*. Thrown away, abandoned, lost, buried things belong to the category of things[e] to be found. The finder has a *titulus* that all his actions in this regard are right until he becomes aware of the situation. He is not required to return more than whatever is still remaining. – When the owner wants to prove that it is his, the other cannot withhold it, and if the other hinders the owner he is *mala fide possessor* {possessor in bad faith}.

Tit: III.

De dominio[f]

{Of ownership}

Everyone has things as *res propriae* {private property}, all exercise *actus possessorias* {acts of possession} to the exclusion of all others. Regarding

---

[a] Kant's three terms here are *nicht recht* (not rightly), *unrecht* (wrongly), and *ungerecht* (unjust).

[b] KI: *besitzt*. KS: *besetzt*, for "occupies"   [c] *apprehendiren*

[d] *occupation*

[e] *Dinge*. All references to "things" earlier in the paragraph are "Sache."

[f] Achenwall has simply *Dominium*

res nullius {unowned things} I also have the right to make use of a thing but not to exclude others. From my right there arises for each the obligation to leave the thing alone. *Summa jurium in proprium* {The highest of rights over one's own property} is *dominium*, dominion,[a] and whoever possesses it is *dominus*, owner.[b] Here[c] the owner is of another human being. Thus Augustus never let himself be called *dominus*.[31] Each has *jus in re* {a right in a thing} or *in rem* {a right over a thing} insofar as he is *dominus*. *Jus in personam* {a right in a person} cannot be called *dominium*. But the Romans also took slaves as *res*. *Dominium* is thus *jus in re* and *jus in re propria* {right in a thing as property}. No one is *suimet ipsius dominus* {the owner of himself}. That will be covered later. One is certainly *sui juris* {a law to himself}. *Dominium* is not *jus connatum* {an innate right}. For this refers only to my person and is[d] negative. A *dominium* is *affirmativum* {ownership is affirmative}, thus it is *jus acquisitum* {an acquired right}. It is the essence of all rights in a thing. I can do what I want with my things as long as I do not harm other persons and their rights. *Dominium* is complete or incomplete. A house, e.g., that another has sold me but which he still has some money invested in has *condominium* {co-ownership}. I cannot have all *actus possessoriae*. *Dominium minus plenum* {ownership less than full} is *limitatum* and the author says also *restrictum*. But that is different, for *dominium plenum* {full ownership} can also be *restrictum*. When I want to sell a good and must first ask a neighbor whether he will buy it. The *dominium* is still *plenum* in this regard. *Naturaliter* {by nature} *dominium* is already *restrictum*, e.g. I am not always free to throw a stone out the window. *Occupationes sunt origines dominii* {acts of taking control are the origin of ownership}. – If I am not in possession of the thing then I can coerce another to allow me into possession and I am always owner. I cannot lose *dominium* through the will of another. I can resist if the other wants to make improvements and to the extent that I want to. Disposition refers to the substance, *usus* {use} to the *accidentia*. *Usus* is *salva substantia* {preserving the substance} and *dominio* {ownership}. *Dispositio* when I also consume something. *Dispositio* is also connected to alienation[e] for that does not always occur *salva substantia* and *salvo dominio* {preserving the ownership}. *Dispositio* is *usus rei* {Disposition is a use of the thing} but not every *usus* is *dispositio* {use is disposition}. *Jus utendi et disponendi* {The right to use and the right to dispose} are different, the leaseholder has *jus utendi* in every way but not *disponendi*.

27:1346

---

[a] *Herrschaft* [b] *Eigenthümer*
[c] KI: *Hier*. KS: *Er*, for "He is the owner of another human being"
[d] KS: *dieses geht ... ist*. KI, MS: *diese gehen ... sind*, for "For these refer ... are"
[e] *Veräußerung*

Tit: IV.

De jure fruendi, utendi et accessione[a]

{Of right of enjoyment, use, and accession}

Accessio {accession} is a special type of acquisition in that it does not pre-suppose a *factum* {deed}. We can acquire either *facto* {by deed} or *lege* {by law} or *pacto* {by contract}. – Taking control[b] was a *factum*. Every *augmentum utilitatis rei* {increase in the usefulness of a thing} is accession of the thing. That which also makes possible the increased use of the thing is *accessorium* {an accessory} and the thing itself is called *res principalis* {the principal thing} in relation to *accessorium*. *Accessorium* presupposes *dominium rei principalis* {ownership of the principal thing} and acquisition presupposes that taking control[c] is connected to *dominium*. This means: *accessorium sequitur suum principale* {the accessory comes after his principal property} because *accessorium* {the accessory} and *principalis res* {the principal thing} are necessarily connected to each other. The *eventus* through which a thing becomes *alicujus accessorium* {an accessory to something} is *accessio*. *Accessio* is seen *juridice* {juridically} as a *modus acquirendi* {way of acquiring}. For there to be *Accessio modus acquirendi* {accession as a way of acquiring} there must be *res principalis* and *altera accessoria* {a distinct accessory}. Further the *res principalis* must be part of the property of whoever wants to acquire the *accessorium*. *Accessorium* must not be *res aliena* {another's thing}. It must be *res nullius* {an unowned thing} or something that did not exist at all beforehand, like the form and what comes from me, e.g. when someone else casts bells from my [mold[d]], then it is *accessio res aliena* {accessory to another's thing}. I cannot acquire *per accessionem* {through accession} that of which I was already *dominus* {owner}. If I discover a new use for a thing then I do indeed acquire the use but not *accessorium*. – Insofar as it is connected to *res principalis* {the principal thing} the *accessorium* must also come under the control of the *dominus* of the *res principalis*. The ocean washes[e] something onto the shore and then washes it away again so I do not have it under my control. – I can shoot animals on my land and then they belong to me. It flees from my land, then I do not have it in my *potestas* {power}

---

[a] Achenwall has *De jure re sua utendi fruendi et accessione* for "Of right of use, enjoyment, and accession of one's property."
[b] *occupation*   [c] *occupation*
[d] This sentence added in MS margin. Adding *Form* as "mold" to fill a large space between *meiner* and *Glocken*. *Form* as mold is a more specific instance of *Form* as form in the previous sentence. KI notes the space and suggests "Bronze," for "when someone casts bells from my bronze"; KS does not note the space, for "when someone else pours from my bells."
[e] KS: *spült*. KI, MS: *spielt*, for "ocean passes"

anymore and so have no right to it.[a] b)[b] It is necessary for *dominus rei principalis* {the owner of the principal thing} to want to have it be that way. Taking[c] is already a sign of appropriation and we can always assume it if he does not otherwise declare. Having *titulus acquisitionis per accessorium* {title by means of acquiring an accessory} constitutes *dominio rei principalis* {ownership of the principal thing}. One can ask whether acquisition *per actionem* {through an action} requires a special *factum* {deed}, namely taking[d] of the *accessorium* {accessory}. – The author correctly says no. He acquires nothing but the thing but he acquires *jus rei suae* {a right to his thing}, i.e. it is acquisition that occurs *lege* {by law}. – If the fruits hang over a fence and fall off the tree they still belong to the owner[e] of the tree even if they have fallen on another's land. To the *accessoria rei* {accessions of a thing} belong 1) *effectus rei, aut* a) *naturales aut* b) *industriales* {the effect of the thing, either a) natural or b) from activity}. They are *accessoria stricta* {accessories in the narrow sense}. Fruits are in this class. 2) *Accessoria fortuita* {fortuitous accessories}. What comes with a thing accidentally as long as it is not *res aliena* {owned by another}. The accession of *accessoria stricta* and *fortuita* is *modus acquirendi originarius* {an original way of acquiring}. For it is *modus acquirendi rem nullius* {a way of acquiring an unowned thing}. Accession is not taking control.[f] *Occupatio* is *modus acquirendi simpliciter talis* {taking control is a way of acquiring of this simple kind} and *accessio modus acquirendi originarius secundum quid* {accession is a way of originally acquiring what comes later}. For the right to take control[g] is derived from *domino*. Thus one cannot genuinely call it an *originarius modus* {original way} but *derivativus modus acquirendi* {a derivative way of acquiring}. Regarding this one can say that all acquisition is *originaria* or *derivativa*. The first is *occupatio* {taking control} for through it *dominium* first arises and nothing[h] precedes it, the second is *accessio* because it stems from *dominium*. Accession produces, as it happens, acquisition and I do not receive *jus acquirendi* {a right to acquire} this way but I have already acquired it. Accession cannot be considered as *res jacens* {a thing in abeyance}. *Res jacens* is what someone has when he can exclude others from the use or acquisition of a thing *absque suo dominio* {without being its owner}. If someone is designated as heir then he has the right to exclude others from it even if he has not yet received it. The Romans called this *hereditas jacens* {an estate in abeyance}. Now jurists have liked to consider accession as *jus*[i] *in re jacente* {a right in a thing in

27:1347

---

[a] *kein Recht darauf*
[b] KS: *b)*. KI, MS: *6)*. In either case there are no antecedents for a series.
[c] *apprehension*   [d] *apprehension*
[e] *Herrn*   [f] *occupation*
[g] *occupiren*
[h] KI: *nichts*. KS: *nicht*, for "and does not precede it."
[i] KS omits *jus*

abeyance}, that he simply has the exclusive right to acquire something. But *per actionem* he acquires a thing that now belongs in his *dominium*. Labor is also *modus acquirendi* {a way of acquiring}. *Accessio putativa* {putative accession}, if someone takes a foreign object which he does not know is torn from something as *accessorium suae rei principalis* {accessory to the principal thing} he acquires without it being *absque culpa* {negligence}; then that is *accessio putativa*. I can acquire *res aliena per accessionem* {a thing owned by another through accession} if it cannot be separated from the things *salvo dominio meo* {while preserving my ownership} e.g. if someone has made a painting on my canvas against my will I can acquire it. But if someone has poured wine in my glass then I cannot acquire it for the wine can be separated *salvo rei dominio* {while preserving ownership of the thing}. If *res aliena* {an unpossessed thing} cannot be separated then its *dominus* can demand only *operam* {the work} and if it occurs against my will not even that. It is thus merely *acquisitio operae cujusdam* {the acquisition of the work of another}.

27:1348

Tit: V.

De jure disponendi de re sua

{Of right to dispose of one's property}

Dominus disponens {the owner is disposing} if he carries out *actus* {acts} that cannot subsist with *dominium* {ownership} and through which the thing ceases to be his property. *Jus utendi* {the right to use} refers to *accidentia disponendi* {the accidents to be disposed} but here it refers to the substance.[a] With this belong destruction, deterioration, reduction in use, and corruption, complete supersession of use. I can also further alter its form so that the thing becomes another particular,[b] that is, *specificare* {specification}, which is otherwise the term for bringing many things under various classes. *Specificare* is in general when I give a form to a formless thing.[c] *Dominus acquirendi speciem* {the owner will acquire the particular} or *jus rem suam specificandi* {the right of specifying his own thing}, i.e. to make things which belong to *genus* {a kind} into *species* {a particular}. Every *dominus* has the right to waive and renounce his *jus* {right}. He renounces when he states that he no longer wants the thing to be his.[d] Abandonment[e] is supersession of possession, when one gives up the *possession*. It is similar to *renunciatio*. One can indeed conclude

---

[a] *Substanz*

[b] *species*, here related to the difference between *in species* (in particular) and *in genera* (in kind)

[c] *einerrohen Sache eine Form gebe*

[d] KI: *sein seyn*. KS, MS: *seyn*, for "wants the thing to exist"

[e] *dereliction*

that he also renounces but it is merely *tacita renunciatio*. *Res derelicta* {an abandoned thing} becomes *res nullius* {an unowned thing}. If one ceases being *dominus* so that another begins to be *dominus* this is *alienatio* and to this belongs *translatio dominii* {transfer of ownership}. If I *derelinquo* {I abandon} something then it is *res nullius* and another takes control[a] of it. But that is not *translatio dominii*. For in transfer there is *dominium continuum* {a continuous ownership} and the thing is not *res nullius* even for an instant. But how this is possible is obscure. The other can still not acquire *res mea* {my thing} as long as it is mine, I also have to relinquish ownership. Must I first relinquish it before the other acquires it or do I keep it until the other acquires it? In the first case it is *res nullius per occupationem* {an unowned thing until the taking control}. The second is obscure. If the thing always remains mine then the other cannot take control[b] of it. – If I still have the thing and the other does also that would be a *condominium* {co-ownership}. But if I have the thing in one instant and the other in the following then the thing itself is still *res nullius* because between the instants there is some time. How the end of my property can be at the same time the beginning of the other's we will show in the following title *de pacto* {on contract}. It has a similarity to the skeptics' objection against the possibility of motion. They say that if my body moves another the other is either in movement or at rest. If it is the first then the movement will be twice as large, e.g. if the body has two degrees of speed then the first body imparts it to the other body. Does the first now give it to the second as the first itself had it? No – the first had lost it so it could not give it to the second. A body could receive movement this way in that it reacts and acquires what the other loses. A testator dies and then the thing becomes *res nullius* because the heir has not yet entered into the inheritance. It is not *alienatio* for I maintain ownership. My will alone does not constitute alienation but the other must himself also will to accept it and another will must thus exist at the same time. In *communio dominii* {ownership in common} I can *transferre*[c] {transfer} to another and this is called *condominium*, joint property.[d] Every *condominus* has *dominium limitatum* {limited ownership}. All *condomini simul sumtim* {co-owners purchasing at the same time} constitute *dominium plenum* {full ownership} or *morale* {moral ownership}. – By *moral* one here means *late* {broadly} all[e] that concerns the free will. If someone sells a house but keeps money invested in it then he can stipulate a *condominium*, e.g. that if the other owner also wants to sell it he is not permitted to sell it for less than the money the first still has invested

27:1349

---

[a] *occupirt*   [b] *occupiren*
[c] MS has blank. KI, KS suggest *transferre*
[d] MS is unclear. KI, KS suggest *Gesamteigenthum*
[e] KI: *alles*. KS: *vieles*, for "many"

in it, etc. If *dominus* keeps his property but allows others to get some use from the thing while he reserves his ownership that is known as him creating an easement.[a] In Roman law[b] it comes from *plenum* or *morale*[c] {abundance or morality}. *Servitus est*[d] *jus in re aliena* {an easement is a right in another's thing} from which I get some use, either positive or negative, so that no damages can accrue to me. If the previous owners of my house made an agreement, e.g. that my house should be only two stories high and I build it higher then those who made the agreement with them can hinder me. This means I have an easement in my house. I have the right to hinder another in a particular *actus* of his *dominium* i.e. negative use. But I can also really use *dominium* of another. The first is *servitus non faciendi* {an easement precluding something from being done}. The other is *faciendi* {something being done} regarding the owner, to tolerate another doing something with my thing, e.g. as in Königsberg in many houses the timbers for one house are in the wall of another house in which case I can coerce the other to maintain the wall in good condition. –*Fundus liber* {a free piece of land} one that has no easement, *servus* {an encumbered piece of land} is one that does. The jurists take the easement from things; they say that one good has an easement in the other. If by *condominium* someone has only *jus utendi* {a right to use} but has *disponendi* {a right to dispose} with another, then he is *dominus utilis* {the owner of the use}, the other *dominus directus* {the direct owner}, the first is owner of the land,[e] the other proprietor of the interest.[f] It is this way in all kinds of landed property, e.g. inheritance law.[g] That is *dominus dominorum subordinatus* {the owner is subordinate to the other owners}, in a house *dominus dominorum coordinatus* {the owner is coordinate with the other owners}.

If I have a right to[h] another's *dominium* {ownership} then I can exercise it or not. I can restrict it, give it up completely, dispose of it however I will. For in *jus* {right} a right is considered as a thing since one can do with a right everything that one can do with a thing. – Such rights are called *res incorporales* {incorporeal things} and regarding them one has *quasi dominium* and regarding *res corporales* {corporeal things} one has *dominium*. *Possessio rei incorporalis* is called *quasi possessio*. – *Dominus* has a right to transfer a part of his right to another, e.g. to rent a house, which lies in the authorization to dispose of it, alienate it, to concede *usus*, etc. which constitutes *dominium*.

---

[a] MS has blank. KI, KS suggest *servitut* (easement)
[b] *römischen Recht*
[c] MS has blank. KI, KS suggest *plenum oder morale aus*
[d] reading *est*. KI, KS, MS: *et*, for "and"   [e] *Grundherr*
[f] *Zinsherr*   [g] *Erbrecht*
[h] *ein Recht auf*

Tit: VI.

De jure facto bilaterali vel pacto[a]

{Of a rightful bilateral deed or contract}

We have talked about *acquisitione originaria* {original acquisition} which occurred *facto unilaterali* {by means of a unilateral deed}. I do not derive my right from another. Further we talked about *acquisitio jure rei meae* {rightful acquisition of a thing as mine} or *lege* {by law}, i.e. about *accessione* {accession}, which is not *acquisitio originaria* but *derivativa*. – Now we come to a *factum bilaterale* {bilateral deed}. A *pactum* {contract} is   27:1350 *promissum acceptatum* {the acceptance of a promise} where one promises and the other accepts, *promissoriae* what is promised. For accepting is a *modus acquirendi* {way of acquiring}. He has a right to acquire the promise. This right, however, is derived. The author talks first of *declaratio sufficiens mentis* {sufficient declaration of intent}. *Declaratio est significatio, se quid velle* {a declaration is a sign of what one wills}. But it is sufficient if I declare that one should consider what I have said to be my will. Through this there arises a right for each to proceed in accordance with the will as *declarans* {declaring}. But the one who is *declarans* also does not wrong another when he immediately declares otherwise. For through the first action the thing becomes *res nullius* {an unowned thing} and if he immediately reflects and takes it back then he acquires it first of all. – That agrees with the universal condition of freedom, if I do that which the other has declared as his will. For everyone has a right to[b] *res nullius* {unowned things}. If I still resist the action which can subsist with universal freedom then I act wrongly. *Volenti non fit injuria, damnum non est nisi quod infertur invito* {he who wills it cannot receive an injury, it is not harm unless it is inflicted on the unwilling} say the jurists. *Uti partes de jure suo disponunt, ita res est* {as the parties rightfully determine their own affairs, so be it}. The reciprocal will between two persons determines their right. *Voluntas communis* {a communal will} resolves validity. *Voluntas communis concludit* {a communal will is decisive}. From *voluntas communis* arises a right through which the recipient of the desired object can coerce it to be supplied and the relinquisher can coerce the recipient to accept it. The only[c] way that I can transfer a thing to another is if I declare that it should be his. This is thus *actus* of freedom which is hindered if the relinquisher does not keep his word, also if the other does not accept it.[d] Both can be coerced. They are free to do it or not. But they would also be free if they are not coerced. Their freedom is restricted

---

[a] Achenwall has simply *De pacto*   [b] *hat Recht zur*
[c] KS: *einzige*. KI, MS: *einige*, for "agreed upon"
[d] *es* is ambiguous between referring to the object and the word

only by universal freedom. If one makes a promise then he gives to the other the freedom to judge in accordance with his promise. If he does not then he infringes on this freedom. The latter can coerce the promissor for he does not limit the freedom of the other because the other has limited his own freedom himself. The author has a lot to say about this, always about the benefits that would be lost if the promise were not kept, but this has nothing to do with it. If I coerce the promissor then I physically limit his freedom, for morally he has limited himself. What is in question is: how does *translatio dominii* {transfer of ownership} occur here? Through a promise the right should be transferred to another. Not through mere *jus* {right}. My freedom is limited if the other agrees with my will but not before. Thus a *promissarius* {promisee} must first accept it. *Promittens* is the promissor, *promissarius*, the one to whom the promise is given, and if he accepts it then he is the accepter. *Promissio* and *acceptio* constitute transfer,[a] both must be together. In[b] the instant that the *acceptans* has accepted it the other must still be *promittens* {the promissor}, the *voluntas* {will} must be simultaneous. If I have just promised and the other has not yet accepted then I can still always retract the promise.

27:1351 *Consensus in promissum* is accepting. There is a simultaneity of the will. One assumes that his act of promising would have lasted long enough for the other to accept it. *Promissarius* {the promisee} acquires only *acceptatio* {by accepting}. This *modus acquirendi* is *derivativus*. He derives his right from another. *Titulus alienationis* {a title of alienation} consists in *in jus renunciandi* {a renunciation of a right} on the part of the promissor and *in jus acceptandi* {an acceptance of a right} on the part of *promissarius* {promisee}. *Promittens* promises either *res* {a thing} or *opera* {work}, i.e. he provides[c] either *rem* or *operam*, juridically *aliquod dandum aut faciendum* {something to be given or something to be done}. There must be a simultaneous will. If there is some time between the promise and its acceptance then there is *res nullius* or *jus in re jacente* {a right in a thing in abeyance}, a right that I exclusively have in a thing. – Now the question is how does accepter acquire? Through the promise of the other or his renunciation of the right? No, then he would attain only *jus in re jacenti*. It must be *voluntatis simultaneitas* {simultaneity of the will} for otherwise the right cannot be transferred. I cannot receive an affirmative right through a single will nor through the will of a stranger but only through the will of the one who has a right in it. When both wills agree then it is right. Whatever *voluntas communis* {the common will} determines is right. Both were free to do it or not. The common will agrees with universal freedom if that will is accompanied with coercion. Each determined his will by himself and limited his will. Both must will in

---

[a] *translation*

[b] This sentence in margin in MS

[c] *praestirt*

one instant that the thing should belong to him. The accepter acquires a right. *Promittens* takes on an obligation. *Pactum est servandum, promissis standum* {the contract is to be kept, promises to stand}. To *pactum* belongs 1) *consensus mutuus pactiscentium* {the parties in mutual agreement}, 2) that it be a *pactum licitum* {permitted contract} not opposed to the rights of others, 3) that it be *physice possibile* {physically possible}. For a *pactum* it is necessary that the *paciscentia*[a] {parties} have *usus intellectus* {the use of their intellects} and that is because freedom is required, which presupposes the use of the understanding. There must be *facultas physica* {a physical means}. *Consensus* as well, for which 1) will, 2) a sufficient declaration of will, 3) determined object, 4) the wills of both being able to make an agreement[b], 5) agreement of both wills. When I am deliberating I have not yet willed. Declarations of will in jest also do not count. Whoever reserves his freedom steps back from his promise. He has still not promised. The *promittens* here has no coercive right. *Consensus expressus* or *tacitus* {express or tacit consent} can exist through agreement; the first is through words. *Consensus tacitus*, which is signified in a deed to which I consent. But it must be such that it can be stated as an actual[c] *consensus*, then it is an actual *consensus*. *Factum praesumptum* {a presumptive deed} is where no *consensus* at all can be sufficiently declared and it is merely a probable *consensus*. But mere probability cannot give me a right to coerce another. I can never wrong another based only on a probability. The action through which I do something to obligate another is called *quasicontractus* in Roman law.[d] If I do something that is in another's interest under the presumption that the other would certainly have agreed with it, e.g. if my neighbor gets everything out of my house when a fire develops and incurs costs for it then he is *negotii gestor* {bearer of the activity}. This cannot at all be considered as formal *contractus*[e] simply from the *titulus pacti* {term "contract"} in that it is a mere probability. But 2)[f] the *praestandum* {thing to be provided} is unknown when it is undetermined. I want to reward him well. To will something and to

27:1352

---

[a] KI: *paciscentia*. KS, MS: *pacientia*, a clear error

[b] *paciscendirenden*

[c] *wirklicher*, here and in the next clause. Presumably Kant meant "express" in the first instance.

[d] *römischen Rechte*

[e] Literally translated, the Latin *pactum* is pact, agreement, compact, and other similar terms denoting less formal arrangements, *contractus* is contract, the more formal arrangement. But Kant, following Achenwall, uses the word *pactum* where in English and in German the word "contract" (*Vertrag*) is generally used. In Roman law, a *contractus* but not a *pactum* was susceptible to civil remedy if breached. See also below at 27:1360 for another distinction Kant offers.

[f] There is no preceding "1)"

promise something are *res merae facultatis*.[a] These are *juridice res indifferentes* {juridically indifferent things} to which I cannot be coerced at all. *Pollicitatio* {pledging}. Under this one means the promise before accepting or when one imposes[b] the reservation of withdrawing it. – In all cases which one promises *gratis* one must presume that it is merely *pollicitatio* in the strictest sense. Yet it is not absolutely strict. It is not credible that I would give another a right *gratis* to coerce me. For *pactum* a three-fold deed is not required, namely *promissio, acceptatio*, and confirmation. The last is not necessary but we will see that in a strict sense a confirmation is necessary. – *Promissarius* {the promisee} must will what I will and further he must will it at the same time as the promissor. Also not *voluntas simultanea* {a simultaneous will} but a will which is the same will for both.[c]

Error in pacto nocet ei paciscentium, qui causa est erroris {An error in the contract harms the party who is the cause of the error}. If the *promissarius* {promisee} has deceived the *promittens* {promissor}, then *pactum* is *dolo superstructum* {based on deceit}. A *pactum* has no effect if *promissarius* is guilty. When neither is the cause of the error or both have erred then the *pactum* is negated, for then it never was really a *pactum*. A *pactum* that is physically impossible is null and void and if it is nonetheless promised then it is *dolo superstructum* and is still not valid. The *pactum* must not conflict with other rights *in justitia currere* {in the rush to justice}. Those are *pacta illicita* {impermissible contracts}. A few *pacta* are called *turpia* {immoral}, those that are void unconditionally such as those which sell sexual pleasure. An object that is *legaliter* {legally} impossible cannot be promised. The accepter must have a right to acquire. When he coerces the other to promise something contrary to all right it is *invalidum*. It is *pactum vi extortum* {a contract extorted by force}. One can do wrong without doing wrong to that to which the *pactum* is directed or to any person. All wrong is of course related to persons but in general to the rights of humanity. Someone has cheated me, pained me. I get upset about that and cheat him back, e.g. he sells me a blind horse and I give him a false bill of exchange. I still do something wrong but I do not do anything wrong to the cheater. If a robber coerces me to make a promise and I do not keep it I do not do anything wrong[d] *juridice* {juridically} for he had no right to coerce me. But I do something wrong to humanity for that is still a means to choose to do a small ill in order to get revenge for a larger one. I thus offend the freedom of humanity. If that occurred often enough then the robber would not believe the promise, will rob him and kill him. This right to humanity is not strict but is still always a right. If I promise to do something after a war such as surrender some land, etc.,

---

[a] The legal term *res merae facultatis* indicates something discretionary or at will.
[b] KI, MS: *belegt*. KS: *klagt*, for "sues"   [c] *ein Wille, der beider Wille gleich ist*
[d] KS adds *ihm*, for "wrong to him"

and the king does wrong and I am also coerced to it, I must nonetheless still keep my promise. It is *vi extortum* {extorted by force} but I cannot be *injuste* {unjust} for there is no outer law for states. They are considered to be *in statu naturali*. So one says, but then it is also unclear whether I do a wrong if I again break the *pactum*. But according to the law of humanity I must not do that. Otherwise there would be constant war, one would not trust another's promises and absolutely nothing would be safe. *Civiliter* {in the civil sphere} a *pactum* that is *metu aut vi extortum* {a contract extorted by fear or by force} is *injustum* {unjust}. But the question is whether civil laws also have jurisdiction over that, for it[a] is certainly supposed to be concerned about safety and that undermines safety. If a robber assaults me then I am in the *status naturalis* for the authorities cannot protect me at all. If I am in a *statu necessitatis* {a state of necessity} then I am always in the *status naturalis*. Such a civil law is absurd because it can punish me only by taking what is mine, putting me in prison, etc. And also threaten me with death, but even that will not hinder me because here my life is also in danger, and I cannot here avoid that fate which afterward I might yet be able to avoid in court.

27:1353

Tit: VII.

De effectu[b]

{Of effect}

After a *promissio* {promise} the *pactum* {contract} still has no effect. *Effectus pacti* {the effect of a contract} is when someone acquires a right through it. To revoke is to declare an intention which is contrary to the earlier one. *Revoco* {I revoke} my promise means that I now will that it should not be so.[c] I can do that prior to accepting. If I have done something irrevocable then he has *jus in re jacente* {a right in the thing in abeyance}. *Irrevocabiliter* is when I say that I will that my promise is to persist and be valid until you have accepted it. But one says that I can revoke without reserving to myself *jus revocabile* {the right to revoke}. Further I can revoke up to the time that the other has accepted but then the accepter has no right. A *promittens* {promissor} states his future will, he judges provisionally. It remains in existence up to the time that the other accepts. But if I have heard that the other wants it then I must confirm[d] my will. – So the will is first complete if the condition holds that another wills it. Still I must first know that the other will accept before I can give it to him

---

[a] *es* in context might refer to the set of civil laws
[b] Achenwall has *De effectibus pacti*   [c] KS omits *so*
[d] KI: *confirmiren*. KS, MS: *conformiren*, for "conform to"

and I must hear that from him first. That's how long the thing belongs to me. —*Confirmatio* of the will appears thus not to be necessary. If I revoke at the last instant when the other accepts it then to whom does it belong?[a] For the Romans *stipulation*[b] was also a kind of confirmation. The Romans had for *pactum* a *stipulation* using *stipula* {straw}, a straw which would be broken.[32] Yet it is a mere formality. Perhaps they had obscure reasons for confirmation. When he promises, he wills to give it to him in the event that the other declares. It is thus a conditioned promise. Because he was free for so long he is still free when the other has also promised. For his will was *conditionale* {conditional} on whether the other would also will it. If the other makes it known then he still must confirm it in his will, the earlier is *voluntas antecedens* {an antecedent will} and the other is *consequens* {a consequent will}. He wills provisionally when he will give it to the other if the other wants it. A categorical will must come from a conditioned one, otherwise the thing could not be transferred. *Promissarius* {the promisee} has *jus revocandi* {a right of revocation} before accepting. According to the jurists revocation has been given up in the instant of accepting; since this instant is common to both, the *acceptans* can then say that I will it and the *promissor* can revoke[c] it in the same instant. Then who receives it? The *promissor* declares before he knows the condition, the *acceptans* in this case already knows. They are thus different and the *acceptans* cannot revoke it for his will was categorical. *Pacta dant legem* {the contracts give the law}. [They] are grounds of an obligation. He is *debitor* {a debtor} if he is obligated by *jus strictum* {strict right} *alicui aliquid praestandum* {to provide someone with something}. *Creditor* who has a right to coerce the *debitor*, *ad aliquid faciendum aut praestandum* {to make or provide something}, *praestandum* {the providing} is *creditum* {crediting}. The author says that through accepting the *promissor* becomes *debitor* and the *acceptans* becomes *creditor*. If I promise something I am not thereby *debitor* and the will alone cannot make me into *debitor* but only both wills, thus I must consider my will to be categorical. *Debita sunt solvenda* {debts are to be paid}. In *ethica* there are no *debita*[d] but obligations are duties. Fidelity in *pactia* is rightful fidelity. *Fidem obstringere* {to obligate one's trust} is to promise *valide* {validly} that a right arises in another to coerce me, i.e. having rightful force,[e] *valide*. If I also renounce my *jus revocandi* {right of revocation} regarding a promise, then I am already *obstrictus* {obligated} without my promise, for the other has *jus*

27:1354

---

[a] KI, KS, MS have a period
[b] *Stipulation*, the most formal oral procedure for concluding a contract in Roman law, will remain untranslated.
[c] *widerrufen*
[d] KI: *debita*. KS: *delicta*, for "offenses"   [e] *rechtskräftig*

in re jacente, jus proprium {a right in the thing in abeyance, a proprietary right} to acquire something, *exclusis aliis* {to the exclusion of others}. – *Perfidia* {perfidy} is not the failure to keep a promise one has made but *violatio dolosa datae fidei* {the deceitful violation of trust}. Have trust in others. *Fides activa* {active trust}, fidelity which each possesses, *passiva* {passive trust}, the opinion which others have of our fidelity *in fruendis pactis* {in the enjoyment of a contract}. That is *credit. Quilibet praesumitur fidelis, donec probetur contrarium* {assume that someone is trustworthy until he shows the contrary}. Even if someone has broken his *pactum* I am not permitted to treat him as absolutely faithless. But because of it I am not obligated to trust him and to give him *credit* but I must assume him to be a promise breaker, or believe he is one, because he has already done it. I am permitted to assume that he is not faithful. The rule of prudence is *quilibet praesumetur malus, donec probetur contrarium* {assume that someone is evil until he shows the contrary}. I am not obligated to believe that he will keep his promises. One trusts a human being if he is unable to cheat not because he does not want to cheat. *Jus personale* {a personal right} is a right against a certain person to necessitate that person *ad praestandum* {to provide}, *jus reale* {right in a thing} right against everyone to necessitate him *ad praestandum*. If a book of mine is stolen then I am not able to demand it from this or that person but only to take it where I find it. *Jus reale est jus exigendi ab unaquaque persona* {a right in a thing is a right to demand something of each and every person}. My right is in the thing and I can take it where I find it. Really I do not have a right against a thing. For if that were the case it would be obligated to me. It will later be shown how one must understand this. The *effectus* {effect} is the same. We could keep talking about it. Obligation is *in re* {in regard to a thing} and the thing makes absolutely no difference for it. In each *punctum* {specific approval} *acceptor*[a] {the accepter} acquires *jus personale* {a personal right} against *promissor* to coerce him *quid faciendum aut praestandum* {either to make or to provide something}. Must something still come in addition to *punctum* for *jus personale* to become *reale*? The Romans said yes, delivery,[b] the moderns no; here the Romans had it right. He must exercise *actum possessorium* {an act of possession}. *Jus reale* he would acquire just at the conclusion of *pacti*. If someone has sold me a book do I then have *jus reale* in the thing?[c] If it has not been delivered[d] it is in the *possessio*[e] {possession} of *debitor* {the debtor} or of the promissor. He is the legitimate possessor because the other has still not yet received

27:1355

---

[a] Reading *acceptor*. KI, KS, MS: *acceptation*, for "the acceptance"
[b] *tradition*   [c] KS: question mark. KI, MS: period
[d] *tradirt*
[e] KI: *in possession*. KS, MS: *im possessori*, for "in the owner"

it. Does he possess it *quo titulo* {by title}? Is it *jus rei suae* {his by right} or not? If it belongs to the other then I do not possess it *jus rei meae* {as mine by right} but *suae* and I wrong the other, but that is not the case. Before the other's concurrence that I should possess it the thing is *res mea*. He must exercise *actus possessorius* for he is a possessor. He must say, "I am keeping that horse there as long as I want until I will let it go." That is an exercise of *actus possessorius*, we do not have *titulum* of possession even if it is not *jus rei suae* {his by right}. Otherwise the other must exercise an *actus possessorius*. Why should I keep the horse for another gratis? If it is hit by lightning then I am not required to pay the seller. The difference between *jus in re* {a right with regard to something} and *jus personale* {a right with regard to a person} is important. In the latter there is a right only against the promissor, e.g. I have bought something from someone. Soon I come to pick it up and he has in the meantime already sold it to another. Do I have here the right to take that entailed thing[a] wherever I can find it? Roman law[b] agrees with this very well. It says that I still do not have the right to coerce him to get the thing back, not before the delivery[c] has occurred. Indeed the seller was no longer[d] *dominus* {owner} but always still *possessor*. We can also call delivery[e] *stipulation*. Each *possessor* must have a title. If after the sale the possessor does not have a title then he does a wrong if he possesses it. And yet that is not true. Should his possession have a title then it is none other than *jus rei ipsius* {a right to the thing itself}. For it cannot be *jus alterius* {a right with regard to the other person} because the other has said nothing to him. If the buyer exercises *actus possessorius* he must first assume possession, e.g. if he says, "You keep the horse until I am able to pick it up," that is *actus possessorius* and *eo ipso* {by that very act} it is transferred[f] to him. Now the other is *detentor* {the detainer} but not *possessor*, through this *jus reale* is transformed *in personale* {into a personal right}. *Pactum privi derogat posterius* {a separate contract modifies what follows}. There is a difference between promising things *in genere* {in kind} and *in specie* {in particular}. Through promising *in genere* {in kind} nothing is alienated but it is through promising *in specie*. So the author says. The question is which kind of right is acquired by one who is promised *in genere* {in kind}? *Jus personale* {a personal right}. If someone buys a part of a bolt of cloth and another later the entire bolt then the latter one who was promised the thing *in specie* acquires *jus in re* {a right in the thing} and the one who was promised it *in genere* {in kind} acquires *jus personale*. If the *pactum* is concluded and the time when

---

[a] *jenes bedungenes* – the conditioned thing, that thing which I have entailed by purchase
[b] *römische Recht*   [c] *tradition*
[d] KI: *nicht mehr*. KS, MS: *noch nicht*, for "still not"
[e] *tradition*   [f] *tradirt*

acceptans should acquire it is left undetermined then the thing is from that instant on *res acceptantis* {the property of the one who accepts}. *Conditio in jure* {in right a condition} is an uncertain event on which a right depends. E.g. If I say, "You should pay me such if this is the case," and the other agrees, then I can later coerce the payment. *Conditio potestativa* {a condition involving authority} is when it depends on the will of that one to whom *promissum* has been made. *Pacta sub conditione suspensiva* {contracts with uncertain conditions} are in games, in cards, lotteries, where the one who is lucky and wins receives the right to control[a] the winnings. It is a future uncertain event.　27:1356

One makes two types of bets, one in which the result is uncertain and the right depends on existence of this result. That is a future event. It is *pactum in conditione suspensiva*. In every bet *eventus* {outcome} must be *incertus* {uncertain} to both. The *eventus* can be certain but the certainty about it is only in the future. *Eventus* can already have been. If someone bets that a person will soon get a husband and he is himself the bridegroom, then that is not valid because he was certain and it is *dolus* {deceit}. In bets where *eventus* has already happened one could always turn out to have knowledge about it. E.g. if someone argues about which book this is in. The bet is here a penalty[b] for the reason that another has simply opposed what I said although he had no basis. One thinks that if one is certain one cannot bet. But this type of bet is made. If, however, the event is in the future then it is otherwise. In §197 the author discusses *pactum*[c] *putativum* {a putative contract} and *acquisitio, alienatio* through such *pactum putativum*. If someone accepts something *bona fide* {in good faith} which the other promises[d] because he believes that the other has a right to promise it, *acceptatio est putativa*[e] {the acceptance is putative}. If *absque consensu domini sine culpa acceptionis* {without negligence he accepts something without the consent of the owner} or *a non domino* {from a non-owner}, then it is *putative* and *pactum putativum*. If I buy a horse I don't know whether he is owner[f] or not. I am not obligated to discover that for myself. As long as my error, which is no fault of my own, lasts, everything I do with the thing is right – But if I hear that I have bought a thing *a non domino* {from a non-owner} or *absque suo consensu* {without his consent} then I cannot withhold it from *dominus* for I would no longer

---

[a] *zuzueignen*　　　　　　　　　　[b] *Strafe*

[c] KI: *pacto*, following Achenwall. KS, MS: *facto*, for "putative deed." Repeated twice more in this paragraph.

[d] *promittirt*

[e] KI: *acceptatio est putativa*. KS, MS: *acceptatio e putativo*, for "acceptance resulting from the putative"

[f] *Herr*

possess the thing *bona fide* {in good faith} but rather *dolose* {maliciously}, then I wrong the other.

Tit: VIII.[a]

Pacta gratuita, promissa absque repromissis {gratuitous contracts, promises without counter-promises}, and further *pacta onerosa* {onerous contracts}. *Gratis praestat, qui praestat alicui quid, pro quo nihil recipit* {whoever supplies something to someone for which he accepts nothing, supplies it gratis}. He provides something useful. Without another doing something useful for him in return. If I promise something that is something[b] neither useful nor harmful to the other then it is not a promise. – *Pactum* {a contract} where there is *promissio* and *repromissio* {promising and counter-promising} is *pactum onerosum*. It is also called *permutatorium, quia ibi res aut operae permutantur* {exchange, because there things or works are exchanged}. In *pactum onerosum* one can assume that everyone hopes for the same benefit as others unless they state otherwise. If they wanted only a part then they would have declared so. Every buyer always acts as if the shopkeeper should be more obligated to him, give more attention to him, than he to the shopkeeper because it is easier to find wares for money than to find money for wares. A buyer thinks as *gratis* that he gave this shopkeeper preference over others. The value of things is a ground of usefulness. Dignity is inner value which is based on satisfaction in the thing itself. *Valor determinatus* {the determined value}, says the author, is price. But what is the value of a thing which is the same as the value of another thing and which thus can be put in place of the thing as equivalent? A thing has no price at all although still a determined value if no equivalent can be set for it. Many human beings have a price for their virtue; if one will give it to them for it they will forsake their virtue. But virtue has no price at all but only dignity. The human body also has no price. A person cannot take anything as equivalent for it. One cannot put a price regarding *punctum servati*[c] {a case of preservation}. Things which are heterogeneous could have the same value but only if they are homogeneous in usefulness. The *valor* {value} of things[d] does not consist in their properties but in the opinion that one has of their usefulness. The value of things is thus mostly *arbitrer* {judged}. Adam Smith says in his book on national character that the universal measure of value would be a bushel of grain.[33] – Indeed that has a certain value in itself, a natural value, but it is still not a determinate value. Some eat more, some less.

27:1357

[a] Achenwall also has *De pretio et pecunia* {Of price and money}.
[b] KS: missing second *etwas*, for "something that is neither useful nor harmful"
[c] KS: *servati*. KI, MS: *servali*, for "a case of a slave"
[d] *Dinge*. Kant switches back and forth between *Sache* and *Dinge*, usually with *Dinge*.

In[a] England one calls[b] corn "wheat," in Scotland "oats," in Sweden "barley," and in Germany "rye." Grain is in general whatever provides sustenance.

Some love finery more than eating. In Spain ladies have themselves carried around in port chaises and beg for makeup. In Moscow they walk around wearing shifts and beg for makeup. Everyone determines the value of things in accordance with his own judgment while contracting.[c] If we agree on value then the *pactum* becomes correct. That whose value is determined in accordance with the common judgment of human beings is *pretium vulgare* {the common price}, market price. If now and then I do not see any value *in specie* {in a particular} but it is used in exchange[d] with something else useful, that is **money**, accordingly it is regarded as very handy for exchange for all other things. It is an equivalent for all other things. *Pecunia est res, cujus usus ordinarius consistit in alienando* {money is a thing whose ordinary use consists in alienation}. I can get some benefit from lending out other things but not money for if I lend that to him he will just give me other money in return. The *usus* {use} of money is merely possible in *sublato meo dominio* {taking away what is mine}, it consists merely in *alienando*. Its usefulness is just that. It is the means for exchange[e] of all things. Suppose I have rye and go to the tailor but he does not need any rye. So I go to the baker who has bread but I do not need any bread, so he gives me money and I give money to the tailor. For money I can get all things which are not illegitimate and are under our control.[f] Money has *pretium eminens* {eminent price}.

[*Tit: LX*[g]]

The *pacta beneficia* {beneficial contracts} are three: *donationes, commoditates,*[h] and *depositiones* {donations, loans, and deposits}. Here *promittens* {the promissor} promises merely *in gratiam promissarii* {a gift to the promisee}. In donation *res gratis* {a gift} is alienated. In *commodatum* {lending} the thing is not alienated, instead it allows only *usus rei meae* {the use of what is mine}. In lending but not in giving I remain *dominus* {the owner}, what is promised is *donum* {a gift}, the promissor is *donans* {the donor}, and *acceptans donatarius* {the one who accepts is called donee}. Thus also there is *commodatum, depositum, commodans, deponens,* 27:1358

---

[a] This paragraph is in the MS margin with no insertion marker. KS, KI place it here.

[b] KI: *nennt.* KS: *nimmt,* for "takes corn as"   [c] *paciscenten*

[d] *permutation*   [e] *permutation*

[f] *Gewalt*

[g] Here Achenwall begins a new section: *Tit: IX, De pactis beneficis et onerosis* {Of beneficial and onerous contracts}. KS, MS: body of text is continuous with previous paragraph

[h] KI: *commoditates.* KS, MS: *condomationes,* for "curbings" or "tamings" (likely error)

commodatarius, depositarius {the item lent, the item deposited, the lender, the depositor, the borrower, and the trustee}. If the *donatarius* {donee} acquires only through *acceptatio* then he can coerce the *donans* to hand it over. But he still has no *jus* {right} to coerce the *donans* if the latter does not give him the right, then he does not have *jus in re* {a right in the thing}. If the *donans* has promised and the other has accepted then the *donans* cannot take it back. With regard to one who has promised something to someone completely *gratis* can one presume that he would want to give a right to the other to coerce him? For no one would throw away his freedom for nothing.[a] *Nemo velle jactare suum praetenditur* {it is assumed that no one wants to throw away what is his}. On this one can assume it would be entirely contrary to the inclination of the promissor to allow himself to be coerced to his promise rather than him wanting to act here voluntarily. I promise someone a book, the other accepts it and requests the book and I say that I have changed my mind, should the other then coerce me? If I have already given him the book then he possesses *jus rei suae* {his by right}; under what other kind of title ought he to possess it? For then I would have to want to coerce him back to return it. And I do not have that right. If someone counter-promises[b] something to me then I limit my freedom but so does the other and I enjoy the advantage. Whatever can be foreseen as belonging to the way of thinking[c] of the parties[d] does not need to be declared. Roman law[e] means by the donation also the transfer[f] and before the transfer grants to the *acceptanten* not a single *jus personale* {personal right}. The author already assumes *jus in re* {a right in the thing} after accepting. Up to this transfer[g] the *donans* has *jus revocandi* {a right of revocation} unless he renounces it. For this he must make a special declaration. In common life one already sees that one has retracted *donans* {the donation} without needing many words.

In *pactum de commodando* {a contract for loan} the *usus* is conceded, the *commodans* {the loaner} then remains *dominus* {owner} and he requires that the thing be repaid *in specie* {in particular}. *Usus* is conceded *gratis* and is certain. *Mutuum* {a loan for consumption} is when I lend something to another but it will be repaid *in genere* {in kind}. E.g. if I lend money, the other is not expected to give me the same money but the same amount. *In specie* the lender is *dominus* of the thing and *in genere* the thing belongs to the borrower.[h] If I lend someone a garment I lend it to him for a determined amount of time and he must repay me then *in*

---

[a] *umsonst*
[b] *repromittirt*
[c] *Gesinnung*
[d] *paciscenten*
[e] *römische Recht*
[f] KI: *will bei der donation auch tradition.* KS: *will die donation auf tradition,* for "has the donation in the transfer"
[g] *tradition*
[h] *mutuanten*

specie. If the thing I lent is broken then according to Roman law he must bring me the broken thing and not another. For he must always repay the garment *in specie* not *in genere.* He is supposed to give it back to me as it is. With money, however, it is otherwise, so if I have stolen it from someone I must give back the same amount of money *in genere.* But if I lend a thing to someone and it is stolen from him then according to Roman law he cannot give it back to me because I lent it to him *in specie* and not *in genere.* But that is a juristic subtlety. I do not see why the *condition* of *commodans* {the loaner} should be *deterior* {worse} than that of *mutuans* {the borrower}, in fact it must be *melior* {better}. For when *mutuo* {I lend} the thing has[a] lost none of its usefulness, as with clothes or other things; when he takes them, I lose the usefulness which he gets from it. But if I   27:1359 lend something to someone I understand as part of this that if the other cannot repay me *in specie* he should still repay me *in genere.* One says here that *casum sentit dominus,* the owner carries the risk. If I say that you must get it for me when it has been stolen, that is another matter. For however[b] *contrahenten* {the parties} agree to settle it is also *jus* but it is not necessary to say that I will that it should be repaid to me *in genere* when not *in specie* for then I allow him the advantage that he may just use the thing but not consume it, it being already understood that I do not want it spoiled and would in that case want restitution. The Romans stuck to the letter of the law. In *jus strictum* {strict right} there must be a basis in every case which is declared either expressly or *tacite* {tacitly}: for the disposition refers to ethics. All *pacta* whose *praestandum* {performance} is undetermined are null and void. This is because in this case the substitution is not determined so it cannot be valid *in jure stricto,* for *commodans* {the lender} must say how much he would value[c] the thing and on this *commodatarius* {the borrower} could judge whether he would accept the thing given such a great danger. Here Roman law is valid *in jure civili* {in civil right}. *Justa commutativa* and *distributiva* {commutative and distributive justice} are different; in the latter all conditions must be express. The determination of value depends neither on the market price nor on *commodans* {the lender} but on the value which the thing has in the eyes of *commodatarius* {the borrower}. And that cannot be determined after the fact. In strict coercive right *pactum* would be *incertum* {uncertain} for the agreement is uncertain. *Pacta incerta* {uncertain contracts} are invalid in accordance with external right. Presumptions are not valid here. Can one assume that *commodans* has assumed responsibility for loss just by lending it if he has not stated it? In accordance with equity that is not to be assumed but in accordance with strict right it is otherwise. Equity is in

---

[a] KI: *hat.* KS: *Ich habe,* for "I have lost none of the usefulness of the thing"
[b] KI: *Denn wie.* KS: *wie,* for "however." MS: illegible
[c] *schätzte*

this way to be distinguished from strict right in that strict right[a] refers to expressed state of mind and he must declare or demand:[b] in strict right everything must be externally valid. If I have not declared my will then I have no external basis on which to prove that the other knew it, consequently the other cannot be coerced externally. The *commodatarius* is free as long as the *commodans* has not yet made a declaration. Before this he is to be considered as completely free from any obligation. Declaration is the externally valid sign for the other to know my will. In equity it is always wrong. I cannot assume that I have also conceded indemnity to him, that I thereby have promised him two things when I only promised one. The jurists make equity into something arbitrary. But it is a real right, one, however, about which the judge can say nothing. In accordance with strict right the *commodatarius* has greater advantage than *commodans*, or the owner. If someone has lost some *commodatum* {item loaned} then the other requires of him that he at least give him a good word. But if I am not responsible for something I am not required to give him a good word. If I also know that the thing will perhaps be lost to me then I still lend out the thing, but if I know that he will defy my right then I will not lend it to anyone. One still feels in this case an inner right. Whoever leaves it up to another *gratis* to preserve a thing is *deponens* {depositor} and the one who promises to do this is *depositarius* {trustee}. The thing is *depositum* {the deposit}. *Depositum* occurs as *in gratiam deponentis* {a gift of the depositor}. We have stated that transfer[c] is not unnecessary for possession of a thing as modern jurists believe. If the thing was not yet transferred[d] then it is detention, this occurs as what is *res sua* {his} or *aliena* {another's}. The first occurs *jus rei suae* {his by right}, the second can have no other title than the will of the owner. That is the *depositum*. Consequently in a sale, before the transfer,[e] the possessor must be seen as *dominus* or as *depositor*. For this, however, *pactum deponendi* {a contract for deposit} must have already taken place. This *pactum* is transfer.[f] For here he exercises *actus possessorius* when he says "I want you to watch over it." *Depositarius* is not *dominus*. Only *custodia* {custody} is allowed to him and not *usus* {use}. He is not obligated to watch over a *depositum* longer than the set time. *Pactum onerosum* {an onerous contract} contains a double *pactum*, each promises and accepts, they promise and accept *vicissim* {in turn}.

Contractus {a formal contract} is distinguished from *pactum* in the following way: in *pactum* always only the *promittens* contracts obligation and *acceptans* merely accepts. *Contractus* is *pactum onerosum*. A *pactum donationis* {contract for donation} is not a *commodatum* {loan}, *depositum* is

27:1360

---

[a] KS: *dieses*. KI: *diese*, referring to equity   [b] *exigiren*
[c] *tradition*   [d] *tradirt*
[e] *tradition*   [f] *tradition*

contractus {a deposit is a formal contract}. *Jus acquiritur, obligatio contrahitur* {a right is acquired, an obligation is contracted}. I can acquire a *jus* without obligation to make a contract[a] with someone, this above all in *pacta gratuita* {gratuitous contracts}. In every *contract* one must assume that both want to provide[b] *aequalia* {what is equal}. The judgment of a third regarding the value of the thing is thus not necessary and if one of the parties[c] later believes that he has received less than the value of the thing that counts for nothing. My previous declaration is already sufficient. *Laesio enormis* {great harm}, according to Roman law,[d] belongs among the civil rights[e] where the members are to be considered as minor[f] children. The doctrine[g] of caring for the citizens and their happiness like a father is completely contrary to the first principle of right, of civil freedom. *Laesio ultra dimidium* {harm greater than half} or *laesio enormis* is if the thing which I receive is not worth half as much as the thing I have given, for *pactum* is also necessary in accordance with local law.[h] But that is false. Clearly no wrong is done to him and he is himself the cause of the problem, but *error in pacto illi docet, qui caussa erroris est* {the error in the contract is a lesson for the one who is the cause of the error}. In *pactum oneroso* {an onerous contract} *praestatio* {provision} is of *res* {the thing} or of *opera* {work}, the first is *dare* {to give} and the second *facere* {to do}. If there is a second *do* {giving} in *pacta onerosa* then it is called *do ut des* {I give that you may give}, if there is a second *facio* {doing}, *facio ut facias* {I do that you may do}, if *do* and *facio* occur only once, then it is called *do ut facias* {I give that you may do}, *facio ut des* {I do that you may give}. These latter two are one and the same for the one says *do ut facias* and the other *facio ut des*. Thus the author is right when he assumes three [kinds]. *Pacta onerosa* are: 1) *Emtio, venditio* {buying, selling}. It is similar to donation except that in this *pactum beneficium* {beneficial contract} *promissor* is *emtor* {the promissor is the buyer}, *acceptans, venditor* {the one who accepts is the seller}. The thing on which an alienated property takes place is *merx* {a commodity}. Some property cannot be alienated, as a husband cannot alienate his wife. A human being cannot be alienated unless he has committed a crime and has forfeited his freedom. *Res* can be sold *in specie* and *in genere*. I sell a house and a load of grain, the former *in specie*, the latter *in genere*; *acquisitor in genere* {the one who acquires in kind} acquires only *jus personale* for it is up to the other what grain *in specie* he will give him; the other who acquires *in specie* has *jus reale* {right in a thing}. All things whose use consists of *consumtion* {consumption} or *alienation* can be promised only *in*

27:1361

---

[a] *kontrahiren*
[c] *contrahenten*
[e] *Civilrecht*
[g] *Meinung*

[b] *praestiren*
[d] *römischen Recht*
[f] *unmündige*
[h] *hiesigen Recht*

genere. The buyer is *debitor* and is obligated to pay the seller when he supplies it. The seller has *jus personale*, but would he have *jus reale*, i.e. if he sold *a comptant*,[a] that is, for cash? But if he has still not paid me and it has come time to remit the money then it is *a content* {for satisfaction}. If I just sold it a short time ago then I have already acknowledged receipt. But one means here that he would have *jus reale* and if he were not able to give me the money the seller could not take it away from him. To sell *a comptant* is when one sells it bit by bit,[b] if he also will do it a hundred times just *a comptant* then nothing is missing whether I give him receipt in a short time or in a year. I can require nothing of the other except that he should fulfill his[c] promise. Through the accepting of the thing he becomes *dominus* {owner} and whoever buys from the *dominus* buys legitimately and so I cannot take the thing from him. But merchants call it selling *a comptant* if the money must be raised within four weeks. Hiring out,[d] *locatio*, is when for a certain amount of money the use of a thing or the effort of a human being is lent. If I alienate a use of a thing then I contract for an easement[e] and not hiring out.[f] In an easement there is also no determined time and it is for various uses. But if I give a thing to a human being for a certain time and for a certain use then I hire it out. If a human being lends the use of *opera* {his work} for money, etc., then he is hiring himself out. A contract for hiring out is when I grant to another the use of my powers[g] for a determined price. I do not alienate my powers to the other. For when I grant I simultaneously determine *opera* but if I alienate the *usus virium mearum* {use of my powers} then I put myself into service for an undetermined *opera*. A human being is authorized to grant but not to alienate. For that accords with a human being as human being. Because a human being cannot alienate[h] himself he certainly cannot alienate the use of his powers. *Locatio – conductio* {letting – hiring} is either of *res* or of *opera*. It is labor and money. *Locator est aut rei aut operae* {what is let is either the thing or the work}. *Locator* is the one hired out, *conductor* the one doing the hiring. The *locator* gets *jus personale* from the *conductor*. From the *conductor* I generally get no *jus reale* before the transfer.[i] The one hiring has the right that the other has granted to him for the use of the thing. If the lessor sells the thing during this time then the lessee has no *jus reale*, e.g. in a house he must

---

[a] KI: *a comptant* (French). KS: *a content* (French), for "for satisfaction"
[b] *Zug für Zug*   [c] KI: *sein*. KS: *mein*, for "my"
[d] *das Verdingen* and *locatio* cover leasing (letting) of movable things as well as hiring out of human labor, and in a few sentences Kant incorporates leasing real property as well.
[e] *servitut*   [f] *vermiethen*
[g] *Kräfte*
[h] *veräussern*, rather than the usual latinate *alieniren*
[i] *tradition*

move out if another has bought it but he has *jus personale* regarding the lessor. The Romans said a sale breaks a lease; that appears to be unjust but it is not for in a lease I have only *jus personale* {personal right} and not *reale* {in a thing}, but if I have made a contract to live there, e.g. three years, then if it is sold I must ask for my *hypothece* {mortgage} and this creates an easement for the owner. If I have *jus personale* and I want to demand compensation, then it must be determined in the *pactum*. Otherwise the *pactum* is *incertum* {uncertain}, i.e. *pactum sub resolutione resolutiva* {a contract with uncertain resolution}. In every *pactum onerosum* {onerous contract} there is exchange. Everything in *pactum onerosum* is trade and trade is either barter or sale. Barter is thing for thing and sale thing for money. If I *statuire* {determine} with someone *usum rei* {use of a thing} yet in such a way that he gives me the thing back in kind {*in genere*} it is *pactum de mutuando* {contract for loaning for consumption} or a loan for *mutuum* {consumption}. To these belong *res fungibiles* {fungible things}, things which are either consumed in use or are those whose use consists only in being *alienando* {alienated} which thus cannot be given back *in genere*. In loaning for consumption[a] *mutuatarius* {the borrower} is not *dominus* any sooner than after the transfer[b] when one has a right through the *commodatio* {the loan} to a thing *in specie* immediately after accepting; if the *mutuatarius* loses the money he is still obligated to pay it for it is called *res interit domino* {the thing perishes while I am owner} and *mutuatarius* is here the lord over the money but not the *commodatarius*. The *mutuatarius* {borrower} thus has *deterior conditio* {a worse condition} than the *commodator* {the lender}. The use of a thing is *beneficium* {a benefit} i.e. *commodatum* {a thing loaned}, or[c] *onerosum* {a burden}, as *locatio conductio* {letting and hiring}. So it is with money and every other thing which can be repaid in kind {*in genere*}, I can loan something for consumption[d] *gratis* or *pro certo pretio* {for a certain price}. *Pactum quod pro usu rei mutuae pro aliquo pretio sit* {a contract that is for the use of a thing for consumption at a certain price} is *usura* {a loan for interest}.[e] *Pactum de mutuando sub usuris* {a contract for loan for consumption under a loan for interest} is *foenus usurarium* {interest on a loan for interest}, *usuratitium*.[f] It is interest.[g] We call interest what would be given *in specie* for the use of *rei*. How far does the right to require *pretium* {a price} from each for the use

27:1362

---

[a] *mutuation*   [b] *tradition*

[c] KI: *oder*, following Achenwall. KS, MS: *und*, for "and"

[d] *mutuiren*

[e] Strictly, the Latin *usura* translates as usury, and means a loan for interest. The contemporary connotation of usury as illegally high interest rate would distort Kant's meaning.

[f] *usuratitium* is ungrammatical and does not occur in Achenwall. It could be read as *usura titium*, for "a loan for interest to Titus."

[g] Kant has two words: *Zins, Interesse*

of a thing extend? It extends to infinity for *uti partes de jure suo disponunt, ita jus est* {as the parties rightfully dispose of what is theirs, so be it}. It must only not contradict the rights of humanity. Thus there is in *jus naturae* no *usurarium limitatio* {limit on a loan for interest[a]} or *praetium* that is too high. That cannot[b] be right in ethics but this does not matter in *jus*. The valuing here is each particular evaluation. The Indians say that taking ten percent is virtue, thirty a burden, twenty common, and one can also get benefits from high interest, but in *jus* one must not[c] really talk about benefits.

I act through another if his action can rightfully be seen as mine. This occurs when I empower him to take my place. The one who is authorized to do a thing is *mandatarius* {agent}, the one who empowers him is *mandans* {mandator}. The full power is *mandatum* {a mandate} and the empowering is *demandatum* {mandating}. If someone does something for another by his will and in his name then *mandans* is to be considered as the source of the thing. *Mandatum* represents the person of another. He must not exceed his *mandat*, if he does he is considered the originator of the excess. *Mandatum* can be *beneficium* or *onerosum* {a benefit or a burden}. I can act for another *gratis*, also *pro pretio* {for a price[d]}. The last is a type of *locatio conductio*. But one always views a *mandat* as a part of a *pactum gratuitum* so that one calls *pretium* {the price} not *merces* {a payment} but an *honorarium*. In *merces* I determine the labor and can coerce it. But in *mandat* a lot is left up to circumstances and to conscientiousness which of course one cannot coerce; thus *mandatarius* always bestows on the other a part of *beneficium*. He can thus act in accordance with a rule but he could perhaps act in more ways than that. So one pays professors, attorneys, tutors, etc. *honoraria*.

27:1363

Tit: X.

De cautione

{Of guarantee}

Cautio {a guarantee} is a *pactum* {contract} which can be included in all the others in that it gives security to a *pacti* {contract}. I do not acquire any right but do acquire the security of my right which I possess, thus it is still a type of equivalent. Every *pactum* could[e] include a guarantee,[f]

---

[a] KI: *limitationem*. KS: *promittentem*, for "promise in a loan for interest." MS: unclear
[b] KI: *nicht Recht*. KS: *Recht*, for "That can be an ethical right but not in *jure*"
[c] KS: *nicht eigentlich vom*. KI, MS: *nicht eigentlich nicht vom*, for "not really not talk"
[d] KI: *propretio*. KS, MS: *pro patio*, for "taking on a burden"
[e] KI: *können*. KS: *kann*, for "can"   [f] *Gewährleistung*

an oath[a] (juridical guarantee[b]). It is a promise to protect someone from a particular wrong. That is *cautio in specie* {a guarantee in particular}; whoever promises security is the *promittens* {promiser} of the other, the *creditor* for the other.[c] Every *cautio* is *pactum sub conditione suspensiva* {a contract with a suspensive condition}. In the event that the wrong occurs I will hold you harmless. *Conditio suspensiva* is *eventus incertus* {an uncertain outcome}. It has the intention of an already established right. The right of *cautio* against the *cavens* {guarantor} is *jus subsidiarium, in subsidium juris alterius* {a subsidiary right, one that reinforces the other right}. The immediate *debitor* is *principalis* and has *jus principale* {the right of the main party}. Thus here *creditor* has *jus principale* and *subsidiarium* {subsidiary right}. *Cautio* is always *conventio accessoria* {an accessory convention} and is only for confirmation of *conventionis principalis* {the principal convention}. The right that I have toward everyone due to a guarantee[d] only exists if *jus principale* exists. E.g. suppose I have also made a *pactum* in which he is supposed to sell me a stolen item and another takes precaution,[e] then *jus subsidiarium* {the subsidiary right} is missing because *principale* {the principal right} is void. In a *factum illicitum* {illicit deed} there is thus no guarantee.[f] Because in *factum illicitum* I acquire no right, I cannot have been promised security for it. Here I act wrongly. *Conventus accessoria, quae conventu principali invalide accedit, ipsa est invalida* {An accessory convention that is invalidly added to a principal convention is itself invalid}. *Conventus* whose *object*, that is *conventus principalis*,[g] is null and void is itself void. *Jura subsidiaria* {subsidiary rights} are constituted in a thing or a person, the first occurs though a security deposit which yet gives him no right to use the watch[h] but serves only for my guarantee,[i] or it is a person who secures for me my right in another, this latter is warrant,[j] *fide jussio*. If *debitor principalis*[k] {the principal debtor} is not rendered what he is due, he, *fidejussor* {the one entrusted}, will render whatever I promise *creditor* in its place. A security deposit is *pignus*. The *fidejussor* is only obligated to render it *in subsidium* {as a subsidiary}. The other cannot demand it of me but first from *debitor* and if he does not do it then I go to the guarantor.[l] One cannot immediately approach the guarantor. He is not liable for the money but for the security. If *creditor* has applied all possible means then he can go to the guarantor. The 27:1364

---

[a] *jurament*   [b] *caution*

[c] KI: *ist des andren promittens, der andre creditor*. KS: *ist des andren creditor*, for "is the creditor of the other"

[d] *caution*   [e] *cavirt*

[f] *caution*   [g] KS puts these four words in parentheses

[h] Kant is using a pocketwatch as an example of a security deposit, or pawn.

[i] *caution*   [j] *Bürgschaft*

[k] KS: *principalis*. KI, MS: shortened *princip:*   [l] *caventen*

139

fidejussor tenetur {the one entrusted is bound} if *debitor principalis* does not pay, *fidejussor liberatur* {the one entrusted is freed} if he does pay the money for the *debitor*. It is a promise that *debitor* will keep his promise. *Pignus* {security deposit} is that through which one establishes a *jus in re* {a right in the thing} that if I do not pay he can make payment through the thing. The thing through which someone creates a right and indeed merely *in subsidium* {as a reinforcement} of the right of another is *pignus*, *res oppignorata* {a thing given as a security deposit}. *Haec pignatore obligatur* {this is binding on the one giving the security deposit}. *Debitor* is the one who gives the security deposit. *Creditor* the one who accepts it. The latter has exclusive right in the thing. Either the thing comes into the hand of *creditor* or not and is given to him only as security, the first is a *pignus stricte* {security deposit in the strict sense}, and the other *hypotheque* {mortgage}. I cannot have a house but only a mortgage[a] given me by someone under my own control. There is *detentio* {detaining} in *pignus* {a security deposit} and he has the right not to give the thing until he has the money; in the case of *hypotheque* he must ensure that if the *debitor* does not give it to him he still receives it. The *creditor* does not have *jus utendi fruendi* {the right to enjoy use of the thing}. If instead of the loan for *usura* {interest} he gets the use of the thing, that is *antichresis* {antichresis}. When the *debitor* pays, then *hypotheque* will be dissolved, *luitor* {will be paid}, free, and thus also the *pignus*. It can be paid only to the one who accepts the security deposit. But is the *debitor* free from it if the creditor sells the security deposit? He has a double right in the *debitor* and the person, the security deposit is only *subsidium* {a reinforcement}. If the creditor sells the security deposit and does not receive as much as he has given then he has a right to demand the difference from me. His right against the *debitor* {debtor} always remains. But couldn't one arrange it so that if the debtor cannot pay the creditor no longer has a right to that? That is possible. But in *jus* that is not customary. *Cessione pignoris, debitor non liberatur* {the debtor is not released with the surrendering of the security deposit}. If I give my security deposit to another so that if I do not pay he has no claims on me, then *debitor* is free upon giving the security deposit. In this case he has not given the thing as *subsidium*. It would really be *pactum de retrovertendo* {a contract of exchange}, a kind of *emtio venditio* {buying and selling}. I reserve the right to buy it back. I have only three kinds of promise: 1) *res (dominium)* {the thing (ownership)} 2) *usus (salvo dominio)* {use (retaining ownership)} and 3) *custodia* {custody}. I can promise everything *gratis* and then it is a) *donatio* b) *commodatum et mutuum* {loan and loan for consumption} c) *depositum*, but also promise through *pactum onerosum* and then it is 1) *emtio venditio*, *permutatio strictius dicta* {buying and selling, and exchanging in the strict

---

[a] *hypothequen*

sense} 2) *locatio conductio et foenus* {letting and hiring, and interest}, if I give money 3) *pignus* {a security deposit}. – In *pacta gratuita* I promise everything *in utilitatem alterius* {for the benefit of another}, in *onera* {onerous ones} everything *in utilitatem meam* {for my own benefit}. In *pignus* the bearer of the security deposit has *jus in re* {a right in the thing} to make payment on his security deposit as far as it reaches but also *jus in persona* {a right in the person} to coerce the one who gives the security deposit to pay the rest if the security deposit is not sufficient. There can also be a *pactum* in which the other demands nothing from me if I do not release the security deposit but that would be *pactum de retrovertendo* {a contract of retroversion}.

Tit: XI.

De juramento

{Of oaths}

27:1365

I can make an affirmation[a] in presumptuous ways in which I invoke things for punishments which are not in my control. Affirmations show the attentiveness and the importance which one places in the truth and the consciousness of all that which belongs to truth. If affirmations are holy they are *juramenta* {oaths}. If a human being does a wrong and the judge knows it then he must punish *ex officio* {out of duty[b]}. A human judge can often lie that he does not know it. But when I have done it and the judge knows it, it is absurd[c] if I say, "I will to be punished." Your volition does not help here at all, if the deed is proved then you will be punished whether you will it or not. People[d] say, "May God punish me if I lie" but that is nonsense for God will punish me even without me saying that. Perhaps, however, one may understand it this way, "I will renounce all requests for forgiveness and pardon if I lie." For some human beings also believe the greatest sins can be forgiven. But that is also presumptuous. He cannot renounce anything except what he has a right to.[e] Answering prayers is a beneficent act of God and further I cannot know whether I will be able to keep my promise in the future. Atheists cannot swear. But Plutarch says, "I would rather believe in no God than in one who forgives all vices for with the former there still remains a feeling of right and wrong but with the latter I can perform misdeeds and yet become holy if I only ask for forgiveness."[34] The atheist cannot believe he will become happy through vice, but one who believes in God can

---

[a] *betheuren*
[b] alternative: "from the office," i.e. the judge has the power qua judge
[c] *lächerlich*   [d] *Die Menschen sagen*
[e] *als wozu er Recht hat*

commit vices and yet still think of becoming happy. The habit or belief that I can ask for forgiveness for everything is the ground of *fides* {the belief} that in this case I renounce asking for forgiveness in the future. That is the most harmful principle for the world, and supposing it were true would it not be something appalling to get a human being to take an oath? A human being would thereby be completely damned. An oath thus runs completely contrary to the principle of morals. One swears by things which one does not have in his control. So Christ (Matthew) says "you swear by your head but you can make no hair black and white."[35] An oath also does a juridical wrong. The *creditor* is compelled to believe in the conscientiousness of the *debitor*. It would be much safer if each judge spoke in accordance with the circumstances. I am not obligated to believe the other is conscientious and if someone coerces me to do this he does a wrong to me. An oath serves for nothing but *terriculamentum* {a means to create terror in the mind}. Sensibility is put into a state of terror and a human being will know that God is already punishing it[a] this way. The Tungusi swear by laying bear paws on the head and saying "may a bear kill me if I" etc. Negroes swear to a fetish, which are sometimes bird feathers, that it should break his neck.[36] The Romans said one can swear by any superstition but to swear by a religion is too holy. Every human being even when he is innocent may thus be reluctant to swear, he feels the wrong. There is *juramentum promissorium* {an oath of promising} and *assertorium* {of assertion}, *assertorium* is always difficult. *Juramenta promissoria* are not valid, they are not to be and cannot be held to like oaths of office. *Perjurium*,[b] perjury,[c] falsehood in *juramentum assertorium*, and *pejeratio* {false promising}, falsehood in *promissarium*. If one is disposed with *promissum juramentum* to hold to everything, but he has not considered that he cannot hold to it, then that is not as culpable as *juramentum assertorium*. But if he knew ahead of time that he could not hold to it then it is just as culpable. Here the *magister* must swear[d] that they will not attribute any errors to Aristotle.[37] In England the clergy must swear to 39 articles of which no one accepts a third.[e,38] Oaths belong to ethics and not to right. I am obligated to view no one as evil if he has not been proved evil. One must judge in accordance with the circumstances of the case. If the swearer in this case has no conscience then the oath is invalid and it serves only as a means to create *terriculamentum* and there is still

27:1366

---

[a] KI: *daß sie*. KS: *daß*, for "that God is already punishing in this way." Grammatically the *sie* cannot refer to "human being" but only to "sensibility"; otherwise in this context the former is possible.

[b] KI, KS: *Periurium*. MS has only "Pe" with blank space.

[c] *Meineid*

[d] *beschwören*, here and in next sentence   [e] KS: *3e*. KI: *sie*, for "which no one accepts"

the question whether I can coerce someone to an oath in accordance with the rights of humanity. An impartial witness could get one to swear and sharpen his conscience but not one who is partial.[a] For indeed the incentives are conflicted in him and where am I then obligated to believe that this incentive will be outweighed?[b] One can also judge with regard to the circumstances of things and that is much more difficult. *Juramentum obligationem vitiosam non sancit* {An oath does not commit one to an obligation to perform a vice}. If someone has been coerced into making a promise strengthened by an oath is he obliged to keep it? Ethically yes but not juridically for the *promissor* has no right to demand it of me because he can acquire nothing *in injusta* {unjustly}. Otherwise one wrongs humanity in that one robs it of the means for one to save oneself through a promise in a case of necessity. An oath strengthens[c] consciousness of the obligation but the obligation does not become any greater. If the promise does not give an obligation then neither does the oath.[d]

Tit: XII.

De successione in bona defuncti[e]

{Of succession to the goods of the deceased}

Bona {goods} are all *res* {things} to which we have *jura* {rights}, the totality of the *bona* {goods} is *patrimonium* {that which can be inherited}. Should I die ownership ceases and another succeeds, that is the *successio in bona defuncti* {succession to the goods of the deceased}. The legitimate *successor* is *haeres* {the heir}. I can take control of *bona defuncti* {the goods of the deceased} as *res nullius* {unowned things} but then I am not *haeres*. *Bona defuncti* is the estate[f] and the right of inheritance[g] is the right to succeed *in bona defuncti* {to the goods of the deceased}. When the *dominus* dies, then either he states who will succeed him, in which case he had disposed *de futura[h] haereditate* {regarding the future inheritance}, or he has not made any disposition. Now the question is whether I can dispose *de re mea in eventum mortis* {of my things in the event of my death}. My will is void if it is not active. Then it is a mere wish. Thus after my

---

[a] *der Interesse hat*
[b] KI: *diese Triebfeder überwogen werde.* KS: *diese Triebfedern überwogen werden*, for "these incentives will be outweighed"
[c] *roborirt*, based on Latin *roboro*   [d] *jurament*
[e] Achenwall has simply *De successione*   [f] *Erbschaft*
[g] KI: *Erbrecht.* KS: *Erbschaft*, for "inheritance"
[h] KI: *futura.* KS: *sartura*, for "regarding the inheritance about to be settled"

27:1367　death I can give nothing to him. In this case I have a mere wish and not a practical will. But mere wish does not give a right. After death my faculty of desire cannot give rise to anything. But if he cannot dispose of anything at all, i.e. if he dies *intestatus* {intestate}, then his things are all *res nullius* {unowned things}. There is no lawful *successio in bona intestati* {succession to intestate goods} but instead the thing is *res nullius* and the first can take control[a] of it. Yet nevertheless children follow the parents in inheritance, as we will see later. But the author, who falsely contrasts the *status naturae* {state of nature} with the *status socialis* {social condition}, says about this that no relative has any special right to inherit. If someone disposes it can occur either *per pactum* or *contra pactum*. The former is *bilaterale*, the latter *unilaterale*. In a *pactum* it is necessary that it be *bilaterale*. The *dispositio per pactum unilaterale* {disposition through a unilateral contract} is *testamentum* {testament}. It is a mere declaration through which someone is appointed as heir. *Pactum bilaterale* is *onerosum* and *beneficium*. The author says that it is understandable how someone would inherit through *pactum successionis*, for I already make myself obligated here in my lifetime and it cannot be revoked if he has not made it revocable, the other thus acquires *pacto* {contractually}. But how can one inherit with rightful force through a *testamentum?* There has been no *pactum*. The *testans* {testator} can always revoke it during his lifetime so *successor* has no right during the lifetime. If he has no preferential right in the lifetime he also has no right after the lifetime of the *testator*. The Romans were right that one would be able to inherit through a testament. Of course the *testator* always had the ability to renounce it and the other has then no right to acquire it, but if he just[b] did not take back his word the other has the right, which is namely *jus in re jacente* {right in the thing in abeyance}. This right is the right to choose whether I will or not in an exclusionary way, and here no one could possibly waive it because he has complete freedom regarding it. In *articulus mortis* {the moment of death} the promise of *testator* still exists and now *successor* has *jus in re jacente* even if he has not accepted it. The difficulty is here due to the *voluntas simultanea* {simultaneous will} which simply cannot exist. But *jus in re jacente* and *promissio* can exist at the same time. The Romans named it *haereditas jacens* {inheritance in abeyance} when one has still not accepted the inheritance. Through the death of *testator* the promise becomes irrevocable. Thus one always looks at the last will. The decision of yes and no, and that is *jus in re jacente*, is accepted by all. *Testamenta non sunt juris naturae* {testaments are not under natural right} say the author

---

[a] *occupiren*

[b] KI: *wenn er nur aber sein Wort nicht zurückzog.* KS: *wenn er nun aber sein Wort zurückzog,* for "but if he now took back his word"

and others because *promissio* cannot be simultaneous with accepting and thus there would be no[a] *translatio dominii* {transfer of ownership}. But I receive here *jus in re jacente* and taking control[b] of it is not necessary for it cannot be waived by anyone because one offers freedom and each wants to be free. If someone makes a testament then the *promissio* always extends *in articulo mortis* {up to the moment of death} when it becomes irrevocable. *Irrevocabile promissum jus in re jacente* {irrevocable promise [leads to] a right in a thing in abeyance}. If I have promised something with the addition that it will never be revoked then the other still has not acquired but he has a right to take from another. The author takes inheritance *per pactum successorium* {through a contract of succession} as valid and not *per testamentum* {through a testament}. But if the latter is not possible then neither is the former for he cannot say, "If I cease to be   27:1368 then the things should not be mine any longer." But that follows already. For the thing is already not mine and I cannot dispose past a point of time when the thing is no longer mine. The *translatio* is when I cease to be *dominus*, through this the other becomes *dominus*. The *translatio* occurs *laeso dominio* {to the detriment of the ownership}. But here the *dominium* as *domini* {owner as owner[c]} is not wronged for he would retain it until death, thus there is a contradiction.

Tit: XIII.[d]

De praescriptione

{Of prescription}

There is *successio in bona alterius* {a succession to the goods of another} about which one presupposes that he has forsaken it. In death one does not go willingly but one does in abandonment.[e] Nonetheless it is still *analogie*. If *derelictor* {the one who abandons} has not made any *pactum* someone could still succeed *per occupationem* {by taking control}. This is why it is attached to [the discussion of] *bona defuncti* {the goods of the deceased} as an *Appendix* [by the author]. The *defunctus* {deceased} cannot remain *dominus* of the thing or, in the case where the one he had specified had not accepted *bona* {the goods}, keep another away, but

[a] KS: also has *besteht*, for "and thus no *translatio dominii* would obtain"
[b] *occupation*
[c] KI: *dominium als domini*. KS: *dominium des domini*, for "ownership of the owner"
[d] In Achenwall the section *de Praescriptione* is not a separately numbered section but, as Kant notes in his lecture, an addition to the previous section *de Successione*.
[e] *derelinquiren*

derelictor can do this because one also presupposes that he is alive. I possess something in *bona fide* {good faith} without knowing that another has the thing. For I possess it *putative* and my *possessio* is no *vitium* {fault}. If I possess something for a long time and the rightful[a] *dominus* has known it and is also able to know it then the question is whether I have not attained *jus quaesitum* {a right of claiming} through the length of the possession because the prior *dominus* has not spoken against[b] it and one can here assume that he has thereby abandoned[c] it. But I cannot presuppose a consensus because my opinion of the will of another would then impose[d] an obligation on another. I say he is obligated to declare that the thing ought to be his. But no one is obligated to declare his will regarding the continuance of his ownership. Yet the ownership endures until proven otherwise, and declared by him; I can prove ownership but not its opposite. He is thus also not *in culpa* {negligent}. *Praescriptio* means abandonment of the property on the part of the old owner ____[e] is *jus acquirendi* {the right to acquire} a thing that possesses a *dominus putativus* {putative owner} who thereby becomes *merus dominus* {unqualified owner}. How much time should elapse until the *dominus putativus* can acquire it? That cannot be determined in *jus naturae* and a *pactum* that is indeterminate with regard to time is invalid. According to *jus naturae praescriptio* is nothing; that it is found in *jus civile* {civil law} is based on the following:[f] in the civil condition[g] one wants to have the security that one does not have in the *status naturalis*. For *possessor putativus* there must still be a time when he would be able to secure his right, otherwise his heirs could thereby still[h] suffer. In *status civilis* it is necessary that there be prescription or a statute of limitation. Otherwise all rights would be uncertain. In *jus naturae* this ground is not valid for then I can expect no security. If something is supposed to be right in *civile jus* {the civil law} it must at least be possible in *jus naturae*, and it 27:1369 is that. For us prescription is set at 30 years. We do not know the genuine owner of any land and all are *domini putativi*. Thus there would be no security of right if there were no prescription. This is a principle[i] in *status civilis* but not *naturalis* {the state of nature}. For the time in prescription is arbitrary and arbitrary legislation cannot occur in *status naturalis*.

---

[a] *rechte*   [b] *contradicirt*
[c] *derelinquirt*   [d] *kontrahire*
[e] MS has blank space between *Eigenthümers* and *ist*. Neither KI nor KS suggest any obviously missing words.
[f] KI: colon. KS: period   [g] *Civilzustand*
[h] *noch* missing in KS   [i] *princip*

Tit: XIIII.[a]

De modis, quibus jus et obligatio tollitur[b]

{Of the ways in which right and obligation are removed}

The right and obligation of a person do not cease after his death. *Mors adimit omnia jura et liberat ab obligationibus* {Death annuls all rights and frees from obligations}. Some rights can be transferred. They are *jura transmissiva* {transmissive rights}. I can let another live in my room in my stead. So it is with most rights. But a few *jura* cannot be transferred, such as the right of a father toward his child by which he can require deference from him, the right of a husband toward his wife, the right of an author that his work is his he cannot transfer to another. Regarding an author we think the thoughts always still belong to him even when he is already dead. *Jus non transmissibile* {a non-transmissible right} is *jus personalissimum* {the most personal right} from which *obligationes personalissimae* {the most personal obligations}. In these right and obligation depend on the person. *Jura transmissibilia non exstinguuntur morte domini* {Transmissible rights are not extinguished with the death of the possessor} also[c] *obligationes* {obligations}. If I have *jura transmissibilia* on which an obligation depends then obligation is also transmissible because it depends on the thing. If I bequeath a house that is encumbered with debts to someone then the heir must also pay the debts. If the heir accepts the inheritance he also accepts the debts; he must state beforehand the limitation that he does so under the condition that he will pay no more debt than the inheritance itself covers. A right to a particular thing,[d] *jus in rem* {a right in a thing}, *perit pereunte re* {is lost with the perishing of the thing} or when the use ceases. If something has vanished or even more so been burnt then my right ceases. When *utilitas rei meae* {my use of a thing} ceases through *factum injustum alterius* {another's unjust deed} then indeed I do not have *jus in rem* but *jus in personam* {a right in the person} regarding an equivalent of the thing. He must replace the *damnum* {damage}. *Casus* {chance} is an *eventus* that does not arise from a free human choice or at least not the choice of those involved for it requires an *eventus involuntarius* {involuntary event[e]} that one could not foresee and prevent and which is the cause of *damnum* {damage}. Blind

---

[a] The roman "XIIII" is used in MS instead of "XIII" in Achenwall because Feyerabend mistakenly numbered the previous section *De praescriptione* as Tit: XIII.

[b] Achenwall has *De modis quibus jus et obligatio ex pacto contracta tollitur*, "Of the ways in which right and obligation having been contracted are removed from a contract."

[c] KI: *auch*. KS: *sind auch*, for "are also"   [d] *Ein Recht auf eine bestimmte Sache*

[e] KT: *eventus involuntarius*. KS: *eventus involutus*, for "surrounding event"

fate can ruin my thing, this is called *res mea perit casu* {my thing perishes by chance}. Here I have no *jus in laedentem* {right regarding the harm} at all. From this follows the proposition *casum sentit dominus* {the owner carries the risk} because he has no recourse.[a] If the thing is in the possession of a *non dominus* {non-owner} and the thing is ruined[b] *casu* {by chance}, this is called *casum sentit dominus* {the owner carries the risk}. Thus *casum sentit deponens sed non depositarius, non mandatarius sed mandans, non commodatarius sed commodans* {the depositor, not the one who receives the deposit, carries the risk, likewise the mandator not the one who receives the mandate, the lender not the borrower}. Not the bearer of the security deposit but the one who gives the security deposit. For otherwise they would have to have settled beforehand that the *acceptans* has to bear the loss. The proposition *casum sentit dominus* {the owner carries the risk} is a principle[c] for the administration of right *coram foro externo* {in the public realm}. *Casum sensit is, in cujus utilitatem aliquid datum est* {He for whose use something was given carries the risk[d]} is *principium coram foro interno* {the principle in the private realm}. The latter is a principle[e] of equality. To *jus strictum* belongs *facultas moralis quem cogendi* {the moral means of coercing someone} and that the grounds are externally declared and so externally valid. If that is not so then it is *pactum incertum* {uncertain contract}. For *pactum certum* is when *consensus* is sufficiently external. So for *commodatum* {a loan} I can indeed presuppose that *commodans* {the lender} merely lends to me and does not want to bear the loss if it is damaged. But if he has not declared that then it is *pactum incertum*. *Commodatarius* {the borrower} could say, "I did not accept it under that condition and how is it now determined how much ought to be paid?"[f] The *commodans* must declare that he will not bear the loss, then it is understood that *commodatarius*, if he accepts it, bears the loss himself. The *commodatarius* is not required to declare, but he who has a use for it must declare, but *coram foro interno* {in the private realm} is otherwise. The *commodans* lends that *in utilitatem alius* {for the use of another} and I cannot assume that he should also bear the responsibility for loss himself. He will not bear any more loss himself in order to please me. For it could be that *commodans* is richer and *commodatarius* poorer. Each views it as an obligation and if one is poor and the richer one bears the loss then he sees it as a *pactum beneficium* and wants the other to give him a good word. Here I do not acquire *lege* {by law}, otherwise it would have to follow from what came before. If one knew that *commodatarius* considered it obligatory that *commodans* must bear the loss then no one

[27:1370]

---

[a] *cedenten* [b] *interirt*

[c] *Grundsatz*

[d] KI: *Casum sensit is*, "he carries the risk." KS: *Casum sensilis*, for "the perceptible risk"

[e] *princip* [f] KS: question mark. KI, MS: period

would ever lend anything to anyone. The judge cannot do otherwise in accordance with strict right yet he sentences in accordance with equity. But I cannot coerce for equity. But equity could influence legislation and one could make laws that harmonize with equity, but in the administration of the laws I cannot use equity. One would separate *praestatio debita*, i.e. *solutio* {fulfillment of the debt, i.e. the resolution} from obligation. Obligation is canceled. It can also cease if I become as much *creditor* as I was previously *debitor*. If I were to give something to someone equivalent, but *creditor* and *debitor* must agree. Compensation,[a] when the *debitor* deducts from the *creditor* that for which the latter is responsible to him. This requires *consensus* of both. *Compensatio* is called *in solutum* {having been resolved} for both. *Liquidum* {liquid [debt]} cannot be compensated for by *inliquidum* {non-liquid}, not a bill of exchange for an obligation, for a bill of exchange is *liquidum, obligatio illiquidum* {an obligation is non-liquid}. An illegitimate delay in fulfillment[b] is *mora* {default}. In *jus* {right} it is *laesio* {wrong}. *Debitor est in mora* {a debtor is in default} if he cannot pay in a determined time. The reminder that he is in *mora* is *interpellatio*, a demand for payment.[c] Demand for payment is not necessary in itself. *Debitor non interpellatus tenetur ob moram* {The debtor not having received the demand is still in default}. *Mora* is wronging the *creditor* through the illegitimate delay[d] of the *debitor*. Demand for payment is not necessary, the *pactum* already obligates him. If the *creditor* does not take it at the time when *debitor* offers it, then *debitor* has paid the debt and he can then deposit the thing anywhere. For then he does everything   27:1371 that is in his control, namely if he takes leave of possession of a thing the *creditor* can take it up if he wants. One who releases the debt, *aliquid dandum aut praestandum* {any giving over or performance}, rescinds. That is here a new *pactum*. The *debitum* is canceled if somcone says, "I will never demand it of you," then it is a juridical release by which he cannot sue[e] him. The *pactum de non petendo* {agreement not to sue} transforms the strong right into an imperfect one. Then I still certainly expect payment but only from his [sense of] equity. Release from an obligation is acquisition of a right. Through a new *pactum* a prior one can be annulled. *Pactum posterius derogat prius* {the later contract limits the earlier one}. So it is with *remissio debiti* {rescinding of debt}. But if I have promised something in an oath then can a second *pactum* break the oath? But the oath is only conditioned and the oath is only a confirmation.[f] But a second can absolve no one of obligation. The clergy believe they have a right to

---

[a] *Gegenrechnung*
[b] KI: *Aufschub der praestation*. MS: blank space instead of *Aufschub* before *der praestation*. KS: suggests *Gebrauch der praestation*, for "use of fulfillment"
[c] *Mahnen*   [d] *dilation*
[e] KI: *verklagen*. KS: *anklagen*, for "accuse"   [f] *roboration*

absolve one of an obligation to which one had sworn with the strongest oath because they believe they are able to forgive sins. The *obligation* can be reduced by another as long as it concerns *quoad caussam et modum debendi* {the provisions and the manner of the debt} yet in a way so that the *debitor* and *creditor* remain; this is called *novatio* {novation}. When I am indebted to someone on the basis of an I.O.U.[a] and afterward on the basis of a bill of exchange. *Assignatio* {assignment} is when *debitor* changes[b] and *creditor* remains the same. The one for whom the other substitutes in his place is called *assignator* {assignor}, the one who is substituted *assignatus* {assignee}. When the *assignatus* does not pay[c] *assignator* always still remains *obligatus*. *Expromissor*, substitute debtor, is the one who promises that he will pay in the place of the other. For I am no longer *debitor* and *expromissor* has taken my obligation upon himself. That is delegation, when I put someone in my place as debtor, *expromissor* is *delegatus* {the one delegated}, I, *delegans* {the delegator} and *creditor*, *delegatarius* {the subject of the delegation}. Through delegation *debitor* is changed. Through the cession *creditor* is altered, which is the abdication of a right of *jus personale* to a second. One can cede his rights. Rents are *jura personalia* {personal rights} according to the *jus romanum* {Roman law}. *Pactum* is here called *cessio*, the first *creditor*, *cedens* {the ceder}, the second *cessionarius* {the cessionary}. Can I cede *invito* or *inscito debitore* {with the lack of consent or the ignorance of the debtor}? Yes. My right in his person[d] is not *obligatio personalissima* {the most personal obligation}. But if other rights of *debitor* are wronged thereby, then it is different. Is *debitor* freed from all obligation toward *cedens* as *creditor*? Yes, those are *modi* {the ways} through which *obligatio* is transformed or canceled.

27:1372

Sect: IV.[e]

Jus naturale belli

{The natural right of war}

Tit: I.

De modis jus suum persequendi

{Of the ways of obtaining one's rights}

We have talked about the *acquisitio* that we attain *facto justo alterius* {through the rightful deeds of another}, now we want to talk about acquisition that we attain *facto injusto* {through a wrongful deed}, that is,

---

[a] *Handschrift*
[b] reading *verändert*. KI, KS, MS: *vermindert*, for "diminishes"
[c] KS inserts a period here   [d] *Mein Recht an seine Person*
[e] Sect. III in Achenwall

jus cogendi {a right of force}, or *coactionis illicitum contra laedentem* {a right of coercion against unlawful wronging[a]}. If someone does violence to me[b] then we act rightly if we coerce him but if he does not do anything wrong then it is wrong for us to coerce him. Coercion is a hindrance of freedom which is possible in accordance with universal laws. A hindrance to a hindrance to universal freedom increases universal freedom and so is right. Each *laesio* {wrong} is a coercion and hindrance to freedom and counter-coercion is thus right. If someone infringes upon my rights, does not fulfill his *obligatio*, does not repay me for a loss inflicted on me, then I can coerce him with force.[c] *Actus quo jure meo utor contra laedentem* {An act which I rightfully use against a wrong} is called *jus suum prosequi* {a right to pursue what is mine}. *Instatu civili* {the civil condition} that occurs through a trial, *instatus naturalis bello* {in the natural state of war} through war. A wrong[d] that I prevent through force must not be preventable in any other way except through force; otherwise it is also unjust,[e] that is, *laesio indeclinabilis* {unavoidable wrong} is always presupposed. How certain is the right of *laesus ad universum laedentem* {the one wronged against everyone doing wrong}? It is *jus infinitum* {an unlimited right} for in general one cannot fix how far he should go but he must go so far as is necessary to defend his right. How great and strong the violence must be I must leave up to him, he does not do the least wrong to the *laedens* {one doing wrong} even if he kills him when he has no other way to defend what is his. One can practice force secretly and publicly, whichever is the one the *laesus* finds most convincing, although the latter appears to be more commendable. *Declaratum*[f] *propositum, laedenti vim inferendi* {declared intent to use force against the one doing wrong} is *hostilitas. Status hostilitatis mutuae per vim manifestam* {the state of mutual hostility through openly displayed force} is *bellum* {war}. For *laesum* {having been wronged[g]} makes appropriate *contra laedentem jus bellicum* {a right of war against the one who wrongs} to proceed[h] according to a declared or undeclared *propositum* {intention}. If the *laesus* {the one wronged} does not need defense against *laedens* {the one who would wrong him} then it is not war. We could thus conceive of a just war for one party and a just enemy. I cannot go to war against anyone unless he has wronged me. The possibility that he could wrong me is not a ground. *Intentio laesionis* {the intention to wrong}. When I know about this can I

---

[a] reading *coactionis*. KI, KS: *coactio ist*, for "or coercion is something unlawful opposed to wrongdoing"
[b] *mir Gewalt thut*
[c] *Gewalt* rendered as "force" in this section unless noted
[d] *laesion*   [e] KI: *ungerecht*. KS: *unrecht*, for "wrong"
[f] MS has blank space. KI suggests *declaratum*, following Achenwall. KS provides no words but inserts a period and begins a new paragraph with *propositum*, leaving out "declared"
[g] KI: *laesum*. KS: *laesio*, for "wronging"   [h] *agiren*

consider it as a *laesio* {wrong[a]} and use violence, e.g. if he gets equipped for war?[b] *Jus belli contra hostem injustum est infinitum* {The right of war against an unjust enemy is unlimited}. I must be able to use any available means to coerce him and cannot in this way ever wrong him. For if a means were to be excluded then its use would be wrong and he would have had the authorization to *laediren* me, which is *contradictio*. I have a right to use his goods, his person, and his life as a means to my own. Through war I can also acquire something and *occupatio bellica* {taking control in war} is *modus acquirendi patrimonii laedentis* {a way of acquiring the patrimony of the one wronging me}, he further has *jus indemnitatis* {the right of indemnity} of the *laesus* {one wronged} that he should make good all damages which can be done either *restitutione rei ipsae ablati* {through restitution of the thing taken} or their equivalent *quod satisfactio est* {which is satisfaction}. But the damage must *injuria datum* {have been inflicted as a wrong}. In this regard *principabiliter* {principally} the *laedens* is first obligated to restore,[c] and if that cannot be done then *in subsidium* {as reinforcement} to give satisfaction. The amount of *satisfactio* is based on the judgment of *laesus* {the one wronged}. The one who initiates the *laesio* {wrong} is *aggressor*, the one who begins hostilities is not always *aggressor* for in *bellum* the one being *laesus* has *jus praeventionis* {a right of prevention} to initiate hostilities. *Melius est praevenire quam praeveniri* {It is better to prevent than to be prevented} is a rule of prudence. *Juridice* {juridically} this *defensio* is war, *bellum laesi contra laedentem* {a war of the one wronged against the wrongdoer}, and *laedens* engages in offensive war *contra laesum* {against the one who is wronged}. In a military sense the defender is the one who does not initiate hostilities and the other is offender. Besides the right to require restitution, *laesus* also has a right *poscendi securitatem, de non laedendo in futurum* {to be able to have security that he will not be wronged in the future} for the *laedens* is *laesionem intentans* {threatening wrong} until he has obtained security. I can, however, conduct a war in such a way that I greatly weaken him, that is *bellum per vindictum* {a war of vengeance} when *bellare* {waging war} is *dolosum* {malicious} so that he is so frightened or so weakened that I do not have to fear him anymore. But if someone wrongs me *culpose* {negligently} or *inculpose* {non-negligently} then I can also wage war against him to compensate for the damages but I cannot practice *ultio* {vengeance}, for that would only serve to get him to renounce *animus laedendi* {the intention to wrong} but here he has not had *animus laedendi*. *Hostilitas* {hostility} goes no further. Bare right[d] without the aim of security but intending

27:1373

---

[a] KI: *als eine laesio*. KS: *mich als ein laesus*, for "consider myself as one wronged"
[b] *er Zurüstung macht*　　　　　　　　　[c] *restituiren*
[d] *Bloße Rechte* with singular verb. Perhaps *Macht*, "power," is intended.

to ruin the other is unjust and *laesus* receives a[a] right to defend himself. If he compensates me for all damages and promises security then all of my right is fulfilled. One says this is true *in thesi* but not *in hypothesi*, i.e. one can indeed give a rule in general but not determine how it should be applied in particular cases. Generally I can say[b] I must or can coerce the enemy until I am compensated for the harm to me etc. But in particular cases it is hard to determine how far this should go. *In casu* {in the event} a particular judgment must still be applied. *Qualität* is determined through a rule of *qualität* not *quantität*. In war I can seek help but *auxiliator hostis injusti* {the helper of the unjust enemy} is to be seen as *laedens* {a wrongdoer}. *Neutral* is one who helps neither of two powers engaged in a war. The question "Is it permitted to be *neutral* or must everyone stand by those who appear to have a right?" presupposes that we are obligated not only to remedy injustice but also to increase universal justice or *status externus* {an external state}. It appears that we must also think about universal justice but in the *status naturalis* no one is authorized to set himself up as judge over another. Defense of life and limb is an application of my legitimate force[c] to prevent force by another who might endanger my life, that is *inculpata tutela* (an inculpable protection}, self-defense. How far is this allowed? The right is *infinitum*, I can use all types of violence[d] against him; none is too much or too strong against him. It extends up to *internecio aggressoris* {killing the aggressor}. The jurists believe that in the *status naturalis* a human being must limit himself to the point where it just reaches[e] *defensio*, i.e. *moderamen inculpatae tutelae* {moderation of inculpable protection[f]}. That means only that I should not use external violence needlessly if a lesser degree is all that is necessary. That is right in accordance with ethical laws. In accordance with *jus strictum* I can never be obligated to treat another that way if he threatens my life. In *jus naturae* I am not obligated to use a moderate means for here *moderamen inculpatae tutelae* is not valid. But in the *status civili* it is, for the state can require of me a writ of preservation.[g] But if my death is possible, although uncertain, the state cannot give any law at all to make me limit[h] myself, for 1) The greatest punishments that the state can give are not greater than the ill that I presently face. The law cannot deter me on this account. Such a law would be absurd. 2) Such a law would be unjust, for where the state cannot defend me neither can it order me. Thus the state can command me because it protects me. It forbids me from using force because it promises to keep me safe from the force of others. In a

27:1374

---

[a] KS: *ein*. KI: *nun*, for "now"
[b] KS adds *ihn*, "to him"
[c] *Gewalt* in this paragraph
[d] *violenz* in this paragraph
[e] KI: *gereicht*. KS: *reicht*, for "suffices for"
[f] The literal translation of the phrase that stands for the restricting of violence to reasonable limits in self-defense.
[g] *Erhaltungsbürgen*
[h] *moderiren*

case of aggression if there is a means which is certain to obviate the need for force, then I can be limited.[a]

Insults[b] are *laesiones bonae aestimationis* {wrongs to a good reputation}. There are real and verbal insults. The following constitute satisfaction: 1) that he did not intend to insult[c] me, that is *declaratio honoris* {a declaration of honor}, 2) *decantatio revocatio* {revocation of what was said}, apology, if one admits that he did have that aim and asks for forgiveness. This is not belittling, 3) *recantatio*, recanting, when he says that he lied, here his insult to me is recompensed by his insult to himself, i.e. thus already punishment by *jus vindicandi* {right of vindication} or *evincendi rem* {of recovering the thing}. If someone possesses something *absque jure* {without right} and *proprietarius possessionem* {the proprietary possessor} excludes *rei suae a possessore injusto* {an unjust possessor from something that is his} it is *evictio* {recovery[39]}. Now the author talks about the circumstances under which someone can be *possessor putativus* {putative possessor}. What kind of *proprietationes* would he have against *possessor bonae fidei* {a possessor in good faith}? He has a right to demand the thing and also all the fruits which he still has. *Locupletior* {richer} is one who has more than previously. One who is *locupletior re alterius* {richer through another's thing}, from that which belongs to another, or *ex re alterius* {from another's thing}, when he draws out the fruits of the land for his own benefit yet which the previous possessor did not yet have. *Possessor bonae fidei re alterius* {A possessor in good faith of another's thing}. He must surrender all fruits which he has but he does not need to give back the ones he has eaten or consumed. No one can become *locupletior damno alterius* {enriched through another's loss}. By *fructus consumtos* {consuming the fruits} I am not *locupletior*. For this judgment[d] it is presupposed that *possessor* possesses *rem injuste* {a thing unjustly}. Thus he is obligated to place the true *possessor* back in possession. If *possessor* is *injustus* but not *dolosus* {malicious} then he can have become *locupletior* through the possession either *re alterius* {through another's thing} or *ex re* {from another's thing}. E.g. if one has 10 bushels of grain and sells it as 11 then he has become *locupletior ex re*; this *possessor* must restore the *res* to the genuine *possessor* and all fruits that he still has. But if *possessor* is *dolosus* then the rule holds that *tenetur facto* {he is bound by the deed}. He must be held to the restitution *omne quod interest domini* {of everything that concerns the owner} i.e. 1) *lucrum cessans* {the missing profit}, 2) *damnum onerosum* {onerous damages}. The first means all advantages which the owner could have in it. If, e.g. through cunning someone has come into

27:1375

---

[a] *moderiren*
[b] *injurien*. KI: new paragraph. KS: continuous text. MS ambiguous
[c] *laediren* [d] *dijudication*

possession of a garden whose owner has gone away on a trip, then he knows the benefits which the owner could have derived from it. Afterward he must restore the benefits but also *damnum* {damages} which have been done to the garden in that time. A *bona fide possessor* {good faith possessor} is obligated only[a] to provide the amount that he became *locupletior* {enriched}, either *re* {itself} or *ex re* {from the thing}, and to restore only as many of the things as are there, he is not required to restore *damnum* {the damage} *emergens deteriorationem* {from deterioration}. *Dominus rem vindicans* {the owner claiming the thing}, however, must compensate for the damages of *possessori putativo* which arose from the acquisition of the thing. E.g. I unknowingly buy a horse from a *non domino* {non-owner}. My *factum* is *injustum* {deed is unjust[b]} and in a *factum justum* {a just deed} I can lose nothing. Indeed *dominus* has the right to demand the horse from me but I also have the right to demand indemnification from him. True, *dominus* does not bear the guilt of *possessore putativo*, instead the thief does. Roman law[c] has worked this out very well and our law errs in this and accords with the English law. In England the *dominus* {owner} must give indemnification to *possessori putativo*, from this it would follow that the *jus in re* {right in a thing} does indeed have limitations. *Jus in re* is the *jus in possessorem* also *possessoris bonae fidei* except for the condition that *dominus* would have to restore the *dominium* {the property} to the *bona fide possessor*. The *bona fide possessor* cannot become *locupletior* but neither can he become *deterior* {poorer}. He has *jus indemnitatis* {a right of indemnification}. The latter is grounded in the nature of the thing, the former on convenience. From this it actually follows that every *dominus* is only *dominus putativus*. The *debitor* is required to meet[d] a certain deadline. If he does not then a new right against the *debitor* arises for the *creditor* because he sins *in mora* {in delay} (*debitor morosus* {a wayward debtor}). He must pay *lucrum cessantem* {the missing profit} and *damnum emergentem* {resulting damages}, *tenetur ad interesse morae* {he is obliged to pay interest for the delay}. Whoever does not keep to his promise gives the one who accepts *promissario* {the promise} a right *exigendi ad praestandum omne quod interest* {to demand of the provider everything that was in his interest}. Now he has *jus optionis* {a right of option} whether he wants the *pactum* extended or not. *Praestatio evictionis* {completion of recovery}. If someone has bought something *absque culpa* {without culpability} from another who is a *non dominus* {non-owner}, then according to Roman law the true owner also has to claim[e] it. Roman law still endures in the right to coerce the *non dominus* {non-owner} *ad praestandam*

---

[a] KI: *nur*. KS: *mir*, for "to me" (twice in this sentence)
[b] Presumably *justum* {just} is intended   [c] *römische Recht*
[d] *praestiren*   [e] *vindiciren*

evictionem {until the recovery is provided}. In *jus civile* one is allowed to obtain a promise for recovery[a] to have security even when the seller promises to replace the damage resulting *e re vindicata* {from the thing claimed}. If I buy, e.g. a house, I do not know whether there are any debts attached to it; consequently the seller must promise recovery. If I have that then I am secure so long as the promise itself is right.[b] It is customary to put that in the formal contract[c] but it is useless for in accordance with *jus naturae* it is already understood.

Tit: II.

De modis lites finiendi

{Of the ways of determining lawsuits}

A dispute,[d] *lis*, is *in sensu juridico* {in the juridical sense} the reciprocal opposition of rights which one has against another. *Jus praetendere* {to allege a right} is to claim a right to something that another has. A falsehood through which some harm is done is *falsiloquium*. Protesting[e] is a declaration that another's practices are wrong. *In statu civili consensus* is inferred from the withholding of the protest. All litigation[f] occurs *in jure certo* or *incerto* {in certain or uncertain right}. The first is if it is certain that one of the two is due the right. But it is apparent that no lawsuit can arise over this, thus the concept *in jure certo* is itself *laesio* {wrong} and the other can exercise force[g] over him as over a *laedens* {wrongdoer}. The mere litigation alone is thus a wrong.[h] The *laesus* {the one wronged} can demand that *laedens* {the wrongdoer} be held responsible for all costs. Thus a lawsuit is allowed only in *jus incerto* or *dubium* {uncertain or doubtful right}. If there is any doubt *modus jus prosequendi* {the way of prosecuting the right} cannot occur with force. One who uses force *in jure dubio* {in a doubtful right} is thus *laedens* {wronging}. Whoever initiates a legal action against me *in jure dubio* wrongs me. He must first provide grounds. If I am not persuaded then the legal action is allowed to begin. *Onus probandi* {the burden of proof} is the obligation to prove something because that is always difficult. Whatever does not need to be proved is *in jure connato* {in right innate} and one is not required to prove his innate right. If there is a lawsuit over that then the one who initiates the lawsuit must prove it, e.g. something is demanded of me, I am supposed to supply some labor to him. Here I am not

---

[a] *eviction* in this paragraph   [b] *richtig*
[c] *contract*
[d] *Streit*, rendered in this section as either "lawsuit" or "dispute"
[e] *protestation*   [f] *Rechtsstreit*
[g] *Gewalt*   [h] *laesion*

obligated to him so he must prove it. I base[a] it *in jure meo connato* {on my innate right}. If someone claims that I must know something then I base it *in jure connato ignorantiae* {on the innate right of ignorance}. A lawsuit over a *jus acquisitum* {acquired right} can be either about *veritas facti* {the truth of a deed} or *injustitia facti* {the injustice of a deed}. Now if *factum* is uncertain who should prove it? The one who denies[b] an action through which he has incurred an obligation is not obligated to prove, in accordance with the *jus connatum* that no human being has by nature any obligation to another. The one here who denies that the other has acquired a right against him is also not required to prove it; he bases it on *jus connatum ignorantiae*. But if *factum* and *justitia* {justice} are doubtful then the rule must hold *adfirmanti factum dubium et neganti, justitiam incumbit probatio* {proof falls on the one who asserts a dubious deed and denies justice}. *Possessor* is never required to prove, he grounds himself on his innate right that he does no one any wrong. The *onus probandi* {burden of proof} lies in each case on the one who wants to have something decided against the *possessor*. *Possessor* always has priority. This is the basis of the rule given by unscrupulous lawyers: *Fac et excusa* {act and then make excuses}. The proofs of a *factum* {deed} are 1) if one has seen the *factum*, 2) produces a witness or 3) *instrumente* {documents}, or 4) takes an oath. If there is a lawsuit that does not allow for a decision, at least not without great difficulties, then the settlement of the lawsuit follows and this is either friendly where each one gets something or else one of them relinquishes his right completely (*compositio litis onerosae* {resolution of an onerous lawsuit}). One can also 27:1377 reach the resolution[c] of a dispute through the judgment of a third. It would be constituted by him voluntarily. His judgment is called arbitration. The *pactum* through which he is named arbitrator[d] is called *receptio* {arbitration}. *Superarbiter* would be one who judges about rights of distinction.[e] One can further decide by drawing lots. Assemblies, *colloquia* {meetings}, *tractatus* {negotiation} etc. also contribute to the ending of a dispute. The *mediator* is not *arbiter*, but assumes the place of both parties and seeks a way to support and to reconcile them. He must thus be impartial. The *litigantes* {litigants} are not obligated to let it rest by the judgment of the *mediators*; the latter has only attempted to see whether he would be able to find a path to a resolution.[f] The *litigantes* have a right to coerce the other to a settlement.[g] If neither of the *litigantes* relinquished their demands then *bellum* {war} ensues. In the *status naturalis* it is legitimate since neither of them is obligated to let it rest on the

---

[a] *fundire*
[b] *negirt*
[c] *composition*
[d] *Schiedsrichter*
[e] *Unterschiedsrechte*
[f] *composition*
[g] *transaction*

judgment of another. Then no other judgment remains except the use of force.[a] *Alter jure aggreditur, alter jure resistit* {one attacks by right, the other resists by right}. How both should have a right to war is paradoxical. The one who is coerced to back down from the dispute is called the vanquished. Now the question arises whether *utrum victoria finiat litem* {victory may end the dispute}? One must see here whether force would have the right to settle the dispute. The vanquished foe has certainly lost the power to seek his right but not yet the right itself, he has not surrendered his right. For this there must be *pactum vi extortum* {an agreement extorted by force} yet which is *validum*. Earlier we spoke of *pactis vi injusta extortis* {contracts extorted by unjust force} which are *invalida*. War has here arisen from *justus aggressus* {rightful aggression}. Every war is considered as a means to seek his right; whenever a superior coerces the other into a valid *pactum* then he attacks him with *justo aggressu*. The *pactum pacis* {the peace pact} is thus considered as *pactum vi justa extortum* {agreement extorted by just force}. The concurrence of the vanquished is at its basis only a formality. A province is seized and the subjects[b] swear allegiance. Are they now obligated not[c] to turn in a spy? This question can also be raised without any oath of allegiance for the victor has ordered this allegiance based on the idea. We will see later, however, that every procedure[d] in the *status naturalis*, consequently also all war, is wrong.

Libr: II.[e]

Jus sociale universale[f]

{Universal social right}

I et Tit: I.[g]

Jus sociale universale in genere

{Universal social right in general}

The name of this second book is unfortunately inaccurate for there can also be societies in the *status naturalis*. Here is the appropriate place to answer the question, "What is a society?" It consists in the unity of many

---

[a] *Gewalt*　　　　　　　　　　　　　　　[b] *Unterthanen*

[c] KI: *keinen Spion*. KS: *einen Spion*, for "obligated to turn in a spy"

[d] *Verfahren*

[e] The second part of Achenwall's two-part *Jus Naturae*, Kant's copy of which survived and his notes in which are included in *Kants gesammelte Schriften* volume 19, begins here.

[f] Achenwall has *Jus sociale universale speciatim jus societatum domesticarum* {Universal social right, in particular the right of domestic societies}.

[g] The name given is for the Section. The name of Title I is *De societate in genere* {Of society in general}.

persons in order to attain an abiding end. The supreme law of a society   27:1378
is the well-being of the society. *Salus civitatis suprema lex est* {The welfare
of the city is the supreme law}. Permanence is the supreme law. So *salus
societatis* {the welfare of society} does not consist in every *socius* {mem-
ber} becoming rich but in the continuance of the society. One could say
status socialis suprema lex est {the endurance of the society is the supreme
law}. Here we must always look to the form. The true *bonum commune*
{common good} is *status socialis*. Every society can be a voluntary or a necessary society. A society between parents and children is *societas necessaria*
because the parents have rights over their children which they acquire
lege non pacto {by law not by contract}. Whatever is acquired *lege* is what
follows from other laws and does not require a new *pactum*. Marriage as
a society is voluntary. We will see later that *matrimonium* {marriage} is
necessary and a society cannot subsist *per societatem*. Every society which
thus has unity has authority[a] over *socius* {member of society}. The society
has duties to every *socius* {member} and every *socius* to the society. *Jura
socialia* {social rights} could be either internal or external. Such a society is then called *persona moralis*: a person *in sensu practico* {in a practical
sense}. –

Tit: II.

De societate aequali

{Of equal society}

All societies are either equal or unequal; the one who determines all
duties is called *imperans* {sovereign} or *superior*. *Inferior* is the one who
is obligated to act in accordance with the will of the *imperans*. *Imperans*
is a member of society. God and human beings therefore do not stand in
society. The *leges societatis* {laws of society} are called *conventiones*. *Pacta
conventa*[b] are thus those that were established at the founding[c] of the
society. *Jus pacti conventi* is *perdurabilis* {permanent}. A *votum* is declaration of a member of society regarding his will, whether his will is in conformity with the will of society. *Votum deliberationis* {a deliberative vote}
is one which has no obligation to the remaining *socios* {members of soci-
ety}. This *votum* is only required for better deliberation. It is thus to be
distinguished from *votum decisionis* {a deciding vote}. Something is *con-
cludirt per majora* {decided by majority} or *per unanimia* {unanimously[d]}.
In Poland there is no conclusion unless every *socius* is in agreement. In
every society there is an *imperium* and that is treated in [the next section].

[a] *Gewalt*
[b] literally "contracts agreed to" but refers to foundational agreements
[c] *bei Errichtung . . . gestiftet sind*
[d] KI: *per unanimia*. KS: *per mandata*, for "by mandate"

Tit: III.

De societate inaequali

{Of unequal society}

The *imperans* {sovereign} can be either the entire society itself or a member of it. Supreme authority to give a law is called *potestas* {authority} and the obligation to give obedience, *obedientia*. *Imperium* {sovereignty} is thus a genuine prerogative. *Imperans legibus a se latis, non tenetur* {The sovereign is not subject to laws he himself has given}. The *imperium superioris in subditum* {sovereignty of a superior over a subordinate} is either *despoticum* or *temperatum* {despotic or restrained}. *Despoticum*, if it extends to all actions and times; we can well call the latter *patrioticum* 27:1379 {patriotic}. If we consider *subditum* {the subordinate} as subordinate to *imperans* in all his actions; he is a slave. Every society has a right to punish that falls on the sovereign.[a] Punishment is not as a power that maintains *subditi* {subordinates}, it is *vindicta societatis* {society's revenge}. Punishment occurs only where there is an intentional violation of the laws. *Laesio dolosa* {malicious wrong} is the ill that is punished. The *maleficus* {criminal} must make amends[b] either through an action or through suffering,[c] the latter in particular when he is sentenced to death. Can a *factum inculpabile* {inculpable deed[d]} be punished? If one calls that which only has the aim of improving *laedens* {the wrongdoer} "punishment" then the one who *culpa* {negligently} wrongs must also be punished. The *corrective* punishments are usually milder.

Sect: II.

Jus societatum domesticarum[e]

{Right in domestic societies}

Tit: I.

De matrimonio

{Of marriage}

Societas domestica encompasses 1) *matrimonium* {marriage}, 2) *parentalis* {parental}, 3) *herilis* {of a master}. *Matrimonium* is a society between man and woman[f] who unite with one another for the business of procreation.

[a] *imperanten* [b] *satisfaciren*
[c] *Leiden*
[d] KI: *inculpabile*. KS: *culposum*, for "negligent deed"
[e] Achenwall has *Jus societatum domesticarum universale*, followed by one paragraph introducting the three-fold division for the subsequent Titles.
[f] In this section, *Mann* and *Frau* are translated as man, woman, husband, or wife according to context.

But they enter into sexual society not merely for the business of procreation but first for the use of their sexual organs. That is called *commercium sexuale* and it is *pactum licitum* {a permissive contract}. The husband can offer his sexual attributes to no one else but the wife[a] and she hers to no one else but her husband. *Pactum matrimoniale* {the marriage contract} is something voluntary. The man can make no other use of his sexual attributes except in society with the other sex. All violations of this type are *crimina carnis contra naturam* {carnal crimes against nature}. But is *pactum* into which one enters with the other sex completely voluntary?[b] The jurists consider it as completely voluntary. *Matrimonium* is *contractus commercii sexualis continui et mutui* {a contract for recurring and mutual sexual intercourse}. Is it permissible for a woman[c] to be able to place her sexual abilities into service by contract?[d] A person who has promised [this] cannot be punished.[e] She is a human being not a thing. I can place myself into service by contract only for labor, it is a duty that no human being can dispose over his own self. Is marriage thus also impossible? No, this is the single exception, and that because the man acquires the woman and the woman the man in return, thus they acquire themselves back again; for this reason *nullum sexuale licitum commercium, nisi matrimonio* {no sexual intercourse is permissible except marriage}. This is now based on the ethical rule according to which a human being cannot alienate himself.[f] A *matrimonium* is possible if both partners are beyond the procreative years for the use of sex always remains. If one partner is incapable of sexual intercourse then it is called *casum sentit dominus* {the owner carries the risk}. From all of this it follows that *concubinat* would be wrong and polygamy is likewise annulled[g] and so also polyandry, which is found in Tibet. The *jura* {rights} of married people[h] are *personalissima* {the most personal rights}. From this it also follows that marriage can be dissolved. The *delictum* {offense} through which alone a marriage can be terminated is called *adulterium*.

27:1380

Tit: II.

De societate parentali

{Of parental society}

Quaestio:[i] Do parents acquire children through procreation? Is procreation thus a *modus acquirendi* {way of acquiring}? I acquire a calf with the

---

[a] KS: missing *als der Frau*
[b] *arbiträr*
[c] *Frauenzimmer*
[d] *verdingen*
[e] *Eine Person die versprochen hat kann nicht poenitiren.*
[f] *sich selber nicht veräußern kann*
[g] *aufgehoben*
[h] *Eheleute*
[i] KI: *Quaestio*. MS: sign for *Quaestio*. KS: omits *Quaestio*

161

cow, and this is also the way a man would have to acquire a child with his wife. But I[a] cannot acquire a rational being and a child is a rational being and it thus never belongs to *dominus* {an owner}. From this it follows that parents are not able to expose or harm their children. Hence procreation of children is not *modus acquirendi*. Children acquire all rights. The rights of parents regarding their children are not grounded on procreation. The child is genuinely in the *status naturalis* {state of nature} and bears no obligation to anyone. Thus it is also quite wrong for one to have thanked God for being the cause of mere existence; mere existence is still not that for which one ought to be thankful. The rights of parents regarding their children are based on their own obligations.[b] They produce[c] the child in order to make the child's existence happy. They have produced the child, this is *actus*; if they do not care for the child then they wrong the child just as does someone who brings someone who is asleep to an unsafe place. They have a right against the children to everything which is necessary for the fulfillment[d] of their own obligation. To the children belongs obedience to the parents. The rights of parents cease when the children are in a state in which they can care for themselves. Consequently after this the children can lead the kind of life that they want. Do parents have a right to demand a return of the costs of upbringing? In no way, for what they have done they were responsible for *lege* {by law}. Anyway most parents raise their children out of love. Consequently they do more than what their *stricte* duties obligate them to. But they are not to demand reimbursement for it. What concerns *tutel* {guardianship} [in the book] is very simple.

Tit: III.[e]

De societate herili

{Of the society of a master}

Domestic labors[f] are those that are necessary for domestic life. A *subject* who is obligated to perform domestic labor for his keep[g] is called *famulus* {a servant} and *superior famuli* {the superior to the servant} is called *herus* {master}: *hera* {mistress}. *Famulus* can be obligated *ad omnes praestandas operas per totam vitam* {to provide all his labors throughout his entire life} or to particular labors *per spatium* {during intervals}. In the

---

[a] KI, KS: *kann ich nicht.* MS: *kann nicht,* for "a rational being cannot acquire"
[b] KI: *Verbindlichkeit.* KS: *Verbindlichkeiten,* for "obligations"
[c] *procreiren* in this paragraph
[d] KI: *Erfüllung.* KS: *Erhaltung,* for "maintenance"
[e] Achenwall also has Title IV: *De familia* {Of the family}, which Kant skips.
[f] *Die häuslichen Arbeiten*   [g] *Unterhalt*

first case the *famulus* is *servus* {a slave} and *herus* is *dominus* {owner} but 27:1381
in the latter case he remains *famulus* (a servant[a]). The *herus servi* {master of the slave} is to be looked upon as *despot*. Is it possible to acquire the *famulus* as *servus* {slave}? *Per delictum* {through an offense} it is possible for through this he loses his rights. A *servus* is subject to *dominus* in everything. The author admits that *servus* cannot be mutilated or sentenced to death because he has his natural rights. He can never relinquish his natural rights, otherwise he ceases being a person. If he makes himself obligated *ad omnes operas perpetuas* {for all his works in perpetuity} then life, limb, etc. are included. Slavery is therefore impossible in *jus naturae*. A *servus ultroneus*[b] {voluntary slave} and a *servus obnoxius* {slave through liability}, the latter is one who is made into a slave, especially in war. A career criminal has brought it upon himself by his principles. Are the children of such *servi* who are born into slavery also *servi*? The author says that the child is *servus* until such time as he can pay back the cost of his upbringing. The child comes into the world, has a claim for upbringing, and is thus never obligated to give back the costs of upbringing.

Libr: III.

Jus civitatis universale speciatim[c]

{Universal right of the state in particular}

Sect: I.

Jus publicum[d]

{Public right}

Status naturalis is not in contrast to *socialis* but to *civilis*. In order for a judgment or right to be valid for another we need in addition an explicit[e] condition in which what is right for everyone is determined externally. *Status naturalis* is the one and only state where *leges externae* {external laws} are observed. Here many different opinions about right are possible and it is thus a condition[f] of childhood, *status justitiae privatae* {a condition of private justice}. *Status naturalis* is thus one of

---

[a] *Dienstbote*
[b] MS: blank space between *Ein servus* and *und obnoxius*. KI, KS: suggest *ultroneus*. KS: also retains blank space after *ultroneus*
[c] Achenwall has *Jus civitatis universale*, *speciatim*, and *Jus publicum universale* {universal public right} on three separate lines.
[d] Achenwall has *Jus publicum universale in genere*
[e] *apparter*　　　　　　　　　　　　　　[f] *Zustand*

bellum justum {just war} for if each one seeks his right then nothing can be settled except *bello* {through war}. Thus *status naturalis* is not always *pacis* {peaceful}. It is not voluntary but necessary to leave *status merae justitiae privatae* {the condition of mere private justice} and enter *in civilem* {into the civil condition}. *A natura* {by nature} a human being is not obligated to enter with another into *societatas civilis*. If I assume that the nature of a human being is just, i.e. that as such a human being would not have the intention to wrong anyone, then I would posit that all human beings would have the same insight into right and the same good will and *status civilis* would not be necessary. But since what we have now is just[a] the opposite, each does have the right to attempt to get others to leave *status naturalis*. Otherwise no human being is secure because each can have a different opinion about right. E.g. I have a right to seek security consequently I can coerce each to enter the state where each is secure. This state is *status civilis*. It is indeed not an absolute duty but only a condition in that it holds only if we stand in *commercium* with others. I work a field; another says, "What is the basis of your claim to it? Do you also have a right?" He can coerce me to give him security for his rights. Universal security develops when human beings make a universal right, set up a judge, and provide him with authority. Hobbes is completely correct on this when he says *exeundum est e statu naturali* {one must leave the state of nature}.[40] How does civil union[b] develop? One must not start it from a *facto* {deed}. An original *contract*, which is an idea that lies necessarily in reason, grounds all civil unions. One must represent all laws in a civil society as given through the consent of all. The *contractus originarius* {original contract} is an idea of the agreement of all who are subject to the law. One must test whether the law could have arisen from the agreement of all, if so then the law is right;[c] the supreme legislator must thus be one who can do absolutely no wrong. Now if human beings unite with one another then they can do no wrong; consequently the law is so constituted that it is not wrong, for the will of all is the law. They are all legislators.[d] There also can be no other possible case where a law could be just. Thus every law which does not arise from concurrence is unjust for this alone is the supreme legislator who can do no wrong, the supreme legislation is thus by those who comply with the law. Now it is not in question whether human beings have ever come together for this aim and have made their laws this way. Laws given by a despot could be just if they are made so that they could have been made by the whole people. A law can thus not possibly be just if a despot

27:1382

---

[a] KI: *nun eben das Gegentheil.* KS: *nun das Gegentheil,* for "now is the opposite"
[b] *Verbindung*   [c] *richtig*
[d] *Gesetzgeber*, lacking either *der* or *die* ("the") could alternatively be singular

places taxes[a] on merchants but exempts his favorites from them. It is not necessary that he judges whether the people in this case would have made such a law but whether they could have made such a law. *Legislator* is *summus imperans* {supreme sovereign}, *souverain*. The *souverain* is thus the people. What is the end of a *republique*?[b] Some say happiness, but that is as false as it is false to say that God created human beings for their happiness. The end of a *republique* is administration of right. Not individual happiness but the state of public justice is its main point. The *summus imperans* is always the people, the individual person who is *summus imperans* is only *repraesentant* of the people. Otherwise one also calls the *souverain* αὐτοκρατής {an autocrat}. Are the people authorized to scrutinize the rightful authority of the *souverain*? If we are talking about a group of human beings who still do not constitute a commonwealth then they are in the *status naturalis*. Such human beings still always have a right to ask why another wants to rule them. Yet *status civilis* is possible only through a *pactum subjectionis* {contract of subjection}. Whoever does not attain to *imperium* through this *pactum* is *usurpator imperii* {a   27:1383 usurper of sovereignty}. But if a group of human beings does constitute a people who are already in the *status civilis* can they still ask about the legitimacy of the *summus imperans*, thus also about the *pactum subjectionis*? This allows of an answer to some extent. Where the people are once in the *status civilis* they have a *summus imperans* {supreme sovereign}. Should the people now want to judge the *summus imperans* {supreme sovereign} then there would be two parties, the people and the *summus imperans*. *Questio* {the question is[c]} who now should decide? Certainly the *summus imperans* who has the power.[d] If the people want to judge the *summus imperans* then they would have no *summus imperans* but they themselves would be it and after that it would be a *democratie*[e] for he would have to cease being *summus imperans*. *Salus reipublicae* {the welfare of the state} does not consist in the ease[f] of each *individuus* for the state of nature is not the state of unease but of injustice. Consequently the *status civilis* ought to be a state that ought to prevent injustice. *Status reipublicae* {the condition of having a state} is thus freedom and indeed as public freedom and this must be the aim of the *imperans summus*. Each ought to be as happy as he can be, but the duty of the *imperans* must be to establish public justice. *Summus imperans* is thus either the people themselves or the *repraesentant* of the people. Who is the ruler? The *executor* of the

---

[a] KS: *Abgaben*. KI: *Aufgaben*, for "duties" or "tasks"
[b] This French word for "republic" will remain untranslated in italics.
[c] KI: *Quaestio*. MS: sign for *Quaestio*. KS: Z.E., for "e.g."
[d] *die Gewalt*
[e] The French words *democratie*, *aristocratie*, and *monarchie* will remain untranslated in italics.
[f] *Gemächlichkeit*

general will[a] of the people. Genuine *souvereneté* rests in the people. But the government or the exercising of legislative power can be either in the people, and then the state is a *democratie*, or it is in a single person, and then it is *monarchie* and the ruler *monarcha*, or it is in *collegium* {a council}, and then it is *aristocratie*. Even here there is no difference in legislative power but only in the governing authority.[b] The *monarch* is not one who can command generally but the one who does not stand under the law. There must be one who executes all laws. The *monarch* who also gives laws is also *souverain*. In England legislative authority rests in the people, the nobility, and the king. Here the king can do no wrong because he is the supreme *executor* of the law. But although he is not subject to the laws he is still not above the law. If the people represent themselves then the government is democratic. This is the basis of the idea of the supreme will. Even in *democratie* itself there must be a few who represent the people. In *aristocratie* the nobles[c] represent it. Types of government are in their basis one and the same. The government is always good where laws are given that the whole people could have given. One type of government is as legitimate as the other. Another question is of efficiency. This is difficult to decide. Human beings are so corrupt that they always make themselves exceptions to the rules. Mixed types of government appear to be the best. Governing is called the idea of realizing a *status civilis*.

27:1384

Sect: II.

Jus publicum universale absolutum

{Unconditional universal public right}

Tit: I.

De potestate legislatoria, executoria et inspectoria

{Of legislative, executive, and oversight powers}

One can divide the *potestas legislatoria* {legislative powers} into *rectoria* {governing} and *dijudicaria* {dijudicating}.[d] The last two stand under the first and constitute the government and the form of justice. Now what authorizations does the *souverain* have? Can he determine the law regarding particular citizens? Can the *monarch* administer his state himself? He cannot. He must have [civil] servants[e] for that. He can also

---

[a] *die allgemeinen Willens*
[b] *der gesetzgebenden Macht ... der regierenden Gewalt*
[c] *Vornehmen*
[d] *Die potestas legislatoria kann man unterscheiden in rectoria und dijudicaria.*
[e] *Diener*

not judge, for that he is in need of magistrates.[a] The *souverain* lowers[b] himself beneath his dignity when he exercises *actus* of *administration* and decisions regarding *jurisdiction*, for majesty rests in the holiness of his person and holiness in turn rests on his will always being just. Whoever administers stands under law. Indeed it can even be said of such a person, "You do wrong." To administer right[c] is also against his majesty for the judge stands under laws. He can judge only in accordance with the law and be coerced to judge that way. *Voluntas imperantis est irrepraehensibilis* {The will of the sovereign is without blame}, thus his law is *lex civiliter valida* {valid civil law}. It is *positive* {positive [law]}. Everyone in a people is either *subditus* {subordinate} or *civis* {citizen}. In the first case the *imperans* is despot. *Civis* is a subject but not *subditus*. He is to be treated as if he is governed in accordance with his own will. Accordingly a *monarch* can rule over subjects just as over citizens. The laws must be promulgated.[d] *Imperans* has the right to abrogate laws, also to exempt someone from laws. An exception[e] *in casu singulari* {in particular cases} is immunity. One asks whether *summus imperans* can give dispensation from observance of the laws? *Privilegium* is to be distinguished from immunity; through the latter someone is given dispensation from observance of his duties, through the former a new right is granted to him, both can occur in conformity with the universal will. The *summus imperans* alone has the right to interpret his laws and the judge to apply them. The interpretation made by the legislator is called *interpretatio authentica* {authentic interpretation}. Interpretation is either extensive or restrictive. *Interpretatio doctrinalis* is given by scholars about a doctrine with the aim of knowledge.[f] The former is irresistible and thus also has *vis executoria* {executive force}. *Imperans* further has *potestas inspectoria* {oversight power}. He can make inquiries if something is hidden from him.

Tit: II.

27:1385

De jure circa munera et dignitates civiles et circa reditus publicos

{Of right concerning civil posts and positions and concerning public revenues}

All *negotia publica* {public roles} are either *negotia majestatica* {roles connected with majesty} or *officia civilia* {civil offices}. *Negotium publicum* is an

---

[a] KS: *Magistrate.* KI: *Majestäte*, for "majesty"
[b] KI: *erniedrigt.* KS: *bringt*, for "gets control over his dignity"
[c] *Recht zu sprechen* [d] *publicirt*
[e] *exemtion* [f] *in scientifischer Absicht*

office. A civil servant is *persona publica*, which is in contrast to the private person.[a] Goods of the commonwealth are *publique*[b] – or private goods; *reditus* (revenues) are two-fold. The goods which serve for maintenance of the ruler and his household are called *domainen* and for maintenance of the commonwealth *bona publica* {public goods}. Revenues of the *imperans* himself are called his personal *fiscus* {treasury}. All *reditus*[c] {revenues} are either *onera* {burdens} or *tributum* {tribute}.

Tit: III.

De potestate judiciaria et jure armorum

{Of judicial power and the right to arms}

Summus imperans {the supreme sovereign} has *jus armorum* {the right to arms}. He has the right to ensure inner as well as outer security. Which[d] right does the ruler have to care for the happiness[e] of the people? This is only an imperfect duty. His perfect obligation is to care for the security of his people. The subjects may afterwards themselves think of their happiness.[f] It must not remain unsaid that he does not rule over children but over citizens, thus each can already care for their own happiness.[g]

Tit: IV.

De jure circa facultatem publicam[h]

{Of right concerning public resources}

The happiness of the state must always be differentiated from the happiness of particular members. The state thrives when it is in complete security. Its happiness consists in its continued survival. Its imperfect duty is also to care for the happiness of each private citizen. For this it must have guards[i] in order to manage inner security. It must have armies in order to create outer security.[j] There must be money in the land. The state can thus impede foreign products from being brought in. But whether it can entirely forbid this is another matter. Even so there is the question whether the right to forbid emigration belongs to the

---

[a] *Privatpersonen*
[b] This French word for "public" will remain untranslated in italics.
[c] reading *reditus*. KI, KS, MS: *onera*, for "all burdens are either burdens or tributes"
[d] The remainder of this paragraph appears to belong to the following Title on happiness.
[e] *Glückseligkeit*, assuming copyist error and conforming with the context. KI, KS, MS: *Sicherheit*, for "security"
[f] *Glück*   [g] *Glückseligkeit*
[h] Achenwall has *circa felicitatem publicam*, "concerning public happiness"
[i] *Wachen*   [j] entire sentence missing in KS

rulers?[a] One cannot comprehend why a citizen should not be free and should enter into any union that does not please him.[b] Citizens alone have rights against each other. Then they could say to the others, "You cannot leave and expose those who stay behind to the danger of being attacked." The right to do that is in any case still very ambiguous. It lies in the nature of freedom that each must put a value on[c] his labor himself.

Tit: V.

27:1386

De jure circa religionem et ecclesiam

{Of right concerning religion and the church}

Rights regarding religion. *Summus imperans* cannot have more rights than the people themselves as a whole have. Now do a people have the right to keep their accepted religion always in one perpetual form without alteration? A people cannot do that. Religion always ought to give vigor and *effect* to our will. Thus it is natural that we must endeavor more and more to increase our insights. They would thus have to renounce all knowledge already attained. The *souverain* can thereby neither command nor forbid any religion. He also cannot stop human beings from avowing their religion. Thus it follows that he can indeed protect the ruling religion and appoint teachers but he can make no law that would place any religion in a state of inalterability. The dogmas of a religion are no concern of the state. But were they to be such that they contradicted the rights of humanity then the state could get involved in them. But suppose a clergyman later followed other insights and put forward a doctrine that contradicted his *contracte*? His contract[d] does not say that he may not think otherwise but only that he may not speak otherwise; he has the obligation to conceal[e] it but not to pretend.[f] In the meantime he is not obligated to teach something opposed to his principles. The lord of the land[g] can still say, "You can enlarge your insights as a scholar but as a priest you must conceal it." The teacher must always remain free as a scholar in order to be able to make suggestions for the improvement of religion, this has nothing to do with his being a teacher in government service.[h] One cannot ever call him a hypocrite in his office for this, let alone remove him from his office. Also it is absolutely not within the power of the *summus imperans* to forbid enlightenment. His duty will be

[a] *Fürsten*
[b] KI: *die ihm nicht gefällt.* KS: *die ihm gefällt,* for "that pleases him"
[c] KI: *schatzen.* KS: *schütze,* for "protect"　　[d] *contract*
[e] *dissimuliren* in this paragraph　　[f] *simuliren*
[g] *Landsherr*　　[h] *daß er Lehrer im Amte ist*

to prevent interference by external religion so that he keeps the clergy from becoming *despoten*.

Tit: VI.

De jure circa administrationem reipublicae extrinsecam

{Of right concerning external administration of the state}

The right that the *souverain* has with regard to the external condition of the commonwealth is that he can give laws which concern relations with other states. He can maintain solders and has the right to levy soldiers.

27:1387

Tit: VII.

De jure eminenti

{Of eminent right}

The right of the *souverain in casu necessitatis* {in a case of necessity} to disregard the preservation of a citizen in favor of the preservation of the whole is considered here. They[a] unite themselves with all powers specifically to give laws to protect themselves. Every law must have been able to have arisen through universal agreement; a law which preserves the majority but disregards the welfare of the remainder is thus unjust. Can a state sacrifice a few citizens for the good of the state? No, for not everyone would have agreed to that. It is possible that human beings prefer to sacrifice their preservation for the good of the fatherland but that is *officium amoris* {a duty of love} but not *necessitatis*. The author says that the *souverain* has a right because the law to preserve the whole is the supreme law which must come before the law to preserve particular citizens. It would not be from *favor necessitatis* {a favor of necessity} but an actual right. *Homo perducitur in casum necessitatis* {A human being finds himself in a case of necessity} if the preservation of his life is not possible except through violation of another's rights. Here all right ceases. But the action is always wrong for *laesus* {the one being wronged} can oppose it. But it is a legitimate *jus externum* {external right} because it cannot be coerced through any penal law. For penal laws are here impossible since they can punish me with nothing more than my death and here I am also in danger of death, thus the ill which I escape is not smaller than the punishment. It is not really right[b] and for this reason it is called *favor*

---

[a] There is no referent for the plural *sie* in the preceding sentence. Likely "the citizens" is meant.

[b] *eigentlich nicht Recht*

necessitatis. It is absurd to say, "You are going to lose your life later" when you do not want to lose it now. The present danger is greater than the future one. No law can forbid an innocent from using all conceivable means to save his life. In the *status naturalis* {state of nature} one attacks and the other defends himself. Regarding penal laws which also include capital punishments, we could give complete approval with the intention of never doing it and because I know that it is wrong. But to will to give one's life for the good of another is *pactum turpe* {an immoral agreement}. But one can do it thinking he will still survive because in the majority of cases one survives anyway. But that is hard to believe. Who can judge that the state would be *statu extraordinario* {in an extraordinary condition}. The commonwealth will be preserved but not the remaining citizens for otherwise he would have to be preserved along with it. How many must there be in the commonwealth for whose preservation others ought[a] to be sacrificed? The proposition is very pernicious and indeterminate.[b] To this belongs *dominium eminens* {eminent ownership} to dispose over the goods of a few in a case of necessity, the right to dispose over freedom, life, etc.

Sect: III.   27:1388

Jus publicum universale hypotheticum

{Conditional universal public right}

Tit: I.

De monarchia

{Of monarchy}

A *monarch* is *solus princeps* {single ruler}, the only one in the state who does not stand under the laws, the head of all executive power.[c] The *souverain* is the one who can also legislate. The *monarch* is also the ruler, thus he cannot be subject to the laws because he executes the laws; he is *solus exlex* {the single individual bound by no law}. Were these separate then they could do something wrong and then there would have to be a third who would be unable to do any wrong. In England the king is *monarch*, all executive power rests with him and for this reason one also says that he can do no wrong. How can it be that the *monarch* really

---

[a] KI: *sollen*. KS: omits *sollen*
[b] KI: *sehr schädlich und unbestimmt*. KS: *sehr schädlich und sehr unbestimmt*, for "very pernicious and very indeterminate"
[c] *Gewalt*

does no wrong? England shows how; the king must have ministers[a] and they must always act in accordance with the laws. If he[b] does not, then he can be accused outright of high treason before the courts.[c] Thus if the king wants something which is against the laws the minister resigns. The court[d] appoints the king but cannot remove him. The king, who is *souverain*, has unlimited dominion.[e] A *monarch* can have his own share of sovereignty as in England. The king, the nobility, and the people make the laws. If the king says no then nothing can be made into law. The king in France is *souverain* and unlimited. Limited sovereignty is *contradictio in adjecto* {a contradiction in terms}. Can a *monarch* abdicate without the consent of the people? No, he stands under the *pactum fundamentale* {the fundamental contract} and because of that has obligations. *Actus* of a prince are *regii* {royal} and *privati* {private}. Regarding the latter he is to be considered as a private man and thus if he buys something he has to pay for it.

Tit: II.

De modis habendi imperium monarchicum

{Of the ways of coming to have a sovereign monarch}

One can ascend to a monarchy through birth alone (*hereditarie* {by heredity}) and through election (*electiva* {by election[f]}) and through *mixta successio* {a mixed succession} when the people still must give their concurrence although it is still a hereditary kingdom.[g] If this is in the fundamental law[h] then no one can alter it. If the *monarch* dies then the people set up a *vicarius* {successor}. If it is an elective kingdom[i] then one makes an election agreement[j] with him, which is the *pacta conventa* {appropriate contract} for him. One might think that the elective kingdom would be the most fortunate. But it is often the reverse, for 1) corruption is often the decisive factor and further if the king does not know whether his descendants will rule then he does not have much concern for the welfare of the land. The hereditary kingdom is either a patrimonial kingdom where the *monarch* can bequeath the kingdom[k]

27:1389

---

[a] KI: *Ministers*. KS: singular *Minister*
[b] *er* is ambigous between the king or one of his ministers.
[c] *Landesgerichten*   [d] *Gerichte*
[e] *Herrschaft*
[f] KI: *electiva*. KS: *selectiva*, for "by selection"
[g] *Erbreich*   [h] *Fundamentalgesetz*
[i] *Wahlreich*
[j] *Wahlcapitulation*, originating in the late Holy Roman Empire, an agreement made by the new emperor with the electors delineating the emperor's authority.
[k] *Reich*

to whomever he wants. He treats it as a *patrimonium*. It is complete *patrimonium* when he can also divide it. [Or] Hereditary is usufructuary when he cannot name his successor. Russia is a patrimonial kingdom. Rulers often say, "Does that agree with the *contractum sociale*?" Whoever inherits the government still does not inherit the kingdom, but the one who treats it as *patrimonium* does. The inheritance which ends the right of a state to exist for itself, done without the will of the people, is against the *pactum sociale* {social contract}: in this way it[a] becomes a part of another kingdom. A land that secedes[b] in order to be a whole does not want to be a member of any other kingdom. If a larger state unites with a smaller one then the personality of the latter ends. That has great influence on its welfare. The concerns of the monarch are always first directed[c] to himself and then to the whole kingdom and of it only a small part. Through inheritance a state can become so powerful that it soon overshadows the others. It would thus be better to do away with inheritance. If there is a conflict in the succession then the parties are called pretenders.[d]

Tit: III.

De reliquis rerumpublicarum formis

{Of the other forms of states}

The question arises whether *monarchie*, *aristocratie*, and *democratie* are to be understood as all three types of state constitutions[e] or of governments? If one is talking about state constitutions then none can be mixed. But there can be mixed types of governments. In *democratie* the legislative power[f] rests in the people. But because the people cannot always gather together to administer the commonwealth a government must be founded and this can be none other than the *doge* {doge} or a *collegium* {council}. – *Aristocratie*, whose legislative power rests in a *collegio optimatium* {council of nobles[g]} as e.g. in Venice. This *collegium* is then called the supreme *senat*. Such a *collegium* is not subject to the law but the individual members are. *Aristocratie* can be hereditary and can also be elective. In Bern there is a hereditary *aristocratie*. Mixed types of government are good. England is *democratie* mixed with *monarchie* and *aristocratie*. The execution of the laws is monarchical, the upper house and the minister limit the power[h] of the monarch, and that is aristocratic.

---

[a] *es*, referring to the former independent state
[b] *sich absondert*
[c] *concentrirte*
[d] *praetendenten*
[e] *Staatsverfassungen*
[f] *Gewalt*
[g] KS: *collegio optimatium*. KS: *collegio primatum*, for "supreme council"
[h] *Gewalt*

Republics are in the *status naturalis* regarding one another, for here there are neither public laws nor public rights nor public punishments. One can also consider a general league of nations[a] (*foedus amphyctionum* {the Amphictyonic League[41]}). E.g. Holland is a league of nations. For it consists of seven particular *souverain* provinces which are in a league. This does not work on a large scale. That would be a *status civilis* in which states are individual citizens.

Tit: IV.[b]

De modis jus suum prosequendi in republica[c]

{Of the way of prosecuting one's right in a state}

In the *status civilis* there is an external right. *Suum cuique tribue* {give to each what is his} subjects you to *justitia distributiva* {distributive justice}. *Justitia commutativa* {commutative justice} in *status naturalis* is the state of war, for no one need follow another in his judgment, and thus *alter jure aggreditur, alter jure resistit* {one attacks by right, the other resists by right}. In *status naturalis* what right is cannot be determined so that it is universally valid. – *Justitia distributiva* determines right through *lex publica* {public law}, applies it in each case, and coerces compliance. Give up the right to follow your own judgment but instead allow the legislator to determine it and the judge to judge it and give up your power[d] with which you could coerce another. Here no one is his legislator and judge. The ill that is connected with the violation of a law is punishment and the laws are *leges poenales* {penal laws}. These constitute the essential difference between *status civilis* {the civil condition} and *naturalis* {a state of nature}. In the *status naturalis* the law is used only for appraisal. *Transgressio legis dolosa est delictum* {Malicious transgression of the law is an offense} and *culposa quasi delictum* {a culpable transgression is similar to an offense}, and both are punishable. *Maleficia* {Malicious acts} in *status naturalis* {the state of nature} are not crimes. The *laesus* {one wronged} has a right to defend himself but not to punish. Punishments always already presuppose *superior* {a superior}. *Delictum publicum* {public offense} is when the security of the *summus imperans* {supreme

---

[a] *Volksbund*

[b] Achenwall has *Sectio IV* rather than *Tit: IV*.

[c] Achenwall has *jus suum persequendi*, for "pursuing one's rights." After this section Achenwall has *Jus privatum universale in jure naturali exul* {universal private right of isolation in natural right}.

[d] *Gewalt*

sovereign} or commonwealth, as a state, suffers. Such an action is *Crimen* {a crime}. Prostitution is *delictum privatum* {a private offense} but adultery is *publicum* {a public one}. Fraud is *delictum privatum* because I do not necessarily have to get involved with anyone but thievery is *publicum*. Stealing is thus *delictum publicum* but making off with something when one seeks enjoyment more than the property and embezzling are not thievery and are thus not *delicta publica* because here the general security is not endangered. Robbery is even more criminal because there is absolutely no security in it. *Potestas legislatoria* {the legislative power} has *potestas sanciendi leges poenales* {the power to determine sanctions for the penal laws}. The *summus imperans* has that. But do the ground and the nature of the punishment lie in the choice of *summus imperans?* Laws are also a matter of choice.[a] Punishment presupposes desert of punishment and one must see whether a *crimen* {crime} is merely against *positive* or also against the natural laws,[b] for in the latter case the *dolus* {malice} is greater and so the *leges* must certainly be different. Also regarding the nature of punishments he is already connected to certain punishments[c] by the nature of the thing. He must punish in order to obtain security, and here he must make such punishments that measure the security of the *laesus* {one wronged} in future cases, he must find that in accordance with *jus talionis* {the right of retribution}, e.g. a thief robs someone of his whole property, one must accordingly also take his property from him and, because he frustrates the other's endeavors to acquire property, one must also place the thief outside of the condition[d] where he can acquire his own property. Thus he will be exiled into labor and will be provided for like an animal. In such a way the best security is obtained. Capital punishments would be given only for murder and for wronging the *imperantis* {sovereign}. Does *summus imperans* have *vis necis* {the power of death}? Beccaria[42] says that all laws must be viewed as if they arose from the unanimous will of the people. They could impose punishments, fines, etc., on themselves but they have no authority to dispose over their lives. In accordance with the same grounds one could not consent to perpetual imprisonment. For of course no one can dispose over his own freedom. Flogging could also never be approved because it dishonors humanity. But a human being does not need to consent to punishment, he has not said, "I would very much want to undergo the punishment." He assents only to the penal law and thinks he will get away

27:1391

---

[a] *Willkürlich*, tied to the *Willkür* (choice) of the previous sentence
[b] *Naturgesetze*
[c] KI: *gewissen Strafen.* KS, MS: *gewissen*, for "knowing" or for "conscience" were it capitalized
[d] *Stand*

with it. Rousseau assumes that a human being acquiesces in the punishment and says that it is permissible to risk my life in order to preserve it.[43] Because citizens' lives are not always secure they seek to preserve their lives, as when they risk it when they can think that they could do some things. It is absurd to ascribe a right of preservation to a human being who has killed another and to hold that the one who executes him is actually a murderer. *Summus imperans* must provide security and he can obtain this regarding a murderer in no other way except his death. Death is also the worst for with it all hope ends. In the worst prison the offender still has hope and often gets away. *Summus imperans* does not have *jus aggratiandi* {the right to grant clemency} because he is not the judge. He can grant clemency[a] for a punishment that concerns his security. Then can a people use force[b] against *summus imperans* when he is ruining them? *Summus imperans* whose government is leading to the decline of the commonwealth is a tyrant. None of the people can *valide* {validly} determine this and he is the head of public justice so he does not stand under any coercive laws and also cannot be punished[c] for otherwise he would not be supreme. Where no coercive law is necessary no coercion is allowed. The people must first be the supreme judge and have supreme power,[d] which is however not the case. It cannot be impossible that a people ought to be allowed that through a law. For if that is not so then indeed all of humanity is in danger. The difficulty rests in a disingenuousness[e] innate to human beings in which human beings wish to have laws but want to exempt[f] themselves from them. That eventually leads to a will which stands under no coercive laws and cannot be limited. Everyone requires a master[g] to coerce him; the master in turn must be coerced. Now there must be a supreme one who cannot be coerced and he is thus also a human being. It is impossible to discover[h] a right in which the head of state is also coerced to act. Perfect justice is impossible. If the people have a tyrant, that is *casus necessitatis* {a case of necessity}. A right that I have in that regard but which is not possible as a public right is *favor necessitatis*. It is not possible to make a law that can coerce the ruler; that is *contradictio*. But it is clearly a necessity and a duty for the subjects[i] to maintain themselves. No law against that is possible for this would contradict itself since the subjects would be threatened with death. But a tyrant is one within whose state no citizen is secure in his goods and his life.[j] Here on both sides no laws are possible. Human beings are in

27:1392

---

[a] *aggratiiren* [b] *Gewalt*
[c] KI: *gestraft werden*. KS: *strafen*, for "he cannot punish"
[d] *Gewalt* [e] *Unlauterkeit*
[f] *exhibiren* [g] *Herren*
[h] KI: *auszufinden*. KS: *auszuüben*, for "exercise"
[i] *Unterthanen* [j] KI: *Lebens*. KS: *Landes*, for "land"

lawlessness and a *status naturalis*. If the people punish their superior he is wronged because it does not occur in accordance with the judgment of a public judge. Of course the people can attack but the monarch can also use force.[a] *Alter jure aggreditur, alter jure resistit* {the one attacks by right, the other resists by right}. If a human being values[b] the right of humanity as the highest priority then he would rather endure all tyranny than defy it. A people will never be in complete agreement; even then they would be permitted only to say, "We will not obey you." Thus only a few are able to take up arms[c] and they have no right to take up arms against the state and the others, in fact often a monarch is led to tyranny this way. The rebellion[d] brings about a *status naturalis* which is *bellum omnium contra omnes* {a war of all against all}. Thus there must be passive obedience if there is to be a lasting form of government. In the greatest tyranny there is still some justice. Machiavellianism is the principle[e] where the people should have passive obedience, but Machiavelli claims that a ruler has a right to conduct himself tyrannically, yet this is false.[44] In a rebellion no wrong is done to him but the people act wrongly for they do not have the right to do it. Monarchomachism is the principle where the people can oppose the tyrant.[45] The whole people can be in opposition, but in *rebellionen* only a part of the people is in rebellion. *Monarchie, democratie*, and *aristocratie* can be corrupted. *Monarchie* can become *despotismus* where he considers the land as his *patrimonium* and the subjects as things. *Aristocratie* can become *oligarchie* where not all *primates* {the nobles} but only a few lord it over the others. *Democratie* can become *ochlocratie* in which the people get hold of only a part of the power.

Libr: IV.

Jus gentium[f]

{The right of nations}

This right has still not yet been brought to universal principles.[g] The best book to read about this topic is *Vattels le Droit des gens 2 Tom. 4to*, translated into German by *Joh. Ph. Schulin. Frankfurt und Leipzig 1760 in III Tom. 8*.[46] – Of these rights we will talk only about the rights of war, which our author treats.

---

[a] *Gewalt*
[c] *empören*
[e] *princip*, here and next few sentences
[g] *principien*

[b] KI: *schätzen*. KS: *schützen*, for "protects"
[d] *Empörung*
[f] Achenwall has *Jus gentium universale*

27:1393

Sect: IV.[a]

Jus belli gentium

{The right of nations regarding war}

Here it mostly depends on customs and treaties.[b] The rights of nations regarding one another would be just as powerless[c] as those of human beings in the *status naturalis* {state of nature} where there is no public justice. Each nation[d] is its own judge and must obtain right through its own power.[e] No laws are valid and the *jus gentium* {right of nations} is merely the possibility of a league of nations.[f] All laws are thought in accordance with this idea. The idea of a communal will[g] can alone be valid as a law for a will.

1) All *gentes* {nations} or states are equal to one another. *Gens* {a nation} is to be considered as *res publica* {a state} internally and a state externally.

2) A state can acquire *res nullius* {an ownerless thing} yet the ocean is *res nullius* {an ownerless thing}, i.e. *mare est liberum* {the sea is free}. But as far as the law can extend from the land the sea is not free, say the states, thus only as far as their power[h] reaches.

3) With a state as in the *status naturalis* no prescription holds. Indeed in the *status naturalis*, according to the author, no *testamente* {testaments} are found, how can he here grant a right of inheritance to the state?

4) States can make *pacta* that endure without end[i] because the state is considered without end.

5) A guarantee can hold for states in which one promises to help the other.

6) States give one another persons for security, they are hostages.

7) They send envoys who represent their states anywhere they pass through. To accept or refuse an envoy is a privilege of every state.

---

[a] The lecture skips the following sections of Achenwall: *Sectio I: Jus gentium universale in genere* {Universal right of nations in general}, *Sectio II: Jus gentium universale absolutum* {Unconditional universal right of nations in general}, and *Sectio III: Jus gentium universale hypotheticum* {Conditional universal right of nations}. *Sectio III* in turn includes three titles: *Titulus I: De dominio et jure territoriali gentis* {Of dominion and the right of a nation to territory}, *Titulus II: De jure pactorum publicorum* {Of right of pacts among states}, *and Titulus III: De jure legationum* {Of right of embassies}. Kant nonetheless discusses some of these issues under *Titulus IV*.

[b] *Hier kommts mehrentheils auf Gewohnheiten und Traktaten*

[c] *so wenig in Kraft*　　　　　　　　　　[d] *Volk* in this section

[e] *Macht*　　　　　　　　　　　　　　　[f] *Völkerbundes*

[g] *des gemeinschaftlichen Willens*　　　　[h] *Gewalt*

[i] *ewig*

178

The *mandatarius* {delegate} shows his *mandat* {commission}, the envoy his credentials. Because an envoy has *character repraesentativus* {the character of a representative} one cannot refuse to accept his *passeports*.

Before a war begins there are disagreements. One sees a few *actus* of the other as wrong,[a] there a state satisfies itself if it does the same in return. These are reprisals done for compensation for the offense. Retorsion[b] is when I just want revenge. *Jus in bellum* and *ad bellum* {right in war and right to war}.

1) A war is unjust which is waged merely because of its benefits. *Sola laesio est causa belli justifica* {only wronging is a cause justifying war[c]}.
2) One cannot wage war for the sake of religion for no one is wronged through religion.
3) Not the increase in power of another nation, that would strain[d] *aequilibrium* {the equilibrium} of all nations. That is clearly no *laesio* and thus no *aequilibrium* is necessary. But in accordance with the rules of prudence a state can make sure that it is impossible and on this basis almost all wars arise. There is still a right to seek security and when a very powerful state is always overpowering[e] such a war is legitimate. Granted, since one cannot determine the ground on which to say a state is too powerful there can be no law. It is merely a general authorization. A declaration of war is necessary, but the one who first begins hostilities must not also be *laedens* {the wrongdoer}. For war is *modus jus persequendi in statu naturali* {a way of obtaining rights in the state of nature} and each *juste* {justly} disregards what another takes for reasons so all act in *bona fide* {good faith}, thus every war is just, but in this each is persuaded of the truth of his own opinion. In war is the use of deceptions, treachery, spies, etc. allowed? Are assassination, poisoning also allowed? The author says yes, *in bello justo* {in a just war}. But one cannot determine if it is *bellum justum*. In war whatever either side determines is valid. – Every kind of force[f] is used in war in order to get the upper hand over the other but no one is permitted to punish the other. If I get a prisoner I cannot allow him to be hanged if he ceases to fight. Poisoning, burning to death, etc. do not belong to the means through which one can resist the

27:1394

---

[a] *laesion* [b] *retorsion*
[c] KI: *sola laesio est causa belli justifica*, following Achenwall. KS: *sola laesio est causa belli justa*, for "only wronging is a just cause for war"
[d] *intendirte*
[e] KS: *übermächtig*. KI: *übermüthig*, for "out of control"
[f] *Gewalt*

power of the other; instead they count only as extermination; such acts could thus be formally punished. Because states wage wars by using their subjects[a] who have to defend the security of the state, plundering of the citizens and farmers[47] who are subjected is not allowed. But in a conquered state someone can order it as lord of the land. Anything which one personally takes away is really robbery. *Quaestio*: whether an ally[b] of an opponent can be considered as an enemy? One has assumed that when the time comes[c] it will not be an enemy, but in effect[d] it is viewed as an enemy. In wars each state can[e] remain *neutral*. *Pacta* {pacts} made before the war lose their rightful force[f] but those made during the war retain it. When the war is over one can still remain *in dubio* {in doubt} about who was right. Thus victory decides. But *pactum pacis* {the peace pact} still belongs to this matter. A peace for a determined time is called an armistice. It is merely suspension of hostilities. In peace complete amnesty is promulgated[g] which is also necessary. So one never identifies the rights prior to the war. It is greatly to be wished that a statute of limitations is included in *praetensionen* {claims for recovery}. If future claims are not refused and settled then they are annulled. If one does not do this it is always a new source of wars.

---

[a] *Bediente*
[b] *alliirter*
[c] *Wenn die Zahl bestimmt ist*
[d] *im Grund*
[e] KI: *kann jeder Staat*. KS: *kann ja der Staat*, for "a state can surely"
[f] *Rechtskraft*
[g] *publizirt*

Drafts for published works

Editor's introduction

Kant forced himself to write for a certain amount of time every day. At least from the time he was able to afford to have a servant, he woke at 5:00 a.m., drank some tea, pondered things while smoking a bowl of tobacco, and worked on his lecture preparation and on his other ideas, then after his two hours of morning lectures returned to work until the midday meal, then after a break for a walk and to spend more time with his friends he returned to work or to read.[1] To be certain of getting this work time he reportedly had his servant Lampe, who had earlier served in the military, enter his room just before 5:00 a.m. and shout with full military seriousness, "It is time!"; Kant was so proud of this routine that he sometimes boasted to guests that Lampe never had to try to awaken him twice.[2] The notes Kant worked on for his lectures in these early morning hours were inscribed into his textbooks. Other notes would appear on loose sheets. Kant clearly worked out his ideas in writing, given the large number of fragments offering similar but distinct arguments and approaches to a single topic. One can trace the subtle changes in his thoughts as he works from lecture preparation through general reflection to draft material to the final published work.

The transitions one can find in the various modes of Kant's handwritten notes show that there is no firm line between a Reflection for a course and some preparatory work or a draft for particular published works. But such a distinction was presupposed in Erich Adickes's original plan for the third part of the Academy edition, since he planned two volumes of *Vorarbeiten und Nachträge* to be separated from the remainder of Kant's handwritten notes. (German distinguishes between *Vorarbeiten*, or preparatory work in general, and *Entwurf*, or a draft closer to the finished product; the material in Volume 23 is identified as *Vorarbeiten* but includes *Entwürfe*, and in keeping with English terminology, are all considered as drafts here.) The general introduction to this volume discusses Adickes's plans in more detail. Here what is important is that Adickes had two criteria for identifying a draft in order to separate it from the Reflections: 1. The relation to a published work was "fairly certain." 2. All material on a sheet was considered a draft if any of it was. He had two more criteria for excluding apparent drafts from the volume of drafts: 3. If the piece could be assigned to more than one work, it would be printed with the Reflections on that topic rather than one or the other work. 4. If it was material toward the *Critique of Pure Reason* it would be placed along with Kant's other notes on metaphysics as a Reflection (14:xxvi–xxvii).

Most of the material Adickes identified as drafts, excluding those for the *Critique of Pure Reason* which constitute the bulk of Volumes 17 and 18 of the Academy edition, were eventually printed in Volume 23. Volume 20 includes a few drafts of essays that Kant himself never published along with the final surviving version seemingly ready for the publisher.[3] The drafts for Kant's unfinished final project known as the *Opus Postumum*, unavailable for inclusion in the Academy edition when Adickes made his plans, constitute Volumes 21 and 22. A very telling indication of the importance of political philosophy to Kant is that his surviving notes reveal that the three projects which seem to have demanded the most effort from him, as measured by the quantity of surviving draft arguments for material destined for books, are the *Critique of Pure Reason*, the unfinished *Opus Postumum* project, and the *Doctrine of Right* of the *Metaphysics of Morals*, the drafts for which constitute over a third of the material in Volume 23.

The actual work of preparing Volume 23 fell to Gerhard Lehmann after Adickes's death and the short tenure of Friedrich Berger as his immediate successor. Lehmann arranged the drafts in chronological order by publication date of the corresponding work. Within the material for each work, however, Lehmann does not include any specific dates even on the rare occasions that the same loose sheet contains material that provides some dating information such as a letter. These dates are added to the translation in this volume when available by other means.[4] Lehmann also leaves out some material that can be identified as a draft that was certainly available to him, being parts of loose sheets already printed in Reicke's collection; the remainder of these loose sheets had also been included in earlier volumes in the Academy edition. This translation includes some of those other fragments that were published in various places after the publication of Volume 23 of the Academy edition. For the drafts for the *Metaphysics of Morals* Lehmann arranged the material with two conflicting ideas: first, he presents a single long draft that extends over six loose sheets, and second, he arranges the remainder of the material in correspondence with the sections of the published work to which they correspond, even though the extended draft clearly falls under a specific section of the published work. The translation in this volume reorders that material as explained in the specific introduction to those drafts.

* *
*

The process Kant used in committing his thought to publication had several identifiable stages. One contemporary described the process in this way:

He first conceived a general outline in his head; then he worked it out more explicitly; added some passages here and there, writing on little pieces of paper, which he inserted into the hastily written first draft. After some time, he revised the entire manuscript again, and then copied it for the printer in its entirety in his clean and clear writing.[5]

Lehmann himself describes six stages in the process toward a published work (23:516):

1. isolated, somewhat related Reflections that have as an object the theme of some later work;
2. loose sheets that approach an interrelated form;
3. loose sheets that are joined to one another and contain a single draft;
4. drafts on folio sheets;
5. *Reinschriften* (complete version in Kant's own script);
6. *Abschriften* (a copy of the *Reinschrift* in another's script).

As he notes, the first two of these stages are hard to define in relation to one another. In addition, the overlap in themes of some of Kant's works – he mentions similarities in *Theory and Practice* and *Toward Perpetual Peace* – make this early stage in the writing process problematic. Since all the volumes of Reflections had already been published, Lehmann could not treat any of the fragments he had before him as Reflections but had to include them in Volume 23. He assigned them to particular works as best he could.

The full range of material of all six types is thus included in Volume 23. Lehmann used this classification to order the material as well: loose sheets that were closer to the published version were printed after loose sheets in the earlier stages. Since that ordering is plausible for rough dating as well, the drafts of *Theory and Practice*, *Toward Perpetual Peace*, and *Conflict of the Faculties* included in this translation are arranged using his order, corresponding to the Academy edition pagination. Additional material that was published outside the Academy edition is included where appropriate. Any identifiable correspondence to the published version is noted using Academy edition pagination.

The material in the final stage is generally not included here. When Kant was satisfied with the draft of a book, he would have a copyist produce a *Reinschrift* (this term often encompasses *Abschriften*) to send to the printer. Kant usually reviewed these manuscripts and made small changes before they were sent off to the printer. The changes Kant makes in those *Reinschriften* are generally only stylistic improvements involving word choices, some of which are even within the margin of variation that any two translators might have translating the same text into English. Those who wish to examine the minute changes Kant made at the last minute are advised to compare them in the German original. Only in the cases where the *Reinschrift* includes significant additional material that did not make it into the printed edition is the additional material included here.

The material related to the *Metaphysics of Morals* was ordered differently by Lehmann (23:517). For the most part he arranged the material in relation to the topics in the published text in order to provide a more coherent ordering of the nearly-200 pages of drafts. This translation alters Lehmann's arrangement somewhat as explained in the editor's introduction to those drafts.

The loose sheets printed in Volume 23 include almost no commas or periods; one is tempted to say that Kant's thought process moved so quickly that he did not have time to set down the punctuation. The truth is that he routinely omitted punctuation when writing and instead relied on journal editors, copyists, and printers to include it for him. Adickes had added punctuation to the Reflections he prepared for publication but Lehmann did not. Kant's formulations are often highly condensed and elliptical, increasing the challenge of parsing the numerous phrases and clauses he used. The translators have nonetheless tried to retain Kant's division into sentences (when apparent) and only rarely break the material into sentences not indicated in the text itself either grammatically or through punctuation. The result captures the complexity of Kant's arguments as he set them down.

Each of the four sets of drafts translated here is given its own more particular introduction discussing the provenance of the work, dating issues, and other specific information. They are arranged in chronological order of the publications themselves. The reader is reminded, however, that identification of some of the loose sheets with particular works is open to some doubt given the overlap of topics and uncertainty in the dating.

Drafts for *Theory and practice*

Editor's introduction

Kant had long held that rebellion against any state, even a tyrannical one, was wrong, as evidenced from his course lecture notes reaching back into the 1770s.[1] He argued in 1784 in "Idea for a universal history with a cosmopolitan aim" that any move from a worse state to a better would come about through indirect means rather than direct force. He believed that human history was moving toward a state that maximized and protected the freedom of each citizen yet thought that such progress depended on unintentionally progressive, self-interested acts of sovereigns trying to sustain and increase their external power rather than on any conscious acts of the citizenry directly intending to realize political ideals. He did argue that individual citizens ought to be able to call publicly for progress in the essay "What is Enlightenment?," but still insisted that citizens are allowed only to attempt to persuade the sovereign and must always still obey the laws.

The outbreak of the French Revolution and its Declaration of the Rights of Man in 1789 would appear to have challenged Kant's position, since direct action aimed at increasing citizens' rights led to the deposing of the French sovereign and to a state much closer to Kant's ideals. Kant privately praised the French Revolution and must have worked through its effect on his position but was reluctant to enter into the public debate about its legitimacy. When the publisher Johann Carl Spener suggested in March 1793 that Kant revise his "Idea" essay by discussing "the present circumstances" (11:415–16), Kant declined, citing both despair at having any influence over political actors and a desire to save his own skin (11:417).

Something changed Kant's mind. Within a few months he began draft work discussing the relation between the principles of a just society and the legitimate means for realizing them. He avoided direct reference to the "present circumstances" while nonetheless working through the question of when and how philosophical principles of right can be applied to actual states. This material became the second part of "Theory and Practice." While these issues were of interest to Kant already, two different triggers, both of which he notes in *Loses Blatt* C 07 below, might

189

have caused Kant to decide to go public with an essay about them. One trigger is the claim by a certain "professor of mathematics," likely Abraham Gotthelf Kästner, who scoffed at thinkers who believe that their ideas will have any impact on the state, particularly mentioning those whose writings championed "pedagogy, enlightenment, critical philosophy, and human rights" as means for progress.[2] The other is a conservative philosopher, August Wilhelm Rehberg, who wrote in an essay collection in 1793 that metaphysics caused the French Revolution.[3] These opposite charges placed Kant in a difficult position: he had to try to show that principles such as his are not mere idle chatter but can have an effect on existing political institutions, thus answering the mathematician, while also showing that his principles do not have such authority that they justify revolutionary means to realize them by violent transformation of political institutions, thus avoiding Rehberg's indictment. The result was the second part of "Theory and Practice."

Just as important is Kant's effort to provide a summary of the *a priori* principles of his philosophy of right. Prior to "Theory and Practice" Kant's published writings on political philosophy consisted mainly of hints: a very brief statement of the idea of right in the *Critique of Pure Reason* (A316/B372–73), a short discussion of the ideal civil society in the "Idea" essay, a defense of freedom of thought in "What is Enlightenment?" Kant's drafts for "Theory and Practice" include discussions of freedom, equality, and independence, but also touch on freedom, equality, and unity as a necessary principle for a state. He includes a discussion of property that does not reach the printed version. These drafts show Kant's first attempt to present his own "Theory" of political right to the world of readers.

The drafts below are concentrated in the period from early 1793 until the publication of "Theory and Practice" in the September issue of the *Berlinische Monatsschrift*. Drafts for the first part of the work, the essay concerning Christian Garve's claim that Kant's moral principles cannot motivate action, are not included. Some of the material also concerns the third part of the work in which Kant answers the charge attributed to Moses Mendelssohn that the human species will not improve itself morally. The bulk of the material relates to the second part that Kant subtitled "Against Hobbes."

Drafts for Theory and practice

TRANSLATED BY FREDERICK RAUSCHER

Loses Blatt C 07 (1792–August 1793). *Loses Blatt* C 07 is composed of unrelated notes that appear in different volumes of the Academy edition. The first page consists of a discussion of the cosmological argument, which flows into a discussion of the ontological argument and the nature of reality and was printed in Volume 18 as R6324 (18:643–47). This is followed in C 07 by material identified as drafts for "Theory and Practice," which Adickes planned to include in Volume 23 (18:643, note). As it turns out, Adickes's successor as editor of Volume 23, Gerhard Lehmann, failed to include the first few paragraphs of this material from page one when he presented other material from C 07 in Volume 23. Werner Stark included this overlooked material in *Nachforschungen zu Briefen und Handschriften Immanuel Kants* (Berlin: Akademie Verlag, 1993) pp. 244–45. The selection below, then, begins with the initial portion of C 07 on Theory and Practice using the pagination in Stark, *Nachforschungen*, and continues immediately with the remainder of C 07 from Volume 23.

[*first page*]   Stark 244

The principles of freedom, equality, and independence[a] for each member of the state hold by themselves and do not depend at all on old contracts or unilateral taking possession, thus not on empirical conditions whose actuality and conformity with right cannot be proven by identifying the first rightful acts.[b] Yet the constitution[c] in accordance with these principles, one that specifies how everyone's mine and yours ought to be determined and protected, does depend on empirical grounds, namely the receptivity that human beings have to such a first arrangement. Now those principles[d] cannot in any way be rejected and denied as illusory (metaphysically) and unfeasible, indeed they cannot even once be curtailed, because they are duties that stem from reason and they must thus also be assumed to be unavoidable as a basis for action,

---

[a] *Selbstständigkeit*   [b] *Acts*
[c] *Constitution*   [d] *Principien*

191

and so the originally subjective temporary arrangements of convenience are valid until all enter into the condition in which these principles can be fulfilled. This fulfillment must itself lie as the germ of the existing state constitution[a] and so it cannot be thrown out to establish another, because this kind of forceful activity would be contrary to right. Thus there is nothing to be reformed through a rebellion, still less is it permissible to create something completely new.

Stark 245   (The equality of subjects under laws that command and protect all equally.) except only that the one who exercises legislative authority does not stand under that authority, and no subjects can attain this independence.[b]

The independence[c] that is required to be a citizen of a state is the rightful condition of not standing under another's orders (*imperium* {sovereignty}), thus not wife, child, and household servant. The set of capacities which makes this independence[d] possible rests upon one who, regarding his subsistence, has within himself a part of the state's powers[e] that rests upon his free choice (a household).

[*second page*]

Whether the political concept of civil freedom, which is grounded on natural, innate freedom, has objective reality or, along with morality, does not.

[*continuation of above in Academy edition:*]

23:127   Of course it would be a professor of mathematics who discusses his ignorance (that he shares with all human beings) as if it were dogmatic science or scientific belief, claiming that writings are innocent of any responsibility for any revolution. Whether it is all just pedantry and the empiricists, shining bright with their insight into the world, are the genuine possessors of wisdom about the principles of the state, and the rationalists rightly banished to their school where they must leave the judgments entirely to whomever has power.[f]

[*a line here divides the above from the below*]

I do not know whether I ought to judge the recent but unanswered accusation against metaphysics that it could be a cause of revolution against the state,[4] it is burdened with aspersions of too much unmerited honor or too much undeserved blame; for it has long been the case that people of business have referred to principle as pedantry in the schools.

---

[a] *Staatsverfassung*   [b] *Unabhängigkeit*
[c] *Selbständigkeit*   [d] *Unabhängigkeit*
[e] *Staatsvermögen*   [f] *Gewalt*

The art of groping toward morality [*added:* teachers of statecraft fumbling around]. When right is under discussion, one cannot proceed from the empirical but only from the rational. One is not allowed to treat them in a way that makes these bold principles of freedom superfluous. Limitations will be set in application after each knows that his right is protected in civil society. – For it must not be that everyone gives up a part of their freedom in order to save the remaining part, for freedom is not like an aggregate that can be divided up but an absolute unity as the principle of a system in which one does give up a part of his rights, i.e. will the rightful limitation for others through our choice, but each wills only this unrestricted freedom, not that which can be given up in its entirety or in part.

The results of the old principles[a] remain but with the proviso that little by little one allows them to lapse.

One whom it is impermissible to coerce to do something for another's benefit without it also being in his interest in his own judgment is naturally free. One who has not entered into and so does not stand under any contingent obligation is morally free. But can the latter not find it in his own interest to yield out of love for another? No! There are only two ways: right or power.[b] A love that is not limited or curbed by another's right is power, and another's power to yield himself and his condition is called abandonment of humanity,[c] where one can never again complain that one has suffered a wrong. This is called making oneself into a mere means.

23:128

Loses Blatt C 15, First Page. Written on a letter to Kant dated April 27, 1793

23:128

It can no longer be in the manner of a gracious lord.

What kind of duty is leaving the state of nature for those outside society? It is a coercive duty, but only to resist all community between the savages and us, not for them to enter into civil society with us. What kind of duty for those who do not resist?

There is no coercive right of subjects against the *souverain*, for the latter alone has all coercive right, and only through him does each have a coercive right against his fellow citizen. Of examples of the wrong that subjects would commit against the republic that of permitting deterioration of the ruling authority.[d]

There can be only one gracious lord. For if there were two of them, the right of one of the two over us could contradict the obligation that we have to the other. There could be many who together possess coercive right over everyone but that is only one single moral (legislative or

[a] *Grundsätze*
[b] *Gewalt*
[c] *Auf die Menschheit Verzicht thun*
[d] *Landesherrschaft*

executive) person; I could have a coercive right toward each of them by means of the moral person.

[four paragraphs that treat solely moral issues omitted]

23:129   [*second page begins with note in margin:*] not merely the concept of outer freedom but also actual freedom does not depend on the choice of others without his consent.

All laws of right must proceed from the freedom of the one who must obey them. For right itself is nothing other than the limitation of the freedom of human beings (in its outer use) on the condition that it harmonizes with the freedom of everyone. The civil constitution, as a rightful state under public laws, contains as a first condition the universal freedom of each and every member of the commonwealth (not ethical, nor just juridical, but political freedom). This consists in each being able to pursue his welfare as he conceives it, and also that he can never be used by another as a means for the end of his own happiness in conformity with the other's concept of happiness but only in conformity with his own. Likewise when the preservation of the whole *status* {condition} [is] one that protects freedom (which must also include the security of property), then this is a *salus publicum* {public good}, i.e. the preservation of this condition of freedom. No one can alienate this freedom, for he

23:130   would then cease to have a right and would become a thing. This occurs with servants who certainly can try to make the work they undertake for another abide together with their wishes for self-preservation.

Regarding happiness in general I cannot say "I absolutely ought to" because it is doubtful whether I also can. With regard to the establishment of a commonwealth I cannot say "I absolutely ought to" because as a private individual I actually cannot. But I should still meet all the moral conditions which now lie in my free power of choice in order to approach this condition as far as I can.

The right of humanity as coercive right must not only rest on the concept of a duty which one can impose on everyone but also presupposes a power[a] to constrain others to satisfy our right. Now this power is either the kind that is in accordance with merely private laws of each (which reason itself prescribes for him alone) or public laws (holding in a certain community) of one commanding will above all. The former is a private power, the latter a public power. The rightful condition (*status juridicus*) of human beings under public laws is the civil condition, and the whole of the many human beings united in this condition is the commonwealth. Thus the commonwealth also has a public power (*vis publica*) for itself.

[a] *Macht*

[*before the next paragraph Kant writes:*] to sheet D, p. 4.[a]

The three propositions of theory are correct.[5] So can the subjects of a constitution that is not in conformity with these principles change it? No, neither through secret disloyalty nor through rebellion, because it 1. would occur without right (in that there is no law authorizing it), 2. is also contrary to right if not the ruler but fellow subjects would act.

But it can never be improved in this manner and that proposition is valid in theory but not in practice.

One could say with regard to *N. II lit. c*[b] If something valid in theory must also be valid in practice (as it is in *N.I*), then would one be able to say if a constitution not in conformity with the social contract is established then the subjects have authorization to overthrow the existing one and exchange it for a new one. Or is it also in accord with the saying to hold that it is easy to move from a state of nature to such a lawful state, which in fact is refuted by history? Answer: I can only conclude with certainty, derived necessarily from theory, how the thing ought to be and afterwards turn to feasibility, but without being able to show when I ought to do something personally. But now whether I ought to do something that presupposes others who are also obligated to do this thing is uncertain and not in my own power, so far this theory is not practical. An already existing constitution cannot be overthrown by the insurrection of the people as *turba* {a mob} and the ruler[c] will certainly not create an opposition himself.

23:131

The possibility of action follows from the absolute ought regarding each individual, but not from the absolute ought regarding a society to be established through that action. Yet what follows from that is the necessity of promoting the means for having the capacity to approach that condition, for that is what ought to happen.

[*remainder of LB C 15 are notes for the first section of Theory and Practice omitted here*]

Loses Blatt F 2. Written on a letter to Kant dated July 13, 1793

23:133

[*first page. Omitted is a draft of Kant's footnote on Garve (8:278)*]

I do not believe that one would find fault with me; I have quite strongly flattered rulers with the inviolability of their rights and person, but one must not fault me for this since I flatter the people so strongly that I have vindicated their right to at least make public their judgments about the mistakes of the government.

---

[a] It is not clear what sheet Kant is referencing

[b] Presumably *Number II, letter C*, but it is not clear what Kant is referencing here or in the next sentence. Given that a few paragraphs later "III" is associated with the third part of "Theory and Practice" on the right of nations and cosmopolitanism, "I" and "II" might refer to the first two parts of this work.

[c] *Oberhaupt*

Hobbes claims the people have no right at all after their commitment to the social contract.[6] But he must say not only the right of resistance but also announcements of opposition and espousing of the idea of progress. For the latter has to precede the former.

That the people could not silently declare their opposition.

The *souverain* cannot resolve for the people whatever a people cannot resolve for itself.

23:134 The people have no right to hostility against the ruler[a] because he represents the people itself. No subject has any coercive right against him and therefore must obey his commands.

Because all coercion of a citizen against another can be practiced only by means of the one against whom there can be no coercion, the ruler; yet the minister is the one through whom complaints (*gravamen*) can be brought to the ruler, so no coercive right of a citizen can be exercised against him either, for the minister would have to understand that he himself is a means to be coerced. All **types of government** are only **forms** of the presentation of an idea.

Whether the can that follows from the ought would apply to the regent or the people.

Against Hobbes and his Machiavellianism claiming that the people have no rights at all.[7]

Reform must originate from the will of the sovereign himself. But this is *in facto* not the united will of the people, instead it should emerge gradually. Writings must enable the ruler, like the people, to examine injustices. – Concealing.

First of course the universal will of the people, without distinguishing among persons, must be the basis for deriving qualifications for citizenship. Wives, children, day laborers, etc., would agree to this because they are not independent enough to live if they were to dedicate themselves to public business.

[*second page*]

What is metaphysics? Philosophy of the supersensible, i.e. whatever cannot be given in any experience. This applies also in right. – God as the basis of nature, freedom as the basis of moral laws, immortality to enable God, as author[b] of the moral law, to give it its corresponding effect in nature. III.[8] What is valid etc., in the right of nations as a cosmopolitan community.

The principles[c] of a state constitution must be derived from concepts of right as principles and that is theory. It is false and harmful to claim 23:135 that something is right because up to now it is known through experience as the only means to reach the end. It puts the cart before the horse.

[a] *Oberherrn*   [b] *Urheber*
[c] *Principien*

Because right contains within itself an equality of action and reaction, which is a product of laws of freedom, so it is also practical for the single valid principle to make a persisting whole possible even under senseless actors; thus theory is here simultaneously practical in maxims but its realization depends on experiential trials.

Nothing can be accomplished through morality or a state constitution from the bottom up. War exhausts everyone, with the increase in culture and ever higher costs, and many human beings involved in a balance of power, and the necessary weapons. But it is possible that states will enter into a republican condition from above starting from the aggregate of states, which themselves, in line with the jealous lust for power inherent in human nature, war among themselves until they have exhausted their energies.

III. On the relation of theory to practice regarding the right of nations.

Of that which is true in *thesi* but does not have all conditions for its possibility in *hypothesi*.

Were one to try it with practice but not theory or construct theory in conformity with practice, one would ascribe to the ruler nothing but rights and instead of duties of right nothing but good will. But since the subject must also have rights, one would make the *souverain* and the subject into opponents. – What is metaphysics? The science of *a priori* principles of the use of reason through concepts, not constructed through intuition. Now one can also judge rationally without metaphysics, i.e. without principles expressed abstractly, through concepts that themselves can be presented in intuition, because they can be verified through intuition and experience. Duty and right alone are concepts which concern freedom and its laws and do not belong to nature like cause and effect whose reality can be proved in experience since experience is possible through them alone.

Thus every doctrine of right must contain metaphysics and without   23:136
a doctrine of right there can be no doctrine of the state and prudence.

Clearly theory does not become practice without trials and examples.

Loses Blatt F 7. Written on a letter to Kant dated April 6, 1793
   [*first page*]

Every member of a people
has a three-fold quality
in relation to the government

1. **Freedom** as a **human being** according to the innate right not to be subordinated merely as a means for the choice of another, instead it must be assumed that he himself authorizes the government to

treat him as if he acts in his own interest and only mediately for another's interest. For right is really an authorization to coerce insofar as it follows from the concept of the freedom of everyone. **Against hereditary subjection.**

2. **Equality** with other members as **subjects** in relation to acquired rights: everyone must be able to attain any rank in the state to which his talent, merit, and luck could bring him, and no one has hereditary right to occupy certain posts in the state. This is equality regarding acquisition of right. This does not apply to equality of external property, of honorary positions, of talents themselves. **Against privileges regarding their status as subjects.**

3. **Independence**[a] **as citizen:** everyone whose existence as a member in the state depends upon his own power of choice (thus not wife, child, or servant subject to another) must be considered as standing under laws that he himself has a part in creating. **Against despotic government.**

[*second page*]

Whether freedom and equality are found in a state, i.e. whether the idea of such a state has objective reality, one cannot determine from experience but only from moral principles of the vocation of the human species. Objective reality is secured through a command that it must be brought about.

23:137   *Loses Blatt* F 21. Written on a letter to Kant dated March 7, 1793
         [*first page*]

On the preservation of property

Through long immemorial possession. For if someone can prove that he has more right to it or can derive it from another's possession by bequest, then the thing[b] belongs to him.

Another is if it is uncertain whether the thing in itself is right or wrong or more so whether such an alleged right contradicts the right of humanity.

Of the citizen

A citizen is a human being in society who has his own rightful independence, i.e. can be considered as himself a member of the universal public legislative authority.[c] Consequently every servant[d] is a human being who, like a parasitic plant, is rooted only on another citizen. The question is whether only those who own land can be citizens, i.e. whether the quality of being a citizen, hence of membership in the public legislating

---

[a] *Selbständigkeit*   [b] *Sache*
[c] *Gewalt*   [d] *Knecht*

authority, must precede ownership of land or whether it must be based on ownership alone. In order to have something external as one's own a civil constitution must already exist. This therefore depends merely on persons in relation to one another, able to engage with one another according to outer laws, and here one must first be a citizen.

Every right to an object,[a] e.g. the salary of a civil servant, can be considered as a right to the substance.[b]

Of citizens of a state[c]

The possessors of land[d] are the genuine state subjects because they depend on the land[e] for *vitam sustinendo* {sustenance of life}. To the extent, however, that they farm only as much as they need to live they are not citizens of the state. For they could not contribute to the commonwealth. Only possessors of great amounts of land who have many servants, who themselves as servants cannot be citizens, could be citizens, and yet they are citizens only to the extent that their surplus is purchased by others who, as free citizens, do not depend on the land. But one must already have citizenship before one can be the subject of a state. Thus in regard to the commonwealth the *pactum civile* {civil contract} comes first, with the caveat that those whose existence depends on the will of another, thus those who do not enjoy a free existence, have no vote. Many owners of goods together do not constitute a commonwealth. There must be a supreme owner[f] under whom they all have their subordinate property and who is the head of the state.[g]   23:138

In a despotic state, i.e. a *souverain* monarchy, there are no citizens but an independent ruler[h] and subjects.

[second page]

Of the way to obtain something as one's own – i.e. to acquire
Any acquisition other than the first is thereby not *acquisitio rei alienae* {acquisition of another's thing} for one can [acquire] *pacto* {by contract} the deed of a *[breaks off]*

Whether first acquisition would be through unilateral power[i] and not more *acquisitio rei concessae* {acquisition of a thing permitted}.

What is yours or mine cannot be derived from *possessio originaria* {original possession} without a juridical act. Yet what is yours or mine is presupposed for land because one cannot consent without it, however no one else can be restrained by it.

[a] *Object*	[b] *Substanz*
[c] *Staatsbürgern*	[d] *Grundbesitzer*
[e] *Boden*	[f] *Obereigenthümer*
[g] *Staatsoberhaupt*	[h] *Selbstherrscher*
[i] *eigenmächtig*	

I can also acquire *jure rei meae* {my thing by law} without a juridical act.

[*remainder of L.B. F21 concerning the first section of Theory and Practice is omitted*]

23:139　*Loses Blatt* D 13 (not dated). Two short sections of drafts for *Religion* appear at 23:101 and 23:108.

[*first page begins with two omitted paragraphs concerning moral motivation*]

23:139　　Freedom, equality, and cosmopolitan unity (fraternity), where independence[a] is inwardly assumed without contract. One does not move from good to evil through moral indifference, instead there 23:140　are two distinct principles, personified as locked in struggle. *Aut–aut* {either–or}. – Cosmopolitan not federalist through contract. – The implementation works this way:

The old despotic possession remains and will be gradually transformed into a system of freedom only if principles really take hold.

Should the good in the world (the cosmopolitan) start from the formation of the subject, i.e. from the people, or from the government which first improves itself? The first principle[b] starts from the struggle of opinions so from the bottom up, out of which nothing orderly is composed. Thus only from the top down.

If we build a state by composition (*aggregatio*), thus synthetically, then the order is: 1. independence of the members, 2. equality of action and reaction, 3. freedom in the use of their powers (the highest). Legislation – dominion[c] – society, the last of which is not the obligation of subordinates but of equals.

Whether peace could exist perpetually if it is not universal. Whether it would not be strengthened through a contract and also reciprocally guaranteed.

[*several short paragraphs omitted*]

23:141　　[*second page*]

1 freedom, 2 equality, 3 independence[d] are the *singula* {separate} requirements for being a citizen. But instead of 3 **unity** is the requirement for all to constitute a state. *Requisite universorum* {required of all}.

Equality (namely rightful equality) is the degree of dependence of powers of the one on those of the other (in accordance with laws of freedom) according to which no one is required to bear more from another

---

[a]　*Selbständigkeit*
[b]　*Princip*, referring to the principle that improvement ought to come from the people.
[c]　*Herrschaft*　　　　　　　　　　　[d]　*Selbständigkeit*

than the other must endure from him in accordance with laws of freedom. All human beings are equally subject to one another and also with all higher rational beings (the *Aeons*[9]). Everyone has a duty and also rights concerning the other to whom one is thus obligated, except against God: no one has a coercive right against the head of state.[a]

Freedom is independence from the power of choice of another except in accordance with laws to which one agrees.

Innate or inherited rightful inequality (not merely temporary as with children) would be an inherited relation of those who obey (*subdita* {subjects}) toward those who have command, and is simply a contradiction because it is not based on laws of freedom, hence not considered rightful, thus also not obligatory.

[several paragraphs about freedom of action omitted]

Freedom, equality, and union[b] (*unio*) are the dynamic categories of the political so that the last, i.e. the state constitution, lies at the basis of everything practical through reason. The law arises from outer freedom; necessitation must harmonize with the law, harmonize with the principle of equality, so as to resist, in accordance with the law, the influence of members' behavior on one another; union from the community of the will of all in a whole of the state (*substantia, causalitas (influxus) commercium actio et reactio*) {substance, causality (influx), community of action and reaction}.   23:143

No one can foresee how without the principle[c] of equality a duty of a member of the state though the other as obedience to orders would be possible, for the former [is subject] only to the law that he himself has made, thus only through his own will that harmonizes with others and that determines the boundaries of duty.

[the following three paragraphs in the margin:]

The lord of hosts. Hymns and noises, unharmonious sounds. Comforter.

The human being should draw good out of evil himself. This is most clearly manifested in states.

The will concerns the law which is not in my control.[d] The power of choice concerns actions that are in my control. Regarding laws I am not free but I am free regarding the maxims I take up.

---

[a] *Oberhaupt*   [b] *Vereinigung*
[c] *Princip*   [d] *Gewalt*

Drafts for *Towards perpetual peace*

Editor's introduction

Kant thought of improvements to his approach to ideal political relations soon after his essay "Theory and Practice" appeared before the reading public in the famous *Berlinische Monatsschrift* in September 1793.[1] Likely within a month he penned a fragment he titled "Something on the relation of theory to practice" (F 23 below) that discusses theory and practice (treated in the newly published essay) as well as the republican type of government (treated only later in *Towards Perpetual Peace*). Between that time and August 13, 1795, when Kant wrote to the printer Friedrich Nicolovius that he would send a manuscript for a new book before the end of the week that Nicolovius could publish for the next book fair (12:35), Kant formulated what would become his most sustained look at international relations and the possibility of peace based on republicanism, a federalism among states, and cosmopolitanism. During that time he gave no indication in any surviving letters or other sources that he was working on a book on the topic, so it is unclear precisely when he decided to transform his afterthoughts into preparatory drafts. Scholars have long suggested that the Peace of Basel between France and Prussia, signed April 5, 1795, was the immediate trigger for Kant's decision to create the new publication.[2] While it could be that Kant took the opportunity provided by that decidedly non-perpetual peace to complete his work for publication, he may have had the short book in mind long beforehand. The topic concerning international structures to ensure peace had been brought to prominence in 1713 by the Abbé St. Pierre, who inspired many others over the following decades and whose proposals Kant knew of for most of his career.[3]

The drafts translated here range from the early one discussing theory and practice to parts of the *Reinschrift* that did not make it into the final published version. Dating of these drafts is not included in the Academy edition but is taken from Werner Stark's study of this material, mentioned in the general introduction.[4]

Drafts for Towards perpetual peace

TRANSLATED BY FRED RAUSCHER

Loses Blatt F 13. This loose sheet also contains R8100 (19:642–43) on   23:155
determinism and religion and R159 (15:57) on anthropology, both dated
1794–95. This passage appears after R8100 and before R159.

[*first page*]

Of Perpetual Peace. Means for it. 1) Do not retain old claims. 2) Do
not conquer any independent countries.ᵃ 3) Do not maintain standing
armies (*perpetuus miles*). 4) Do not accumulate a treasury. 5) Do not create
any national debt. – These are negative means. Positive 5 every state
reforms itself.

Here the practical ones [say] that one can become prudent through
experience alone and consider the way things are always done as real
and expedient; for those who think metaphysics is vain theory and empty
dreaming are in possession of the ~~principles~~ means that the world can use
for perpetual peace; still they must consider this dreaming with peaceful
hearts, and as something which has absolutely no influence on business
people, and they draw attention to the schools. – Play with ideas.

The metaphysician, who in his sanguine hopes to improve the world
will always be juggling ten balls (i.e. doing the impossible), will be viewed
with a shrug of the shoulders. Harrington's *Oceana*.⁵

Loses Blatt F 20. This appears to be a draft of the footnote on   23:156
8:347–48.

Objective practical necessity to act in a certain way (to do or to refrain
from doing) ~~as long as it does not contradict the laws, that is, can be
thought merely as possible not as necessary; consequently a permissive
law, a necessity of the contingent in accordance with laws, that, if they
are laws of reason and the permitted action~~. But if it is considered
merely as not forbidden (as permitted) consequently also not as necessitated, then the action conceived this way is not thought as standing

---

ᵃ *Länder*

207

23:157 under that practical necessity and the concept of a **permissive law of pure reason** contains a contradiction if freedom, which in this case is not restricted by any law, is yet at the same time represented as something that needed to be restricted through a law. – But here (N. 2, 3, 4[a]) only a type of acquisition that is entirely forbidden by reason is under discussion, in which reason allows the persistence of an illegitimate **state of possession**[b] for some time to be permission for it, because in a particular permissive law it is not the same object (even the same right) but another that is meant.

A permissive law would say: illegitimate possession of a thing (or a right) in a lawless condition (*status naturalis* {the state of nature}) can persist as putative possession as long as this lasts (for in itself the rightful authority which is required for any condemnation of this as an illegitimate possession is lacking); but **taking possession** in such a way must cease after leaving that condition (of nations) and entering the condition of a prevailing right of nations[c] (which in accordance with the law of reason *exeundum esse e statu naturali* {one must leave the state of nature} is just as necessary for states in relation to one another as for individual human beings). – Otherwise one does not need a law anywhere to be able to say that something is permitted, and if this exact thing is found in our civil constitution as an exception to a prohibition, then that is proof of the great juridical deficiency of its legislation, that it is to be understood as containing in the form of a prohibition, but not at the same time, the condition under which alone it is valid (as in mathematics), and so it is seen as necessary to add to the positive laws still more particular permissive laws restricting each in his own range; where it cannot be foreseen where it will end. – Therefore it is regrettable that one had to abandon the idea of the worthy and clever Herr Grafen von Windischgrätz, who made determination of this exact formula into his prize question,[6] because it alone can reveal the genuine touchstone of firmly determined legislation (and what one counts as *jus certum* {settled rights} still always counts as pious wishes).

[Laws[d]] contain a ground of objective practical **necessity**, but permissions a corresponding ground of contingency, of actions, hence a permissive law necessitates to that which no one can be necessitated by another,
23:158 which would contain a contradiction if the object of the laws were to have the same meaning in both kinds of relations. Now, however, the prohibition of the permissive law has to do only with the future **manner of acquisition** of a right (e.g. through inheritance), but release from

---

[a] There are no preceding numbers in this draft. These references do not appear in the published version of this footnote.
[b] *unrechtmäßigen Besitzstandes*　　　　[c] *herrschenden Völkerrechts*
[d] added by Academy edition editor

this prohibition has to do with the present **state of possession,**[a] which finally can be still further extended in accordance with a permissive law of reason in the progress from the state of nature to the civil state as an illegitimate, although still honorable, possession (*possessio bonae fidei* {possession in good faith}), although a similar **manner of acquisition** is forbidden in the resulting civil state in accordance with this process; the authority for the extended possession would not exist if such an acquisition were to occur in the civil state, for there illegitimate possession as an infringement must cease as soon as it is discovered. – Here I make this remark only casually in order to get the teachers of natural right to see the concept of a *lex permissiva* {permissive law}, which a systematically organizing reason itself presents as a test, often used in particular with regard to the civil laws (which are admittedly only statutory); e.g. if it says in the law that this or that is forbidden and then it follows that in number 1 this and in number 2 that circumstance would prevail, etc. where no end of exceptions is in sight and it is easily perceived that this is not in accordance with a principle – for otherwise the conditions would not have to be added by tapping around the prohibitive law but instead would have to be part of the form itself. – it is therefore regrettable that this unresolved remaining prize question of the Herr Grafen von Windischgrätz, as wise as he is clever, had to be abandoned so soon. For the possibility of such a formula (similar to a mathematical formula) is the single touchstone of a determined, consequently lasting legislation and is that which alone can bring a pious wish to a state of *jus certum* {settled right}.

[*second page*] In general the permissive law can be defined as such: it is the law of an illegitimate possession of that which is capable of being acquired.

Loses Blatt F 15   23:159

In all three forms of the state the form of government can be republican. This is one in which all burdens which the people should carry are distributed with their own consent[b] (in accordance with *justitia distributiva* {distributive justice}). E.g. requiring personal service in lieu of military service, payment of excise taxes, and customs duties. Whether such a burden should in general be imposed is a matter for the sovereign as legislator, e.g. that there should be war. – The government is despotic (*titulus* {so titled}) if it is not the servant of the state and trustee of its affairs but is lord for itself[c] (*souverain*), because it can in this way do something wrong and no lawful means (*remedium juris*) are possible against it

---

[a] *Besitzstand*   [b] *Stimmen*
[c] *Selbstherrscher*

in that it, as *executor* of the *souverain*, has all executive power.[a] Republicanism is thus the right of the people to refuse obedience to the minister or magistrates if the people believe that it would not be in accordance with the laws to obey them, until they are convinced otherwise. Over that[b] there must be no status or dignity whose authorization to coerce could not be formulated through the right of the subjects in equilibrium.

[*the following two paragraphs are related to the first paragraph of footnote at 8:349*]

Whether a human being is authorized to demand security from others that the other will not injure him only when the other has already injured him, or whether he is permitted to demand this security beforehand. The latter is clear. (For otherwise I would never be able to have security for I would not know whether he will injure me this time.) for I would have to first be obligated to put my trust in him that he will never aim to injure me, but I am not obligated to do that. Thus I am allowed to first obtain security regarding his upholding my rights before I would have to prove the harm of not having such security. [*In margin:* The ideas must be kept holy.] It is an imperfect duty to treat other human beings well. ~~I can demand this security out of my innate right of freedom. But in the state of nature that provides me no such security.~~

23:160   That the other is allowed no right against me (which I could violate) may also be what one would think if I have no **reason** to assume that he does not want to respect what is mine, but it is not a ground for being secure that he would not harm me just because he has not yet done it ~~yet~~, for why should I adopt that favorable opinion of him, e.g. to lend him something and trust his word that he will return it, if I have in this case no security from him. For the merely natural human being, his proximity to others[c] is itself an infringement, he can be necessitated to leave because his existence threatens others with danger (that is the cause of the diffusion of human beings in the state of nature). It would not do for me to wait to see whether he would injure me, for supposing he were to do something it would still always be uncertain whether he would do it a second time. His promise is unreliable. – Therefore first a public right then private right. – But as far as the first is concerned, everything begins from power,[d] although it should not or at least should not remain so.

But wherever there is no security that he **will** not **injure** me (or the other assumes this), there can be no obligation on my side to tolerate him unhindered next to me. For there would already have to be a public right, which obligated me to it, for by myself I cannot do anything to keep myself from exposure to danger. ~~There is no special~~

---

[a] *Gewalt*
[c] *Nachbarschaft*

[b] *das*, could be "the people"
[d] *Gewalt*

~~section of the doctrine of right in~~ The division of outer right into that in the state of nature and that in the civil condition is completely inadmissible. In the first case there is no rightful condition (it is not a *status juridicus* {juridical condition}), instead in it one abstracts only from the way in which rightful laws in general can be given force[a] for their realization, this is referred back to in civil right, above all in the way the civil constitution in general is classified in accordance with the various forms of **sovereignty**[b] (*forma imperii*) and of **government** (*forma regiminis*). In both the supreme head of state and the people are considered to be in a lawful relation to each other for the supreme head of state is either only one over the people, or a few of the people, or all of the people constitute the sovereign authority[c] together (monarchy, aristocracy, and democracy); this difference in regard to the ends of a lawful constitution is not essential, for it can be attained by means of all, although by means of one it is easier than by means of the others; in contrast the forms or types of government, whether they are **republican** or **despotic**, i.e. whether they are based on the spirit of general will of the people or on one or another private will. The first, **in a representative system** of state constitution, realizes[d] a republican constitution and is the only one which is fully in accord with concepts of right, because it is also the only one of these fully derived from these concepts. But democracy (in the genuine sense of the word), as the power of the people without representation, is directly opposed to freedom and thus also to the concept of right, since it is necessarily mob rule,[e] because the supreme head and the people as ruler[f] can never be one and the same person in that the latter only **obeys** while the former only **orders**, (how, then, under these two there can be thought only a union, *unio*, but no society of *superior* and *subjectus* {superior and subject}), hence the people cannot rule[g] by themselves but instead only through the voice[h] of certain representatives among them.

23:161

The majority do not allow it to be said that it could be better with the established order, for otherwise there could be a better *codex* {code}.

If, as the politicians say, war is not ended by victory but by treaty (the conclusion of peace), they are absolutely correct insofar as it concerns formalities, for without the latter reservations for future wars could still remain. But to hope to find one's security in this formality would be to put so much trust in the sincerity of human beings that if it could really be taken as real, there would be no more war at all.

---

[a] *Kraft*
[b] *Beherrschung*
[c] *Herrschergewalt*
[d] *beweist*
[e] *Ochlocratie*
[f] *Herrscher*
[g] *Herrschen*
[h] *Stimmgebung*

[*this paragraph added in the margin:*] Possession 1, in accordance with an analytic principle[a] of right, is one grounded in general in the concept of freedom, originally *a priori* 2. in accordance with a synthetic principle that no one can require me to make use of something but instead I myself have a right to be able to use other things.

23:162   [*second page*]

[*in upper margin:*] On the argument that human beings are not angels. War is a kind of crudity, imprudence, barbarity just as with savages there is fighting instead of arguments.

The state constitution[b] is in the end based on the morality of the people and this in turn cannot properly take root without a good state constitution, because war, by means of force, does away with the rules, so: [*breaks off*]

If someone departs from the principle[c] of freedom and equality, I want to know where he wants to determine their boundaries through laws. That which he alone can choose is that he sets absolutely no principles[d] over his choosing, and he makes the harmfulness, about which each has a different opinion, in accordance with the circumstances (which are left to the judgment of each) into a principle, if it deserves such a name.

To reform the state in accordance with principles is not merely to patch it up.

To recommend improvements to the state forbidden by the jurists – how they are not suitable for political legislation.[e]

Whether inclination to war would indicate evil and hatred of humanity or more vanity and lust for power.

[*remainder of this Loses Blatt in margin:*]

Here the topic is not the promotion of morality, certainly not the promotion of happiness, but merely to forbid war.

The practical politician reaches conclusions about how it will go in the future based on how it has always gone in the past, without considering that this precise assumption, if it is accepted universally, is the cause of things never improving. But if that is not the genuine ground of their dismal assertion, then they would do well to stop hiding the deep insight into human nature that they possess. They know (they say) **human beings**. – That is to be expected because they deal with many of them, but whether they also know **the human being** is quite doubtful. Their knowledge may well be like that of which La Mettrie and his

23:163   colleagues the anatomists boast. Like those who must carry others about

---

[a] *Princip*
[c] *Princip*
[b] *Staatsverfassung*
[d] *Principien*
[e] *sie* is indeterminate between the jurists being unsuitable as legislators (i.e. in Kant's opinion) or the improvements not being suitable as legislation (in the jurists' opinion).

in sedan chairs, he says, we know where all houses on the street are, but have not been in any.[7]

Exhortations reach great lords but not their administrators.

Where the state and the people are two different persons it is despotism.

Loses Blatt F 23. Written on a fragment of a letter to Kant the content of 23:163
which suggests that it was written October 1793.

Something on the relation of theory to practice[a]
in questions of right (*quaestiones juridicae*)

It is remarkable that *a priori* principles[b] of practical reason still count as theory and are differentiated from those for practice. The first are as a whole **moral-practical**, those which stand under them, which consist of principles for **practicing**[c] a certain imperative (of skill), are **technical practical**, and if practicing these concerns one's own happiness, **pragmatic**. Thus imperatives of morality, of skill, and of prudence.

Technical practical imperatives are either pure rational principles or empirically conditioned; the first kind are those of pure art of measurement (*geometria*), the second kind are those for the art of measurement in the field (*agrimensoria*), e.g. whether one could best survey the field with a small surveyor's table or with an astrolabe.

Whether the claim that the best state constitution[d] is a republican one is really based on principles of practical reason, namely the right of human beings in general, does of course belong as such to theory; but while this claim is not yet realized, one must institute reforms little by little to gradually realize it and indeed it must be understood with the prospect of perpetual peace in mind, thus in accordance with *a priori* principles, and thus it belongs to the practice of the right of states.[e] Without such principles, which have this idea of the pure republic in mind, it would just as well be called a patching up of the state as the so-called "practitioners" are so used to considering it all. – The doctrine of right is treated either juridically or philosophically. The first has empirical principles (the law of the land) as its basis, the other pure rational principles from concepts. Only jurists and empiricists can make judgments about right in accordance with positive laws, only philosophers can make judgments about that which is contained in the *a priori* principles, as in general how the law of the land must be constituted and how a constitution must be constituted so that it contains the prerequisites for 23:164
the best law of the land. The jurist as such (*purus putus*), in order to do

---

[a] *Praxis*, unless otherwise noted   [b] *principien*
[c] *Ausübung*   [d] *Staatsverfassung*
[e] *Staatsrechts*

his business, has to resist the great urgings of the philosopher about the nature of the matter, and that is the so-called conflict between theory and practice, which is based on a misunderstanding. The jurist wants obedience to the laws of the existing constitution not to be weakened by anything, but he himself does not know that these laws are followed grudgingly, and he resists the plans of the philosopher for the best constitution. The philosopher, if he remains true to his aim, strives not to oppose the jurist in observation of the laws of the land, but freedom of public opinion regarding the best possible constitution will lead the current legislators to it by means of the idea.

Not much depends on the different forms of the state regarding the ruling person, whether one or several or all in the state possess the legislative power. For the law, if it is to be a rightful ground of duties, must still be considered in all of these forms as if it proceeded from the general will of the people. All the more depends on the type of government, and it is also in particular all the more crucial how the one to whom the exercise of this power[a] is entrusted can be bound to the law, for this in the first place requires much power of judgment and, because he is the supreme executive power, there is none higher above him. Judicial authority, which in its pronouncements derives a given case of governing from the universal rule of legislation, is heavily involved in this.

In order to make the republican **constitution** discernible in comparison with every other one, I must remark that the constitution (*constitutio*) of a state (*civitas*), insofar as it is measured with regard to the right of humanity, will at bottom be based on exactly the same principles[b] (of freedom and equality), i.e. its spirit must be in accordance with **republican** constitution, the opposite of which is not in accord with these principles and is called a **despotic** constitution.

[*the following paragraph relates to 8:351–52*]

The civil constitution[c] (*constitutio civitatis*) can be considered either in regard to the **person** (whether it is one or a few or all) who possesses supreme power (thus being autocracy, aristocracy, democracy) and

23:165   through whom the people are **ruled**,[d] and here it can be almost equally valid whether it happens through one or a few together or all of the people together – or the division has to do with the way it is **governed**, which is much more important; and so there is a two-fold form of civil constitution, the form of **sovereignty**[e] (*forma imperii*) and the form of **government** (*forma regiminis*); and although it can be the case that the first makes a difference to the second being good [*in margin*: war (belongs to the right of nations) The Bulgarian prince: a blacksmith who

---

[a] *Gewalt*
[b] *principien*
[c] *bürgerliche Verfassung*
[d] *beherrscht wird*
[e] *Beherrschung*

214

has tongs[8]], so that we could even consider the former more as means and the latter as the end, whether the supreme power may be the power of a prince, the power of the nobility, or the power of the people,[a] the main question is how many kinds of form of government can there be based on laws, and which apply the laws, and the answer is it is either republican, if the legislator is not at the same time the executive, [*breaks off*]

[*second page*]

The first division has to do with the substance of the state, the second with the form. – If there must once be a state constitution, i.e. a supreme constituted power[b] which determines and secures everyone's right (*justitia distributiva* {distributive justice}), then what must be seen to first is the person who could have this power; for in accordance with the course of nature this must happen prior to the rightful contract because this contract presupposes peace, without which the voting people[c] could not be gathered together at one time to express their general will unless they were to subject to coercion. The substance of the most supreme power (the ruler[d]) can be either one, or a few, or all together who find themselves next to one another for this purpose[e] (autocracy, aristocracy, democracy); now here is the way they can rule the people, i.e. in accordance with the universal laws of their common will regarding administration of right, which really originates with those who have subjected themselves to a supreme power although as yet undetermined. Thus to form one of these three types of state power,[f] either the power of the prince or of the nobles or of the people is assumed, each of which constitutes a distinct form of state (*forma imperii*); still, a distinct form of government stemming from the state constitution is necessary (*forma regiminis*). It can indeed be based on one just as on another of the three forms of state in accordance with the concept of right, but importantly this does not make it tied to such empirical grounds; rather the form of state would not be so badly chosen if it were to have to be chosen and created *a priori* from pure rational grounds, instead of in such a way that the form of state would depend greatly on the empirical conditions under which it comes to be, and would not stem from the choice of the people. The third rightful power is that which determines the division of property to each in accordance with the consent of the government with legislation (*justitia distributiva* {distributive justice}) and is the tribunal for the administration of right (*potestas judicaria* {judicial power}) which authority likewise constitutes the third member of a rational syllogism where the *major* {major premise} is understanding, the *minor* the

23:166

---

[a] *die oberste Macht mag nun Fürstengewalt, Adelsgewalt, oder Volksgewalt sein*
[b] *Gewalt*
[c] *Stimgebenden*
[d] *der obersten Gewalt (der Beherrscher)*
[e] *Absicht*
[f] *Staatsgewalt*

power of judgment, the *conclusio* is reason. But the form of government as the kind of power applying the law can only be divided into two types: namely it is either republican, i.e. measured by freedom and equality, or despotic, a will not bound to this condition. The first is a democratic constitution in a representative system; however, pure democracy as a type of government is despotic, as are the two others if they have not intentionally accepted the principles of the republican type of government as an overarching restriction on the power of the state through the voice of the people.

The first two forms of state represent the people as at the same time the supreme head, the third is in itself absolutely not representative and thus the government rules **at the same time** as sovereign, which is despotic.

A king who represents the people with rightful force, i.e. unites the power belonging to them, is the best of all despots, a nobility is worse, because its interest deeply divides it from the people, but worst of all[a] democracy, which is the people themselves.

23:166   *Loses Blatt* F 12 (after June 1793). The fragment mentions a fact about Greek government that Kant likely drew from the *Berliner Monatschrift* of that month.

    [first side]
    [related to footnote on 8:352–53]
    The exalted epithets bestowed on a *souverain*, e.g. "the divinely anointed," "the administrator and representative of the rights of God on earth" and the like, have commonly been bitterly censured as inexcusable, gross, dizzying and common flattery of the monarchy,[b] but, it seems to me, without grounds. For far from these titles making the absolute ruler of a people arrogant, they would rather have to humble him in his soul if he is intelligent, and make him reflect that he has taken on the most sacred office on earth, that of trustee of the right of human beings and yet must always still himself be only a human being.

23:167   *[written upside down:]* In the end more depends on the type of government being good than on the form of the state, which is better only insofar as it provides a better ground for government. – The Greeks did not know of the representative system.

    [second page]
    [see 8:362–63] But before we determine more closely the type of affording of the guarantee, it will be necessary first to examine the condition that nature has first prepared for the person acting on its great stage, which would finally make its assurance of peace necessary; only then shall we examine the way it affords this security.

---

[a] *am Meisten*   [b] *das königliche Haupt*

Loses Blatt F 16   23:167
   [*first page*]
   [*see 8:355*]
   The way in which states pursue their right (*modus jus suum perse-quendi*) can never be through an external court by which they seek their right through legal proceedings, but through war; and its outcome, victory, can never determine right, and the peace treaty itself (*pactum pacis*), which indeed follows, rightfully makes an end to this war which has just been waged but not an end to the condition of war,[a] to finding causes which are used as pretexts that must always count as valid, because in the state of nature each is judge in his own case; however, what holds in accordance with natural right for human beings, they ought to leave the state of nature as a state of publicly declared injustice in order to submit themselves to an externally legislating power,[b] cannot hold for states in accordance with the idea of the right of nations,[c] yet reason, from the throne of the highest morally legislative power, delivers an absolute condemnation of war as a procedure for determining rights, and, on the contrary, makes a condition of peace[d] a duty, but one which has no obligating force without the rightful consent of human beings and without a contract – so there must be a league of states which is posited only for reciprocal preservation of the peace with each other. [*next two sentences added:*] Association in this league obligates them together only through negative obligation, namely to wage war neither against all others nor united with others, and to do their part for perpetual peace (whose concept is itself merely negative). They do not obligate themselves to provide help to one another against any state (who may be within or outside the league). – This is a right of the nations themselves in the state of nature, for they also have a right to that which   23:168
they are uniformly obligated merely as human beings. But this is a right of states against all others who necessitate them to leave the state of nature, to submit to them, and to enter along with other states into a single civil state; states are of course permitted to resist this because public right has already been established within these states, whereas nothing of the sort is to be found in the state of nature for individual human beings. Preservation of peace also involves a merely negative contract and not a positive obligation, like the civil constitution it requires. – The following moments determine the characteristics of this contract.
   1. There is no external right without securing for the other party[e] his right. 2. In accordance with the right of nations this security

---

[a] *Kriegszustande*   [b] *Gewalt*, in this paragraph
[c] *Völkerrechts*   [d] *Friedenszustand*
[e] *Theils*

cannot ~~under free states~~ be expected from a union in accordance with civil laws, hence subjection under one supreme power[a] ruling over states (a great body of states), for that is contrary to the concept of the right of nations, ~~thus instead it should be a free combination~~ and consequently security presupposes a union of the wills of all with this aim, but these wills are free and must remain so. A federal association (Federalism)[b] is such a combination. 3. Such a federalism presupposes free states as such and is merely negative, namely the aim is only to end war and at the same time the annexation of one state by another. [*in margin:*] also the coercion of others to necessitate this state into a civil constitution with others. The federal association is thus directed only to peace.

[*second page*]

4. A right of nations which has effect can thus take place only under a federalism of free states as such; under this title is to be understood a combination of powers[c] that, without coercive laws, guarantee for one another nothing more than the freedom on which perpetual peace can be grounded.

A union between states simply to preserve the freedom of a state and also to guarantee freedom to others has the aim to do it without subjection to external public laws. Such a league is ~~union of pure federalism, commanded by reason, of human right~~ the synthetic principle [*written above:* the synthetic concept] of the external freedom of states without lawful coercion (in contrast to that of the independence of its choice from others which is analytic). If the concept of a right of nations means something and is not to be completely empty, then it cannot be thought of otherwise than as a *foedus pacificum* or *pacis* {league to make peace or for peace}, which is distinct from a peace treaty (*pactum pacis*) that only means the end of a single war, in that the state would stop all wars and enter into society.

23:169

The order of nature wills that power[d] and coercion precede right, for without them human beings would not even once be brought to unite themselves for legislation. – But the order of reason wills that afterward law regulates freedom and brings it form.

[*The following paragraph is draft for 8:356–57*]

The concept of a right of nations as a right to go to war, is, strictly speaking, unintelligible (since it is supposed to be a right to determine what is legitimate not by universally valid external laws of freedom but instead by unilateral maxims of force[e]); one would have to mean that human beings so disposed destroy one another and find perpetual peace in the vast grave that swallows up all the horrors of violence along with

---

[a] *Gewalt*
[b] *Bundesgenossenschaft (Föderalism)*
[c] *Verbindung der Mächte*
[d] *Gewalt*
[e] *Gewalt*

their authors. In accordance with reason there is only one way that states in ~~right~~ relations with one another can leave the lawless condition, which involves nothing but war; it is that, like individual human beings, they give up their savage (lawless) freedom, likewise subject themselves to public coercive laws, and so form an always growing state of nations (*civitas gentium*) that would finally encompass all the nations of the earth. But they are discouraged from acting in accordance with this idea, not merely because of the difficulty of carrying it out, but more because of the opposite hostile idea of a supposed right of nations as a right without being a public, lawful constitution, and a right to decide single-handedly what will count as right under this idea; so they can posit (what was completely correct *in thesi* is unattainable *in hypothesi*) instead of the positive idea of a world republic only the negative surrogate of a league of the vicious, that alone itself averts war by being a constant counterweight to inclinations tending toward an eruption of war (*furor impius intus – fremit horridus ore cruento* {within, impious Rage . . . shall roar in the ghastliness of blood-stained lips} Virgil[9]); [*remainder in margin:*] which can yet be built into a pure republic that is by its nature inclined to perpetual peace, so this can serve as a middle point for other states that have not themselves completely taken on that form that would commit them to peaceful intentions.

Loses Blatt F 9. Written on the cover of a letter dated June 3, 1795.　　23:170
   [*First three paragraphs relating to a footnote on 8:367 on different religions are omitted*]
   Differences of races, of languages, and of religions make so many separations, but even worse the last of these leads to offensive war.
   Unity of languages and of religions and of types of governments would soon make for migration and a melting together of peoples, hence universal monarchy, which is harmful. Thus nature arranges it so that the relation of states, in accordance with the right of nations,[a] a state of war [*breaks off*]

Worship of God

Separation of the states makes federalism necessary as a means for the right of nations in the war that arises from the state of nature of nations.
   The idea of a right of nations presupposes that there are various　　23:171
neighboring states that are separated from one another because their rights could come into conflict with one another, because this state[b] of discord is still better than the concord that would result from the melting together of many states into a great one with a universal monarchy,

---

[a] *Völkerrecht*　　　　　　　　　　　[b] *Zustand*

which has many times been attempted but which can have no stability, because the weaker the capacity of governing in accordance with laws becomes, the more it approaches mob rule and so despotism breaks out into an anarchy that will destroy itself. – Every state, even the smallest, is always striving to view itself as the centerpoint of expansion over all others, but nature wills that this occur without mingling, like a bunch of pebbles thrown on a still surface of water – each wave spreads out endlessly from its starting place and, in conformity with rules, crosses but does not mix with others. Nature has used the means of differences in language and religion for the end of bringing about the segregation of peoples.

[*Relates to 8:363–64.*] Distinct languages and religions prevent states from joining together. – Who knows what power[a] still lies in the background. Mounted nomads have expelled civilized peoples from their lands. On the prohibition of blood against the hunters (herding, farming, and fishing peoples) – On pressures from contact which divide Samoyeds and Finns from one another.[10]

That nature would of itself agree with the final end as if it were determined in accordance with moral laws of right. – For culture is when human beings are necessitated to be next to each other, progressing in natural ways. – Progress of human beings, however, inevitably raises up conflict in the aims of human beings because there is no universal principle that has the power to make their efforts unanimous (i.e. without conforming to the moral law), and one's aims negate those of another, i.e. because evil is itself always in the way. Thus nature agrees negatively with that which the law of right prescribes, i.e. it coerces to an analogue of the moral law; e.g. in the foundation of a civil society of states, an analogue of the right of nations. – Third there is in nature also a positive or contingent ordering of purposiveness of its own determinations, namely as when reindeer and moose in the most extreme regions find provision everywhere.

23:172

[*The following paragraph relates to footnote on 8:350–51*]

It depends namely on the answer to the question whether the rank granted by a state, of one subject being above another, would have to precede merit, or whether the latter ought to precede the former, and whether it is possible for a people to settle on the first alternative. Now it is obvious that if rank is connected with someone's birth, it is quite uncertain whether this human being will have merit (skill, good will, and diligence) suitable for the post that he is to possess, hence it is the same as if he were to have it granted to him without any merit (to order his subjects who would be bound to obey him), which no general will of a people in an original contract would decide upon. A nobility of office

[a] *Macht*

220

(as the rank of a higher magistracy could be called which is acquired for oneself by merit) is not opposed to equality, for there rank adheres to a post, not as property to a person, and if he retires from his business, he goes back to the status[a] of the people in general, and so someone who one year is merely a citizen of the state and was obedient can the following year become a civil servant who now gives the orders.

How trade increases freedom, contraband, strength, excise taxes, but marriage alone preserves the number of human beings.

[The following relates to the Third Article at 8:357]

In this article, as in the previous two, it is not a question of philanthropy but only of right, so that hospitality (hospitableness) means the right of a foreigner ~~newcomer~~ against the owner of land ~~wherever they resided (human beings or people)~~ not to be opposed with hostility just because he ~~wants to participate~~ has arrived on his land.[b] – This right is the consequence of the right of the whole human species to the land (for this has a determinate quantity as the surface of a sphere), since they cannot disperse infinitely, hence to be permitted to take a place in vicinity to others, so that these others are also justified in necessitating him (nonetheless peacefully) if he again leaves this vicinity. So the Bedouin Arabs recognize the duty of hospitableness toward a foreigner who finds himself at his tent even though he is turned away after a peaceful reception.[11] The foreigner can invoke this hospitableness (but not invoke a right to be a guest whom his host must invite) as a right to visit, which is given to all human beings in virtue of the freedom of space assigned to them by nature.

23:173

Inhospitable stretches of the earth's surface, such as the sea and the deserts that belong to no one, divide the community of human beings, but in such a way that ships in the one case and camels (the ships of the desert) in the other make possible a visit by one people to another. Whoever does this voluntarily can in any case be turned away, but not fought, by the inhabitants, whoever is involuntarily forced into it (a ship that seeks haven in a storm or the crew of a stranded ship) cannot be again chased into driving danger from the coast or the oasis in which he saved himself, still less can he be captured, but he must be able to find shelter until a suitable opportunity for his departure arises. – A foreigner can rightly claim this degree of sociality, but only limited to the mere hospitality of the inhabitants of each land not to oppose him with hostility.

Compare this to the actual behavior of civilized, especially coastal people on the seas, one sees that they recognize no limitation to their presumptions except whatever their own powerlessness[c] prevents them

[a] *Zustand*   [b] *Boden*
[c] *Ohnmacht*

from doing, and all the foreigner's goods, indeed even the person of the foreigner himself, are treated like booty thrown into their hands by nature. – If we also look over the inhospitable inhabitants of the Barbary Coast who, in an element that belongs to no one, take control of ships of all nations, none of which they have purchased, and also enslave any of these people who get stranded, hence perpetuating war on their part,[12] then one will note with horror the ills that overstepping the bounds of hospitality ~~whose observance would have spared distant nations from so much inner war and violence~~[a] has brought to the human species, and indeed to Europe, which brought all this commerce to all people on earth under the tutelage of the most active part of the earth, through wars which Europe has not merely waged against others but finally brought upon itself, wars that with the awakening of commerce threaten to become more and more frequent and to follow faster upon one another.

23:174

Trade in negroes, which is in itself already an offense against the hospitality of black peoples, will be even worse for Europe in its consequences. For the result of the amount of sea power and the increased number of sailors used for commerce with the sugar islands, and adding in the war which could be waged using them, is partly the burial of a number of human beings *en masse* in the sea, partly the emptying of all coasts or also of whole peoples, and partly slow starvation through obstruction of the circulation of food. – The lands of America had barely been discovered before the inhabitants were pushed aside or swindled to make room for settlements, still worse the inhabitants were themselves in part made into slaves as goods without owners,[b] and in part forced out of their territory and wiped out by internal wars through which they were made unhappy because driven by jealousy and concern for the supremacy of one part in a multitude of long wars, because of which the commercial inhabitants grew in power[c] at a manifold of new opportunities. The visits from our part of the world to the East Indies, on the mainland as well as on the islands, began with separate, peaceful settlements and resulted in the subjugation of a substantial part of the old inhabitants, but even worse the internal wars, from which only China and Japan were spared, which the European powers provoked from such a great distance and which finally reached their own territory itself, and which were concluded with the people of our lands no longer allowed any territory in their lands.

The principles that allege conformity with the right of possession applied to newly discovered lands that are believed to be barbaric and inhabited by unbelievers, as goods without owners, acquired without

[a] *Gewaltthätigkeit*   [b] *Herrenloses Gut*
[c] *Macht*

the assent of the inhabitants and even with their subjugation, are completely opposed to the cosmopolitan right to limited hospitality; and since Europe is the continent that placed itself in reciprocal trade so that the gains or losses in whichever region of the world they may occur are always and often felt very sensitively in Europe, so Europe receives new and never diminishing material with which to expand and perpetuate war instead of peace in this part of the world.

A spark of a violation of human rights suffered in another continent,   23:175 in accordance with the flammability of the material of thirst for power in human nature, above all in their leaders, lights the flame of war that reaches the region where it had its origin.

It is quite necessary to extend the concept of human rights not merely to internal matters of a state constitution in one people or to the relation of nations to one another in a right of nations but finally also to a cosmopolitan right, because the right of states as well as the right of nations[a] [are needed] for external human right in general; without them the prospect of approaching perpetual peace would be completely cut off.

Now that a community that would encompass the nations of the earth is coming to be more or less prevalent so that the violation of right in one place on the earth is gradually felt in all, the idea of a cosmopolitan right is a necessary extension of the *Codex*.

FRAGMENTS OF THE PRINTER'S COPY

Parts of the manuscript sent to the printer, the *Reinschrift* (see editor's introduction to this section of Drafts), survived and are included with the preparatory material for *Toward Perpetual Peace* in the Academy edition, (23:175–92). These fragments correspond to 8:362–68 and 8:370–75 in the published version. While most of the changes are relatively minor, those interested in specific details regarding last-minute alterations in the passages are advised to consult the Academy edition, where annotations to the text of the printer's copy identify the alterations. Here are included only a few full paragraphs crossed out in the printer's copy that were thus left out of the published version.

[The following paragraph appears in the printer's copy at the end of the second paragraph of the Appendix (8:370), the final sentence of which does not appear in the printer's copy. The Cambridge translation in the volume Practical Philosophy has ". . . (though it is sufficiently enlightened to hope they will be in conformity with its wish)," after which the following paragraph appears only in the printer's copy, crossed out.]

---

[a] *sowohl das Staats- als das Völkerrecht*

What the appearance of a conflict between both principles shows is 23:18 above all that one confuses having that moral idea before one's eyes as an unshakeable goal in order to realize it in practice with a supposed obligation to do this immediately (impetuously); e.g. to want to transform through revolution an imperfect state that was established in a way contrary to right, a violent operation that will dissolve the state into complete anarchy. Danger lurks there, and since it is better to have some right 23:184 rather than none at all even when excessive arbitrary power impedes it, it is a duty for the subjects to allow the state to persevere until the sovereign authority[a] itself is moved gradually to reform it by the nature of things and by the pleas of the subjects, or also by a duty of the sovereign toward the state to consolidate the state's powers, even were it by means of lawless despotism, in order to preserve the state by reducing external threats. But some object to this and set practice and theory against one another, claiming that those in power as well as those who obey would not sacrifice their selfish inclinations for the sake of concepts of right, that even if they ought to and could do it they would not will to do it, i.e. if one takes the human being as he is (*cereus in vitium flecti monitoribus asper* {soft as wax for molding to evil, peevish with his counsellors[13]}), as unjust in himself, not tamable through laws of right, and even the wrong in the type of government is made into justice in relation to such a tainted being: then one says more than one can prove, e.g. in the proposition powerful princes are willing to establish their rights only through war. For that this lies provisionally in human nature in their crudity (regarding culture) it is not also proven that he would be precluded from being an inseparable means for the final end for human beings, and it is only an excuse of the practical man to bedeck and embellish himself in merely mechanical knowledge of the state and of right.

[*The printer's copy and the published version now continue with* "But now the practical man . . .", *8:371*]

[*The following paragraph appears in the printer's copy at the end of the fourth paragraph of the Appendix (8:371). The Cambridge translation in the volume Practical Philosophy has "*. . . *can alone hope to find a sure ground for its edifice of political prudence," after which the following paragraph appears only in the printer's copy, crossed out.*]

23:186 But empirical propositions, because they actually teach how things work and may have always worked in the world but not that it **necessarily** had to be so, could not be the basis for moral principles that carry necessity along with them, and thus it cannot be the natural necessity of the actual behavior of the human beings, which would contradict the moral law, that would be the basis for maxims, and to act

---

[a] *Herrshergewalt*

contrary to right with the excuse that one must treat human beings conforming to the way they now are (and have ever been), first, does not follow from the theoretical proposition that even though they **should** and also **will** to improve they could not because of their more powerful nature, hence second it does not follow that one should cobble together maxims of alleged state prudence taken from power politics[a] and a pliant morality with those of a miscarriage of a similar kind (from which one can make what one wants) in order to derive a public **right**, instead of subordinating the former, which can vary with the circumstances, to the latter, which is independent and sacred without any leeway. I can conceive of a moral politician (who [puts] politics after morality) but in no way conceive of a political moralist (who puts morality after politics); and although maxims universally grounded on what is right still allow exceptions for inclination now and then, however reluctantly, and in that case if the need arises there is hope for forgiveness by the grace given by the highest judge, there are yet some who intentionally distort the idea of duty or scorn it as pedantry, which is such an heinous violation (*injuria atrox*) against the highest power legislating in us that it must be seen as the only wrong that insofar as we can judge can be forgiven neither in this nor in a future world.

23:187

[*The printer's copy and the published version now continue with "Admittedly, if there were no freedom . . .," 8:372*]

[*The following paragraph appears in the printer's copy at the end of the last full paragraph on 8:375. The Cambridge translation in the volume Practical Philosophy has ". . . namely the honor of augmenting their power in whatever way they may acquire it," after which the following paragraph appears only in the printer's copy, crossed out.*]

One does best when assuming that nature in human beings works toward the same goal that morality strives for, better than if one slanders humanity, especially regarding their essential predispositions, in order to cajole human beings who are adorned with power,[b] and better than focusing on the belief that the current stage in the progressive improvement of the human race is the highest that our species is destined for in order to excuse the wrong done by the powerful.[c]

23:192

[*Added in the bottom left corner but not in published version:*] When the incentives of realpolitik[d] negate and annihilate one another moral incentives will begin to display their effect and the idea of perpetual peace will be realized.

[*The printer's copy ends here*]

---

[a] *gewalttätiger Politik*
[b] *Macht*
[c] *der Oberen*
[d] *Naturpolitik*

Loses Blatt Schubert. Part of this sheet is identified as a likely draft for *Perpetual Peace*. It might, however, be Kant's response to Friedrich Schlegel's review of *Perpetual Peace* in which he said "I cannot grasp how Kant can consider the concept of the majesty of the people absurd."[14] The pagination is from Stark, *Nachforschungen*, pp. 246–47.

[*Corresponding to 8:354.*]

Stark 246   Majesty is the authority[a] of a person insofar as that person has power[b] over all other powers[c] in the state. Now this cannot be a merely moral person, e.g. be a republic, which indeed does exercise sovereignty over

Stark 247   itself but which simultaneously represents the whole sum of the subjects, where no one possesses the highest authority but instead each has equal rightful power relative to all. Thus the title **Majesty** applies only to a single physical person who has power **over all others** in the state (a monarch). When one hears talk of the sovereignty of the people, one should take it to mean this. In contrast the expression **the majesty of the people**, which deceptive republicans often toss around, borders on the ridiculous. Clearly majesty is that authority in a people that can be limited by none higher. Now there is no one among the people whose standing would not be limited by a higher authority, namely that of the whole people as a **moral person**: for the people is the sum of all subjects. Now if, as in a monarchy,[d] this authority is transferred to a single physical person who will be his own lord, then the liberation of this person from any possible reluctance of the people gives him the luster of a luminescent star, whereas all those subject to the dignity of the state are eclipsed by the reflection of that luminescence.

Loses Blatt G 17. Written on a letter dated September 18, 1793. Missing from Academy edition, printed in Stark, *Nachforschungen*.

Stark 246   That only one single proof of the laws of duty insofar as they belong to morality is possible – raises the question whether this is also true in relation to the laws of right.

Rightful equality can also be explained this way: it is the relation of a human being toward another in which no one can give him orders unless he himself wills it. Thus merely negative. But he cannot will that someone would give orders to him except through a contract which he can void, hence he cannot put himself in the condition of subserviency.

[a] *Auctorität*   [b] *Macht*
[c] *Gewalten* in remainder of paragraph   [d] *Königthume*

Drafts for the *Metaphysics of morals*

Editor's introduction

Kant first mentioned his plan to write "Metaphysical Foundations of Practical Philosophy" in a letter to Johann Heinrich Lambert on New Year's Eve, 1765. This work, for which Kant claimed to have already thought out the contents, would appear alongside a parallel "Metaphysical Foundations of Natural Philosophy." Both were to function as introductions to Kant's newly devised "proper method of metaphysics" by providing "examples to show *in concreto* what the proper procedure should be." Only after these "little essays" were published would Kant publish the denser work on method, which would then "not have to be burdened excessively with detailed and yet inadequate examples" (10:56).

As it turned out, not only did Kant abandon the plan to publish the illustrative works in practical and natural philosophy *before* the systematic work on method in metaphysics, spending much of the following decade and a half formulating that proper method and transforming the project until its culmination in the 1781 *Critique of Pure Reason*, he also wrote and published eight books and over a dozen essays – nearly the whole of his critical scholarly production – before finally returning to the work on a metaphysical foundations of practical philosophy over thirty years later.[1] The *Metaphysics of Morals* is not itself identified as "metaphysical foundations," though its two parts are: the *Metaphysical Foundations of the Doctrine of Right* and the *Metaphysical Foundations of the Doctrine of Virtue*.

The 210 pages of draft material for the *Metaphysics of Morals* in Volume 23 are third in quantity among drafts, exceeded only by the material for the *Critique of Pure Reason* and the incomplete and inchoate *Opus Postumum*. Three-quarters of this material is devoted to the *Doctrine of Right*, and about half of the remaining is aimed at the Introduction and Preface of the *Doctrine of Virtue*, prominently concerning the distinction between right and virtue. Generous selections from these drafts are included here.

Some other drafts were apparently inadvertently included in the published version of the *Doctrine of Right*. Bernd Ludwig has argued that the copyist preparing the final version to be sent to the printer, or the printer himself, misunderstood some of Kant's signs and notations in Kant's own full handwritten draft in which Kant had marked intended deletions and shifting of text.[2] Kant presumably was too busy working on the *Doctrine of Virtue* to review the material again before printing. Ludwig's own edition of the *Rechtslehre* incorporates the revisions and deletions that he determined better fit Kant's intentions, placing the deleted material as a supplement and identifying those passages as "probably preparatory work."[3] The Cambridge Edition of the *Doctrine of Right* follows only two of Ludwig's suggested changes, only one of which involves deleted material, and includes the deleted material in a footnote to pages 404–405 of that edition.[4]

Text from one loose sheet that was not included in the Academy edition but that has been identified as preparatory work for the *Doctrine of Right* is also included. *Loses Blatt Hagen* 23 also includes some material identified as preparatory for the *Conflict of the Faculties* on religion and material on physics and chemistry that constitute R74 (14:517–21). The portion of Hagen 23 translated here appears in Werner Stark, *Nachforschungen zu Briefen und Handschriften Immanuel Kants* (Berlin: Akademie Verlag, 1993). The text of Hagen 23 is split into distinct parts in order to place relevant discussions under the proper topic; it does not read as a single extended argument. Its importance lies in the fact that it is dated 1794, making it one of the earliest fragments of work identified as preparatory work for the *Doctrine of Right*. Other material included among the Reflections that were written after 1788 – the last year in which Kant is recorded as teaching his course on Natural Right – are possibly preparatory material rather than lecture notes as well.

The selections are arranged largely in accord with the topics in the published *Metaphysics of Morals* rather than in their unfortunate order in *Kants gesammelte Schriften*. Gerhard Lehmann, the editor of the volumes from which these drafts are drawn, included separate parts in two volumes. Most of the drafts for the *Metaphysics of Morals* are in Volume 23; however, only one of the two drafts for the Appendix added to the second edition of the *Doctrine of Right* appears in Volume 23. Appearing in Volume 20 is Kant's long draft for the Appendix written in direct response to the review of the *Doctrine of Right* by Friedrich Bouterwek. Lehmann's reason for placing this draft in Volume 20 rather than 23 is that it is part of the *Rostocker Nachlaß*, a set of manuscripts also including several unpublished yet largely complete drafts appearing in that volume: the First Introduction to the *Critique of the Power of Judgment*, the writings against Eberhard, and prefaces for the *Religion within the Boundaries of Mere Reason*. Perhaps to make Kant's response to Bouterwek appear parallel to those other works, Lehmann included a mock-up of a full title page as it might have appeared when published, drawn from Kant's own handwritten sketch although presented as a facsimile of a published book without any indication that it stems only from Kant's pen.[5] This material clearly ought to have been published with the drafts for the *Metaphysics of Morals* in Volume 23 alongside the loose sheet also identified as a draft for this Appendix. This translation includes it in its proper place.

Another counter-intuitive arrangement appears within Volume 23, where Lehmann placed a long draft on property that extends over six sheets, which he called a "continuous signed draft," not with the drafts on private right where it belongs but prior to all other drafts, as if in some way it stands alongside them and is not a part of drafts for particular sections. Following this continuous draft, the remaining sections collect independent loose sheets roughly according to the corresponding sections of the published book: the Preface and Introduction to the entire *Metaphysics of Morals*, the Introduction to the *Doctrine of Right*, Private Right, Public Right, Explanatory Remarks (the Appendix), a selection on honor and duels omitted from this translation – also out of order since it corresponds to material in Public Right on punishment – and then the various parts of the *Doctrine of Virtue* of which here only the Preface and Introduction are included.

The present translation arranges these selections more closely with the order of the published *Metaphysics of Morals*, with the exception that drafts for the *Doctrine of Virtue* are included immediately after the drafts for the introductory material for the *Doctrine of Right* because they concern the distinction between right and virtue treated in that material.

   I: Prefaces and introductions
      A. to the *Metaphysics of Morals*
      B. to the *Doctrine of Right*
      C. to the *Doctrine of Virtue*
  II: Private right
      A. Continuous, signed draft
      B. Other loose sheets
 III: Public right
 IV: Appendix added in 1798
      A. Loose sheet from Volume 23
      B. Direct responses to Bouterwek's review from Volume 20

Kant's direct responses to Bouterwek's review are distinct from the remainder of these drafts because they were written after the publication of the *Doctrine of Right*. As if making up for the decades-long delay in composing and publishing his *Metaphysics of Morals*, Kant did not wait to complete the entire book before publishing the material on right. The *Metaphysics of Morals, First Part, Metaphysical Foundations of the Doctrine of Right* appeared in early 1797. Within weeks a review by Kant's supporter Friedrich Bouterwek[6] appeared in the *Göttingsche Anzeigen von gelehrten*

Sachen (Göttingen Notices for Scholarly Matters), a journal published by the Göttingen Royal Academy of Science devoted to reviews and discussions of books and other publications rather than to original articles. Bouterwek's review is largely a summary of Kant's book interspersed with parenthetical objections to specific points. Kant respected Bouterwek's views. After the review was published, Kant mentioned in a letter to his friend Johann Heinrich Teiftrunk in October 1797 that he thought it "as a whole is not unfavorable to my system" in contrast to the "many enemies" the *Doctrine of Right* aroused, and noted his plan to publish a supplement to clear up misunderstandings and "perhaps eventually to complete the system" (12:207). Kant's supplement was published separately from the *Doctrine of Right* in 1798 – Kant wanted to spare readers the duplication involved in buying a completely new copy of the whole book[7] – as "Explanatory Remarks to the Metaphysical Foundations of the Doctrine of Right," and it was also included as an Appendix at the end of the *Doctrine of Right* in its second edition that same year.[8] The preparatory drafts for this Appendix can thus be dated with confidence between February 1797 and mid-1798.

The entirety of Bouterwek's review is included in *Kants gesammelte Schriften* 20:445. A complete translation of Bouterwek's review by Kenneth Westphal is available elsewhere.[9] Selected passages from the review are quoted or summarized below prior to Kant's responses. Page references to the *Metaphysics of Morals* in the review have been converted to the pagination of *Kants gesammelte Schriften*. Selections from Bouterwek's review are printed in italics. He presented his own objections to Kant's positions in parentheses.

Drafts for the *Metaphysics of morals*

TRANSLATED BY KENNETH R. WESTPHAL

I. DRAFTS OF PREFACES AND INTRODUCTIONS

A. *TO THE* METAPHYSICS OF MORALS

[Pagination is from Stark, *Nachforschungen*]
Loses Blatt Hagen 23. Between February and May, 1794.

1. The laws of actions 2. the maxims of actions. Duties of right and   Stark 252
duties of virtue. A. toward itself, B. toward others.

Jus {right} 1. The right of humanity in our own person, 11. the right of   Stark 253
human beings. Both negative duties, the former as a limiting condition
of the possibility of the latter.

Ethica. A. The end of humanity in our own person, B. the end of
human beings. Both affirmative duties and extended to the matter of
duty of ends. To the first the fitness to all ends, thus to cultivate talents,
hence to physical but also to the moral end, namely the conscientious
performance of all duties of right out of respect for the law, the cultivation of the disposition for which is a duty of virtue, although the actions
themselves are duties of right.

The duties of virtue toward oneself could also be called bodily duties,[a]
however not *amoris benevolentiae erga se ipsum* {benevolent love toward
oneself}, (for no duties are given for that because each wills his own well-
being himself) but *amoris complacentiae in semet ipso* {sympathetic love in
himself} in which we are conscious of having fulfilled the physical and
moral ends of humanity.

Loses Blatt E 22 [*first page*]   23:246
All laws of right (concerning what is mine and yours) are analytic (due
to freedom) – all laws of ends are synthetic

---

[a] *Liebespflichten*

233

For ethics: Schema of the division
Lawfulness – moral disposition
Duty of virtue
One's own perfection – others' happiness
Law – Duty
End
One's own perfection – others' happiness

All ethical obligation is *latus* {wide}. The extent of performance and the kind is not determinate. – Exceptions are those obligations not to violate the laws of right even if they be merely inward – An end which is made a duty for us by others is impossible, though of course a duty which we make into an end is possible. This end is the morally good in the disposition and the action has morality.

The duty corresponding to right is
    always negative
The duty corresponding to the end is
    always affirmative

The duties of justice follow analytically
    from outer freedom
The duties of virtue follow synthetically
    from inner freedom

} Because inner freedom is only known to us through the moral law

23:247   Virtue merits reward; vice a punishment. The observed duty of justice is $a - a = o$

Of unforgivable crime. Justice[a] shall be satisfied as a public accuser – Of unforgivable sins. Larceny, embezzlement, theft, robbery.

Monarchy and pure republic are the only tenable constitutions.[b] The others (aristocracy and democracy) are merely provisional arrangements. – The republic when coming to be is a Pandora's box, hope rests on its ground.[c] For this alone is what makes conquest into a burden, and other nations can and will add themselves to it, because it hates war, in order to enable themselves to share in the good deed of perpetual peace. It is a moral constitution. To initiate one is a crime.[d] But if fate brings one about it is yet a greater crime not to follow it. For it arises from the original source of all right, the will of all.

23:249   *Loses Blatt* E 38 [*first page*]
    1. **Axiom** of freedom: It is possible to possess something outer **rightfully** (*lex justi* {law of justice}). For a connection with an outer object[e] in space [is] what makes its use possible, i.e. holding is

---

[a] *Gerechtigkeit*
[b] *Verfassungen*
[c] *Boden*
[d] *Frevel*
[e] *Gegenstand* in this *Loses Blatt*

physically possible, yet the initial taking possession is always in accord with the law of freedom.

2. Postulate of means: It is possible to possess something by right (*jure*) i.e. right is an actual object of the power of choice (*lex juridica* {juridical law}) which in effect says I have the capacity to take into my possession outer objects of the power of choice in accord with laws of freedom.

[*second page*]   23:250

3. The will's edict: It is possible to possess **rights as things**[a] regarding outer objects, i.e. to possess them merely by right (*lex justitiae* {law of justice})

Loses Blatt E 60 [*first page*]

Freedom in general under necessary laws of agreement with itself is the obligation or the limitation of freedom by law.

An obligation determined by law is duty. There are various duties though only one obligation overall in regard to the totality of duty. This latter has no plural. The possibility of an action which is not contrary to duty is authorization. An action with authorization is allowed. Agreement of freedom with universal ends of humanity and of human beings or with others' freedom through coercion mediated by the common power of choice. That duty for which coercion is allowed (that which is connected to coercion) is strict duty or coercive duty.

The obligation to perform actions insofar as they are not regarded as coercive duties is morally free duty; insofar as they are regarded as such they are legal or strict duty. The voluntary [*breaks off*]

* *
*

B. *TO THE* DOCTRINE OF RIGHT

Loses Blatt E 29 [*first page*]   23:257

Right regarded as authorization, as something which, being universal, can only be singular, concerns, independently of obligation, merely the **freedom** of the power of choice etc. **A right** to provisions – to acquire them by contract is an **object**[b] of the power of choice although there are many particulars, just as the former is a mere form of the power of choice. – Through the **former** one simply does not act against any duty (perhaps because no one obligates him, e.g. towards God); through the **latter** he obligates others as God obligates subjects to obedience to authority, to beneficence etc.

[a] *Rechte als Sachen*   [b] *Object*

The categorical imperative: act according to the maxim of the agreement of your freedom with that of everyone else in accordance with universal law, leaves undetermined which ends human beings have – however to act so that you can will that your maxim shall become a universal law is an imperative connected to an end which we have or **should** give ourselves.

The principle of the right of **humanity** is absolute and without any subject who conditions **human beings** because, since the former is the *homo noumenon* which has no empirical determinations, it is merely formal. In contrast the latter is empirically conditioned or, further, determined.

Ethics is the doctrine of morals which contains the law of the agreement of the will with its end insofar as the will is regarded universally – hence the *latitudo*.

The best form of government is not that in which it is most commodious to live (*eudaemonia*) but rather that in which best secures the rights of citizens.

23:258 The human being is *sui ipsius imperans* {his own sovereign} (of the *phenomenon* of the *noumenon*) and yet equally well *subditus* {subject}. – However though regarded *sui juris* {as his own master} in both nevertheless not *dominus* (property owner) of himself. – Whether God himself could be regarded as property owner; I doubt one could say this; for in the case of a free being one cannot comprehend that it be made by another, except of course the body but not his spiritual being.[a] For just this reason one can say God could have no unconditional **right** over such a being.

Duty in relation to right } of human beings
Duty in relation to an end *Jus et Ethica*

Connection to the freedom of the power of choice or to its object.

It is not enough to act conforming to law (*legalitas actionis* {legality of the action}), instead this conformity to law must in addition also be the end of the action, and hence by itself alone must be its incentive (*moralitas*). This quality of the disposition (the ground of the maxim) is **virtue** (*ethica rectitudo* {ethical rectitude}); here the will is expanded beyond the laws of the power of choice, which only concern its freedom, and the necessitation of the subject by the law in general is raised above inclination as the principle of happiness, which costs sacrifice and resistance so that the strength of the resolve is called virtue.

[a] *geistiges Wesen*

The disposition (maxim) to perform an action in general, i.e. only because it is a duty, is the morality of the subject in regard to this action, and the firm resolve so to act is virtue, regardless of whether the obligation may be juridical or ethical. – However, only that duty in which the obligation consists in making the object of the power of choice as such into one's own end is called a duty of virtue, which is thus distinct from duties of right.

[*The remainder of the page consists of short thoughts in the margin, some of which are omitted here:*]

A dignity, a status, a caste.[a] 1. office 2. innate dignity 3. a status which no one of lesser dignity can obtain.

It is impossible for all to be equal within a state. Offices already distinguish between those who are higher and lower. That they are born to inequality so that they cannot raise themselves to equality with all others is opposed to natural freedom.

23:259

Of the division of all relations of right in accordance with *a priori* principles of their completeness and order. On this rests the metaphysics of right and a system of reason, otherwise it is merely an aggregation.

Duties that correspond to another's right and those that correspond to another's end

The analytic law of duty is: I have authorization to do anything as long as I do not violate my duty

[*second page*]

Whether it be an error in political science[b] that it speaks more of the rights of the people[c] than of their duties? No! For the people as such are subject to the coercion of laws. He who presumes to be permitted to exercise coercion must prove his right because the human being (who is supposed to be coerced) by nature is free. Therefore that duty which is connected to right cannot be prior to but must be derived from the right of the people itself so far as this people itself should not contradict itself i.e. from the limitation which the people imposes upon itself.

But why does the doctrine of virtue have a lower rank than the doctrine of right regarding the capacity to obligate, although the human being who hones his virtue has greater esteem than he who holds merely to the right? Because the end is an inner ground of determination within the will and makes its material not only the freedom of the power of choice but also its object[d] and hence not merely the form but also the inner content of the law.

---

[a] *Eine Würde, Ein Stand, Eine Caste*
[c] *Volks*
[b] *Staatswissenschaft*
[d] *Object*

23:262   *Loses Blatt* E 41 [*second page*]

Right *justum* is that free action whose maxim can be consistent with everyone's freedom in accordance with a universal law. – The right (*scientia* {knowledge}) is the sum total of laws in accordance with which what is right or wrong can be determined. A right (of which there may be many which one can have) is a capacity rightly[a] to obligate others' powers of choice. Anyone's action through which he obtains a right is rightful action[b] (*actus juridicus*). What is right in accordance with positive laws is laid down as right[c] (*juris est*). That in conformity with right[d] is whatever does not contradict the laws of right.

The Code of Right[e] is the doctrine of mine and yours (in the rightful sense). Someone's own (*suum cuiusque*) is the object[f] of the power of choice, hindering his use of which is an infringement (*laesio* {wrong}) against his right. – That this hindrance be a wrong[g] requires a possession of the object.[h] Possession is the subjective condition of the possibility of use namely the connection of the object with the power of choice which makes it such that if the object is altered the status[i] of the subject is likewise thereby altered.

The action by which something is brought into possession is taking possession (*apprehensio*), that by which it is declared by him to be his is appropriation (*appropriatio*), that by which it becomes his is (*acquisitio*).[10]

1. Principle:[j] all outer mine and yours presupposes an intellectual possession, though taking into possession presupposes a physical possession which is the schema of the intellectual possession and which subsumes the case of mine and yours under the law.

Reason wills the maxim of the power of choice: act in accordance with the maxim etc. this is a categorical imperative for the free power of choice which does not arise from the power of choice.

Desire as *appetitio* and desire as *concupiscentia* {longing}[k] are not the same. The one is the *genus* and can also be entirely intellectual the other is a *species* which is always sensible and precedes the maxim. Thou shall not covet[l] thy neighbor's good is *regula appetitionis* {a rule for the desire} – Refrain from temptation opposes longing.[m]

The postulate of practical reason regarding the outward use of the
23:263   power of choice is a categorical imperative of the will which regarding the freedom of the power of choice is synthetic because the concept of

---

[a] *rechtens*   [b] *rechtliche Handlung*
[c] *Rechtens*   [d] *Rechtmäßig*
[e] *Rechtsbuch*   [f] *Object*
[g] *Läsion*   [h] *Gegenstand* for remainder of paragraph
[i] *Zustand*   [j] *Grundsatz.* There is no matching "2."
[k] *Das Begehren appetitio und die Begierde concupiscentia*
[l] *Begehren*   [m] *concupiscentz*

possession exceeds the concept of the power of choice and in addition to the sensible also grounds the intellectual (*possessio noumenon*) as the condition of the possibility of outer mine and yours.

The concept of right is a concept of reason albeit of practical reason which determines the free power of choice with regard to all its objects,[a] even its outer objects, independently of conditions of time and space with regard to possible mine and yours and which grounds the concept of intellectual possession, i.e. of rightful mine and yours.

Freedom is not a concept which one can draw from experience.

Loses Blatt E 46. On a letter dated March 5, 1794.   23:266
[*first page*]

Nature and freedom
The highest nature and the highest free power of choice
| |

All-capable power of choice   All-commanding will

A duty of *jus internus* {internal right} insofar as it can equally be regarded as *officium juris externi* {duty of external right} is a duty based upon supersensible legislation in which the *Autor* {author} of the obligation in accord with a law (not the *Autor* of the law) must also be at the same time the *Autor* of whoever is subject to the law, i.e. such a duty is connected to the will of the creator of the universe insofar as it con-   23:267 tains nature as well as freedom. This creator must not only be thought of as *summus imperans* {supreme sovereign} but also as *dominus* {owner} of moral beings in the world, and since this relation cannot be represented as physical (in regard to rational beings) and the idea of such a being is transcendent, this relation can only be thought through faith and thus such a duty is a **duty of faith.**

Therefore the distinction between **lawful** (not merely ethical) **duties** as public[b] duties (based upon human or divine revelation[c]) and **duties of faith** rests on this: that one represents an inner duty of right problematically as also being an outer duty, and this manner of representation is morally necessary in order to participate in the end of all moral disposition towards the highest good.

Loses Blatt F 19   23:268
[*second page*]

Division of duties

Concerning the morality of actions all duties belong to ethics, which contains the necessity of actions from respect for the law. However, in

---

[a] *Objecte*   [b] *öffentlicher*
[c] *Offenbarung*

what concerns legality, since what matters is only that actions correspond to the law regardless of whether the subjective ground of determination is the representation of the law, duties are either merely negative, i.e. such as merely restrict freedom in its inner or outer use and are called duties of right in the universal sense of this term, or duties are also affirmative and ampliative through the end which they assign (analytic or synthetic). Yet both kinds are either limitations of one's own or of others' freedom or amplifications of one's own or of others' ends: 1. Of freedom through one's own personality 2. through other persons.

23:269   The doctrine of right is the doctrine of duties so far as they are determined through others' powers of choice in accordance with the principle of freedom – The doctrine of virtue so far as duties are determined through one's own power of choice in accordance with the principle of ends.

The other whose power of choice determines our own in accordance with laws is either the idea of humanity in us or a human being outside us – Of **Schiller's objections**: no monkish moral theory.[11]

The obligation to allow oneself to be compelled would be a necessitation in accordance with laws of freedom not to will to be free which contradicts itself

Of casuistic moral theory – of the Braunschweig fragmentists.[12] Of arch-catholic Protestants.

Predispositions in human nature to hinder the melding together of peoples by differences of religion and disunity of languages. Contrasting predispositions through war to bring about an universal monarchy and despotism.

C. TO THE DOCTRINE OF VIRTUE

23:374   *Loses Blatt* E 21
          [*first page*]

Preface

Even the title of this book: Metaphysical First Principles of the Doctrine of Virtue, appears to be a pedantic artifice of affected cleverness as if what virtue may be, how one can achieve it, and which noble fruits it provides, could not be known as Cicero had tried without allowing oneself at all to enter into the depths of metaphysics, the mere glance at which is already frightening. – The greater precision of the principles[a] of the doctrine of right accords well with metaphysics, of course, because what is mine and yours shall be weighed according to the principle[b] of equality. However in the doctrine of virtue where duty only works on

---

[a] *Principien*   [b] *Grundsatz*

one side without a counter-weight, this embarrassment about determining degree and grounds appears idle.

That the above division into a doctrine of right and a doctrine of virtue is required in a metaphysics of morals is shown in the latter's systematic representation. – Likewise it can be easily seen that the first part namely the doctrine of right requires a metaphysics, though it is not obvious that the doctrine of virtue also requires special metaphysical first principles. For the doctrine of right concerns mere form which is abstracted from the end (the matter) as an object, and formal principles[a] are in all cases metaphysical. In contrast the doctrine of virtue as the doctrine of wisdom discusses ends the adoption of which is represented as duty in order to promote well-being in us and in others, and indeed it appears that the general metaphysics of morals would be sufficient for this, and not that another special metaphysics of virtue would be needed for it, because these merely prescribe the application.

Loses Blatt E 3   23:376
    [*first page*]

The principle of morals is
that the maxim can hold as universal legislation.

1. that it as maxim of the power of choice be law
2. that it as maxim of the will can be willed through the power of choice: it ought to be a universal law, which is lesser and not necessity in the determination of the kind and extent of action.
   a. for myself universally in regard to all actions.
   b. universally for anyone towards one another. *ethic* and *jus*.

Or better. A as a principle of freedom for me and for others (maxim of the power of choice). B as a principle of ends for me alone (maxim of the will).

1. Doctrine of right – maxim of the power of choice as free, for in this way it can have only laws in the relation of human beings to one another.
2. Doctrine of virtue – maxim of the will as purposive will which is only valid for me (in reference to internal or external actions): for I can prescribe an end only to myself not to others.

All principles of duty concern either merely **duty**, whatever the incentive of the action may be, or they concern also duty as incentive so that

[a] *Principien*

the necessitating ground must **be in ourselves**. The first concern duties of right, the second duties of virtue.

In the first others' powers of choice can be determining for my own in the second only my own can contain the determining ground (*jus et ethica*).

Now the maxim of my **power of choice** can be thought of as at the same time universally legislative or merely as my **will** by which I myself determine my maxim so to act, which is also valid for everyone without limiting his freedom, hence as merely lawful though not through my own will legislating for others' wills: That in me and others which is the internal **contingent ground** of a maxim which accords with universal legislation is called the end, and a duty regarding ends (which can be set for each only by himself) is a duty of virtue. Synthetic principle of the extension of morality.

Officia lata {wide duties} are those that are not *praecis* {precisely} determined. For **them** there are thus no laws rather mere determining grounds (*principia*) for maxims because they do not make for necessity.

Coercion can indeed pertain to my power of choice though it cannot make me adopt coercive right as my own determining ground in my maxim – Duty immediately subjective determining ground.

Either a maxim can be at the same time universally legislating or merely the will can give universal lawfulness to the maxim. The latter, namely to be able to will that the maxim be a universal law, determines nothing regarding the maxim.

1. Doctrine of right. The totality of duties which hold independently of all motives to observe them.
2. Doctrine of virtue the totality of duties which make themselves into motives.

1. Duties which command to actions as such
2. those which command the maxims of actions to which we are obligated.

[. . . .]
[second page]
If it be asked why we should assume the qualification of a maxim for universal legislation as the condition of our authorization then no further ground for that can be provided: it is *res facti* {a matter of fact} that this law is in us and indeed is the highest. It can only be shown that because it is a law of freedom in general, reason as the principle of all laws would [otherwise] lack any principle.

23:377

23:378

Res facti est objectum a cuius esse ad posse nobis repraesentamus consequen-
tiam – cuius posse ab esse independenter repraesentatur est **res ingenii**. {**A**
matter of fact is an object for which the transition from being to possibility we represent to ourselves as a consequence – **a matter of the mind**
is that for which the transition from being to possibility is represented
independently.}

Res facti physice tale est per experientiam (testimonio sensuum) cognosci-
bile (cognitum) – huc pertinent **eventus**. {**A physical matter of fact as**
such is cognizable (cognized) through experience (by testimony of the
senses) – to which extent it belongs to **events**.}

Factum practice tale est eventus ex causa libera s. qui arguit auctorem. Fac-
tum practice tale semper est imputabile. {A fact in the practical sense as
such is an event from a free cause or one that indicates [or] requires
an author – a fact in the practical sense as such is always imputable.}

Loses Blatt E 5   23:379
   [*first page*]
   All duties contain an unconditioned necessitation of the free power of
choice through the idea of a maxim which qualifies for universal legislation. Now the determining ground of the power of choice makes either
the action or the maxim to act according to a certain rule absolutely
(objectively) necessary. The first necessitation contains the principle: so
act **as if** your maxim shall serve as the basis of a universal legislation.
The second necessitation states: Make it your maxim so to act as if you
were thereby universally legislating, yet under the condition that in this
legislation you can agree with yourself.
   The doctrine of the former duties is the doctrine of right, that of the
latter is the doctrine of virtue; the former are (good) actions the latter are good maxims (dispositions), i.e. subjective principles to act lawfully. Regarding the first kind of duty one does not notice whether or
not the principle of the legislation itself provides the subject's incentive,
as long as the action occurs in accord with that principle. The second
case, however, considers the condition of obeying duty. – In the former the legality in the latter the morality of the action is demanded
in the law of duty. (Observation of duty as *factum* or such observation
from respect for duty as a *principium*.) [*in the margin:* lex is always *cogens*
{coercive}]
   The doctrine of the first duty is the doctrine of right the second
the doctrine of virtue[.] good acts (of the power of choice) and good
will.
   [. . . .]
   [*third page*]   23:380
   First of all, what is duty? – This necessitation is either merely to a
species of actions (e.g. of benevolence) so that regarding individual cases,

freedom of choice, in both kind and extent, is underdetermined,[a] or the action is precisely determined by the duty. The latter is strict duty the former indulgent duty.

All duties bind the power of choice to conditions which reason prescribes *a priori* and categorically and thereby limits either the freedom or the end of the power of choice. The first are strict duties the others indulgent.

[. . . .]

23:381 Analytic principle of all duty: So act that the maxim in which you take up your action could at the same time be universally legislating.

Synthetic: Incorporate such actions into your maxims which are at the same time universally legislating, hence can be considered as duty, i.e. do what you ought from duty, i.e. because you ought.

Both principles are **laws of causality through freedom**. The first [*fourth page*] is formal in regard to the *nexus effectivi* {efficient causality} of personality (one's own as well as others'). The second is also material in regard to *nexus finalis* {final causality}, an end which could at the same time serve everyone as a rule. – The doctrine of virtue concerns this latter and properly does not stand under laws but rather itself makes a maxim into a law hence regarding ends it is also not strictly determining according to matter.

The duty to assume maxims suitable for universal legislation follows not from the **rights of others** instead these demand only actions as *officia* {duties}. Also not to incorporate into one's maxim the right of humanity in our person, for this (humanity) demands only actions.

All duties are legislating (or contain legislation) for the human will (the intention with which they ought to act) though not all contain at the same time determination of the kind and the extent to which they should 23:382 be carried out (execution). The maxim of the intention is always **ethical** even when the law one has incorporated into his maxim is **juridical**. The law of execution is always juridical even when the maxim of the intention is ethical. Properly, duties can never be connected to reward but rather only to release from guilt.

According to its form duty is limitation of the power of choice through freedom. However, this can only be limited by others' freedom (and conversely) and by nothing else.

This doctrine is the external doctrine of right. According to its matter it[b] is promotion of ends.

---

[a] *Übrig gelassen wird*
[b] *sie* could refer to the doctrine of right or, less directly but more plausibly, duty

Duty is an action which is absolutely **commanded** i.e. made unconditionally necessary by reason. Accordingly there are thus many duties according to differences of their matter, i.e. of actions. – Hence duty is based upon the necessity of making such maxims as admit of universal legislation into the condition of the determination of the will – the limitation of the actions we will to the condition of such maxims is provided by the doctrine of right, the necessity of the maxim itself of such actions by the doctrine of virtue. – Necessity of actions in conformity with duty and necessitation of actions by the representation of duty: virtue concerns all actions in conformity with duty so far as they concern the principle of intention. The principle of action as such can be the right.

Loses Blatt E 9   23:384
 [*second page*]
 Duties are either strictly or *late* {widely} determining; the former stand under the laws of actions immediately, the latter under the law of the maxims of actions (in this way the latter leaves playroom for the power of choice). The former are perfect (duties of right) the latter imperfect, i.e. duties of virtue. *Jus et Ethica* (*propius sic dicta*) {right and ethics (specifically so named)}
 There is one categorical imperative.
 The human power of choice is a free power of choice.
 The doctrine of right as doctrine of strict duty (under specific laws) 23:385
is either the doctrine of inner or outer right, through which a. either freedom in the inner or b. in the outer is limited. The first belongs to ethics for itself regarding content but still to morality in general and thus also to right as limiting highest condition.

Loses Blatt E 76   23:390
 [*first page*]
 Duties are actions which are necessary according to an unconditional command of reason. The necessitation to such actions is called obligation. The moral characteristic of the subject[a] to be necessitated to fulfill duty by the mere idea of duty is virtue; the doctrine of everything which belongs to virtue is the doctrine of virtue (ethics).
 Hence the doctrine of virtue concerns all duties insofar as it contains only that from the universal doctrine of morals[b] which specifically makes the idea of duty itself into a motive. However the universal doctrine of morals concerns all actions in conformity with duty regardless of whatever may be the motives by which the subject is determined so to act. – However that necessitation which does not occur through the idea of duty i.e. which is not one that the subject's reason exercises upon it

---

[a] *Subject*   [b] *Sittenlehre*

(coerces itself) according to laws of freedom, can only be the possibility that is compatible with freedom, to be coerced by others to such actions and reciprocally to coerce others to such actions.

Therefore the doctrine of morals is either the doctrine of right or the doctrine of virtue.

However the authorization of coercion of others (to coerce them) is grounded upon the subject's personality, and the person's free power of choice itself stands under the idea of the person's personality, in accordance with which it is necessitated by itself in self-regarding actions and is morally compelled by analogy with the coercion of another, and this obligation toward itself can thus also be called the right of humanity in our own person which precedes all other obligation.

[second page]
Thus the right of humanity in our own person does not yet belong to the doctrine of virtue because it does not also demand that the idea of duty towards oneself be itself the incentive of the action: However it is the highest condition of all laws of duty because otherwise the subject would cease to be a subject of duties (person) and must be counted among things.

23:391   If therefore the authorization to dispose of objects[a] as one chooses[b] is called right in general then the authorization to dispose of one's own person is limited by the right of humanity within us upon which we may not infringe, and the respect for which does not belong to the doctrine of virtue but rather to the doctrine of right as a merely limiting condition.

However in addition to instructing us to act in conformity with duty from respect for duty in general, the doctrine of virtue also instructs us in particular duties, i.e. it commands a maxim of action that cannot be determined by laws because they do not rest merely on the form of lawfulness, but because an end as matter, i.e. object,[c] is made into a duty of the power of choice (of the will); now this end can be within or outside us. Within us no end can be made our duty except that which is a means to ends to which it is a duty to conform, (one's own perfection); but outside us happiness.

[in the margin:] If a duty is obligatory then the imperative is unconditional, however that an action be a duty i.e. obligation, is either unconditional or conditional: the first under the principle of freedom the second under the principle of ends, in both to conform to the form or the matter of the power of choice.

[a] *Gegenständen*   [b] *nach Willkür*
[c] *Object*

246

[*third page*]

Now this provides particular duties namely those of virtue. Now their principle cannot be called law; since it does not command actions the maxim of which can be universally legislative but rather leaves the maxim undetermined and instead commands the maxim of a certain kind of action. These are not solely grounded on the formal condition of all duties (as that which alone is necessary), namely freedom in accordance with universal laws. Therefore the principle of virtue can only determine actions generally rather than *praecise* {precisely}, and the necessitation which must be found in any duty only concerns the manner of thinking[a] (maxim) so that room for play remains to the power of choice, provided only that it does not specifically alter the manner of thinking and its principle. Such a maxim which determines nothing about the kind and extent of an action is a maxim of ends, and indeed as a maxim of duty of such ends which are one's duty to adopt, consequently not one's own happiness. Therefore fitness of one's own person for all possible ends 23:392 generally (one's own perfection) and conformity with whatever is naturally and necessarily everyone's (others') end, namely happiness. The capacity of desire in connection with that which is not fully within our control is called the will (the good will) (just as that which is within our control is called power of choice). Therefore the law regarding ends is a law of the will, not for the power of choice, whose decrees here can be subjected only to general but not to specific and hence not to universal principles.

[*in the margin:*] That the maxim of my action (subjective principle) be fit for universal legislation (as objective principle) is not the same as the principle that to have this maxim itself be a duty. The former principle merely limits the power of choice, the latter is ampliative. (Hypothetical necessity is either restrictive or constitutive.)

[*fourth page*]

Considered in the concept of duty is either merely the kind (form) of practical necessitation, namely that through an imperative of morality or of the exercise of art (morally- or technically-practical principle), and thus that concept means merely obligation and is the principle which sets the condition limiting the maxim to that capable of universal legislation by which we know that something would be a duty – or the concept concerns an action determined with regard to an object[b] (as matter of the power of choice) and then with regard to the variety of such objects there are many actions and hence many duties. The division of the various actions regarding which we have duties can only be derived

---

[a] *Denkungart*   [b] *Object*

a priori from the manner in which one is or can be made to be obligated at all, and then duties (*officia*) contain either the obligatoriness that makes mere actions into duties or also that which makes the maxim of the action a duty. The first can be called duties of right in general, which rest solely upon the necessary conformity with the law of freedom in relation to one's own person or with others, hence proper laws, i.e. strictly-determining principles, and these laws which limit one's own freedom due to the personality of the human being are the condition of the possi-

23:393 bility of limiting others' freedom. – Now the obligatoriness which treats the maxim itself (not merely the action) as a duty is ethical: one should allow the representation of the law to suffice as one's incentive. (*Formalis* {the form} of ethics.) And here the doctrine of virtue concerns all duties altogether (also those contained in the doctrine of right). However according to its matter ethics also has particular objects of the power of choice which together can be called ends, which are morally necessary. In regard to these morals has no objective laws that provide the determinate actions but rather only maxims for the species of actions so that some play room remains for freedom to determine the action. *admonitiones* {guidelines}.

[*these two paragraphs in the margin:*] The propositions: "this ought to be done by you" and "you ought to will that this be done by you" are distinct like the deed and the maxim to do something. In the first case the principle determines the action in the second only the maxim of the action of a certain kind and leaves the extent undetermined.

The first presupposes that it is within your capacity and determines the action as law based on the ground of freedom and personality without any end. – The second makes the cultivation of the capacity itself a duty without determining its extent in relation to ends and is a principle of maxims not a law of determinate actions.

23:393 *Loses Blatt* F 6
[*first page*]
Thus all duties toward oneself are ethical (not juridical) because, if the incentive of the action were not duty itself, which would otherwise morally necessitate us, then the action should issue from us ourselves, though not conversely; all ethical duties are duties toward oneself although they can also be duties toward others.

That is the division of morals according to its matter, i.e. according to actions in conformity with duty and their incentives.

However in all duties the obligation, i.e. the moral necessitation, is to be considered, which concerns the form of obligation whether it be perfect or imperfect, determined *stricte* {strictly} or merely *late* {widely}.

All obligation of course presupposes a law. If this law determinately   23:394
and immediately concerns the action so that the kind – how to act? –
and the extent – how much to do? – is determined in the law, then the
obligation is perfect (*obligatio perfecta*) and the law is *stricte obligans* {nar-
rowly obligatory}; no choice remains to us either for exceptions if the
law is valid in its universality or for the measure of compliance with it.
However if the law does not directly command the action but only the
maxim of the action, it leaves open to the subject's judgment the kind of
act – how – and the measure – to what extent – the thing commanded
should be realized, provided only that it would be necessary for us to do
as much as is possible under the given conditions, then the obligation is
imperfect and the law is not a narrow but a broad obligation *late obligans*
{widely obligatory}. –

From this one sees that in the latter case not merely the form of lawfulness but also a matter of the power of choice, i.e. an end, is made
a duty by the law which as a physical effect, because as such it always
has empirical conditions, allows for reflection regarding the technical-
practical imperative and for a choice whereby I can do something good
meritoriously, instead of the strict obligation (*obligatio perfecta* which
must not as such be regarded as a matter of possible external coercion) which makes everything in that kind of duty into a matter of sheer
responsibility.

Because the moral concept of right (*rectum*) or wrong (*minus rectum*
{lacking right}) expresses the *minimum* through which an action which
may be performed would follow from a law (rule), so that not even the
minimum[a] about it is neglected, hence the law cannot be lax (indulgent)
in its application, thus the duties one owes can be called duties based on
right while the other, meritorious duties can be called duties based upon
the subject's end. The first kind of duty can in general be called duties of
right *officium juris* the second can be called *officium ethicum* hence duties
of virtue, because virtue is moral strength (of intention and of the act)
to do all that is dutiful to the greatest possible measure.

[*at very bottom of page*] The *minimum* is omission (*negatio*) the *maxi-
mum* is the promotion of the end.

[*second page*]   23:395
Whether obligation be *stricte* or *late* depends on the kind, and because
it depends only on the form of obligation there can also be internal
(just as well as external) duties of right. Both would thus be called *officia
juris*, the first *officia juris interni* (*erga seipsum*) {internal duties of right (to
oneself)} the second *officia juris externi sive juridica* {external or juridical
duties of right} – Regarding duties of virtue they would contain both
officia ethices ethica {ethical duties of ethics} as well as *officia ethices juridica*

---

[a] *Mindeste*

{juridical duties of ethics}, i.e. duties of virtue would contain the observation of all duties whether they be of perfect or imperfect obligation, namely observing them as a moral disposition in fulfilling one's duty in general.

II. DRAFTS FOR PRIVATE RIGHT

A. CONTINUOUS, SIGNED DRAFT [23:211–41]

23:211   *Loses Blatt* E 11
          [*first page, marked "1" at the top by Kant*]
Of first acquisition (*jus in re* {a right in a thing})

In an action one **does wrong** (*injuste agit*) against another even if one does not as such do him wrong (because he had no right or forfeited it) and this occurs when the receiving party is not in a rightful condition. In this case the latter can resist. – However, one thus does wrong because one behaves in a way that prevents a *status juridicus* {rightful condition}.

With regard to original acquisition the principle of the ideality of possession thus holds with regard to *res nullius* {an ownerless thing}. However this holds regarding resistance to others just as if the thing as such were an actual possession.

Those who espouse the acquisition of right through taking control[a] must also espouse possession through mere will and hence that ideal possession suffices for mine and yours. – The principle of the restriction of mine and yours to the condition of real outer possession abolishes all outer mine and yours since this latter consists in the view that ideal possession would be possible and would ground a right.

The principle of the ideality of possession holds *cum effectu* {with effect} only in the *status civilis* {civil condition}, though *absque effectu* {without effect} in the *naturalis* {state of nature}, and yet with a right to resist due to the priority of taking into possession.

Antinomy between the principles of ideal and of real possession. Ideal possession must be presupposed because otherwise no wrong[b] from another's interference could be thought (intellectual-empirical possession). Yet it itself presupposes a pure intellectual possession in accordance with mere categories of control[c] over things and the influence of the power of choice on another, which is not based on conditions of space and time and which can be derived analytically from the concept of outer power[d] over the usable in accordance with laws of freedom. – However to derive from this the rightful reality of ideal possession requires a synthetic principle in accordance with which each is bound, and is also

---

[a] *occupation*   [b] *läsion*
[c] *Gewalt*   [d] *Macht*

reciprocally entitled in his relations to things and to human beings, to limit himself and others to the condition under which their use can agree with the idea of a collective will.

Mine and yours   23:212

Mine is that the use of which by anyone else is precluded by my mere power of choice. This is either the internally mine, if it is something which is attributed to me as myself; the externally mine is the outer object[a] which depends upon my power of choice.

Possession is the connection of an object to me by means of which my freedom precludes others' power of choice from use of the same. (Thus the object I possess is so bound with me that its alteration by anyone other than me are at the same time my alterations.)

From this it follows 1.) that all possession consists in that connection of a person with an object which is in that person's control, that is, regarding which the subject has a physical capacity to determine through his power of choice, for this is the sole condition under which something can be an object of power of choice (not of mere wish) – The act of bringing something within his control is the taking[b] of the object. Thus possession can also be represented as continuous taking.

[*second page*]

1. Proposition. Something outside me is **mine** only insofar as I must be judged by anyone, even without empirical (physical) possession of it, to be in pure intellectual possession of it; for I shall be able to exclude everyone from the outward thing which I designate mine through my mere power of choice and thus regardless of the physical conditions of possession.

Remark: regarding the meaning of intellectual possession, e.g. that I place something out of my control and physical connection with myself and nevertheless am wronged if another uses it. For since this latter only occurs insofar as I am in possession of that thing, a true though non-physical, hence merely intellectual possession of it must therefore be thought. One can call this possession **virtual** as distinct from **actual** possession. Its principle, which is to present itself as sufficient for the distinction of mine and yours, is the principle of the **ideality of possession**.

[*the next three paragraphs are an addition in the margin:*] Schmaltz[13] says: whoever interferes with another's work[c] hinders the other from having acted, i.e. he acts in such a way that if the other had presupposed such a   23:213 course of action in accordance with a universal rule (which he can do in

---

[a] *Object*   [b] *apprehension*
[c] *Arbeit*

accordance with intellectual principles) he would not have been able to work on something at all – thus he does not reduce the other's right to the thing, since he had none, but does him wrong[a] because he hinders his acquisition of something which of course belongs to his entitlements though not to his possessions.

If two parties have such a principle they act wrongly although of course they do not wrong each other. – There is an ideal mine and yours in the acquirability of a right which is infringed.

The difficulty with mine and yours regarding land is because it should rest entirely on unilateral power of choice and thus seems not to require others' agreement, and so is the hardest to solve and only indeterminately relates to the establishing of a unification of powers of choice regarding such an acquisition.

2nd Proposition. All usable outer things stand under the principle of the possibility of a merely ideal possession sufficient for mine and yours. For suppose that this also required what is physically necessary, it would make our free power of choice regarding the use of objects depend upon those objects i.e. not merely the power of choice but rather freedom in use of that which otherwise lies within its control would thus be limited by those objects, which is impossible.

3rd Proposition. Intellectual possession cannot of course be given as required for mine and yours without some sort of physical possession of the same object, that is, one cannot know whether such a determination of the power of choice belongs to the subject without a certain appearance of taking possession as object[b] of experience: but if this is presupposed then no persisting empirical possession is required for judging of mine and yours. – For all rightful relation is a merely intelligible relation of rational beings to each other and **by this means** to objects of the power of choice in regard to which their powers of choice are only restricted by the law of universal validity of choosing for everyone and hence it, as an outer right as such, is based on absolutely no conditions of time and space. Physical acquisition is thus [*breaks off*]

We have no knowledge of the actuality of a possession except insofar as it is made knowable through an empirical connection of the object with the subject in space and time. This possession only becomes **rightful** through intellectual (ideal) possession. Merely rightful possession is one and the same as the ground of mine and yours, [*third page*] only the appearance of the intellectual determination of the power of choice with regard to an outer object which is within the subject's control, but the conditions which ground outer right are based only on intellectual laws of the agreement of that subject's power of choice with the freedom of

23:214

---

[a] *unrecht*   [b] *Gegenstand*

everyone, and thus on his intellectual concepts, independent of anything empirical. Thus I would say: if something within my and no one else's control is subjected to my power of choice I thereby necessitate others to refrain from using it merely through my power of choice. The physical condition of others' influence which this possession may or may not have on my freedom may be as he wants.

4th Proposition. The principle of the ideality of possession in determination of mine and yours is analytic, i.e. is based on the principle of contradiction and is indeed the irreplaceable condition, although insufficient for determining the limits of the empirically-mine and -yours. – For so far as concerns the former this principle is already contained in the concept of outer freedom as independence of the power of choice from any other's power of choice and also from things and can be known from this in accordance with the law of contradiction. As regards the latter, however, the determination of this possession in experience merely as its appearance in space and time and hence possible only by dependence upon the connection of the power of choice of a human being with objects or with others' powers of choice and hence what and how much of them could actually (in the sensible world) belong to mine and yours cannot be determined through this principle which thus cannot suffice for distinguishing the latter.

[*in margin:*] 4th Proposition. The acquisition of an object of the power of choice is possible either 1) by **unilateral** determination of the power of choice in regard to its object or 2) only by bilateral promising and accepting since each for himself wills that something namely just the same occurs or 3) since one must have an effect upon the subject namely through performance[a] only through mutual determination of subjects upon each other.

5th Proposition. The synthetic principle of outer right can be nothing other than: All distinction of mine and yours must be derivable from the unifiability of possession with the idea of a common power of choice under which stands anyone else's power of choice regarding the same object. – For, because the power of choice of the one party cannot as such be assumed to necessarily agree with that of the other in relation to the same object in accordance with a universal law in accordance with mere laws of freedom[b] (and hence in accordance with the concepts of right), unless each regards himself as required to refrain from any use of outer usable things which could also be objects of others' powers of

23:215

---

[a] *praestation*
[b] Kant's grammar is ambiguous between these laws being parallel, the second simply rephrasing the first, or the second modifying the first.

choice (which however in accordance with the above contravenes freedom), thus under the presupposition of the possibility of an outer mine and yours, the condition of their possible agreement in accordance with laws of freedom in the synthetic unity of their powers of choice is the idea in relation to which determination of the limits of mine and yours outside me and thus on which alone can be based all outer contingent [*fourth page*] right: i.e. only through the idea of a unified power of choice can we acquire.

6th Proposition. This idea of a united power of choice as that upon which must rest all presumption of an outer right is qua principle and maxim necessary with regard to right even though the unification itself is contingent with regard to right.

[*in margin:*] 6.) The idea of a united will is thus necessary so that the object remains in someone's possession even if it is separated from the subject by time and space. Only through that will is the thing transmitted to us.

Whether an action may be right or wrong can be known analytically from the above mentioned principle of freedom. However, the question whether an outer object of the power of choice may be **mine** or **yours** does not concern an action but rather concerns: whether someone would have **a right** as outer possession or would or would not have an outer though not physical possession. Thus if a circumstance[a] is assumed in which neither of them can yet possess an outer right, both can still act wrongly insofar as they contravene the condition[b] of the possibility of producing an outer right, though neither of them thus suffers wrong from the other because they both are still in a circumstance in which no mine and yours obtains. – Now, however, the circumstance in which the mine and yours of any one party taken in that relation can first of all be acquired is that of a united will, which thus first makes possible the agreement of powers of choice regarding the same object in accordance with universal laws of the freedom of their powers of choice in outer use. However this uniting is not necessary as such [*added in margin:* namely the uniting of powers of choice through which this unity itself is made into an outward duty and through which all wrong is prevented is the rightful and *status civilis* {civil condition}] but rather only insofar as one will ground a right. Thus the founding principle[c] of mine and yours is contained only in the condition that the action through which this occurs must be derivable from the idea of a unified power of choice.

[*inserted on the right:*] The objects[d] in which one can acquire a right are as various as thinking about possession of these objects allows.

23:216

---

[a] *Zustand*, normally rendered as "condition" [b] *Bedingung*
[c] *Princip der Gründung* [d] *Gegenstände*

1.) Possession of a thing 2.) of a person's declared will 3.) the possession of a person simultaneously as possession of a thing. In relation to the first the uniting of powers of choice may be regarded merely as possible, in the second possession must be regarded as actual, in the third it must be regarded as necessary. The first concerns objects as substance, the second as action, the third as reciprocal influence, the first is founding of a possession, the second is exclusion, the third is the limitation of a possession through the other's right. Finally one against one or one against many or one against everyone.

Taking possession occurs through taking control,[a] through accepting, and through subjection.

Everything within a condition[b] lacking *justitia distributiva* {distributive justice} where instead each is his own judge – in *status naturalis*: because here no *publicum* is thought but instead individuals in relation to one another.

[*in margin:*] *Jus in re* {right in a thing} is a right against everyone, *jus personale* {personal right} a right against one person, *jus imperii* {sovereign right} a right against one person and equally against any possessor of that same person.

Loses Blatt E 12 [*first page, marked "2" at the top by Kant*]   23:217
Possession is the connection of an object of the power of choice with the capacity of the subject to use it (here the conditions of time and space are disregarded; instead all is intellectual) – An outer possession is possession of an object[c] that can also exist as object[d] of the power of choice separated from the subject.

Nota. Possession can be understood in merely an intellectual or also in a physical (empirical) sense. The former is that the conditions of which are merely pure concepts of the understanding (categories) the latter is that the conditions of which are relations in space and time.

[*in margin:*] Objects of the power of choice are within our power.[e]

Mine is everything the use of which by another hinders my own use, I can exclude any other through my mere power of choice because the obstruction of my use contradicts freedom in accordance with universal laws. Hence mine is that which, even without physical possession, precludes use by others that opposes my power of choice in accordance with laws of freedom. – My own is that of mine[f] which no other may use, the mine-in-common is that the use of which by others does not oppose my power of choice.

---

[a] *occupation*	[b] *Zustand*
[c] *Object*	[d] *Gegenstand*
[e] *Gewalt*	[f] *Mein eigen ist das meine*

How is the outer mine in space and time possible, e.g. how can I complain that the use of an object of my power of choice which is separated from it in space or time infringes upon my freedom, since of course that use is merely an influence on a thing outside me? That is otherwise not possible except insofar as intellectual possession is represented as not dependent upon physical possession and thus if this latter has ceased the former is unchanged.

The initiation of physical possession is taking[a] (*apprehensio*), its persistence is retention (*detentio*). As existing in time both belong not to intellectual possession as its determinations – and yet without the sensible conditions of physical possession the existence[b] of intellectual possession cannot be acknowledged because the sensible conditions constitute the presentation of that existence in a possible experience.

23:218 Thus the externally mine can only be acquired through my own mere power of choice through taking and hence the unification of the object with my capacity to use it and indeed through taking whereby the freedom and power of choice of no one is affected, i.e. of an object which belongs to no one or through reciprocal power of choice insofar as it is directly an object of another's power of choice who cancels his connection with the same in view of my taking, i.e. through accepting or

1) through an action with regard to the object 2) through two actions with regard to the object and the subject together 3) through determination of all actions of the subject who is at once also object.

Categories
of quantity and quality of right

1) Mathematically of the freedom of each in the synthetic unity of powers of choice regarding the formal determination of right so that none does the other wrong.
   a. Unilateral, multilateral, omnilateral determination of the power of choice regarding synthetic unity b) command, permission and prohibition.
2) Dynamically of relation[c] and modality regarding the reality of the power of choice in view of its object. A right in terms of matter (not merely the form through which something would be represented as right), a. relation. Right in things, personal right, communal right. b) Modality. The possibility of the unification of the powers of choice regarding an object, actuality of this unification (*im pacto* {by contract}) and necessity of this unification in the *unio civilis* {civil union} as the sole *status legalis* {legal condition}.

---

[a] *Ergreifung*   [b] *Daseyn*
[c] *Relation* in this paragraph

Through his sheer will no one can make into his own what he has taken[a] or also merely received. He must have it durably in his control.

In a purely intellectual sense something is an object of the power of choice which merely can be in my control (apart from conditions of space and time): the usable. It is also a consequence of the freedom of the power of choice that everything externally usable must be such that it can be used i.e. in general he who acts in accordance with a subjective principle according to which what is usable would not have any use whatsoever does wrong. The object of the power of choice, of which object any arbitrary use one may make of it agrees externally with universal freedom, is his own. Thus everything usable must be such that it can become someone's indeed anyone's own.

[*second page*]

That action through which I make it the case that something outer becomes mine is rightful acquisition (NB: I cannot acquire anything through the wrong of another for if I provide satisfaction and a replacement myself then that is not acquisition but rather merely taking my own into possession).

[*in margin:*] Whether acquisition *per accessionem* {by addition} is an action?

Through my acquisition others receive an obligation to perform or to refrain from something which prior to my action they did not have. – However no obligation can result for anyone except that which he himself assumes (*omnis obligatio est contracta* {all obligation is restriction}). Therefore no one can acquire by unilateral power of choice (though of course through unilateral action) but only through the united powers of choice of those who in the acquisition create an obligation and mutually contract[b] themselves. But the possibility and authorization to be able to acquire everything usable is necessary *a priori*: consequently so is the unification of the powers of choice of all human beings regarding all objects. Thus by the same principle of acquirability which all human beings have, they also acquire the obligation to be able to acquire only in accordance with the idea of the unification of their powers of choice regarding the very same object in accordance with laws of freedom. – Thus the principle of all acquisition is also the principle of the restriction of every, including the unilateral, power of choice to the condition of the agreement with a universal possible unification of powers of choice regarding the same object.

The principle of all propositions regarding innate right is analytic.

That of all propositions regarding acquired right is synthetic.

[a] *apprehendirt*   [b] *contrahiren*

For: with the former propositions we do not transcend the conditions of freedom (without providing the power of choice with any further object) namely that the power of choice must be consistent with the freedom of everyone in accordance with a universal rule (thus actions are only considered insofar as they accord with right).

With the propositions of the second kind I augment the power of choice with an outer object which by nature belongs to no one, i.e. is not innate and thus cannot be inferred from freedom analytically as an object of power of choice.

23:220

The synthetic principle *a priori* of the right of acquisition (or of acquired right, since freedom may not be acquired) is the agreement of the power of choice with the idea of the united will of those who are limited by that agreement. For because all right which is not innate is to others an obligation which is not innate to them (to do or omit something) but is placed upon them, though this cannot be done unilaterally by anyone else because it would contravene innate freedom, and thus only insofar as his will agreed to it, i.e. he restricts himself to this obligation, hence only through the united will; thus no right can be acquired without relation of the power of choice of those who acquire it to the idea of a united will.

However we have an innate right to acquire all that we are able to use, though only insofar as it agrees with that condition of the outer synthetic unity of powers of choice: When it is an object that belongs to no one merely by his own power of choice in connection with the possible harmony of powers of choice – if it is the effect of another's deed[a] in relation to actual unification of powers of choice, it is the person himself related to that necessary unity.

[*third page*]

Now in this united will the mere idea of an outer relation of the powers of choice of rational beings toward one another insofar as they, in accordance with laws of freedom, can make use of outer objects, and yet this is no *factum* {deed} but rather merely a norm; all of their actions which ground **a right**, i.e. the acquisition of an object, can and must be regarded as a pure intellectual *actus* {act} prior to our regarding this as an occurrence evident in space and time. – Thus the intellectual taking[b] of an object of the power of choice, the accepting, and the subjecting, the categories of acquiring right or of acquired right in accordance with pure concepts of the understanding are *a priori*.

---

[a] The German *Tat* and the Latin *Factum* are translated throughout as "deed" in the sense of "act" rather than "title to land." Kant uses *Titel* to refer to the latter sense of "deed" in English.

[b] *apprehension*

Subordinate to these are all *actus* of acquiring in space and time, since the possibility of the acquisition of an outer right in general wherein the object is merely thought does not rest on these as *phenomenon*; instead what rests on them is only the presentation in intuition of that which would be acquired so far as this can be given. However, since objects of 23:221 sense cannot be subsumed under pure categories of the understanding as species can be subsumed under their genus, the cognition of a rightful acquisition must be preceded by a schematism of outer intellectual relations of powers of choice to their objects (in accord with the laws of freedom); for only through this schematism alone (which also occurs *a priori* though in connection with relations in space and time) can the condition of the possibility of the right of outer acquisition by human beings be given as an object of experience, so that under this condition alone can the object be subsumed under the categories.

1) I acquire an object which is given as belonging to no one but which I will that it shall be mine and which is a self-subsisting impersonal thing (substance), i.e. as a thing in space, by a unilateral act of apprehension which is the **first** in time. Therefore the priority of taking[a] is the sensible condition of acquisition – all of this under the idea of a united power of choice.

2) I acquire an object of another's power of choice that is also an object of my power of choice from him through the actual unification of the powers of choice through accepting i.e. by taking into possession while the other withdraws from possession (to my advantage): hence **through bilateral action** (giving and accepting)

3) I acquire a personal object of my power of choice as a thing[b] through a unilateral act of taking insofar as this taking makes necessary the bilateral *actus* of unification (these are merely intellectual concepts); the schema of this is the taking of a person as a thing where the **status**[c] of freedom of one of them is abolished by a will which itself through an deed becomes objectively necessary. Hence it is the schematism of the time-order which contains within itself a ground of the necessary durable simultaneity of the condition and the *actus* is a reciprocal influence through multilateral action (of a master and many bondsmen).

[*fourth page*]

Of the antinomy of rights of acquisition

Regarding pure concepts of the understanding mine and yours is empirically unconditioned, in contrast regarding concepts of experience mine

---

[a] *apprehension*   [b] *gleich einer Sache*
[c] *Zustand*

23:222 and yours is limited to conditions of possession which due to acquirability seem to make the former impossible.

Possession is the universal condition under which alone someone can be injured in his freedom hence under which alone he also can possess **a** right. Now, regarding all acquirable objects, he must be in possession if they are to belong to what is his; but on the other hand it is the case that only the connection with the object through which he is not in (physical) possession of the same constitutes the character of what is his.

N.B. can one not say: the *prior occupans* {one who took control earlier} no longer has right in the land to occupy it, as if so many people at the same time were so to restrict the land that even the most necessary use of it were rendered impossible, for then the dire situation, which would result from so many self-important people[a] striving to make a place for themselves and even for their greatest needs, would reach the point when the ills resulting from the opposition because of the lack of land would even the scales.

The first concept belonging to knowledge is that of an object in general. The first concept belonging to a right, however, is the concept of an object of the power of choice, and from an object of power of choice (as a capacity to use an object), that of possession as the condition of the actual use of a **given** object. – An object of power of choice as such is represented either merely as thought or also as given (in space and time). The concept of possession pertains to this. – The possession of an object[b] is either physical or merely a rightful possession. The latter is a connection with the subject through mere concepts of the synthetic or ampliative unity of powers of choice regarding the object. On this is grounded the concept of mine and yours which is identical with the concept of possessing a right, or of the purely intellectual possession of an object[c] outside me. – Now this is either a self-subsisting thing outside me, *res corporalis* {corporeal thing}, or merely the determining ground, lying in my power of choice, of another's power of choice which is not merely analytic. This right is such that it holds against anyone who is in possession of the thing, *jus in re*; which contains the right against a person and finally the right against a person who is at the same time regarded as a thing (since in all synthetic division *a priori* through concepts there must be three members of the division).

23:223 So that a thing outside me may become mine requires first of all a physical connection to it which I bring about and, if it is to be an original acquisition, a unilateral act through which my will is not merely indicated but rather is implemented through taking it into possession

[a] *Mittelpuncten* [b] *Gegenstand*
[c] *Object*

so that it shall be mine. – The first condition of all we possess on earth is the land on which alone our existence and preservation is possible. – If the question arises whether ground may be acquired only through division (in accordance with a *lex agraria naturalis* {natural law of land distribution}) or through taking control,[a] it is thus presupposed that it previously belongs as a whole to the human race i.e. that the race possesses it uncontroversially and indeed through the right of its personality. However because this will is only an idea, such taking into possession can of course only occur by a unilateral *actus*, and this idea would only be the limiting condition of taking possession as a distribution by the common will. A thing cannot be made unusable. Its first use is thus a right.

[*next two paragraphs in margin:*] Usable things must be able to become mine or yours, the condition for which is possession. However, they cannot be mine or yours without their being mine or yours as outer possession as well (and therein consists the *Jus in re*). – The former holds in accordance with the intellectual concept of possession the latter in accordance with the empirical.

The question is whether something outside me can be mine. I have first grasped something, formed it to my ends, altered it; if it is not immediately in my hands it nevertheless has been modified by me – But in this way I can make the entire world my own and by priority of use exclude everyone – The former is true intellectually – the latter also – The answer is that I can appropriate something outer only as my *praerogatio* {prerogative} not as property, the former via intellectual grounds the latter due to the impossibility my making for myself a share of a common land without distribution or in time etc.

Loses Blatt E 13   23:224
[*first page, marked "3" at the top by Kant*]

Antinomy of outer rights

Antithesis

Nothing can be externally mine (*juridice* {juridically}) and there is thus no right of acquisition of objects outside me. ~~For if it were the latter, the use another makes of a thing outside me would infringe upon my freedom, not merely my power of choice regarding an object. Here, however, freedom can be affected only through coercion, hence through the influence of another on the subject; so my freedom would have to be thought as in me, the subject, and yet at the same time as a circumstance found in an object outside me, which is a contradiction.~~

---

[a] *occupation*

261

An object of the power of choice which is to be mine must be able to be in my physical possession so that I am able to use it, as the authorization to use it constitutes an essential part of what is mine. However this possession is of course not necessary (as is the case in what is inwardly mine in accordance with the innate right to freedom), instead the outer mine consists simply in this: that I may without obstruction use a thing which is not in my control, e.g. a place even if am not connected with it, someone's declared will even if it is not concurrent with mine (insofar as the other, if I had accepted his declared will, is already no longer so disposed), or a person who stands under my power of choice as a thing (*jus in persona instar juris in re contra quemlibet possidentem* {right in a person in the form of a right in a thing against whomever possesses the person}) even if this person is either of another will or is possessed by another, though if I am not in physical possession of the object, any infringement by another on my use of it is no infringement on my freedom so that no wrong is done to me, it thus follows that I cannot by any action acquire a right to an object[a] outside me (because if this were the case others who hinder me in its use would do me wrong).

Remark. In the case of *Jus in re* {a right in a thing} one cannot represent why I thereby have a right against any possessor of this thing outside me in any way other than because one has, as if by genius, attached the right to the thing so that it, as it were, becomes bound to me and thereby resists use by anyone else, because my power of choice (as that which I put into the thing) would in this way infringe upon its freedom. – The same holds in our representation of the right against a particular person which I believe I enjoy by means of the promise I have accepted. For if he thus refuses to fulfill this promise, then I do not attain the object of my power of choice but my freedom is not thereby injured. I thought to extend my possession and yet nothing outer has augmented it; thereby it seems that my freedom is not infringed upon so that nothing unjust befalls me. In order for this latter to occur through an action (whether commission or omission) regarding the object outside me and which I call **mine**, it would require my possession of the object, i.e. such a physical connection to the same that it cannot be separated or withheld from me without affecting me myself. However because at issue here is a right whereby I can first of all make claim to possession, this latter cannot already be presupposed.

[second page]

Thesis. It must be that something outer namely everything usable can be mine or yours. For suppose that is impossible in accordance with concepts of right, then the power of choice would, through the concept

23:225

---

[a] *Gegenstand*

of its freedom in accordance with a universal laws,[a] rob itself of the use of everything usable. The law would thus not be merely the limitation of freedom to the condition of the agreement with everyone else's freedom, instead the free use of the power of choice regarding objects outside me, which possess no rights, would be nullified by these objects as if they had a right or by the mere freedom of each. Now because the first in itself contradicts freedom, though not the power of choice in regard to its object, but instead limits the freedom of the power of choice in accordance with concepts of right, it would thus be that right would be such that that freedom would rob the power of choice of its free outer use which also contradicts itself.

Remark. One could well suppose there are beings who in their mutual outer relation of influence can reciprocally use some of another's powers, or who are also able to use things surrounding them as they intend and who nevertheless, because they are self-sufficient, wanted to make no use of them, so that then everything usable outside them would remain unused. However it is impossible that this could be concluded from concepts of right; rather a principle of right that had as a universal   23:226
consequence that any object which is usable in accordance with freedom nevertheless shall be excluded from all use must be deemed false. For all right is not merely a necessary concept concerning all outer relation among rational beings, simply to secure the freedom of the subject so that its freedom may never again be **subjected** to outer wills,[b] but rather because these beings as such will to make use of outer things it is necessary to **act** only in conformity to conditions of right. Thus the need to extend the concepts of mine and yours also to outer objects insofar as this is kept within the limits of universal freedom already lies in human nature simply as rational beings.

[*third page*]

Solution of the antinomy

The use of everything usable, which in accordance with the thesis the free power of choice is entitled to make, is conceived merely under the condition of an intellectual not a physical possession, i.e. that the subject must have the object[c] of the power of choice within its control; this is a pure concept of the understanding containing no sensible condition. Now right, as a pure relation of the understanding,[d] cannot be derived from any empirical grounds nor any such act, but rather only from *a priori* principles under which the empirical possession can only

---

[a] *nach einem allgemeinen Gesetze*, using both the singular indefinite article and the plural noun
[b] *nichts wieder Willen von außen leiden dürfen*   [c] *Gegenstand*
[d] *Verstandesverhältnis*

ground a right insofar as it is thought in accord with the schematism of an intellectual concept and thus is subsumed under it. Consequently the condition[a] of right must be judged in accordance with the intellectual concepts of possession and not in accordance with what is empirical in space and time, i.e. mine and yours outside us can always be conceived regardless of the physical separation of the person from the objects[b] and a right in those things can always be acquired.

Right

[*this paragraph inserted:*] All propositions concerning right which contain a mine or yours outside us are synthetic propositions *a priori*. How are these possible, since our freedom is not affected by the hindrance of an object outside us? – It can be nothing other than the idea, to which freedom obligates us, of the united powers of choice regarding usable objects outside us. – Others do us wrong, i.e. we are entitled to coerce them (this accords with our freedom) not to oppose the use of what is usable in accordance with a universal law.

23:227

To have a right, distinguished from when one says one is right to do or omit something, always signifies possessing an outer object merely by right and thus it belongs to the outer rightful mine or yours. The proposition which states this is synthetic: for it expresses more about my power of choice and its capacities than is thought merely through freedom. That we can **have** something this way, i.e. that an *a priori* ground would belong to my not merely physical possession but to freedom in accordance with universal laws (although it is not contained within the concept of freedom) is a synthetic *a priori* proposition of right.

All right consists in the possibility (the capacity) to necessitate others through the mere power of choice in accordance with laws of freedom (though not merely through these). Thus it consists properly only in the relation of the power of choice to others' powers of choice and not immediately to objects of the power of choice. Thus one can conceive of possessing something rightfully even though I may not possess another's power of choice; but to possess merely rightfully is tantamount to possessing it without my having the object but rather merely others' powers of choice within my control (and in this way the thing) to necessitate them to something that is not necessary in accordance with the laws of everyone's freedom.

Therefore all synthetic propositions of right are only possible because 1) to have an outer mine and yours which does not contradict freedom in accordance with universal laws so that one may not act against this principle. 2) that such a merely rightful possession can however only be met with in a unified power of choice, so that the *a priori* condition of

[a] *Bedingung*   [b] *Gegenstände*

the unifiability of powers of choice regarding any object also constitutes the condition of the possibility of a merely rightful possession of things and of the outer mine and yours, for which the categories of possession of the thing, of another's action, and finally also of the person other than me, are the kinds of synthetic unity.

[*from here to the end of the page in the margin:*] Of the intellectual acquisition without involving the idea of time merely to be the author or to accept.

Of the category of community in the 3rd number.   23:228

Of acquisition through first taking possession.

This is nothing other than acquisition of a prerogative for the conferring of a right prior to all civil society, although in anticipation of a prospective civil society to be established around it. – He who wills to compel the present virtual possessor does him wrong, though without encroaching upon this his property (which he does not have). For he hinders him in making the first step toward establishing all property in things.

Qui prior tempore potior jure est {whoever is earlier in time acquires the right}, i.e. even though he has not acquired any property, nevertheless he has still acquired a right to be judged by a judge.[a] He does not wrong the other whom he resists.

[*fourth page*]

However these concepts of *a priori* synthetic unity of the powers of choice are not yet sufficient to know that something is either mine or yours and the categories of quantity, causality, etc. could be empty. Therefore *a priori* conditions under which objects of the power of choice are given must be provided, i.e. intuition must be added in order to obtain a cognition of mine and yours outside me; though intuition *a priori* to serve as the schema of the concepts within the principles of mine and yours which pertain to objects[b] of possible experience. Now this schematism of an outer right is

a) the relation of the object[c] of the power of choice outside me in space, b) of another's power of choice to my own in time c) of persons against each other insofar as the one can belong to another's mine or yours – and indeed insofar as their powers of choice are separated from the object through space or time or through their own capacity to determine their own situation[d] in space or time.

Therefore things (because they have no free power of choice which can conflict) can be acquired through unilateral power of choice though

---

[a] *Von einem Richter geurtheilt*   [b] *Gegenstände*
[c] *Gegenstände*   [d] *Zustand*

only a possession limited to the conditions of the **possibility** of the bilateral power of choice with regard to the same object. Performances of another person only through the **actuality** of a bilateral agreement. Finally persons *ad instar* {in the form} of things only through the necessity of reciprocal unification.

23:229   The concept of mine includes within it the concept of the possession of an object of the power of choice, i.e. that I have it in my control 1. as a **thing** as something which also exists without anyone's power of choice, 2) which can exist only in the power of choice of a person (and in outer mine only in another's power of choice), a power of choice whose causality can be determined by me. 3) another's power of choice itself insofar as it depends for its determination upon my power of choice in accordance with a law given by me, although my condition depends upon the former determination of his power of choice. – The grounding of this contingent mine (the acquisition of this right) is a) to be sought merely within my *proprio facto* {very own deed} (*unilaterali*), b.) in my rightful capacity to determine the other to an **act**. Acquisition of a right to an *actus* of another's power of choice (*facto unilaterali alterius* {unilateral deed by another}) also only a specific *factum alterius*, NB I cannot acquire through wrong[a] to the other. That is intended acquisition. c.) the condition of another's power of choice *facto bilaterali* {through bilateral deed}.

Within mine and yours empirical possession which depends upon conditions of time and place is to be distinguished from purely intellectual, which properly constitutes the distinction of mine and yours, of which the former is merely its presentation. In the first case I say I possess the object in the second only the right to it. However in both cases the merely rightful possession, namely when one abstracts from all empirical conditions, is that which properly constitutes the mine and yours.

If one takes the empirical conditions of the presentation of mine and yours, i.e. that through which alone one can know this distinction, for conditions of rightful possession as such then an antinomy of right arises.

[*the next two paragraphs are additions in the margin:*] The distinction between a servant and *locator opera* {a contract worker} is this: that I have in the former a *jus in re* against all others with whom he stays to demand his return because he constitutes a part of the household, in contrast to my having in the latter only a personal right that he perform something for me though he may stay where he will.

To possess a right to a thing and to possess a thing itself is *intellectualiter* not differentiated.

---

[a] *Läsion*

Loses Blatt E 14
[*first page, marked "4" at the top by Kant*]

That which depends upon my power of choice in accordance with universal laws is either 1) a thing, or 2) another's action or 3) a condition, to act and to undergo. These are the three kinds of mine outside me, and possession is a) the thing, b) another's action as I please, c) a person, whereby the unification of powers of choice in the first case is merely possible, in the second is actual, in the third is necessary, in order to possess something outside me. However my action is thus α) unilaterally, β) bilaterally active, γ) reciprocally active and passive.

Antinomy

~~Thesis. It is possible for something outside me, i.e. also not possessed, to be rightfully mine, that I would have an outer right, i.e. a merely rightful possession is possible. — For suppose: an object of the power of choice outside me could not be mine in accordance with concepts of right, i.e. my mere power of choice could not make any desired use of any usable objects at all, unless it would happen in this way to infringe upon the freedom of the power of choice in accordance with universal laws, under the condition that I myself at the same time from possession of the thing as unification with~~ — [*breaks off*]

Thesis. It is possible that something outer be mine, i.e. that others' powers of choice, by using an object[a] outside me, would infringe upon my freedom; my mere power of choice, even without possessing the object, resists in accordance with universal laws of freedom whomever obstructs me in the use of such an object. – For suppose the opposite: it would thus be impermissible, i.e. it would contradict universal laws of freedom, for anyone to use whatever is externally usable if I find I am not in possession of it. Thus freedom in its use of something would make itself dependent upon something other than the condition of its universal validity, namely upon the objects[b] of the power of choice which it has the capacity to use: i.e. the power of choice which is limited to the possession of an object as the condition of mine or yours would not be a free power of choice, which contradicts itself.

Remark: if for example the usable outer object of the power of choice be a thing (corporeal thing)[c] then I would not only merely be in possession of it but also must remain so if the authorization to use it and the lack of authorization on the part of others to obstruct my use of it should continue. Thus I would not be able to prevent others from entering upon some land from which I have just left because I cannot carry it with me, and must always carry around with me the piece of wood I have found 23:231

---

[a] *Gegenstand* in this sentence   [b] *Objecte*
[c] *Object ... eine Sache (körporliches Ding)*

so that I can say that it is mine, and the usable itself would, through freedom which restricts use only to the rules of validity for all, be reduced to just the use – Or suppose another's agreement to do or provide something for me, which is a possible use of another's free power of choice, then if you do not receive into your possession what has been promised together with your acceptance of the promise, and thus acquire nothing, and in accordance with your concept of freedom the other party is always free to refuse even that which is to be performed because you have not directly through accepting received it into your possession, and indeed this dependency upon the object[a] of the power of choice together with the consequent restriction of use is a consequence of the law of freedom.

[second page]

Antithesis. It is impossible that something outside me be **mine** i.e. that others' powers of choice infringe upon my freedom through the use of an object[b] outside me. This proposition appears to lie immediately within the expression itself. For wrong can be done to me by others only insofar as my freedom which agrees with theirs in accordance with universal laws is infringed by their action. Now the obstruction of my possession of an object outside me is of course an action which infringes upon my power of choice, though not my freedom, because the latter consists in an influence upon myself. Thus no wrong happens to me when others get an object of my power of choice into their possession against my power of choice so that I am precluded from any use of it. Consequently no object outside me can be mine, i.e. also without my possession of the object I can have no right with regard to it.

Remark. If I cover a spot on the earth (on which we suppose no one has yet lain) with my body, even then it is not thereby mine even if I wanted others to be excluded from it in the future; rather only as long as I lie or sit there (as the word *possidere* also indicates[c]) can no one else compel me to leave it because he thus infringes upon my freedom which is contradicting no one else's freedom. But if I subsequently separate myself from that spot with an intervening space, if I get up and go elsewhere, then I cannot have the opinion that anyone else would be prevented, simply by my will expressed to him in the strongest way, from using it at his convenience to the exclusion of my own; for he does not have any effect on me at all but only on an object[d] outside me and he does not damage my freedom. Thus without (bodily) possession I cannot possess any place and also no thing as soon as I release it from my hands and set it down (on a place belonging to no one) and hence cannot call it

23:232

---

[a] *Object* [b] *Gegenstand* in this paragraph
[c] The Latin "possidere" (to possess) is derived from the Latin "sidere" (to sit).
[d] *Gegenstand* in this paragraph unless otherwise noted

mine. – The same also holds if the object of my power of choice is separated by time from me and from its possession, e.g. someone promises me an object[a] of my power of choice which is in his possession, a bodily thing, or an application of his forces to perform something that I will, and I unify my will with his, in this case there is time between that prior promise itself which we have accepted[b] and the resulting performance, a time within which the promissor can become of a different mind without infringing on my **freedom** because I am still not in possession of what has been promised as that which is the necessary condition under which my freedom can be infringed on by others. Therefore my accepting of another's will is not simultaneously the possession of the same (since this is separated in time) and hence also in this way it is not possible that anything outside me be **mine**. – In other words what is mine without physical possession is not mine (*meum reale*), by not keeping his promise the other does not infringe on my freedom because I am not in possession of the object and hence am not affected if the other does not perform.

[*two lines in the margin:*]
Solution
Of the Ideality of Possession

Loses Blatt E 15
[*first page, marked "5" at the top by Kant*]
Solution of the antinomy
The principle of the ideality of space and time (as well as sensation) does not preclude the point that the pure concepts of the understanding would have objective reality merely in them or under their conditions as appearances. Equally I would say that the principle of the ideality of possession by mere right does not preclude the point that the same concepts of right would not acquire objective reality solely through physical action, e.g. taking[c] and accepting.

23:233

All concepts of right are entirely intellectual and concern a relation among rational beings as such to one another which must be thought without any empirical conditions merely as a connection of free powers of choice to each other, so that in this way what is right can be determined. – This determination therefore does not depend upon conditions of space and time, rather it must have its principles[d] *a priori* in the mere idea of freely acting beings and their relations insofar as they, in their outward use of their capacities, agree with the freedom of everyone in accordance with universal laws. The actions themselves which accord

---

[a] *Object*
[b] *acceptirten*
[c] *apprehension*
[d] *Grundsätze*

with these laws are only to be regarded as appearances of those determinations of the will which lie *a priori* in the pure understanding, under which these determinations can be subsumed by means of the schema of the power of judgment.

Therefore all that is mine and yours as regards its principle[a] must stand entirely under pure intellectual concepts of right, and hence also a merely rightful possession must be thought through just such a concept so that possession must be thought merely as a connection of the object[b] (of mine and yours) with the power of choice (to use it) without allowing any admixture by conditions of space and time. Now indeed such a connection (that it may be) as such and without those sensible conditions cannot at all be known, although in the case of a sensibly conditioned action or of the condition of the subject (regarding possession of the object[c]) I must of course abstract from the latter in order to seek the ground of determination of the mine and yours in the pure intellectual concept of possession; for without this concept no wrong[d] could occur through another's obstruction of my use of an outer object.[e]

[*second page*]

The apparent conflict of reason with itself regarding outer mine and yours (what is not in my physical possession) – **The thesis states** there must be a mine and yours in objects[f] outside me i.e. in objects which I do not possess, which would be absurd if the concept of possession as such meant their connection with my power of choice. However I can and should thereby understand: in that of which I am not in empirical possession, for if I take away this empirical possession, the intellectual (connection with my power of choice) still remains and this is precisely what the universal rule of right grounds. – Now **the antithesis states** there can be no mine or yours in things outside the subject, because I would thus not be in their possession and I would suffer no[g] damage to my freedom when others precede me in their use of the thing. This opposite would of course contradict the preceding if by possession in both cases physical possession must be understood – Now both propositions can be true since possession can obviously be taken in two senses, and here there must be no mine and yours regarding objects[h] outside me without any possession at all, but there could be without physical possession, for of course there remains intellectual possession which indeed makes it possible that I can say I have **a right**.

23:234

---

[a] *Princip*
[b] *Object*
[c] *Object*
[d] *Läsion*
[e] *Gegenstand*
[f] *Objecten*
[g] reading *keinen* for *einen*
[h] *Gegenständen*

Explanation

If I have established for my purpose some land that no one yet possessed, I have bound it with my power of choice which disturbs no one else in his possession.

[*in margin:*] But whether also not the freedom of others to choose a different use for it?

Regardless of whether I now distance myself from this piece of land (interrupt my physical possession), as long as I do not abolish the connection with my power of choice, then the merely rightful possession remains (namely my entitlement to use it exclusively) and the thing is **mine**.

Another kind of mine is that of an object[a] of another's power of choice, or another's power of choice regarding an object insofar as it can become mine. Namely if the other has promised an action and I have accepted this promise, then I possess the other's deed (or its effect the object) intellectually, i.e. in a merely rightful way regardless of whether a period of time intervenes during which I can come into physical possession and the other hinders me in my possession when he denies me his act.

[*third page*]   23:235

** **

The principle of the possibility of mine and yours outside us is therefore the principle of the ideality of possession as the sufficient condition of the distinction of mine and yours. In contrast the principle that only physical possession has objective reality makes outer mine and yours impossible (because this consists precisely in that something which is also out of my physical possession could be rightly bound with my power of choice). Regarding mine and yours physical possession is merely the appearance of rightful possession. But this appearance is necessary only in taking possession (whether taking[b] or accepting) as an outer identifying mark restricting others' powers of choice because a right has been grounded.

Of rightful acquisition (in accordance with concepts of right)

All innate mine or yours is grounded upon an analytic principle of mere freedom – all other mine or yours upon a synthetic principle of right of the augmentation of the power of choice in regard to the object. The question is how is a synthetic law of right possible *a priori*? E.g. can something be acquired by taking control,[c] hence can I place myself

---

[a] *Object* in this paragraph   [b] *apprehension*
[c] *occupation*

in intellectual possession of an object through my power of choice? In relation to the idea of a possible or actual or indeed necessary unity of powers of choice among persons who find themselves in mutual rightful relations through their common will, in which the possession of my thing is secured, it becomes possible that what is physically outside me be mine. – That it must be possible (and through the antinomy the impossibility was not demonstrated) is proven above, but here the question is how and in virtue of what.

[*in margin:*] First something must be the object[a] of the power of choice of whomever shall acquire a right or distribute it to another i.e. he must have it within his capacity. Second he must himself execute an action whereby a right is produced, i.e. he cannot acquire another's object *facto injusto* {by an unjust deed}. Third, he must take control of[b] the object, whether it be bodily by taking or virtually by accepting (Whether this be a derivative right? admittedly provided it is a thing though not if it be merely another's act.) – He must will to receive it into his possession. – He thereby creates an obligation in others by which they themselves must consent to the specific principle[c] that they will to make things outside them into their own.

23:236

The objects[d] of acquired mine and yours are 1. things 2. another's actions 3 persons other than ourselves. Thus 1. rights in things 2. personal right 3. the most personal right, rights of status[e] (*jus in statu personarum fundatum* {right established in a person's status}). The first right is established in a thing. The second is not established at all the third is established in persons as things 3 the right in a person as a thing.

[*fourth page*]

A right in regard to an object[f] outside me cannot as such be acquired; for all acquisition presupposes a right in accordance with which alone it is possible. It is a principle[g] the form of which comes first, even before the matter of the power of choice is given. – Instead this right in an object outside us is in general that from which or in conformity with which alone an object can be acquired. Now the formal right is the determinability of another's power of choice through my own and vice versa in accordance with laws of freedom, yet these do not obtain in outer mine and yours if a single power of choice by itself were to determine the other because then one of them would not be free. Thus the concept of the synthetic mine and yours contains the idea of a unified or unifiable power of choice through which alone what is one's own is determined for each and this synthetic unity is a condition *a priori* under

---

[a] *Object*
[c] *Princip*
[e] *Standesrecht*
[g] *Princip*

[b] *Bemächtigen*
[d] *Gegenstände*
[f] *Gegenstand* in first part of paragraph

which alone something outer can be acquired. – Therefore in relation
to an outer object[a] the appropriation of something, the agreement 1.) to
a possible unification of powers of choice on the possession of the same
object, 2. With an actual, 3. with a necessary unification of powers of
choice in mutual relation, will constitute the condition of outer rightful
acquisition.

The intellectual possession of the object, of which the empirical is the
presentation, can only as from the unified powers of choice [*breaks off*]

The object as a thing[b] (which has no free power of choice) is possible
empirically merely through unilateral, but as a person's *factum* {deed}
through bilateral, finally as a condition of reciprocal performances only
through omnilateral determination of powers of choice in outer relations
toward others (outside this whole).

Loses Blatt E 16

[*first page, marked "6" at the top by Kant*]

23:237

Right in land

Originally I find myself on some land since it is inseparable from my
existence (that I once as it were took[c] it by birth is a related concept
which can be set aside). Thus I am the occupant[d] of this land; whether
by right this occupancy is to continue permanently so that the occupancy is at the same time possession can here remain unspecified. – I
thus have an innate but still created[e] **right in a thing** which yet may
not be regarded as acquired because it is connected with my existence,
I may also have been on this land from eternity. – From this right all of
my *jura in re* (*externa*) {rights in things (external)} must be derivable –
Therefore everyone must allow me some land or other, hence if someone takes away my occupancy, this can occur only on condition that he
assigns me another on which I can live (not to leave to my fate which
land one would grant me).

This *detentio* (occupancy) as such is bound with the use which is
required for my existence, and I do not become obligated to anyone
through that occupancy when it does not depend upon my power of
choice. This even holds if I involuntarily end up on some land, because
I must be able to be somewhere: **even if there are also previous occupants of it specifically in relation to borders.**

Now if I take some land which has not yet been claimed by anyone
I have in this way acquired only a portion of the land at large[f] which
I cannot myself determine: really only the authorization to use it **even**

---

[a] *Object* in remainder of paragraph
[b] *Das Object als eine Sache*
[c] *apprehendirt*
[d] *Inhaber*
[e] *entstandenes*
[f] *allgemeinen Boden*

if I do not physically occupy[a] **it, and** to exclude others from it, but its borders cannot be determined simply through my power of choice. Therefore I can determine my property only in reference to a common will of those who also are by natural necessity bound to that land, and in general the certainty of possession is related to a common will which distributes land and therefore to the *status civilis* {civil condition}.

The antinomy only concerns the possibility of a merely rightful possession in general and thus precedes consideration of mine and yours in general.

[marginal sketches of kinds of rights omitted here]

23:238 *[second page]*

Division of the universal law of right – 1) that of the power of choice in regard to its agreement with the freedom of everyone. 2) Laws of freedom and agreement of the same with the power of choice and with the use of all of its objects[b] (which are everything usable, consequently standing within the control of the object as well as in its faculty of desire.)

23:239 In the first case freedom limits the power of choice in the second the power of choice limits freedom and in turn its law. In this way the former also augments itself because it limits the limitation of freedom itself (e.g. to limit rightful possession merely to the occupying of land) and its principles[c] are synthetic whereas the former are analytic.

In the sensible presentation of the intellectual concept of right 1. regarding *jus in re* {right in a thing} the thing is represented as person, 2. regarding *jus personale* {personal right} the act of a person is represented as use of a thing, 3 regarding *jus consolidatum* {right of attached property} the person is represented directly as thing *instar rei* {the form of a thing}.

Condition[d] (*status juridicus* {rightful condition}) is the relation of one's power of choice to others' powers of choice so that everyone is able to have certain rights. Any condition requires a constitution (*constitutio*), which may now consist merely objectively in the concept of a **principle of possible conditions** or subjectively in an *actus* of the power of choice, nevertheless it is always a relation of unified powers of choice.

For between freedom and the power of choice there are four relations.[e] 1. Of freedom to freedom. **Universality** of the principle of right in general 2. The agreement of the power of choice with freedom, the quality of right 3. Of freedom with the power of choice of each, the relation[f] of powers of choice to objects. 4. Of the power of choice to the power of choice a. the possibility of their unification b. the actuality (*actus*) of unification c. necessity of the durability which already lies in

---

[a] *einnehmen*	[b] *Object* in this paragraph
[c] *Grundsätze*	[d] *Zustand*
[e] *Beziehungen*	[f] *Relation*

the concept. – This modality concerns either the relation of the power of choice to things, or the power of choice to the power of choice, or person to the person as (*instar*) a thing, and acquisition is a) taking b) accepting, c) constituting, i.e. the constitution[a] in private relations among persons.

Difficulty

First acquisition can occur only through a unilateral *factum* {deed}. However, can my own power of choice thereby impose upon others an obligation which they previously did not have and which they have not taken upon themselves? If we are to be able to acquire *factum unilateralis* it must be a universal postulate of the power of choice that we make all things depend upon human beings, but all human beings depend upon each other regarding the use of things with regard to limitations on use.

The acquisition of a servant can also occur without *pactum* {contract}   23:240
through his arrest for debts. That is not the bondsmanship of a *servus* {slave} which can only transpire *ob delictum* {due to an offense}.

[*remainder of second page in margin:*]

1 Right to things
   personal right[b]
   realized right to a person[c]

In a *pactum* I acquire *praestatio* or *factum alterius* {another's performance or deed}.

In *re domestica* {household matters} I acquire persons *instar rerum* {in the form of a thing}. The right to a thing, the right to a person, the right to a status[d] of a person as a thing *jus in personalitatem* {right in a person}.

[*third page*]

What is mine (outside me) is that from the use of which I can rightly exclude everyone even though I am not in physical possession (occupying) of it. Now I cannot exclude such use by limiting others' power of choice through my freedom because the handling of an object[e] outside me does not damage my freedom; aside from freedom there is nothing other than the power of choice that contradicts others' freedom. Therefore if something outer nevertheless shall be mine, it must be preceded by a possession based solely on my power of choice not on occupancy, i.e. a merely rightful possession in the idea of freedom of the power of choice regarding objects in general through which the latter stands in connection with space in general so that the former is subjected to that power of choice, i.e. that his freedom is impeded those who through their

---

[a] *Verfassung*   [b] *das Persönliche Recht*
[c] *Personenrecht*   [d] *Zustand*
[e] *Gegenstand*

275

maxims would not want to allow that some place or other belongs *a priori* to the subject. This prior right is by virtue of one's existence on earth as *possessio principalis* {possession in principle} by which I have a right to acquire everything which happens to be in such a place which I have first occupied, where I happen to find myself regardless of my will,[a] as *accessorius jure rei meae* {an addition to my right to a thing}.

In the pure intellectual representation of mine and yours it is possible to acquire something unilaterally because in that case there are no other conditions for possession than will and one's capacity to use something. However in the sensible presentation of mine and yours each possession is bound to the condition of space because it must be possible to leave the possessed thing though it remains someone's which is necessary for freedom. Now through this freedom other objects[b] of the power of choice are obtained, and this does not contradict the freedom of previous occupant[c] if the thing that is not in his possession is occupied[d] by others: – Hence here is an antinomy – Solution. Every human being, as he is on the earth, must be regarded as the occupant of the entire surface. In this way however he is regarded as possessor in community with all others (*communio originaria* {original holding in common})

Thus there are *res alicuius, res nullius* and *res cuiusque* {things belonging to someone, to no one, and to everyone}. This holding in common[e] constitutes the *suum externum (jus in re)* {what is one's externally (right in a thing)}, only represented as granted by the common will and obtained by the subject's unilateral action.

1. The *communio originaria* is not empirically grounded as a *factum* or event but rather a right to land without which no human being can exist, which itself follows from freedom in the use of things.

One must assume that mine and yours in things can only occur within the universal original possession of the earth's land, for then contemporaries and later generations are limited by the *prior occupans* {one who previously took control} to the conditions of the possession actually taken by the first who master it. The limits of this prerogative, however, are determined unilaterally, yet in relation to those who in the future might take their share.[f]

All synthetic rights in things (for in themselves they are analytic) have as their ground the *fundus communis* {communal land} and thus can be regarded as founded before possession is taken.

---

[a] *wiedermeinen Willen zufällt*	[b] *Objecte*
[c] *Innhabers*	[d] *occupirt*
[e] *communion*	[f] *auf künftig mögliche Theilnehmer*

B. OTHER LOOSE SHEETS ON PRIVATE RIGHT

[The pagination is from Stark, *Nachforschungen*]
Loses Blatt Hagen 23. Between February and May, 1794.

Doctrine of Right   Stark 254

Of mine and yours outside me, 1. right in a thing, 2. personal right,
3. personal right directly as (*instar* {in the form of}) a right in a thing.

Right in a thing

No right in a thing outside me is innate (*a natura sunt res nullius* {by
nature things are ownerless}) yet the right to acquire all usable things
outside me is (*non sunt essentialiter res nullius hic est nihili* {things are not
essentially ownerless, that is, nothing}). The *jus rei quaesibilis* {right to
acquire a thing} is innate, for otherwise freedom would be limited by
things. The *jus in re* is either *proprium* or *commune* {proprietary or com-
munal}. *Jus proprium* is either to make any use of a thing one desires
or only one. The first is *dominium*: the thing is **mine**. The object of
my power of choice in whose mere rightful possession (i.e. also without
physically holding it) I find myself is mine: for without any possession
I would not be affected at all by the use that another makes of it, but
only with physical possession, in which case my innate right and not the
acquired right (as all right in things must be) would be affected by this
curtailment of the freedom of my power of choice.

The right in a thing is thus in fact only the concept of an intelligible possession, i.e. to be connected to the thing through my power of
choice alone without holding the thing yet as if I would be in physical   Stark 255
possession. The intelligible possession thus remains when the link to my
power of choice is not actually severed. But without any preceding physical possession no intelligible (purely rightful) possession can occur, for
without that the thing and its link to me has not been given.

The first taking possession through which something is acquired is
unilateral. It depends only on the manner through which something is
acquired as one's property and is maintained in a purely rightful possession without holding.

* *
*

Loses Blatt E 6   23:273

[*first page*]

1) Right is the relation of persons to one another so far as the freedom
of one limits the freedom of another through his power of choice to the
conditions of universal conformity with law. This limitation rests upon
a synthetic law of freedom if the object[a] is outside me: if it is in me, then

---

[a] *Gegenstand*

upon an analytic one. In the first case I constrain another through the representation of outer laws in the second case through the representation of inner laws through his freedom.

2) Thus there are no rightful relations of things among each other nor between things and persons. For corresponding to right there is an obligation on the other's part – Things however are incapable of any obligation.

3) All rightful relations of persons to things concerns only the schematism of the possession of outer things (in space and time)

4) An outer thing is intellectually mine [*added in margin:* to this corresponds a strong obligation, i.e. dependence on the power of choice of the other who thus has his power of choice in his control and can coerce him] or yours if I would be wronged by the use which another may make of it against my will. Thus **I must be in possession of the thing for it to be mine**.

5) The difference between physical and intellectual or virtual possession is merely the difference between the schematism of the concept of right in mine and yours and the concept of right itself.

[*in margin:*] Regarding outer things a mine and yours must be possible for otherwise they would impose an obligation upon me.

6) The schematism of outer mine and yours rests upon the agreement of everyone to universal principles *a priori* of distribution of things in space through which a mine or yours obtains: hence it presupposes an original common possession.

6)[a] Prior to this distribution however there are indeed rights regarding unequal acquisition [*added in margin:* virtually, i.e. currently and in rightful possession through my mere power of choice], since each free power of choice makes itself the center of the circle of its exercise, and here initial taking possession can create a provisional property if only the possession is identical with the capacity to use – This property only means that one can necessitate all others either to enter into a union or to depart.

[*in margin:*] Right as such as the mere form of the power of choice in accordance with laws of freedom is only singular – Though a right (*jus quoddam* {a specific right}) of which there are many is a right in accordance with its matter and what one can possess, alienate, etc. etc.

7) [*paragraph 7 subdivided for clarity*] The 12 categories of merely rightful possession. My right is:

That of **quantity** 1.) unilateral, 2.) granted by another, 3. derived from everyone's possession –

23:274

---

[a] Kant repeats "6"

That of **quality** 1.) of the capacity to use, 2) of the independence of a thing from use by another, i.e. of freedom, 3.) of the limitation of others' power of choice through my freedom. –

That of **relation** 1.) of substance, i.e. of things, 2. of causality, others' promise, 3. of community, the mutual possession of persons.

That of **modality** 1.) provisional right. 2. acquired right 3. innate outer right.

8) Only the unified will among a number of persons can make an outer mine and yours.

[*second page*]

9) The conflict among principles of right regarding outer objects of the power of choice thus derives from one's taking the schema of right for right itself, which is only an **intellectual** relation of powers of choice in accordance with laws of freedom. The latter must come first as a ground and the rules of the schematism stand under it, rather than the schema being the ground of right.

10) A practical concept of reason is the concept of a ground of action that has objective reality although it cannot be presented to the senses. Of this kind are the concepts of duty, right, and virtue. Right in the outer relation of the power of choice is thus a practical concept of reason. Action (the *actus* of the power of choice) is indeed only a concept of the understanding belonging to the category of causality which can be presented in a schema for sensible intuition, although the ground to act this way and not otherwise, **right**, cannot be given, i.e. presented, to the senses in any corresponding intuition.

11) Because the rational concept of right has of course objective prac- 23:275
tical reality i.e. it must be possible to provide for it a corresponding object (an action) in sensible intuition and hence in space and time, hence there must be a corresponding schematism which however does not **directly** correspond to the concept of right but rather to the physical act of the power of choice, though so far as this power is regarded as free, which, because the freedom of the power of choice cannot be schematized, cannot otherwise be thought than by regarding the physical *actus* of the power of choice (which already has its physical schema) as merely the schema of possession.

"**Physical possession**, holding, must be thought of merely as the schema of **intellectual** possession (of right) through the mere power of choice in (rightful) **mine** and **yours**."

For rightful possession consists merely in the capacity of the power of choice to determine another's power of choice regarding an object[a] of the senses in accordance with laws of freedom.

---

[a] *Object*

12) Of the pure intellectual principles[a] of mine and yours outside me. a. Whatever things outside me I have in my control without infringing upon others' freedom under universal laws are what is mine. b) whatever is to be done by another subject to my will is mine c) whichever person's will in a certain kind of use is subject to my will in accordance with laws of freedom, that person is mine.

* *

I cannot simply say of some land that it is mine but rather only that I have a prerogative to possess it exclusively. For I cannot annihilate it, destroy it, nor carry it away, hence I cannot dispose of its substance; I can only use it exclusive of others. What is one's in land, only that land is mine which I receive in accordance with the original *lex agraria naturalis* {natural law of land distribution} hence as a share of public land through distribution in accordance with laws of freedom.

[*third page*]

All laws regarding mine and yours outside me are analytic insofar as they rest merely on reason in the concept of right, i.e. they rest solely on the concept of the freedom of the power of choice. However the laws which determine possession of mine and yours outside me in space and time (although my right cannot be outside me) are synthetic; and hence just as the former require only agreement of my will with others' wills, i.e. regulative unity, so the latter require unification of powers of choice regarding that which is not originally (innately) mine; and in this community of wills the object[b] that would be called mine is in common possession in accordance with rational concepts, though sensibly it is not in my physical possession (occupying). Thus, in accordance with the analytic law of freedom (as independence) regarded negatively, I can sit wherever I will if it is unoccupied by others; though not in a place **because I previously occupied it**, if another now occupies it, without laying down as a basis the relevant unified powers of choice, which presupposes a public law and which grounds freedom (as capacity) regarding outer objects of the power of choice in the mutual relations of persons. – Distinction between lawful freedom (*legitima*) and legal freedom (*legalis*), the latter requires public laws (not convention[c]).

23:276

How are **synthetic** propositions of right[d] possible *a priori* (regarding objects[e] of experience, for regarding objects of a free power of choice in general they are analytic)? **Answer**: As principles of freedom as a capacity independent of nature through the command of a common will in the idea. 1) **Analytic proposition of right**. Any outer object of the power

[a] *Principien*
[b] *Object*
[c] *conventionen*
[d] *Rechtssätze*
[e] *Gegenstände* in this paragraph

of choice is mine through the agreement of others' powers of choice (without regard to relations of time and place). **Synthetic proposition of right**. The piece of ground **remains mine even when the occupants change** and likewise as regards causality in promising in *pactum*. The owner is such a one and this is the **definition of owner**. If I do not watch over the piece of ground it is preserved in common possession and will. – The **mine of another person** is mutual influence just as the simultaneity of A and B consists in their being **reciprocally condition and conditioned** which occurs in *succession*.

Right

Considered *formaliter* {formally} is the relation of one person to an action in accordance with which the person through **this relation** is authorized to compel someone else in accordance with laws of freedom (*facultatem habet* {authorized}). If the person is authorized only to compel herself[a] then it is the right of humanity regarding one's own human person, i.e. inner right; if the person is authorized to compel others then the person's right is an outer right, the former belongs to ethics the latter to *jus*.

Regarded *materialiter* **a right** (which constitutes part of what one has)   23:277
is the relation of one person to an object[b] of that person's power of choice outside that person according to which that person can exercise coercion against others in accordance with laws of freedom in order to possess the object.

[*in margin:*] **Possession** is the connection of a person with an object[c] in accordance with which it is possible for that person to make arbitrary use of it.

[*remainder of page is an addition in the margin*]
As a concept of freedom, right is directed not toward empirical but rather toward intellectual possession. This latter, however, can only become knowledge through the schematism, otherwise it is empty.

In the *status naturalis*, i.e. where there are no outer limiting laws by which my freedom can be secured against others on the condition that their ownership is also secured against me, to acquire something outer is a contradiction. I can only acquire a privilege of right which consists in this: that my action agrees with the idea of the civil condition.

The possibility of having something outside oneself as one's own, if the outer object[d] of the power of choice is merely thought through intellectual concepts, can be comprehended *a priori*, in which case there

---

[a] In German *Person* is a feminine noun   [b] *Gegenstand*
[c] *Object*   [d] *Gegenstand*

are pure principles[a] of mine and yours. But possession (having) in space and time, hence what is empirically mine, is not thereby determined, consequently all of these concepts as such are empty (as categories) and concepts of right can only become cognitions if the will of another is represented as it appears and reveals itself externally to the senses. Hence taking[b] as a sign of the will for possession. As a rational concept, however, right cannot be made intuitable except through the schematism of **possession**, which can be empirical, not any schematism of right.

[*fourth page*]

Regarding possession of a thing outside me I can exercise no coercion against others in accordance with laws of freedom except when all others, with whom I enter into this relation, can agree with me about it, i.e. through the will of all united with my own will, for then I coerce each through his own will in accordance with laws of freedom. Only[c] the concept of right is a concept of reason that, through the idea of a unified will, is laid down as the ground of all outer mine and yours, and another's outer right against me is a coercion to which I am subjected in accordance with laws of freedom.

23:278

That among human beings whose powers of choice stand in outer relations there must be a right (and indeed a public right), i.e. that they must will that there should be such a right so that one can presuppose this as their will, lies in the concept of the human being as a person regarding whom my freedom is limited and whose freedom I must secure. – Yet for that reason that unification of powers of choice is not always actual. Hence mine and yours is only provisional until this unification is established, although it is of course subject to inner laws of right, namely to limit the freedom of rightful possession to the condition that it make possible that unification.

Regarding an object[d] of my power of choice (so far as another alters it through his power of choice) I can be **wronged only when I possess it** (so that he must alter me in my freedom). Thus I cannot be wronged regarding an acre that I do not occupy nor in the action which another has not performed nor in the child who leaves my house, if **rightful possession** were to depend **upon physical possession** and not conversely. Thus we must regard the physical condition of rightful possession only as the schematism of the latter, which of course is necessary to the subject and yet which also holds objectively without it.

[a] *Grundsätze*
[b] *apprehension*
[c] Reading "Allein" for "Allen"
[d] *Gegenstand*

To have a right means to have something outer the use of which no public universal law (in accordance with principles of freedom[a]) can possibly hinder.

Therefore each has a right as first possessor to have some land: since if the opposite were made a law freedom as a positive capacity would be annulled[b] – It is only a matter of how much land.

That any object[c] of the power of choice outside me must be acquirable is an identical proposition for otherwise it would not be an object of the power of choice, or freedom would altogether exclude itself from its use which is a self-contradiction. – But how much I may acquire remains thereby undetermined, for if I could acquire everything altogether then my freedom would not limit others' freedom but rather annul it. I can acquire only in one way, consequently the proof can only be indirect   23:279 (namely that it is otherwise impossible to acquire, e.g. that from a point on a line only one single perpendicular line can be drawn because otherwise there could be two right angles in a triangle or no triangle at all could result since the sides run parallel. *Problema indeterminatum* {the problem of indeterminacy}: on a given line construct a triangle (without the sides being given): the angles taken together must be less than two right angles. But by how much?) Only the *a priori* necessary unification of the will for the sake of freedom and certain determinate laws of their agreement can make acquisition possible, since the object[d] of the power of choice is previously thought by reason within the unified power of choice, and this unified power of choice determines for each what is his. N.B. By prescription and vindication I acquire the status[e] of my possession only through civil law not through natural law.

[remainder of page in the margin]

1) Of outer mine and yours [as] object[f] of the power of choice. Of the manner of having such. It must occur also without occupying and yet in accordance with first occupying.

2) Of the manner of outer mine and yours. Rights to things[g] – personal right. – From rights to things follows personal right.

3) Of the manner of acquiring something external. Originally (not *factum injustus alterius* {another's wrongful deed}). *Factum, Pactum,* and *lex (naturalis)* {deed, contract, and (natural) law} without a specific *pactum* the child remains the property[h] of the father, and the bondsman namely to accommodate *pro alimentis jus in persona*

---

[a] *Freiheitsprincipien*
[b] *aufheben*
[c] *Gegenstand* in this sentence
[d] *Object*
[e] *Zustand*
[f] *Gegenstand*
[g] *Sachenrecht*
[h] *Das Seine*

(*fundatum*) {personal right to sustenance (fundamental)} when he is not emancipated or does not emancipate himself. – For this only a *quasi contract* is needed.

4) Of how his property is grounded on possession even if this possession [is grounded on] prior property *praescriptio et vindicatio* {prescription and vindication}.

Of the right which has no judge – *aequitas, casus necessitatis* {equity, cases of necessity}.

23:279   *Loses Blatt* E 10

[*KS selection on second page, this passage around the left margin*]

Every human being has an innate right to be on some place on earth, since his existence is not a *factum* {deed} and hence also not an *injustum* {a wrong}. He also has a right to be *incorporaliter* {non-bodily} at several places at once if he has specified them for his use and not through his mere will. However, because everyone else also has this right the *prior*

23:280   *occupans* has the provisional right to coerce anyone who hinders his use to join with him in entering a contract to determine the limits of permissible possession and to use force[a] if others prevaricate.

23:280   *Loses Blatt* E 17. On a letter dated July 17, 1795.

[*first page*]

There is an apparent antinomy between the conditions of the rightful possession of a thing as an object[b] of experience and that of the possession of the very same thing as an object thought merely through reason, hence rightful possession although dependent on space and time and so at the same time physical possession, and for this the concept of **merely rightful possession**.

For in general I only possess rightly that the use of which without my agreement is a violation of my freedom, and thus in accordance with the first concept of possession I can possess nothing outer at all by merely rightful possession; I possess no corporeal thing which I have not so connected with my body that no one can hold it as they choose without altering me in my person, no piece of ground from which I have departed, no house from which I have removed myself, no apple which I have released from my hand, and so nothing corporeal outside me could be possibly mine – for **only that which I possess merely rightly is mine**.

On the other hand however I must of course also be able to possess all of this merely rightfully for otherwise all things would be *res nullius* {ownerless things} and my freedom would indeed consist in independence but would not be a capacity, and I would do wrong to things

---

[a] *Gewalt*   [b] *Gegenstand* in this paragraph

through my appropriation or to other men even if I do not have any influence on them.

Therefore it must be that the mere, pure concept of the understanding of an object[a] of my power of choice which belongs to no one must be sufficient for me to appropriate it, and so to be able to regard it as belonging to my rightful possession and hence also even if is not in my physical possession which is bound with conditions of space and time.

Resolutio. There is no genuine contradiction between these two concepts of possession for the first is possession within the realm of appearance which, as unilateral appropriation (without a lawful corroborating universal will), is not sufficient for merely rightful possession and yet is 23:281 necessary for mine or yours as the requisite **designation** of my legislating universal will within which this possession is preserved even without physical possession.

Loses Blatt E 19. On the back of a letter dated June 12, 1795.   23:281

First the concept of right
1. **Being right** (*regula justi*) {standard of justice} [is] the **possibility** of action in accordance with laws of freedom – the formula of justice (*justitia*) as such.

2. **To have** a right (of which there can be several) [is] the **actuality** of private right of each individual in relation to others [as] outer right, hence justice in *status naturalis* {state of nature} ~~(lex justitiae commutativae)~~ ~~{law of commutative justice}~~ (*lex juridica*) (law of justice)}

3. To be in a rightful condition *lex justitiae distributivae* {law of distributive justice}, right of acquisition, right of possession, the **necessity** of the use of right through the universal will *lex justitiae distributivae*.

Of rights in things[b]
There is no immediate right in things (for they cannot be obligating for us) instead there is only right against persons. Thus there can be no unilateral acquisition, instead **distributive justice** for all is required – Everything depends upon which grounds of right favor my claim that this thing is assigned to me as mine. Yet before those grounds exist the question arises whether I have, prior even to all property, a certain right regarding the **use** of the thing. – Land is first. If I occupy some land this is no right in the thing but rather my innate right to freedom that no one can remove me from that place. – However even where I am not situated, [the product of] my work can nevertheless be my thing, e.g. my acre, for perhaps another may wish to live nomadically. But because in

---

[a] *Gegenstand*   [b] *Sachenrecht*

23:282 this way anyone would be entitled to destroy the work of anyone else so that usable things would thus remain unused, which I cannot possibly will, there must be a provisional right – until that is a *justitia distributiva* {distributive justice} is established – though this cannot do more than organize a possible *justitia distributiva* (and indeed through a unified will of all, *lex agraria* {law of land distribution}). – Accordingly my right is a prerogative of whomever is first to make use of things and is a right of war on occasion of an attack against things which are not yet actually acquired by me, although I possess them intellectually or intentionally even though I lack rightful possession of them. – The thing *qua* thing in itself[a] belongs to me, but possession within appearance does not correspond to the concept of right when I consider this as a thing in itself;[b] then in this case I can possess nothing unless I am its occupant because only then do I suffer through another's interference with my freedom. – The schematism of the concept of right in mine or yours concerns the laws of the free power of choice only insofar as they contain the ground of exclusive use in reason. This is because freedom and right belong to reason and not to the understanding, since right does not at all concern objects[c] of experience and cannot be used on their behalf, in a way like benefits and detriments.

23:282 *Loses Blatt* E 24
[*first page*]
Admittedly it is absurd for all to be equal within the state, though the inequality must be restricted to public offices. – It seems to be that where neither chance nor power has done it, reflection and political intrigue have conceived the plan by which *divide et impera* {divide and rule} is to give inherited advantages to some and to make them into natural authorities in order better to rule the others, or also by jealousy of some toward others to subject both to its will.

Of society in *status naturalis*
hence the *status naturalis* is not *oppositum* of the *status civilis*.

If the three kinds of ideal acquisition were not *jus natura* {natural right} then they would also not be *jus civilis* {civil right} in their execution, i.e. to make them into statutory laws would be against natural right. If it is wrong in the *status naturalis*, i.e. to vindicate what belonged to one in itself without replacing it, then it is also wrong to do so before a court in the *civilis*. However the state of course has the authority to prescribe such laws to the judge, for otherwise the manifold of cases would tend so greatly to exceptions that there would thus be absolutely no general rule.

---

[a] *Die Sache als Ding an sich*   [b] *Sache an sich selbst betrachte*
[c] *Gegenständen*

[five paragraphs omitted]
[second page]

Whatever is wrong according to laws in the *status naturalis* is also 23:283
wrong in the *status civilis* – Yet not conversely because this latter also
contains something further.

Whether the expression *nomine regis* {in the name of the king} is
proper.

Whether there can be hereditary monarchs

Whether the right to property rests on that to land.

If there is an error in administering the state then it must be rectified
as soon as it becomes known. – If instead there is an error in the constitution it is not immediately to be affirmed. – For it could be that this
error may be so linked to others that everything collapses.

Of the difference between the analytic and synthetic universality of 23:284
the will. – The will of each which concerns all and the unified will of all
which concerns each of them.

[four paragraphs omitted]

Loses Blatt E 32   23:284
[first page]
§ 3ᵃ

The problem is: how is a merely rightful possession possible? How is
it possible that I wrong someone by my use of a thing with which he is
not physically connected, or: How can someone through his mere power
of choice preclude me from using a thing?

Answer. I along with all others must have possession, not acquired but
innate, of that which constitutes the condition of all occupancy, i.e. all as
common occupier of the land in accordance with an innate right – since
this cannot be acquired because it is to constitute the ground of all acquisition. – But this ground constitutes that right. – Therefore he possesses 23:285
some land which he does not occupy merely rightly yet not as his own
but of course as potentially his own, i.e. authorization~~unilaterallyhim~~
through his mere power of choice to keep others from it, since he can
necessitate others to unite together with him in a universal will in order
to specify for each the limits of the land each has. As long as others resist
doing so, he has as *prior occupans* {earlier occupant} a right of priority
to use this land and to exclude others unilaterally from it (*praerogativus
juris quaerendi*) {prerogative to seek the right} which represents the role
of the *jus quaesiti* {right being sought} regarding the specific area of land
in accordance with the innate right as such to have something outside
oneself as one's own.

ᵃ There are no other numbered sections.

In order to possess something rightfully[a] (and not merely in conformity with right[b]) a rightful condition is required in which what is right can be specified i.e. what is mine or yours. This condition must be thought *a priori* and indeed in accordance with concepts of freedom alone. – To possess something rightly in space involves a spot or place assigned to me not merely in conformity with right but by right.

Land is the condition of the possibility of corporeal mine and yours since a thing is only mine because it is in my rightful possession even when I have released it and so simply laid it on the ground. Thus no mine or yours can be found in land which belongs to no one. – However it suffices that it belong to someone or other if not me, for then I can have a *pactum* for its use, which however would always be a *meum hypotheticum* {conditionally mine} rather than absolute.

[*second page*]

Deduction

By nature no outer corporeal thing belongs to anyone at all, and thus all things are to this extent *res nullius* {ownerless things}. As a matter of right,[c] however, no one can be necessitated by others to adopt a principle in accordance with which outer usable things as such would belong to no one, which would be the case if each were made dependent upon the physical condition of possession (to occupy it) (§ [d]). Therefore each is authorized to resist those who compel him to act in accord with a principle under which outer things as such could belong to no one (which would thus make him dependent upon things). Now everyone has an innate rightful possession of the condition under which alone outer things can belong to someone, namely land, even though this possession does not yet suffice for mine and yours, because land is communal and as such contains mine and yours only *in potentia* until, that is, a rightful act supervenes, as much on the part of him who will have something as his own as also on the part of all others who agree it shall be his. Yet this agreement is necessary because otherwise all things would remain *res nullius* though also not *suum* {anyone's}.

23:286

All human beings have innate rightful possession of the land which they occupy bodily but of course they are not so dependent upon it that they are not in possession of ground they do not occupy [*breaks off*] ~~The human being cannot make his freedom dependent on things and base a law upon that. But he is naturally dependent on the place where he is.~~

[a] rechtlich   [b] rechtmäßig
[c] *Von Rechtwegen*
[d] Kant left blank space to fill in the § number.

How is *etc.*?

Through the innate possession of land I exclude all others from its use as far as is required for the preservation of my existence (hence not by my mere power of choice), but I am likewise excluded by others from using their place on the land, all through a common will. Therefore the idea of a common power of choice is the determining and limiting ground of each particular power of choice in possession of land, and indeed to the extent made necessary by the independence of freedom from corporeal objects[a] (not to be pinned to their place).

1. An outer mine and yours in corporeal things must be possible, hence it must be possible through one's mere power of choice to exclude others from the use of certain outer things [*added*: through my mere power of choice] in accordance with laws of freedom. For otherwise freedom with regard to the use of outer things would through its relation to others' freedom annihilate all outer things in a rightful relation and make all corporeal things into *res nullius* {ownerless things} in accordance with a universal law. However an exclusion of others through my mere power of choice is a categorical imperative for others to regard   23:287
such things as belonging to me. Therefore such an imperative is actual, since so to speak an obligation can be imposed upon things to obey merely my power of choice, and freedom in outer relation to corporeal things is a ground of outer coercive laws, and indeed without *factum injustum* {an unjust deed} to limit others through my mere power of choice without doing so in accordance with my innate right of the inviolability of my person – However this law is a law of the communal power of choice because without this, their powers of choice among one another would rob itself of the use of outer things. – Therefore a communal will to make outer things, which by nature I possess, into one's own is simultaneously bound with the communal original possession.

Loses Blatt E 33   23:287
[*first page*]
§
The limit of the physical possession of land
is indeed the condition though not the limit
of all rightful possession of land

Possession is a relation of the subject to an object[b] of the power of choice which contains the ground of the possibility of its use. Now this relation can be **thought** either merely through pure concepts of the understanding (of cause and effect) or it can also be represented as **given**

---

[a] *Gegenständen*   [b] *Gegenstand* in this paragraph

in space (and in time); In the first case the presence is merely **virtual** in the second **local**. Without local presence of the subject in space, and so without any physical possession of land, no possession could be recognized as actual; such presence is thus also the condition for each and every **rightful** possession. However, without the **concept of reason** of a relation of the subject to outer objects which is based upon mere pure concepts of the understanding of the connection (as virtual) in accordance with laws of right, no rightful possession can be thought. The possibility of a merely rightful possession thus contains an amplification of the concept of a rightful possession in general beyond the physical (occupying). Now the question is whether the limits of physical posses-

23:288 sion are also the limits of rightful possession or whether possession could also be conceived to extend beyond those limits, hence that under the presupposition of physical possession of some land, I could be thought to possess merely rightly still more land in the same place, and whether I could be thought to expand a space which I physically occupy beyond the limits of this possession so that moreover I can consider myself to possess it in accordance with mere concepts of right. That the latter be possible and that the principle of right regarding use of things outside me must be laid down as a ground, though we have no insight into **how?**[a] this is so, is clarified as follows.

It contradicts the use of freedom consistent with others' freedom in accordance with universal laws, and hence also with the right of humanity in general, for one to restrict another's use of outer objects[b] and mine and yours overall to the limits of their physical possession, for then freedom would make itself dependent upon things in accordance with laws of freedom, which would be presupposed either through the representation of an obligation against things (just as if they too had rights) or by a principle[c] of the free power of choice that no outer thing shall be mine or yours, each of which is a contradiction as a principle[d] of a freedom which robs itself of its own use. Therefore the principle[e] of freedom in the idea of a complete and united power of choice is of itself (*a priori*) ampliative with regard to rightful possession beyond the limits of physical possession.

The possibility of such a principle, however, lies in the presupposition that the free power of choice of everyone must be considered as united regarding corporeal things outside us, and moreover originally without any rightful act, and indeed because it relates itself to a possession which is also original though communal, within which what is possessed by each and thus mine and yours can be determined only in accordance with

---

[a] Kant's "?" in middle of sentence   [b] *Gegenständen* in this and next paragraphs
[c] *Princip*   [d] *Grundsatz*
[e] *Princip* in this and the following paragraphs

the idea of the agreement with a possible collective[a] power of choice. The possibility of merely rightful possession is given as *a priori* although its rightful determination is possible not through anyone's own power of choice but only through outer positive laws and thus only in the civil condition.

[*second page*]

§

A principle to make the outer use of one's freedom depend upon outer things which otherwise would be dependent upon us contradicts 23:289 itself. Now the will that there shall be no merely rightful possession but that instead all rightful possession of land shall be limited to that which we occupy, so that no land could be mine or yours, would contain such a principle, therefore the will which would abolish merely rightful possession as invalid contradicts human freedom (which of course is limited by others' freedom but not by things which do not as it were counter human right through a right of their own). – Hence the question is not whether a merely rightful possession is possible, hence that something outer be someone's own, because to presuppose this is practically necessary, but rather only how this is possible, i.e. how we can think of ourselves as being rightfully in possession of corporeal things and this given their presence on land which we do not physically possess. –

§ ~~All human beings are in common natural possession of the whole surface of the earth; yet this possession is merely an idea of the innate right of each to a place on it which no other has occupied, which all others, hence each, receive in common. But an innate common power of choice is also connected to common possession, which determines for each the use of the land from this possession and whose law is that freedom itself is not made dependent on things and can be limited only through the freedom (of the power of choice) of another. The common power of choice can thus, according to the above, limit possession of outer things not on the condition of occupying them hence only on the condition of a community of possession in accordance with an intellectual principle[b] etc.~~

If I find myself in physical possession of a place on the land, I thus find myself in a place which naturally belongs to the common possession, and likewise if I place myself somewhere else. However, the common possession of the whole of space is also bound to the common will that limits the will of each regarding the free use of the land. Now if this will for using the previous place corresponds with the collective will, then I exercise the natural right to be in that place (as if I were still there)

[a] *gesammten* [b] *Princip*

because my will depends on the universal will and not on things and hence also not upon places.

[*third page*]

Of the independence of freedom from things

When I say I am in **rightful** possession of a thing outside me, this amounts to saying I am bound with it in accordance with a law of freedom pertaining to its use which can co-exist with others' freedom regarding that same use. Here is thus a pure intellectual concept of a possession which holds in utter abstraction from all determinations of my existence in space or in time. – Now whether indeed I am dependent upon these conditions in my existence as a sensuous being concerning my outer actions as holding an outer object,[a] nevertheless the concept of right, which contains an outer relation of my free power of choice to others' free powers of choice as one under a universal law, is in itself independent of that condition, so that I can nevertheless be regarded as immediately connected with a thing located in a place where I am not and as owning it even if my spatial connection in which I was holder of that thing ceases; my power of choice, which necessarily agrees with others' freedom of the power of choice in accordance with a universal law, to retain the thing in dependence upon me is not abolished, and this possession would thus also hold as merely rightful possession and hence the mine in this thing would obtain. – [*in the margin, connected by a symbol*: I am by nature in a common rightful possession of the surface of the earth with all others, and this possession must correspond to a common power of choice as an idea of a principle of right[b].] Now my free power of choice regarding this intellectual possession (without occupying) necessarily agrees here with everyone's freedom, i.e. others would disturb me in a (rightful) true possession of the outer thing (and hence do me wrong) if they were to treat me, because I am not now in possession by occupying, as also not being in rightful possession of the thing, for since I am by nature together with them in common possession of the land, my preservation upon it would be made dependent upon occupying and hence upon things, in which case each would infringe upon all others out of freedom in accordance with universal laws. Therefore the common power of choice which corresponds to the common natural possession of land, insofar as it does not contravene the laws of freedom by making itself depend upon things, can obtain possession of land even without occupying, i.e. as a merely rightful possession.

§ – Land which can be possessed merely rightfully must have unity i.e. to expand outward from the possession of a place across a space, because

23:290

---

[a] *Gegenstand* [b] *Rechtsprincips*

merely rightful possession is only the expansion of possession beyond occupying.

[*fourth page*]

§

A merely rightful possession (hence also mine and yours in corporeal things outside us) is possible.

23:291

No law is thinkable through which the free power of choice in outer relations were to make itself dependent upon corporeal objects[a] so that exclusive possession would necessarily have to be also corporeal or physical, e.g. that I would have to cover with my body, if it is some land, or carry in my hands, if it is something movable, everything I want to reserve for my future use. For first such an obligation cannot arise from my power of choice in relation to others' powers of choice in accordance with laws of freedom (i.e. from concepts of right) since this principle[b] directly opposes everyone's freedom; second it also cannot arise from an obligation toward things since there is no obligation towards things. Thus, either there could be no mine and yours in outer corporeal things at all (all outer things being *res absolute nullius* {absolutely ownerless things}), or a merely rightful possession must be assumed to be possible, no merely rightful possession of things could hold at all. Therefore all exclusive possession required for mine and yours without occupying would be impossible, hence also all of this possession would only be possible in common. Now all human beings are really in common although merely rightful possession of the land, and they are rightfully entitled to make use of it. Human beings would thus first of all not be limited by nature in accord with a universal law to being in a particular place on the land, for on this supposition they possess the land overall in common, nor would they be limited through others' freedom in accordance with laws of right to a merely physical possession, for then the free power of choice would make itself dependent upon things even in accordance with concepts of right, therefore human beings are on the land with the sole authorization of a rightful possession of that land, i.e. a possession that they also enjoy without occupying it, though indeed in accordance with laws of right, and thus they are in possession of it and they could be wronged even without any physical influence upon their person. – i.e. the power of choice of all others cannot exclude a person from the innate possession of some land or other, for they are all in original common possession of it, however this power of choice also cannot tie a person to physical possession in accord with laws of right, i.e. to make physical possession a condition for possession, for this is opposed to freedom; consequently there remains a merely rightful

23:292

---

[a] *Gegenständen* in this paragraph
[b] *dies Princip*, referring to previous sentence

possession and indeed through a common will that is necessary *a priori*. Possession which is given (physical) and that which is merely thought are understood through the mere power of choice grounded upon the original community.

23:292 *Loses Blatt* E 35
[*second page*]

Subsumption under the concept of intellectual possession cannot be regarded as its presentation in a possible experience, since that concept as mere idea consists precisely in its inability to be presented in experience (where it would be empirical possession which it should of course not be), instead it is to be regarded as the presentation of the public law that unites the power of choice regarding mine and yours, and as the presentation of the conditions of their agreement.

3[a] Principles of universal human right – a) Freedom. Each human being in the state qua member of the state has an innate right to act immediately for his own benefit alone and only mediately for the benefit of others. A condition in which the judgment upon this is not his own but is assigned to another is not possible in right.

b) Equality. Each human being within the state is a citizen of the state, i.e. it must be allowed to him to rise to whatever levels of wealth, of offices, and of honor to which talent, service and luck may lead under the dominion of the sovereign, i.e. among citizens there are no privileges before others.

c) Security of one's own acquired in conformity with right. As someone protected by the state, each person within the state exercises through the courts the same power[b] against others as he has suffered from them and in punishment no distinction among persons are valid.

Freedom cannot consist in the authorization to do whatever is not opposed to the rights of a third party (why not a second), for what is another's right? Someone might present himself as having acquired a right through long possession. Ultimately nothing would remain other than the right to keep oneself free of any corporeal harm.[c] In the above

23:293 definition the object of the power of choice is determined in accordance with the conditions under which the power of choice accords with freedom. One may not even benefit someone against his will. For otherwise it would also belong to freedom to give up freedom itself and to surrender one's way of living to another's power of choice. – Equality, the sole condition of which is freedom, is the right and indeed the public means

---

[a] There are no other corresponding numbers
[b] *Gewalt*   [c] *Läsion*

of right. – Therefore freedom, equality, and public capacity of right,[a] i.e. the capacity to protect oneself by means of right.

Provisional right persists in the civil condition in its consequences and is taken up into civil right to the extent that it does not contradict the latter's nature.

a) The freedom of a member of the state (a member is whatever is not a mere instrument of a living being but rather itself has life). He must be able to be legislator and is one potentially. Equality consists in the member being able to raise himself to that position (since in this consists a state in which human beings unite themselves into a whole in accordance with universal laws of freedom). b) equality as subject of the state (for there must be no gracious master other than the *souverain*). c) Independence[b] as citizen of the state (since each is himself legislating and likewise subject to the law). NB. the *souverain* is either the people or represents the people.

Pure principle of reason[c] of the possession of mine and yours. – If something outside me shall be mine or yours then it must be able to be in my possession as subsumption under this principle. – First possession is unilateral but the subsumption under the sensible condition of the former, namely to have something in one's power, presupposes a double meaning.

1. Analytical principle[d] of the possibility of mine and yours in outer objects[e] in general (because otherwise we would make *res nullius usus* {something usable an ownerless thing}).

2. Synthetic principle of the possibility of mine and yours in objects of experience – Here there is a distinction of possession and I can of course only be wronged insofar as I am in possession. ~~My intellectual possession must therefore be rightfully valid even when I am not in physical possession, and indeed because otherwise I would rob~~ freedom ~~of its use regarding outer objects.~~[f] However there is no rightful condition by nature. Yet such should be under outer laws. In relation to this idea as the principle of the possibility of mine and yours within experience, anyone can be regarded as being in intellectual possession.

It is possible to possess the outer merely rightly – but only through synthetic unity of the powers of choice in accordance with outer laws.

1. Analytical principle. It is possible to have something outside me as mine rightfully. For suppose the opposite then ~~in accordance with~~

23:294

[a] *Rechtsvermögen*
[b] *Selbstständigkeit*
[c] *Reines Vernunftprincip*
[d] *Princip* for the next several paragraphs
[e] *Gegenständen* in this and the following paragraph
[f] *Objecte*

~~laws of freedom it would be impossible to have an object~~[a] ~~of the power of choice, hence that which I have in my power to use and which it is possible for me to use. It would thus also be true that something that is an object for the power of choice would be transformed into a practical non-entity (*utile in inutile* {useful to useless}) through the universal law of freedom.~~ either the possession of an outer object of the power of choice would be physically, or its use in accordance with laws of freedom would be practically, impossible. However the former contradicts the concept that it is an object of my **power of choice**, hence something that stands within my power to use, the latter contradicts the **freedom** of use of each and every usable object[b] insofar as freedom is not simply limited to the conditions of agreement with everyone's power of choice in accordance with a possible universal law but more so all use of the usable is abolished. Therefore a principle in accordance with which an outer object of the power of choice could not be someone's own is impossible in accordance with right, and any such object must be able to be someone's outer own.

Remark. To maintain that any object of my power of choice outside me can be mine regardless of any limiting conditions of freedom would be as much as to hold that I shall not be permitted to use an outer object[c] of my power of choice either at all or not as what is mine i.e. to the exclusion of others. The first proposition would convert everything outside me into *res objective nullius* {objectively ownerless things} (because what holds of me holds also of others): the second would oppose anyone's power of choice in the use of an object[d] to everyone else's power of choice and so would rob the power of choice of its freedom and indeed through a principle of freedom just as the former would rob it of its objects.[e]

That this principle lies analytically in the concept of the relation among free powers of choice in general to outer objects[f] is seen from the universal rational concept of right in that relation, namely if it is considered in abstraction from all empirical relations. An object[g] is in my control[h] (is object[i] of my power of choice) and in no one else's control. I will to use it merely for myself to the exclusion of others. The law of everyone's freedom does not hinder me, rather this law lies at the basis of that authorization. Thus I am in relation to them in having them as mine.

23:295

---

[a] *Object* in this and the next sentence
[b] *Gegenstand* in the remainder of this paragraph
[c] *Object*
[d] *Gegenstand*
[e] *Objecte*
[f] *Objecten*
[g] *Gegenstand*
[h] *Gewalt*
[i] *Object*

23:295
   [first page]

Jus in re {right in a thing}

Is the right against any arbitrary possessor of it? But on what basis do
I have a right against a person? Through this: that he has made himself
obligated to me and thus on account of a deed on his part. – However
I can have no right against anyone else on account of his possession of
a thing except insofar as each has made himself obligated through the
possession of a thing in general, because each, considered as being in
co-possession of all things which are brought into any possession, is as
it were subjected by the common will, and all things which can come to
be under anyone's control are subject to this will.

To use something physically is not possible for me unless I possess it.
Still, however, if I am to be authorized to use something regardless of
whose possession it is, then I and all others must be thought of as having
a non-physical possession in accordance with laws of freedom through
which I limit others' freedom to the condition of agreement with my
own freedom. Now it is necessary, and particularly so in accordance with
laws of freedom, that each usable thing must be able to become property
so that they will be in someone's intellectual possession, where only he
who has it in his sensible control limits others through his freedom, thus
admittedly only insofar as this freedom is connected with that thing so
that any alteration of it is simultaneously an alteration of him. If the
beginning of possession is not an alteration of others' freedom, and vice
versa, then others' use is not an alteration of the former's freedom, so he
possesses something exclusively.

Analytic principle[a] that the freedom of anyone is exercised externally
so that it can co-exist with everyone's freedom in the use of whatever is
usable.

Synthetic principle of anyone's power of choice, that through that   23:296
same power of choice one limits others in a way that that the use of
whatever is usable is not thereby abolished in accordance with universal
laws.

How is a power of choice that extends itself beyond self-possession
possible (since of course there is no immediate incursion against freedom, e.g. in possession of a thing to the exclusion of others, or another's
promise as possession of someone else's power of choice)?

If we omit time and space, there still remains a mutual relation of
powers of choice to one another (immediately or as mediated by things)
in accordance with laws of freedom; for through this a relation of anyone's power of choice to everyone else's can first be thought, although
this relation cannot be **known** except under the presupposition of an

---

[a] *Grundsatz*

intuition within which it can be physically given, i.e. in space and time. Hence forces[a] are exercised externally among and against each other in accordance with laws of freedom. – If I consider this action merely in accordance with laws of freedom, nothing other than analytical opposition (of the affecting of persons) can occur. However within space or time alone nothing affects freedom. In both taken together [*second page*] freedom and power of choice (the latter in space and time) first provide principles *a priori* of the extension of the power of choice over others' powers of choice in regard to the use of usable things, since only then in accordance with the conditions of space and time can an opposition first arise.

There is no such relation of the power of choice to others' power of choice through which, if everything is determined in accordance with mere laws of freedom, they oppose each other or could determine everything **regarding the possession of an object**[b] except by unification of the powers of choice, first *potentiale* {potential} (and hence universal) unification or *actuale* {actual} (and hence particular) unification. The first means: it must be possible that in accordance with my principles,[c] my power of choice unifies itself with others' power of choice concerning the possession of objects; the second means that such unification must be actual.

For no one can know composition by taking[d] or through the senses except insofar as one represents the composite through one's own connection. Precisely this is the case regarding the relations among free beings as such through which they can enter into connection. Only here with the difference that the connection is not one whose conditions already lie in intuition, but rather the power of choice itself makes the connection in relation to the possible use of things.

Analytical principle[e] of right (coercion): act so that your freedom can co-exist with everyone else's freedom in accordance with a universal law, since coercion can co-exist with that.

Synthetic principle. It is a duty in itself (also without coercion) so to act that your freedom agrees with others' freedom. – This latter is a duty of virtue, the former is a duty of right.

The principle of the duty of right[f] has, in addition to freedom considered subjectively (innate right), also freedom in objective relation, i.e. the unity of the power of choice in relation to its object, so that consequently this unity is synthetic: – Act so that your power of choice can co-exist with others' power of choice regarding its objects in general in accordance with principles of freedom. Synthetic principle of right.

23:297

---

[a] *Kräfte*
[c] *Grundsätzen*
[e] *Grundsatz*

[b] *Object* for the remainder of this page
[d] *apprehension*
[f] *Der Grundsatz der Rechtspflicht*

This always contains an *intuitus* {something intuited} regarding natural things[a] which can be objects of the power of choice; either they are con-current with the power of choice, or the determination of this power follows upon them, or the former is the ground of the latter. Synthetic unity of right regarding things, persons and the latter as things.

One has a right synthetically through one's mere power of choice to limit others' freedom [*added*: power of choice] even though others do not directly infringe upon one's freedom, e.g. to coerce someone to keep his promise when he does not keep it himself does not thus infringe upon my freedom. It must be possible to possess rights and to acquire them, and the action whose maxim abolishes this possibility is wrong. Now I can have a right 1. to use a thing exclusively, 2. to have others' actions serve my interests, 3. Also against other persons in accordance with my will. Therefore I cannot abolish the possibility of such use.

[*third page*]

I have a right, when by my power of choice I can determine others' powers of choice regarding [*added*: for producing] the object of their powers of choice, and indeed in accordance with laws of freedom inde-pendent of all conditions of space and time, e.g. that I have subjected a thing to my powers[b] and it remains mine regardless of my physical pos-session as well as of any other's consent to my choice that what is his is to transfer to me without the subsequent time making a difference between them.   23:298

Through my power of choice I can as possessor either necessitate all others to grant me the use of a thing, or to necessitate only one other do or omit something, or to necessitate a person to something by which everyone else can be prevented from using this person as a thing.

To have a right means in effect to possess **rightfully** that partic-ular object,[c] i.e. an authorization to compel others through his mere power of choice to do or omit something which otherwise is indiffer-ent to freedom. – Juridical possession of an object does not depend at all on the conditions of the object and its existence, space and time, but instead merely upon relations of my power of choice to others' powers of choice in accordance with laws of freedom, and the sensible conditions of physical possession stand under the categories of right which absolutely determine the power of choice.

These categories are, 1. of quantity[d] universality, to compel anyone who has physical possession of a thing which belongs to me, 2.) of quality how rights become acquired, lost, or limited as the reality of a possession

---

[a] *Naturdinge*　　　　　　　　　[b] *Kräften*
[c] *Object* in this paragraph　　　[d] *Große*

not merely of the freedom opposed to the negation merely to reduce no one's freedom, which is bound to the *actio justa* {just act} and the limitation since the freedom of each is limited by this right. 3. of relation a) of things in substance (which also exist in themselves[a] without effect of my power of choice) b) of another's action: to which my power of choice compels him c) of community, since one person makes himself dependent upon another, i.e. in a certain status of theirs, in which the former is dependent merely through the other's power of choice.

d) of modality since this right either itself is merely possible or also actual or also is necessarily ascribed to each human being.

23:299

The sole physical condition on which we make the acquisition of a right (which itself is a physical *actus* within time) depend is that we connect the object[b] with our power of choice either through taking control[c] or accepting or through an accepting which becomes necessary by taking into possession, because it is possible only in that my freedom is infringed upon by the hindrances which others may impose on my power of choice.

The schematism of acquisition is to be regarded *a priori* as transfer[d] through common power of choice. Potential or actual community of this will. That is the synthetic unity of powers of choice about an object which makes possible acquisition as empirical synthesis.

[*fourth page*]
Whoever acquires some land acquires no right in the land in itself, since such a right would correspond to the land being under an obligation, instead he acquires a rightful capacity (through his mere power of choice) to resist others so that they do not use it as they choose, not even to preserve his freedom against injury, however it is not possible to think this if one does not presuppose that no human being is able, through his power of choice or through its maxim, to make all use of usable things impossible.

A relation which one can conceive only as that between one's freedom and others' powers of choice is a rightful relation. That is a pure concept of reason, i.e. I can only think it through a concept of reason that cannot be presented within sensible intuition at all, instead this latter is merely the consequence. – Therefore someone first possesses something rightfully if it is assigned to him merely due to the relation of his free power of choice to that of others. Thus coercion is rightful when it is based on a necessitation of another solely through his power of choice in relation to others' free powers of choice.

---

[a] *für sich* [b] *Object* in this and the following paragraph
[c] *occupation* [d] *translation*

If it is conceived simply between human beings as pure intelligences and neither in relation to things nor to one another in space and time, right is easy to determine in accordance with universal rules. One only has to arrange freedom and the power of choice in relation to each other either immediately or as mediated by things. Indeed one can say generally that all outer right as possession of others' powers of choice (since one has their powers of choice in one's control) rests upon the idea of a community of powers of choice, which, if the human being is regarded as a sensible being in order to make this right effective *in concreto*, requires: 1. the sensible conditions of the determination of right regarding things by which alone a common will becomes **possible**, 2. the conditions required for it to become **actual**, 3. the condition for the use of persons as things through which a united will becomes **necessary**.   23:300

The difficulty about the supreme principle of right[a] is that one has wanted to examine the right of a human being [*added:* the relation of freedom in space and time] before one had examined the right of a person as such (as *noumenon*). Hence the difficulties in applying these principles have been held to be difficulties regarding pure principles *a priori*. – It is the same as when Aristotle numbered space and time among the categories and the sensory conditions of knowledge among the intellectual conditions, because both contain an *a priori* determination. – The possession of an object[b] as a thing is only possible in space, possession of the affirmation of a performance by a person is only possible in time, and that of the possession of a person as a thing is only possible in both together.

That from which I am distant is, for the intellectual power of choice, in my possession. Likewise for promises.

Difficulties in execution (the unification of wills) cannot be counted as difficulties in principles.

Loses Blatt E 43   23:300
[*first page*]
Of merely rightful possession
Without being in possession of an object, a person's freedom cannot be reduced by hindering his use of the object. Therefore, prior to all physical possession and more so prior to any proper rightful possession, *jus proprium* {proprietary right} regarding an object must be possible, and this possession must be contained *a priori* within the idea of the nature[c] of the power of choice or its relation to objects outside it, or in general within the idea of a rational being. This can be nothing other than common possession, and this because each is in possession of others' powers

---

[a] *des obersten Rechtsprincips*   [b] *Object*
[c] *Beschaffenheit*

23:301 of choice, which concerns the rules of the use of those powers of choice regarding usable objects[a] in general, since each could resist any others in general who wanted to validate a maxim in accordance with which something usable necessarily is placed beyond all use.

[*three paragraphs omitted; fourth page*]

As rightful, possession must be grounded solely upon intellectual connections of the object[b] with the person so that freedom would be wronged even without infringing upon physical independence.

23:302 [*in top margin:*] Wherever control[c] may reach, freedom cannot be limited by nature and natural conditions of possession, but instead only by and on the basis of agreement with others' freedom.

Freedom (external) is the independence of the power of choice from others' powers of choice regarding that which one possesses. The possibility of resisting others' powers of choice by one's own mere power of choice is right in general. A right is the objective ground for resisting others' powers of choice in accordance with universal laws of freedom in possession of a thing. If no action has come first, then each power of choice resists others' powers of choice and no rightful acquisition is possible. A relation in which this mutual resistance agrees with the freedom of each regarding taking into possession must therefore be presupposed, and that can be none other than the concept of a unified power of choice. The *communio arbitrii* {common power of choice} is thus the condition of all acquisition and of mine and yours in general. – Concepts of right are categories of the possibility of this common power of choice. 1. In accord with quantity that of the universality of the agreement to this law, 2. in accord with quality that of possession, the deprivation of which (*res nullius* {ownerless thing}) is limitation, 3. of relation, a. to things, b. persons, c. of persons as things, 4. of modality, a. possible unification, b. actual, c. necessary in accordance with the three categories of relation. All of these precede all relations in space and time, and mine and yours in space and time are determined through those categories.

23:304 *Loses Blatt* E 45
[*first page*]

Of acquired right in something outside me.

This right is the capacity immediately to determine others' powers of choice through my own in accordance with laws of freedom.

The supreme question is: how is it possible that something outside me be mine, i.e. that something be subjected to my power of choice in accordance with laws of freedom? Hence that a thing, a certain action of

---

[a] *Objecte*
[b] *Gegenstandes*
[c] *Gewalt*

a person other than myself, finally also a person herself distinct from me, be mine: so that it would be an infringement of my freedom if others' powers of choice resist my own which determines theirs. –

The principle[a] of the ideality of physical possession suffices for the distinction of mine and yours, for the reality of the rightful. The principle of the reality of the possession required for exclusive use of objects of the power of choice is the condition of possession in space and time, and this condition is sensible. In contrast the unity of many various powers of choice regarding the same object[b] without reference to space and time is the intellectual sufficient condition of rightful possession. However the condition of the presentation of this right *in concreto* is physical taking,[c] accepting, and subjection of other persons, although they can distance themselves by means of freedom.

23:305

In the case of the real principle, the sensible conditions of possession would negate the use of freedom regarding the useful as well as the expansion of the power of choice in general which can co-exist with the freedom of each.

[*second page*]

1.[d] Proposition: That it is possible to acquire *occupando* {by taking control} and that it is wrong generally for anyone not to affirm this title of acquisition, or not to recognize that something remains someone's when there is no physical possession: However that it is impossible to determine the limits of this **virtual possession,** and so it is indeed an ideal right that requires the idea of a united power of choice and is obtained only under the condition of the agreement with the possibility of a united power of choice. And for the acquisition of the deed of another **actual** united power of choice, and acquisition of a person herself an objectively **necessary** united power of choice, i.e. a unification that has become a duty and is contained in the idea of possession of what is desired.

One can take possession of only as much as one can bring within one's control,[e] provided that others respond likewise, since the taking control[f] is intellectual.

How human beings who are distinguished by space, time, and the private power of choice are nevertheless united regarding the objects of their powers of choice is difficult to comprehend. – Mine and yours regarding things, persons, and possession of one person by another as if the former were a thing, are represented through mere ideas of reason,

[a] *Princip* [b] *Objects*
[c] *apprehension*
[d] There are no other corresponding numbers.
[e] *Gewalt* [f] *occupation*

23:306 and are comprehensible and allow their laws to be given. However the limitation of possession to conditions of space and time produces difficulties, indeed the impossibility of the adequate satisfaction of that idea of reason, because freedom cannot be subjected to any sensible laws.

The will that has the object[a] within its power[b] immediately is one creating the object and so against this nothing can be said. – However he who must assume the existence of the object as independent of his will is also not permitted to make something into his own by himself even with the greatest power,[c] nevertheless this is indeed required because otherwise freedom would make itself depend upon things and not upon others' powers of choice. Therefore mine and yours depends only upon the power of choice united in the idea (*a priori*), and no thing becomes mine by taking control but rather by *distributive* power of choice. – Everything is connected to and grounded upon the idea of the united power of choice regarding all things as originally and objectively necessary, although as if it existed. If the powers of choice cannot agree about distribution then no one wrongs another in this *statu praeternaturali injusto* {preternatural state of injustice} though also no one acquires any right.

23:306 *Loses Blatt* E 50

Rightfully mine and yours

is that which cannot be removed from my power of choice without my (or your) consent. – Hence that which exists merely through my power of choice consistently with everyone's freedom (the law for that) is rightfully mine. – Thus that is mine which is subject to my power of choice merely in accordance with rightful relations, the physical relations be what they may. – Mine is that object the alteration of which is simultaneously an alteration of me as subject.

Doctrine of right contains that which can co-exist with the freedom of the power of choice in accordance with universal laws.

Doctrine of virtue contains that which can co-exist with the necessary ends of the power of choice in accordance with universal laws of reason.

The first are negative and analytic in inner and outer relations and contain the inner as well as the outer conditions of possible outer laws.

23:307 The second are affirmative and synthetic in inner and outer relations and admit of no determinate law.

The former duties are *officia necessitatis* {necessary duties} the latter are *officia charitatis* {duties of charity}.

[a] *Object*　　　　　　　　　　　　　[b] *Gewalt*
[c] *Macht*

Whoever is subject to no one is free. A subject, however, is one whose state[a] of being happy or not depends upon another's will.

Loses Blatt E 51

Possession of a right without possession of the object itself.

Possession is that relation of an object of the power of choice to the subject through which, if the former is altered, the latter is simultaneously altered. – If this alteration is merely physical then the possession is called holding[b] (*detentio*) namely a connection through which the subject is altered in his natural determinations. If the alteration concerns the subject's right then the possession is to that extent rightful; a rightful possession which is not as such physical (not holding) is called a merely rightful possession. **Mine** (adjective as determination) is that the alteration of which is an alteration of me. **What is mine**[c] is such an object of my power of choice, i.e. something I can intend to use, and to the extent it is exclusive it is mine **as opposed to** yours or in general to that which is someone's, i.e. the **mine as property** (*proprium*); but this is not what is mine and at once also someone else's, which is **mine in common** (*meum commune*). The beginning of the *actus* of the power of choice through which my physical possession arises is taking[d] (*apprehensio*), which is taking control[e] (*occupatio*) if it occurs to a thing that previously belonged to no one. The determination of the power of choice through which I will that an object shall be exclusively mine is appropriation[f] (*appropriatio*). – Possession by holding can be called **empirical** just as merely-rightful possession can be called intellectual.

§

The concept of what is mine as an object[g] outside me
is grounded upon the idea of a merely rightful possession.

If there is to be a mine and yours in things outside us then there must also be a purely intellectual (merely-rightful) possession of those same objects of the power of choice outside us by which all right to empirical   23:308 objects is possible.

§

There is a mine and yours in things outside us.

For otherwise if we were to bind ourselves to physical possession and did not allow that possession overall has a wider validity than our holding, then freedom would deprive itself of the use of objects,[h] freedom

---

[a] *Zustand*
[b] *Innhabung*, also translated as "occupying" with regard to land
[c] *Das Meine*   [d] *Ergreifung*
[e] *Bemächtigung*   [f] *Zueignung*
[g] *Gegenstand* in this paragraph   [h] *Objecte*

would deprive itself of all objects[a] of the power of choice, or make itself dependent upon things outside itself.

§
Taking[b] is subsumption
under the intellectual concept of possession.

Empirical possession does not contain the first ground of mine and yours since this consists precisely in that I also have a representation of the object[c] independently of its physical possession though indeed in one's control. Therefore an intellectual possession must be possible for itself through mere concepts of the relation of the free power of choice to objects, under which of course the empirically given object can be subsumed, i.e. mine and yours in general are determined a priori through a pure concept of the understanding by categories of mine and yours, and the concept of mine and yours does not depend upon experience.

§
The empirically mine and yours is grounded upon the
subsumption of taking (of the object) under the idea of
the united powers of choice regarding outer objects
as such.

For through a unilateral *actus* of the power of choice I would impose upon others an obligation which does not rest upon their own powers of choice, and that would infringe on freedom in accordance with universal laws. Therefore others' powers of choice must agree *a priori* regarding 23:309 mine and yours, which is only possible when others' powers of choice are united with my own in one will, i.e. through the idea of united powers of choice.

§
The principle of the expansion of what is mine beyond what is innate to objects[d] outside me, and so synthetic *a priori* propositions for this, is the principle[e] of the possibility of outer right regarding objects in space and time.

[*second page*]

In the case of intellectual mine and yours possession is not
distinct from appropriation nor holding from possession of
the right

Our freedom is wronged, though not immediately by others' use of a thing outside us, yet through the maxim by which no thing may be determined to be one's proper use[f] without holding.

---

[a] *Gegenstände*
[b] *Apprehension*
[c] *Object* in this and the following paragraphs
[d] *Gegenstände* in this paragraph
[e] *Princip . . . Grundsatz*
[f] *zu seinem eigenthümlichen Gebrauch*

Intellectual possession is the unhindered connection of the use of an object[a] with the power of choice (as a capacity of desire regarding whatever is within our control) through mere concepts of the understanding. As the sufficient principle of all right conditioned by empirical possession, this is the ground of the possibility and determination of mine and yours. – Therefore if an object[b] is brought under the concept of taking control of an object[c] without any contradiction of the power of choice with itself, then it is mine or yours.

This contradiction-free connection is only possible in the idea of a common power of choice which confirms or constitutes empirical possession.

Right is a pure intellectual concept.

Analogy of the synthetic *a priori* law of freedom with that against idealism

For assume there were no merely rightful possession of the objects[d] of the power of choice outside me, i.e. it is right for anyone to hinder anyone else's use of outer objects which he does not possess, then everything useful outside us would be made unusable through the principle of freedom in accordance with universal laws for everyone (*res nullius usus* {something usable an ownerless thing}) (since all that would remain is only the authorization of the subject to make exclusive use of his own inherent determinations). However because in the relation in which the subject stands to outer objects, the inner determinations of the subject would also depend upon outer things and could not exist without them, it would thus be right to hinder everyone's having those inner determinations without which he cannot even make use of himself in accordance with the principle of freedom, i.e. the dependency of the free use of outer objects[e] upon physical possession at once negates the innate right of self-possession, or the power of choice robs itself of its innate right, which is self-contradictory.

23:310

For assume there could be no mine or yours outside us although there were objects of the power of choice outside us; it would thus be permissible to resist anyone's use of an object outside him, and yet notwithstanding that, it would be impermissible to hinder his use of those of his determinations which nevertheless depend upon those outer objects, namely in a way that everyone would be authorized to prevent others from having those determinations at all. Now since it is an innate right of mine to use myself and all of my inner determinations exclusively insofar as I naturally am dependent upon objects of my power of choice in outer relations, and hence to count them among a possible mine and

---

[a] *Objects*
[b] *Object*
[c] *Gegenstandes*
[d] *Objecte* in first half of this paragraph
[e] *Gegenstände* here and the following paragraph

yours, then the principle which negates mine and yours outside us would rightfully infringe on this innate right, which is self-contradictory.

§ 4.
Third proposition

There must be merely rightful possession of the objects[a] of the power of choice outside us.

This is merely the conclusion from the two previous propositions as premises.

Remark. This third proposition is a synthetic *a priori* proposition whose possibility we shall discuss below. – It deserves note, however, that it shares much in analogy with that of the reality of outer perceptions (which is directed against psychological idealism). For just as the proof of the later rests upon our inability to be conscious of ourselves as 23:311 empirically determined in time if we did not bring time to bear upon the apprehension of a manifold outside us (in space) within our representation, so that whatever is necessarily given as the condition of that self-consciousness is represented by us as an object of the senses rather than of imagination; then analogously without outer objects[b] of the power of choice we could become conscious neither of the possession of our own determinations nor of the innate right to use ourselves, so that we regard our right to make use of outer objects[c] as the condition of the possibility of the inner use of our power of choice, and thus must assume right regarding outer objects *a priori*.

23:311 *Loses Blatt* E 59
   [first page]
   All human beings are in a collective possession[d] of land, not by a rightful act of unification of their powers of choice but instead originally through the unity of the land and by the right which is theirs by nature to occupy some place or other on the earth, which is itself a limited unity of all possible possession of the earth, regarding which the occupants of earth naturally must work against one another for the occupation of their places, and due to which there must be an underlying law of nature which determines what belongs to each so that their opposition does not nullify the proper effect of the right stemming from original possession. – This law can be no other than that of an original collective will[e] not as *factum* {deed} but rather as an idea through which alone that agreement is possible.

---

[a] *Gegenstände* here through semicolon in the following paragraph
[b] *Objecte*   [c] *Gegenstände* in remainder of sentence
[d] *Gesammt-Besitz*   [e] *Gesammtwillens*

From this collective possession, which is not grounded upon any rightful act but instead is innate, follows necessarily the right of each to choose for himself a location as a **particular possession**, though in accordance with laws of freedom, and unilaterally to make it his own, because otherwise freedom would exclude itself from possession and from use of usable things for which would also be required an express act of the common power of choice.[a]

To speak of maxims of right belongs to ethics.

Everyone is entitled by nature to a right to separate possession

Possession as condition of the possibility of a wrong or of use

The universal formal condition of all mine and yours is the principle 23:312 of the agreement of my power of choice with that of everyone else in accordance with universal laws.

The first material condition of mine and yours in an object[b] is possession of it – for without the connection of the object with the subject, the object could be affected by others without the subject being wronged.

That possession of an outer object determined in space and time, i.e. empirical possession, is possession in appearance (*possessio phaenomenon*) because it is a possession containing no concept of right. Possession which is independent of that condition is **intellectual** or merely rightful possession (*possessio noumenon*).

Since the concept of outer mine and yours is a concept of right even though it would have no object to which it could be applied were that object not given in empirical intuition, rightful mine and yours are the ground for a possession in appearance (which is theoretical), and thus of course since reason abstracts from this it contains an intellectual (moral-practical) possession of the object considered in itself namely merely as an object[c] of the power of choice in general.

[*second page*]

Possession in respect to the possibility of the use of an outer object[d] is a connection which is either ideal and the mere connection to the capacity of the power of choice or it is real and an act of the power of choice, namely one that contains the exercise of such a capacity. In the first case one says: the subject has it in his power[e] to do this or that with the object (*in potentia sua positum*) in the second he has it within his control[f] (*in potestate sua positum*) – Therefore *potentiale* {in one's power} possession must be distinguished from *potestative* {in one's control}, and to bring something into the latter form of possession is a rightful act which suffices for mine and yours if the will for it is there, though not in the former case. –

---

[a] *Act der gemeinsamen Willkühr*
[b] *Gegenstand* for most of next three paragraphs
[c] *Object* [d] *Gegenstand* in this paragraph
[e] *Macht* [f] *Gewalt*

Now **bringing within one's control** must first be understood physically (conditioned in space and time) the likes of which one calls mathematically (theoretically) determined though subsequently he must [*breaks off*]

23:313
Apagogic proof

Assume that no land could be acquired originally and hence unilaterally, i.e. could not be brought rightfully into separate possession, then that land could not be brought into any possession at all or at least not into any common possession, hence each excludes all others and all exclude each other from use of land *a priori*. But because this right to a possession of land belongs to each (for without this I cannot be wronged by the use others may wish to make of it) and because the exclusion of others from the separate possession of some particular patch of land is part of the right to a separate possession of it, land would thus be in the common possession of each and yet anyone can be excluded from the particular possession of it, which contradicts itself (since right which is not assigned to any individual also cannot be assigned to all of them taken together.)

23:313   *Loses Blatt* E 55
          [*first page*]

Universal formula of outer acquisition

All taking into possession in space and time presupposes an intellectual taking into possession, having the outer object[a] (distinct from the subject) in his control, as well as right as the possibility of this act in accordance with laws of freedom (which regarding outer things always occurs upon the first taking into possession). Therefore here freedom and capacity are granted. Now for this the will that contains the agreement with all others' wills, which is only possible through their collective unity, is **thought** (not empirically given), and resolved in this way the object is mine.

Of the principles of outer acquisition in general

Acquisition is a rightful act, i.e. an action by which something becomes mine. If the acquirable object (*quaesibile* {acquirable thing}) is outside me then the condition for it is that I am previously in possession of the object outside me, and should the acquisition be original (for there must be this kind of acquisition in general § [b]), then there must be a possession which precedes any rightful act of **free power of choice**, i.e. a **natural**
23:314   yet nevertheless **outer** possession, and this in regard to things outside me is none other than that of **land**.

---

[a] *Gegenstand* until final paragraph of this *Loses Blatt*
[b] Kant left blank space to fill in the § number.

The principle[a] of the original natural possession of land is: "I have the innate right to be upon land (to occupy a place upon the earth) upon which nature or accident (hence without my power of choice) has placed me." However anyone else upon the same common surface of the earth with whom I stand in outer relation of possible mutual influence, because of the unity of the surface of the earth, has like me the same right.

The first rightful act required for outer mine is taking into possession[b] (*apprehensio*) of the object (hence here of some land), i.e. the beginning of use through its connection with my power of choice: which must be the first taking into possession (*prior apprehensio*) in order to accord with right necessarily, because only this agrees universally with the outer freedom of everyone. Possession by empirical taking[c] is occupying, hence my presence in the space where the thing is with the aim of a possible use of it, and hence all others on the same land for all: Consequently taking a place on earth into possession is a particular acquisition from their common possession (*communio*)

[*second page*]

1) the outer freedom of all others' power of choice, that taking into possession is the first (in accord with **time**) 2) the capacity to bring a place into one's possession (in accord with space). 3) the will, i.e. the obligation of all others by virtue of the common possession of the entire surface of the earth.

To these correspond the intellectual conditions which are required for mine and yours.

    a. of the priority of taking, that the object is not yet in anyone's possession

    b. of empirical taking, that the subject has brought it altogether within his control.

    c. of the empirical community of the land (through being next to one another upon one and the same surface of the earth). The common will which alone determines with universal validity what belongs to each.

How are synthetic propositions of right possible *a priori*.

Regarding concepts of right everything depends only upon how and   23:315
how much I possess intellectually, i.e. by the mere will regarding that which I have in my control even without empirical relations in space and time.

Things[d] in space are regarded intellectually only as things[e] **outside** me; possession additionally as something one has **in one's control**. Private empirical taking into control regarded as a determination through

---

[a] *Grundsatz*   [b] *Besitznehmung*
[c] *apprehension* in this *Loses Blatt*   [d] *Dinge*
[e] *Sachen* for remainder of paragraph

the **collective will**, so that in accordance with pure relations of right those mere things which in accord with laws of outer freedom I bring under my control and which I will that they be mine in conformity with the common will, that is mine. – This consequence drawn from those items as reasons is not a synthetic but instead a merely analytical proposition. – If however all of these concepts are taken empirically, if the externality of **space** in itself is taken as a relation[a] of the subject, if possession is to consist in presence in a place and taking or occupying is to constitute **taking possession** as such, then such a proposition is synthetic and must be known *a priori* only within intuition which however is impossible in regard to right.

The empirical conditions of acquisition serve the dynamic and intellectual functions only to undergird them with an object[b] and an empirical relation to which those functions are applied so that they acquire objective though only practical reality.

23:315　*Loses Blatt* E 56
　　　　　[first page]

Principle.[c]

That which I bring under my control in agreement with the laws of outer freedom (hence as the first), and which I will, in accordance with a universal law (of the collectively-universal will[d] in the idea), that it shall be mine, is mine.

Here mere concepts of the understanding of possession and of the object[e] of the power of choice are regarded as *noumen* not as sensible power of choice of the object[f] determinately given in space. – This principle holds for all outer acquisition (whether as rights to things as personal or also as rights to persons as things).

23:316　　　　　　　Principle of first acquisition of some land.

The indeterminate possession of some land or other (place on the earth) is *potentiale* possession, namely the possibility of taking possession of the particular.

Deduction of the right ~~of a principle of acquisition of outer things~~ to an original acquisition of land.

This right is grounded upon a *factum*[g] that is original, i.e. is not derived from any rightful act, namely upon the original community in land.

---

[a] *Relation*　　　　　　　　　　　　[b] *Object*
[c] *Grundsatz*　　　　　　　　　　　[d] *collective-allgemeinen Willens*
[e] *Gegenstand*　　　　　　　　　　[f] *Object*
[g] *Factum*, normally meaning "deed," has the sense here of "matter of fact"

The original acquisition of land must be **unilateral** since if it were grounded upon others' agreement it would be derivative.

Yet the right of the one who acquires cannot stand in immediate relation to things (here to the land) since the obligation of others **immediately** corresponds to right; things however cannot be made obligated. Thus the acquisition of some land is only possible by a **rightful act**, i.e. by one through which the one who acquires is bound to the land not immediately but rather only **mediately**, namely by means of the determination of the will of another person obligating all others negatively in accordance with universal laws, namely to refrain from using a certain piece of land, and this restraint is possible in accordance with universal laws of freedom (i.e. in accordance with laws of right) only insofar as the former has possession of it.

However the one who acquires can in this perspective take possession of some land in order to have it as his own through his private power of choice, i.e. unilaterally, by a rightful act, because otherwise he would obligate all others through his merely unilateral power of choice, hence only consequent upon a possession [*second page*] which he has originally (prior to any rightful act) and which also as a collective possession by everyone who can make the same claim, i.e. a possession which can through a will unify all possible possessions upon the surface of earth, which contains an original community (*communio originaria*) of the surface of the earth upon which alone is grounded the act of the first acquisition as original, which is at once the acquisition of a particular place by unilateral taking possession, though indeed this is not acquisition until   23:317
and unless it agrees with the united will in collective possession of all objects of the power of choice, which in accord with laws of freedom can be brought in someone's control to have as his own.

Now such a common possession *a priori*, prior to all acts of the power of choice, is actually in possession of the surface of the earth, and freedom, capacity and will agree *a priori* (prior to any rightful act) before practical reason to have as its own the outer object (the ground): consequently [*breaks off*]

Not a relation to substance as phenomena, i.e. immediately to things which have no obligations.

Deduction of the concept of right in things
i.e. the possibility of the first acquisition of land.

First acquisition, regarded as original, in accordance with concepts of right (as mere concepts of reason) here, where the possibility of outer mine and yours in things is in question, signifies the unconditioned act, i.e. independent of conditions of time, of the power of choice by which an outer thing becomes someone's own. For the previous time is the condition of the subsequent. – In pure relations of right **possession** signifies neither occupation nor **taking possession**[a] (*apprehensio*) nor the connection of a person with a place in space but rather the act of bringing an object[b] distinct from (outside) a subject into his control (*act* of causality), and the community of possession (*communio*) as an original one with others does not signify the connection of the presence of many persons in all places with the presence of others: but rather of the unified power of choice regarding the same object.

23:317 *Loses Blatt* E 57
[*first page*]
Postulate of practical reason regarding land.
"It must be possible for anyone living on earth to acquire some land originally" (*vid.* § [c])
For suppose that such an acquisition is impossible, then there would be either absolutely no or at least no original acquisition of land for those

23:318 who live upon it. – The first case contradicts the postulate of practical reason, in the second all acquisition of land as a rightful act would always have to be derived in turn from another rightful act so that each would make arrangements for what is his own on the universal land, and there would be an assumed regress in the series of derived acquisitions due to which there is no possible sufficient ground for them.

§
"By their innate right and prior to all outer mine and yours all human beings are in original possession of the land, on which rightful possession, the possibility of the acquisition of land, must be grounded."

The first condition of the possibility of outer mine or yours
is the possession of an object of the power of choice.
However the beginning of acquisition and the first condition of its possibility is **taking into possession**[d] (*apprehensio*) which insofar as it is regarded as a *factum* regarding an object in space ~~and time~~ can be called taking[e] (*apprehensio empirica*), but insofar as these conditions are disregarded and considering only the concept of the understanding **to bring** an outer object **under one's control** (into a connection with the subject by which he is enabled to use it) can be called **intellectual taking into possession**.
Now all human beings by right occupy the place on the earth upon which nature or chance has placed them without any choice, and thus in

---

[a] *Besitznehmung*   [b] *Gegenstand* through next five paragraphs
[c] Kant left blank space to fill in the § number.
[d] *Besitznehmung* in this paragraph   [e] *Ergreifung*

accordance with an innate right (prior to any rightful act) are in possession of the land upon which they find themselves as the highest condition
of the possibility of its use so far as this is absolutely necessary merely
for preserving their existence. – They are thus as a whole in original
possession of the surface of the earth (wholly or in part) by nature. – But
in this no one is also assigned a residence (*sedes*), not immediately, i.e.
a place which one or another may regard as his own; for this requires
a rightful act (of acquisition). – Likewise [*second page*] because this connection of the subject with the land is equally necessarily bound with the
subject's will to use this land on his own behalf, one can make the obtain- 23:319
ing of this possession representable as taking into possession (*apprehensio*) and as an act by which a right to make that land his own, but not
yet the land, is indeed originally acquired, i.e. a right to acquire it, which
act, since it arises immediately from nature, is not yet a rightful act (*actus
juridicus*) as one which must proceed from the outer freedom of will and
its laws, and yet it can and must be represented in accord with an analogy
with such an act.

Remark. The concept of right is not a concept of an immediate
relation of the subject to outer things; since the concept of obligation
corresponds immediately to the concept of right. But things cannot be
assigned obligations. – If one speaks of right in a thing one thereby
understands the right arising from mere possession of a thing to obligate
everyone not to harm me in my lawful use of it. – That mere possession
conforming with right (that which agrees with the universal principle[a] of
freedom) as such already suffices to provide a right in the thing, though
not yet to call the thing mine, i.e. that everyone is obligated, which is
expressed by the formula of juridical happiness: Happy is he who is in
possession (*beati possidentes*).

The possession of an outer thing (such as of some land) can only
ground an outer mine or yours insofar as it can be considered as a common possession, i.e. one following from the common will of all who are
in possession of the object,[b] since a private possession obligates not each
person but rather the whole.[c] – However the original possession of land
for all by nature is such a possession that precedes any rightful act.

Definition. The will of a subject in relation to an object insofar as it is
in his control is the power of choice. – To acquire something unilaterally
is to acquire it by an act of one's own power of choice and hence immediately through relation to the object. – Nothing outer can be acquired
unilaterally; for that would be to obligate others by one's mere power of

---

[a] *Princip*
[b] *Object* in this and the following paragraphs
[c] *der Gemeinsame*

23:320 choice *pro arbitrio* {by choice} which is inconsistent with outer freedom in accordance with universal laws. Therefore not by an act that immediately relates to the outer object, although first taking possession can be unilateral since it is always consistent with outer freedom.

23:320 *Loses Blatt* E 58

[*first page*]

Moral maxims require publicity when their moral end is possible only when all others are likewise morally disposed, which cannot be effected if one does not universally communicate one's principles, i.e. makes them public. – That end which can only be effected collectively through the free cooperation of all others is, e.g. mutual aid in cases of dire need.

[*in margin:*] to derive one's own happiness from the happiness of the whole [is] the finest politics

What I have within my control in accordance with laws of freedom (as first possessor) is not yet for that reason mine even if I will it when this will is not the united will of all, except insofar as I have distributive possession of some land because its division from the common land is made by me since I cannot originally acquire all land because I would thus exclude all others from the right to be somewhere or other.

Due to the naturally determined form and size of the inhabitable surface of the earth (as a globe) he has an innate right to each place upon it, to occupy one or another place, i.e. he is in a potential though merely **disjunctive universal** possession of all places on the earth, hence all who dwell on earth are placed by this unity of their residence in a relation of thorough mutual possible influence and thus have an innate potential collective possession of the earth's land, and this **community of possession** is theirs by an innate **right** and likewise also their inseparable **obligation** – neither that the former is **acquired** by a rightful act, i.e. by choice, nor does the latter result from such an act – instead both are **innate** and indeed as relations of right which cannot be thought as immediately connected to **things** but rather only to persons. Now this collective possession as **collectively-universal** possession, through the resistance in occupying the space which each requires on earth, makes a rightful act possible and practically, i.e. objectively, necessary by which the possession of each be determined **distributively**, though this can-

23:321 not occur unilaterally (by taking[a]) because such an act of the power of choice is not grounded on a law that obligates all others and thus not on any right, hence no land can be acquired by unilateral taking possession.

---

[a] *apprehension*

Equally well, some land must be able to be acquired originally (i.e. without being derived from what is someone else's own) (§ [a]), i.e. practical reason wills that every part of the land could be someone's own. Therefore a common will, which is not an act of the power of choice, i.e. an original-common will which corresponds to the common innate possession must [be] the basis of distributive pos[session] [*breaks off*]

[*the following paragraph written in margins and between the lines*]
All human beings are in original (innate) possession of the land without requiring any rightful act of taking possession, i.e. without it being necessary to bring it under their control which otherwise is required for any intellectual possession. – However this possession is mere occupying, and because it is undetermined which land is occupied, this can be called disjunctive-universal possession and indeed one which is rightful though it cannot be other than a potential possession, i.e. the authorization to obtain a possession by a rightful act (of taking[b]), in order thereby (and by the will bound with the taking) to achieve *potestative* {authorized} possession. Therefore because this right belongs to each and every individual regarding all places on earth, they are in potential collective possession, i.e. under the idea of the united will, for otherwise any one possession would contradict any other, which is thus also original and requires no act uniting powers of choice. Because this is only ~~a necessary idea~~ a regulative principle (as idea) a particular taking possession as original must be possible, if it is to be possible to have something outer in space as one's own without depending upon any other rightful act (such as contract). Now first taking possession always accords with the law of outer freedom and hence also with right, and if this is thought through the mere concept of the understanding it is an act by which the object,[c] if one also abstracts from conditions of space, is in my control, and if this taking control occurs through a will that accords with the idea of the collectively universal will, then it occurs through this latter, hence this object[d] becomes mine.

[*second page*]

23:322

1. All human beings on earth are in an original community of possession (*communio originaria*) of the surface of the earth as a whole, the extent of which is determined and is incapable of enlargement.

All human beings (*singuli* {each individual}) have an innate and equal right to be upon the earth (physically to possess it) wherever nature or chance has placed him without his consent ~~and this innate right which precedes any rightful act (of the power of choice)is innate The right of~~

[a] Kant left blank space to fill in the § number.
[b] *apprehension*   [c] *Gegenstand*
[d] *Object*

each. Hence each human being naturally takes a place on earth wherever or whenever he comes into being,[a] and can himself **think** of this act as rightful, namely as disjunctive-universal taking possession (taking[b] of land) to possess either one or another place upon the surface of the earth (as a globe). Now this relation as a rightful relation is not an immediate relation to the land (as outer thing) but rather to other human beings insofar as they too are upon the same land at the same time (since if the existence were thought of as successive then the first taking would have to be a rightful immediate relation to things, which is impossible) and land cannot be unilaterally acquired primitively.

[*in margin:*] "He has the right" means: he does not act contrary to freedom in accordance with universal laws. "He has a right to a thing" means he obligates others by his mere will in a way they would not be otherwise bound.

However all human beings insofar as they are on earth **at the same** time must for this reason also be in collective-universal possession of the entire surface of the earth, i.e. in possession which arises through everyone's united powers of choice; for otherwise someone's power of choice regarding possession would come into conflict with another's and one would deprive another of his place, with the result that contrary to innate right the disjunctive universal possession would be negated through this defective unity. – Therefore one must **think** a universal united power of choice as a juridical act by which a place for each is necessarily determined through a collective will, hence a collective possession (*communio originaria*) from which is derived each possible possession.

23:323

In the idea of this common possession and in accordance with laws which flow from this concept, a unilateral acquisition of land is always possible in which the common not the private will makes first taking possession rightfully-possible, and not in an immediate relation to a thing but rather to persons. – i.e. land can be acquired by first taking possession.

Apagogic (analytic) Proof – Assume that land could not be unilaterally acquired in the state of nature, then it could not be acquirable at all, not even in the civil condition. – For this condition is only of those who already stand in reciprocal relations of outer mine and yours arising from the contract of all, in order to subsume this acquisition under certain laws through an objectively universal will. Now if there were no outer mine and yours, then there could also be no public law to secure to each his own.

1. Each human being naturally, i.e. prior to any rightful act, takes a place on the earth wherever nature or chance has placed him, and has

---

[a] *zur Wirklichkeit kommt*   [b] *apprehension* in this paragraph

the right, i.e. he obligates all others to refrain from this place not by his relation to an outer thing, to the ground as its occupant,[a] for there is no obligation to things, but rather to everyone else's powers of choice who are in possession of the same surface of the earth and of some place on it through their own powers of choice just as much as he is. – Holding an object[b] of the power of choice, bound with the will to use it somehow, is possession, and everyone who dwells on earth is therefore in original dynamic possession of some land, i.e. he has it in his control prior to any rightful act.

2. Since all human beings on one and the same surface of the earth are originally in possession of one or another place on it, and since the right of possession is originally each person's in regard to any place on earth and so is **disjunctively universal**, i.e. anyone can possess this or that place on earth, hence this possession must also be regarded as **collectively-universal**, i.e. as collective possession by the human race to which corresponds an objectively united will, or one which is to be united, because without a principle[c] of distribution (which can only be ascribed to the united will as law) the human right to be somewhere or other would entirely lack effect and would be negated by universal conflict. 23:324

3. Therefore first taking possession does not contradict the right of others (*lex justi* {law of justice}) just because it is the first, i.e. no one else has already taken possession of that land – though as unilateral it is indeed not yet a rightful act which obligates others because it is only practiced toward things and so is not an act by which any land is acquired. However the taking possession which accords with the idea of a possible and *a priori* objectively necessary collectively universal will, and which agrees with the principle of original collective possession of the surface of the earth, is of course the first rightful act that constitutes the *con ditio sine qua non* of first acquisition (since there must be a first) and is a negative acquisition to prevent others (in accordance with the *lex juridica* {juridical law}) from disturbing those who are in possession of a place (assuming possession to be intellectual) until the united will and the condition of outer legislation are established (*lex justitiae* {law of justice}), which in accordance with the original comprehensive possession determines for each what is his.

Physical possession regarded under the idea of collective possession, which contains the *a priori* condition of the former and is a merely intelligible possession, is a relation to some land, to have it in my control through my mere will and hence to possess it intellectually.

---

[a] *als Inhaber*
[b] *Die Inhabung eines Gegenstandes*
[c] *Princip*

23:324   *Loses Blatt* E 59
         [first page]
         Thesis *Praemissio* {assumption}. Assume it is not possible, then it would be either impossible to possess the object[a] of one's power of choice or it would be contrary to right to appropriate it, i.e. to resist, in accordance with universal laws of freedom, others who hinder one's use of it. – However the former does not hold because it presupposes the outer object as object of the power of choice[b] which I have in my control, and likewise neither does the latter because the same object[c] is equally well the object of others' powers of choice and consequently is entirely consistent with others' freedom to use it in accordance with universal laws. Therefore it is false that it is impossible to have an object of the power of choice outside me as my own; consequently it is possible etc.

         Antithesis. Assume it is possible. Because the object is outside me
23:325   I am thus not in possession of it, though I cannot be wronged by the use another makes of an object which is not in my possession, hence it is impossible rightly to resist others' use of it, consequently it is also impossible to have something outside me as my own (indeed it is contradictory to regard it as an object of my power of choice)

         Solution. The concept of **possession** in the thesis is not the same as in the antithesis, consequently there is no true opposition between the two claims; both propositions can be true. For in the thesis possession is thought in accordance with a pure concept of the understanding as is necessary if I am to subsume it immediately under the rational concept of right (It is the tenth of Aristotle's categories, *habere* {to have[14]}; though in the critical system it is a predicable of the category of cause). It is referred to as *possessio noumenon* in concepts of right. Thereby I think only an object within my capacity to use which is not naturally connected with me, although we here abstract from how this object may be determined in connection with me as an object[d] of my action; however in the antithesis the object is thought as existing in space and time so that the concept of possession is thought as *possessio phaenomenon* (in accordance with the schematism of concepts of the understanding). Now since the pure concepts of the understanding do not as such depend upon their schemata and are not limited to those conditions but rather can be extended to objects in general, while the concept of right as a **concept of reason** affords no schema at all and immediately extends only to the concept of the understanding of possession under which possession in appearance is also found, it is thus clear that what is valid in the thesis could also be valid in the antithesis of possession, though not conversely. If we abstract

---

[a] *Gegenstand* in this *Loses Blatt* unless noted
[b] *der äußere Gegenstand als Object der Willkür*
[c] *Object*   [d] *Object*

from all conditions on which objects of the senses necessarily depend, as when speaking merely of right in general, the universal laws of which issue entirely from pure reason, then these latter constitute the principles in accordance with which right regarding objects of the senses must also be judged. – However because that suffices to know how to judge that within experience which is right or wrong, [*second page*] a particular principle of subsumption of a given case under those principles of right must also be supplied as a basis for this knowledge through which the determination of mine and yours (outside us) within space and time becomes possible. – This principle is that of the agreement of powers of choice with the idea of a united power of choice of those who stand in relations of right towards each other (regarding an outer object[a] of possession). Only by this idea is it possible to make synthetic judgments *a priori* about mine and yours. For right regarding an object of the power of choice is properly the rightful relation of persons towards each other which makes mine and yours possible, and this is purely intellectual.

23:326

Thesis. It is possible to have as my own an outer given object of my power of choice. For assume it be impossible, then that cannot be a physical impossibility (of possession); for it is an object of my power of choice hence within my power;[b] consequently it could only be a deficient basis for right, hence it would be an impossibility in accordance with laws of right to resist those who wanted to hinder my use of an object outside me. However they could not hinder me except by themselves being able to regard such an object, the use of which is at their disposal although it is outside them, as what could be theirs. Consequently the proposition that an outer object of the human power of choice could not be one's own contains a contradiction, hence it is possible to have something outer as mine.

Antithesis. It is not possible etc. – Mine is that through the use of which by another I can be wronged. Now I cannot be wronged except insofar as I am in possession of the object of my power of choice; however I understand by an object outside me that which is not in my possession and through the use of which by another I also cannot be wronged. Therefore it is not possible to have something outside me as mine.

Remark. One must of course note here that "outside me" here means as much as an object the alterations of which are not my alterations.

12)[c] **Solution** of the Antinomy. In the thesis **the concept of possession** is represented as *possessio noumenon*, **intellectual** possession in accordance with mere concepts of the understanding of relation (of the

23:327

---

[a] *Object*   [b] *Gewalt*
[c] Kant appears to resume numbering. He had provided numbers 1–12 at 23:273–75 and it is unclear whether 12 and 13 here refer to that numbering. There is also another 12 on 23:330.

practical category *habere*); though in the antithesis it is taken as **sensibly-determined** (*phaenomenon*) outer relation in space and time, and hence both propositions can be true, and what is absolutely possible in accordance with mere concepts of the understanding of possession can also be impossible in accordance with sensibly determined concepts if one does not add a limiting condition, and this is the synthetic principle of the unification of powers of choice of distinct human beings into a communal power of choice through which alone the extension of human rights beyond innate right is possible. – In this way synthetic propositions of right are possible *a priori*. – In this idealist unification possession always remains as *possessio noumenon* even when *possessio phenomenon* is lacking, as merely rightful possession within the common will.

[*in margin:*] 13) Only in the idea of a united will of two parties, who stand in relations of right toward one another regarding an outer object of the power of choice, is it possible to have something outer as one's own. – For it is only mine so far as I can think of myself also as being merely rightfully in possession of the object, i.e. even when I do not find myself in physical possession. However since then the thing is in no one's possession, it must be preserved in the mere power of choice – however this can only be the common power of choice as the one which is in possession of the object *virtualiter* {virtually} not *localiter* {by location} or *temporaliter* {temporally}.

23:327   *Loses Blatt* E 68. On a letter dated August, 1792.

[*second page*]

Acquisition by taking control,[a] by accepting, by subjection. In the first things are regarded as dependent upon human beings (not conversely) regarding their use. In the second people are regarded as dependent upon each other regarding each of their powers of choice. In the third one's status is regarded as dependent upon another's status, hence his existence (regarding sustenance and protection), 1) The possibility of producing people through carnal intercourse, 2) Relation to those actually produced, 3) the necessity of obedience due to the need for sustenance or maintenance as such: the domestic maintenance of dependants.

23:328   I always acquire[b] through an action and indeed rightly only through an act whereby I limit others' powers of choice, i.e. an action which relates not merely to things but rather through persons to things. 1. Through merely unilateral action to make possible the uniting of powers of choice, 2 through bilateral action to make it actual, 3 through unilateral action which makes necessary the bilateral.

An action by which I obligate another to do something from which I benefit is an acquisition. If the action is unilateral then this is original. –

[a] *occupation*   [b] *acquirire*

Such an acquisition must be possible; for otherwise as regards what is contingently mine I would always depend upon others' powers of choice so that I do not infringe on their freedom. However because others' freedom would of course also be made dependent upon my mere power of choice if it were merely up to me to obligate him in some way or other, then were it to depend upon each individual power of choice to make others obligated (I would do this to others by *acquisitio originaris* of land and others likewise to me since they would hinder my so doing), then a condition must be possible whereby this opposition of powers of choice is negated, i.e. the idea of a possible unification of powers of choice: in relation with which and with its possibility the will of all can become univocal, and this idea contains the highest condition of all acquired rights. This will is the synthetic unity of free powers of choice *a priori* which is the basis of the concept of acquisition.

These propositions presuppose however that the existence of human beings universally depends upon such a possession, and a right to assume others' agreement to such a principle of the possibility of possession is based on this.

Loses Blatt F 14   23:330
[*first page*]

12) Corporeal objects[a] outside me can be acquired through a rightful act (not originally) for if there were things that belong to no one (*res nullius*) I could of course have no immediate right to them ([b]); instead this right must be regarded as derived from the originally united powers of choice regarding mine and yours in general, otherwise I would only acquire originally that whose existence I caused. Therefore all acquisition in time is to this extent (in accordance with the idea of reason of mine and yours) merely derived. However acquisition can within time nevertheless be **originally first**[c] (primitive) because through the idea of an *a priori* united will I do not make mine that which previously belonged to another (*res alienus* {a thing belonging to another}) and then ceases in the same sense to be his. – To acquire something outer originally would be to unilaterally (*propria autoritate* {by one's own authority}) place others   23:331 under an obligation which they otherwise would not have. Yet initially and primitively I can of course acquire it so far as my own right alone validates the *a priori* united will.

Unilateral *actus proprietatis potestatis* {act of one's own power}

Thesis. [*in the immediate margin:* instead of 7] It is possible to have an object of the power of choice outside oneself (*praeter semet ipsum* {in

---

[a] *Gegenständen* throughout first page   [b] Kant leaves the parentheses empty
[c] *uranfänglich*

addition to oneself}) as one's own. This is an identical proposition; for if something is an object of my power of choice then it is within my power,[a] i.e. it is possible to possess it as such, consequently also to resist others' powers of choice through one's power of choice in accordance with laws of freedom. Accordingly it means nothing more than that an object of the outer power of choice, or the outer power of choice itself, is possible. However this possibility cannot be **known**[b] by mere reason *a priori*, instead it is merely a category of the relation of causality, namely of the use of an object in accordance with the law of freedom that I am able to resist anyone else who hinders me in this regard, hence of **possession**. Therefore the proposition would be: It is possible to possess something outside me: Whether such a possession is possible is not to be known by itself alone (without appeal to another determination). – One can only prove it apagogically. For assume there were indeed objects outside me but no power of choice to which they could be subjected, and this simply because they are outside me and my possible possession, ~~then all outer objects of cognition would themselves in accordance with the possibility of res nullius~~ then I could also not be affected or wronged by other rational beings. I would thus stand in no proper outer relations of right. Thus it could also not be asked whether something in outer relations would be right or wrong. Therefore this is already presupposed in the prior question.

Just as in the theoretical where synthetic propositions of right are possible *a priori* only through the categories in application to the form of sensibility, so synthetic judgments of right are not possible *a priori* except as the first two conditions in relation to a power of choice to be united universally, (so that the power of choice of one harmonizes with the powers of choice of everyone in a law) because only in this is possession initiated by *apprehension* also maintained.

23:332   *Habere* (ἔχειν) *est possidere*. **Possessio est vel phaenomenon vel noumenon** {To have is to possess. Possession is either phenomenal or noumenal}. One cannot say "I possess a right" because only I and not the right can be affected; instead "I possess something by right" (*jure*), i.e. not merely in accordance with right (*juste*) but rather **rightfully** (*juridice*), and if this possession is not at once physical *mere juridice* {merely rightfully}. I possess something (in accordance with laws of freedom) **rightfully** if can make use of it in accordance with these laws, hence insofar as this possession is not merely restricted to natural conditions.

[*second page*]

a) An outer merely-rightful possession is possible, i.e. it is possible through my mere power of choice to prevent others from using an object (an analytic proposition of limiting others' freedom through

---

[a] *Gewalt*   [b] *läßt sich . . . erkennen*

my own). – For assume it were not possible, then ~~I would, because the power of choice would still have to have some object or other, be able to prevent other's power of choice only regarding myself and not regarding an outer object; I would be able to rightfully resist everyone else, and they could rightfully resist me, in the use of an outer object of the power of choice~~ my power of choice would be unable to have any outer object whatsoever but only myself and the right of freedom of my own person – However under the presupposition that there are objects[a] of my power of choice outside me which also are equally well objects of others' power of choice who can resist my own in using those objects, there must be a law of right which limits each person's power of choice to conditions of the freedom of everyone. However this law must precede *a priori* all outer use of the power of choice hence prior to all physical possession, which can only be made permissible through that law, and yet it contains the concept of outer possession (as that which contains the condition of right or wrong which someone can do to another). However such a concept is the concept of an **intellectual** possession, i.e. the possession of the right to use an outer object[b] without regard to physical possession, which properly is a possession of the object through reason under laws of right and thus a merely rightful possession. Such a possession is thus possible.

Thesis. Assume that there is an object[c] of my power of choice outside me, then it is possible to have it as mine. For as object of my power of choice it is within my power[d] to use it. However as an outer object   23:333
of the power of choice in general it is also within others' power. – Consequently here is a relation of the powers of choice of distinct persons to one another in the use of one and the same object, which must stand under the law of each person's freedom limited to the condition of all their agreement with the freedom of each. Now were it not possible for me to have such an object as mine, then the law of freedom would limit the power of choice itself to the condition of having no outer object, i.e. not to be an outer power of choice which contradicts the assumption.

Antithesis. It is impossible to have something outer as one's own.

~~Thesis etc. Assume it is impossible. Then merely for that reason it would be impossible for something outside me to be an object of my power of choice. Because I have in my power that which is an object of my power of choice, i.e. it could be possessed, if this is thus outside~~

---

[a] *Objecte* in this paragraph unless noted   [b] *Gegenstand*
[c] *Gegenstand* through the end of the third page unless noted
[d] *Gewalt*

me, i.e. not connected to me at all, then it is to that extent also not in my power, for I do not possess the object insofar as it (as previously explained) is outside me. But something in general, as well as the use of it, can be an object of my power of choice, and so mine, only insofar as I possess it, hence something outer, i.e. what I do not possess, is yet mine to have, which is a contradiction.

[*two sentences in margin:*] by an outer object here I understand always that which I do not possess

Only through a contract can the exclusion from using something outer (not everything) be constituted.

Thesis – – if the concept of an outer object of the power of choice is thought merely as a pure concept of the understanding this proposition is analytic and based on the law of contradiction. For if it is represented as an object of my power of choice, i.e. of my possible use, an outer object[a] is thus at the same time represented as something which I can **possess**; this **possession** as an object[b] outside me immediately contains through my freedom the limitation of others' freedom to use this object[c] to the condition of agreement with universal freedom, hence it contains a right [to resist[d]] others who wish to hinder my use of it, which constitutes the concept of mine.

[*fourth page*]

It is possible to have an object[e] of my power of choice outside me as mine. For an object of the power of choice outside me is the outer object[f] that I can use as I please. However, this object would then be mine if I could exclude others through my mere power of choice even without its physical possession – Now assume it were not possible to have something outside me as mine, then I could not exclude any others from using it through my mere power of choice, though conversely others also cannot exclude me (due to the law of freedom to harmonize with everyone's freedom). If however I cannot exclude others from the object of my power of choice and also they cannot exclude me from it through their mere powers of choice, then there is no relation of right between us regarding outer objects, or in accordance with principles of right the object[g] is not an object of my power of choice, i.e. freedom utterly negates the outer use of the power of choice.

Assume it is not possible, then it would not be impossible in accordance with laws of nature, since it is an object[h] of the power of choice

23:334

---

[a] *Object*   [b] *Object*
[c] *Gegenstand*
[d] Kant does not specify the right but the context implies a right to resist.
[e] *Object* in this and the following paragraph unless noted
[f] *Gegenstand*   [g] *Gegenstand*
[h] *Gegenstand* here and in the next sentence

which thus is within my power,[a] thus impossible only in accordance with laws of freedom, namely that of the agreement of freedom with the freedom of everyone. However this directly opposes freedom in the use of a thing outside me because others' freedom excludes my own just as mine excludes the power of choice of others' freedom from use of the object – *Summa* {in sum} reason's concept of freedom, together with the concept of the power of choice regarding outer objects[b] within its power, makes necessary the concept of a concept of right[c] of possession of such an object.

Loses Blatt F 18   23:334

[*first page*]

Of the possibility **of having** something outside oneself **as one's own**.

Mine is that the alteration of which is my alteration. The **physically mine** (in space and time) is that which belongs to the empirical determination of my existence. This mine is inner if it belongs merely to my determination in time; outer if it is outside me though nevertheless so bound with me that its alteration is also at the same time my alteration. Rightfully mine is that **object[d] of my power of choice** from which I can exclude any others, when it is regarded as object of their powers of choice, through my mere power of choice, consequently in accord with   23:335
laws of right.

[*in margin:*] An object of my power of choice is whatever I can use as I please.

It pertains to having something rightfully mine 1. that it be an object of my power of choice and is equally thought as an object of others' power of choice. 2. That I be in **possession** of it, i.e. in a connection with this object[e] which makes its use possible. Hence if something is an object of my power of choice but equally is within me myself it is **rightfully** and of course also **naturally** mine, hence everything is mine that I possess physically by occupying it is **simultaneously rightfully mine**. In contrast that which must be regarded as mine even if I do not directly possess it physically, hence an outer object regarded as mine in this way, is mine **merely rightfully**.

11. How it is possible **to have** something outer **as one's own**

I cannot rightfully possess that which is outer as an object of my power of choice that can simultaneously be regarded as an object[f] of others' powers of choice, except by means of a common (united) power of choice of those to whom it can be an object of their powers of choice, and

---

[a] *Gewalt*
[b] *Objecte* in this sentence
[c] *den Begriff von einem Rechtsbegriff*
[d] *Object* from here into the third paragraph
[e] *Gegenstand* for remainder of paragraph
[f] *Gegenstand* in this paragraph unless noted

without rightful possession there could be no mine and yours (although this is not sufficient for that). [*in margin:* there is no mine without merely rightful possession] – For through my own power of choice (*arbitrio proprio*) I can limit no one's freedom except insofar as I am physically bound with the object of his freedom. Thus if I am rightfully to exclude others from this object insofar as it is also an object of their powers of choice through my own, then their powers of choice must harmonize with my own and thus I only exclude others via the power of choice united in this way. Therefore no outer object can be mine or yours except where a united power of choice exists. – Now if the concept of outer mine and yours is a necessary concept of right, i.e. such that it lies *a priori* at the basis of all rightful outer relation of the person in relation to outer objects[a] of the power of choice, [*in margin:* i.e. if it is necessary that there must be an outer mine and yours] then an *a priori* united will must also

23:336 lie at the basis of this relation as legislating through which each particular power of choice can necessitate others. – However it is *a priori* necessary that something outer could still be mine as outer, for right is a relation of the power of choice of any one to that of another insofar as they reciprocally limit their freedom in **outer** use in accordance with the idea of a common will. Now if no outer mine and yours were possible, then freedom would make itself dependent upon physical possession, i.e. upon things in space and time, consequently [*second page*] the concept of right itself would be dependent *a priori* upon empirical conditions and hence itself would be empirical, which contradicts the concept of right.

III. DRAFTS OF PUBLIC RIGHT

23:340 *Loses Blatt* E 47

[*first page, material summarizing possession omitted*]

[*in margin:*] If the happiness of all is to be the object,[b] the matter of the law, then it is certainly true to the extent that, were everyone to obey the moral law, then universal happiness would also be better effected than by any other rule, at least if we make the duty of virtue into our principle;[c] we would thus proceed with the greatest confidence despite our ignorance of the natural consequences. Yet how can we make it that if we hold ourselves to this maxim and even make sacrifices for it, others would do likewise?

[*second page*]

Freedom, outer

Explanation: that outer freedom is the condition of a human being in which he can do what he wills if only he does not wrong others is

---

[a] *allem rechtlichen äußern Verhältnis der Person in Beziehung auf äußere Objecte*
[b] *Object* in drafts for public right unless noted   [c] *Grundsatze*

tautological. For no one **can** do everything he wills. (The will does not always presuppose the means instead only the power of choice presupposes it.) Therefore it must be expressed this way: that he is permitted 23:341 to do whatever he wills etc., though this means he does wrong to no one if he wrongs no one. Here freedom should be explained through the formal condition of action. Yet it is a material condition of action.

Outer freedom is a condition of being subject (*subjectus*) to no one except **the law** to which he himself has given his consent. However to give this consent to a law which negates all consent by others is a contradiction. Therefore it is the authorization to determine his own end for himself (to act in accord with his own end and not simply having to act in accord with others' ends). Hence children are not free, nor the mentally disturbed, nor the violent. Hence freedom is the independence of his happiness recognized as not dependent upon others' will.

Happiness is satisfaction with one's entire (present and future) state. The consciousness of the fulfillment of all his wishes (for which what is moral is also considered, since insofar as it succeeds one is happy, though the motivating ground to morality cannot be derived from this). Outer **freedom** is the independence of a human being from others' power of choice so that he is permitted to act not in accordance with their but rather also in accordance with his own ends, i.e. so that he is not **permitted** to serve **merely** as a means to any end of someone else (to be able to be compelled so to do).

Antinomy of the constitution in a political and religious constitution.[a] Antinomy 1. **Thesis.** A constitution once assumed by a people must always remain the same for their progeny and thus perpetuate itself. 2) **Antithesis.** it should not perpetuate itself but instead must each time be regarded as a newly agreed union and the people as constantly **constituting**.[b] Not aristocratic or privileged perpetuation, not perpetuation of sects, not perpetuation of spiritual goods. The people is always free and the individuals are bound by its decrees. Not by rebellion.

Concerning the highest authority the constitution is either 1. **monar-** 23:342 **chy (king)** 2. **polyarchy (senate)** 3. **anarchy (ministers** who constitute no highest authority but instead mere agents). No **pantarchy** or this is instead **anarchy**. That the right of the state must proceed from the idea of the common will is beyond doubt, although whether it shall or could arise from this will is neither to assert nor to deny, though it is certain that all constitutions ought to proceed from it.

[a] *der constitution in politischer und Religionsverfassung*
[b] *constituirend*

[two paragraphs omitted, remainder of page in margins]

All civil systems (*status civilis* {civil condition}) are either autocratic or representative. The former are despotic the latter are systems of freedom and of a condition of the autonomy of the subjects (the people) that constitutes and is constituted by revolution.[a]

Monarchy polyarchy, pantocracy

Equality because each is nothing.

Monarchy aristocracy and democracy. The representative system of **democracy** is that of the **equality of society** or the **republic**, that of aristocracy is that of **inequality** since only some together represent the sovereign – of monarchy that of the equality which is the effect of inequality since one (monarch) represents all. If one thinks of a constitution in which none of these powers[b] is unlimited but instead, because one limits the other, the sovereign consists only in their connection, so the two in such a constitution must always limit the third because otherwise anarchy would erupt if all three limited each another. However the one limiting must have greater authority[c] than the legislature, for otherwise it could not limit. But the third must of course have equal authority with the others because otherwise it would be no power. Therefore the syncretic system of inequality cannot occur instead it must be antagonistic.

23:343

23:343 *Loses Blatt* F 3

[first page]

Of revenge

Punishment is an *actus* {act} of public justice hence an *actus* of those higher in the state against those beneath of inflicting an ill which accords with the wrong which he had done to another (citizen, passive or active). In itself it is always **vengeful** but it can also be connected with the intention of improving the criminal. – Only the government can punish and vendetta is prohibited. – This is to be distinguished from the *jus inculpatae tutelae* {right of self-defense} where the protection cannot be provided by the government, because here a *moderamen* {guidance} must be observed, as *in casu necessitatis* {in a case of necessity}.

Freedom

for punishment outer freedom can be suspended by arrest, and with or without using force[d] – by prison or admonishment.

[in margin:] NB. Rights are connected not merely to duties in general but rather specifically to strict duties as distinguished from remissible

---

[a] *revolutions-constituirender und constituirter Zustand*
[b] *Mächte*   [c] *Gewalt*
[d] *Gewalt*

330

(remissible[a]) which belong to ethics. The former contain the limitation of freedom through the law either of the will of humanity or of human beings:

A rule is the relation of a **concept** to everything that is contained under it (i.e. by which it is determined). Understanding is the capacity of representations under rules or of rules themselves, law is the rule in accordance with which the existence of things is determinable. – Mathematics (pure) thus contains no laws. All laws are either natural or moral laws (of nature or of freedom).

[*second page*]   23:344

What accords with right, *rectum*, is logically opposed to that which is wrong (*minus rectum, pravum* {lacking right, vicious}) just as the lawful is opposed to the unlawful, like A and non-A. Now this is the division of a still higher moral concept; what is it? An action under the moral imperative (of **obligation**) in general.

Now here must be distinguished: 1. what obligates him 2. to what is he obligated, 3. how is he obligated.

What or **who** obligates him. That is his own will regarded as universally *a priori* legislating, moral-practical reason through the categorical imperative.

If it is said I have right [on my side] (in dispute) against this or that, the object[b] is thus already assumed to be known.

However if it is said I have a right against him this means that one owes the other whatever may be due – Hence the perfection of a thing which must be known and a perfection, if also the thing is otherwise unknown and is only determined by the former perfection.

A rational being has duties if the **freedom** of his **power of choice** is limited through a law (what is law?) If it is limited by **another's power of choice** that being thus has **duties of right**; however insofar as its freedom is only limited by the inner law of practical reason of the subject itself it has duties of virtue.

A right of the other to demand something of him does not always correspond to duties towards someone, and these duties are duties of virtue. Right is the capacity to obligate another by one's power of choice.

What is the highest divided concept of obligation? The object[c] of the free power of choice in general? – that of an obligation in general. This

---

[a] *von remissiblen (erlaßlichen)*   [b] *Object*
[c] *Gegenstand* in this paragraph

object is either something (regarding which there is an obligation) or nothing (where there is none, *actio indifferens* {indifferent action}, *adiaphorum* {indifferent things}) *actus mere facultatis* {mere ability to act}

    All obligation is **relation** in accordance with laws of free beings, *necessitantis adversus necessitatum* {the obligated to the obligating} or conversely; the first are active the second are passive obligations, those where the necessitating subject must be another person are rightful, where it must be even the same person, ethical obligation. In the first case the *obligatus* {one obligated} is necessitated by another's **power of choice** in accordance with laws of freedom, in the second merely by the representation of the law. Thus the principle: "act so that your freedom" etc. is a principle of right. In contrast: "act in accordance with principles of right if conflicts with objectively necessary principles occur" is a principle of ethics – where the subject who obligates is the same person as the one obligated. The latter concerns the difference between ethical duties and duties of right in accordance with form.

23:345

    [remainder of page in margin:] **Right** and duty, **end** and duty are relations of one and the same subject though regarded as two persons, namely twice as *obligantis* {the one obligating} namely through his power of choice or through his will; the former accords with the form of freedom the latter with the material of the will which is the **end**.

    Whence have those, who have the fixed maxim to act upon their duty in accordance with laws of their own reason, greater conscientiousness in their actions than those whose duty is grounded upon *statuta* {statute}.

    Why does one oppose right to duties, already even in the division as if there were two kinds of duties? Because obligation in accordance with laws of freedom concerns merely what is *formalis* {formal} – however obligation in accordance with ends (to make these into law oneself) concerns what is *materialis* {material} in obligation.

    Whoever thus has rights and no duties must be able to do everything. The 3 categories of capacity, to persist, to make, and to connect.

23:345   *Loses Blatt* F 4. On a letter dated June 12, 1795.

    [first page]

    In the so-called conflict of principles of right with politics the issue is instead about conflict among laws of right (not about those of ethics and the principles of happiness). Woe to him who acknowledges any politics other than that which holds sacred the laws of right.

    Nor is it an issue of admonishments one directs at rulers or subjects, the most useless and to an extent the oddest thing of all. Instead how

23:346   may public right be established,[a] i.e. a system of private right through a public will and a power[b] which gives it effect.

[a] *zu Stande zu bringen*   [b] *Macht*

Of public right regarding sedition.

[*second page*]

A public law (has a sanction) presupposes a publicly declared will accompanied by a power[a] and makes all individuals into a *universitas* {whole}.

that which one does not trust himself to announce publicly as his maxim and the announcement of which would negate itself is contrary to public right.

~~politics as science is the system of laws for securing the rights and satisfaction of the people with their inner and outer condition.~~

Just as **cleverness**[b] is the skill of using human beings (free beings) as means to one's own aims; so the cleverness by which someone uses an entire free people to his own aims is known as **politics** (art of state).

That politics which uses for its purposes such means as agree with respect for human rights is moral in contrast to that which disregards the point about means (thus that of the pure politician) which is **demagogy**.

All true politics limited to the condition of conformity with the idea of public right (not to oppose it).

Public right is a totality of laws of right that admit of universal proclamation (*declaratio*) for a people. – From this follows that the true politics would have to proceed not only honorably but also openly that it may not act in accordance with maxims which one must conceal (not declare aloud) if one wants to succeed by means that do not conform to right (*aliud lingua promtum aliud pectore inclusum gerunt* {those who say one thing yet have another in their hearts}), and one must even hide doubts regarding the laws or the possibility of their execution.

One can assume this as a principle[c] of universal natural right: act in accordance with maxims which also can be valid as laws of public right.

For without agreement of your actions with public right even your private right has no reality. For your outer rights always relate to other human beings, and if there is no principle of right for both, then in cases of conflicting claims the determination of the rights of each is only possible in a law of right valid for both *a priori* i.e. in a public law of right. 23:347

Public right is the totality of public laws (i.e. such that can be declared by an empowered legislator to all those obliged by a duty). – Now should these laws be cognizable *a priori* by reason then they can proceed from nothing other than the idea of a common will ascribed to the highest legislator (to the idea thereof), except that the declared will must be ascribed to an actual person. Without this ascription the concept of right has no determinate source of execution, namely the actual connection of the will of all to a will of the whole.

[a] *Macht*   [b] *Klugheit*, usually "prudence"
[c] *Grundsatz*

Public right is that of whomever only commands and does not obey. Private right is reciprocal. Without public right there is the *status naturalis* and a mere idea of the possibility of an administration of right.

The state is a people which rules itself. The fascicles of all nerves which together constitute legislation. The *sensorium commune* {common sense} of right deriving from their agreement. 3. The *facultas locomotiva* {capacity to move} of government.

23:347 *Loses Blatt* F 17. Probably after October 1796.

[*first page*]

However the right of pardon, either the reduction or the complete stay of punishment, is harder to comprehend than penal right. In crime of one subject against another there is no such thing since that will which supremely administers public justice can neither increase nor diminish what is assigned to each by right. – However the head of state can reduce or entirely negate the judgment of the civil court concerning punishment for the offense which the head of state itself suffers from subjects (*crimen laesae majestatis* {the crime of treason}) because it can renounce its satisfaction: It may then be that the transgression involves a danger to the people. This right is the proper and sole right of majesty.

23:348   It is remarkable that one has found pardon, which is solely a result of choice, as contrary to justice as the highest holiness that one also imagines, e.g. the blood debt which lies upon a land always crying out for vengeance. – The theologians have found it so inappropriate that crimes should go unpunished that they prefer to assume that an innocent could assume them (for others) simply in order to satisfy justice or that children must atone for their parents' guilt.

The mixed state constitution is that in which the executive authority calls the people together in order to choose their representatives, hence one proceeding from the king as head of state who is not chosen but instead is head by birthright and who has the authority to establish hereditary aristocrats, between whom and the people's representatives a conflict shall occur of such proportions that the king will be empowered to give a law. This form of state is dependent on the principles of government which should of course originally arise therefrom.[a]

To commit crimes without punishment. Services going unrewarded occurs.

The right of pardon is a right to stay punishments. Now this cannot be by staying the punishment resulting from wrong which subjects have

---

[a] The referent for *daraus* is unclear.

done to each other, for among the people the impunity of crime (*impunitas criminis*) is the highest wrong which can befall a people. Therefore it can only pertain to a crime of a subject against the head of state (*crimen laesae majestatis*) which the latter can excuse because and insofar as it concerns only himself. However if it is also dangerous for the people, it cannot to that extent be unpunished. This is the sole proper right of majesty: to exercise by executive authority an act that can be wrong.

Loses Blatt F 18   23:348
    [*second page*]
    Jus sociale {social right} constitutes no particular right even less a particular rightful *status* {status} since there can also be *societas pactitia* {societies based on contract} in *status naturalis* {the state of nature}.
    That society which is necessary due to a physical *factum* {deed} is not   23:349
pactitia {contractual} even though a *pactum* is thus *necessitas* {necessitated}, but instead *societas naturalis*. Likewise with marital society, which makes dutiful a *societas perpetua maris et foeminae* {perpetual society of male and female}.
    Because the time in which children naturally become free can be determined neither solely by the parents' power of choice, by which they want to rid themselves of a burden, nor by children, who want to obtain leisure, hence children must serve as early and as long as they can.

    Doctrine of Duties. 1. as mere doctrine of law without seeking incentives in the law 2. As simultaneously incentives of action – the doctrine of right can be represented as contained under ethics, namely ethics applied to it, nevertheless the doctrine of right does not require this. It concerns the laws that necessitate others by one's mere power of choice in accordance with universal laws of freedom. Therefore it is a doctrine of the equality of effect and counter-effect in accordance with laws of freedom.
    [*several paragraphs omitted*]

                2) Of public right (as distinguished from private right)   23:351

    1. Of the outer condition lacking right
    2. Of the outer rightful condition or of public right
        a. Of public human right within a people.
            Civil right.
        b. Of the public right of peoples as opposed to their condition
            lacking right.

    On the basis of the postulated original universal consent of the people to a certain chosen constitution,[a] and although not all actually agree in this way, the conventional contract[b] presupposes the will of all in that the

---

[a] *Constitution* in this paragraph   [b] *conventionelle Contract*

majority is to decide, and indeed the majority of those who are eligible electors who also are determined *a priori* as **independent members** of the commonwealth. Any extant constitution, even if it is not certified (documented[a]), must be regarded as having resulted from a convention even if it is suspected that it was established by force, and all previous property must be regarded as if it rested upon rightful acquisition and moreover as valid, excepting rights to other persons as subjugated by birth. However this conventional constitution can and should indeed be changed but not by rebellion.

Of crimes of state – the regent can commit this if he acts as the *souverain*; however he is only responsible to the *souverain*, not to the people.

The universal will of the people is not the will of all about a given case but rather that which merely connects these various wills, i.e. the common will **which decides for all** thus the mere idea of civil unity. – If the citizens themselves could be punished merely because they obligate themselves to be punished, then one would still have to impose upon them a punishment if they, contrary to their obligation, want to withdraw themselves from punishment.

23:352   What one inflicts upon another in a crime in which the other does not bind his will with that of the other (e.g. in fraud) he does to everyone, i.e. he the murderer kills everyone so far as he can, hence also himself. However the law is given through the common will and indeed as necessary.

[*next two paragraphs in margin:*] Every constitution[b] must be republican to be just. However the kind of government can be monarchic, aristocratic, democratic, i.e. the executive authority can be organized in various ways under the legislative. – The regent must not be able to do wrong. Thus he cannot involve himself in private decisions. It is against his majesty.

NB. Of civil, religious, and scholarly associations.[c] (the civil servant is not in post if he is removed, the scholar enters his association). Of the connection of the latter two and the related difficulty. No title envy on the part of scholars. Organization of the scholarly association about which kings cannot concern themselves.

[*fourth page*]
Punishment is an ill which someone suffers, but not because he has made himself obligated to suffer it, i.e. as a fulfillment of his duty, since otherwise punishment would be a rightful deed of the criminal in which

---

[a] *documentirt*　　　　　　　　　　[b] *Verfassung*
[c] *Gemein-Wesen*

actus he must endure an ill as a fulfillment of his duty, instead because he committed another act of transgressing his obligation and in this moment of committing the deed the punishment is regarded as the common will coming forth through counter-effect.

All states are entitled to necessitate all other neighboring states to enter with it into a league of nations which is of course not a *pactum societatis civilis* {contract of civil society}, i.e. to federate itself with them, not to concern itself with their internal affairs but rather only to have peace, and indeed to have it for the same reason which authorizes them to demand that savages unify themselves with them into a civil society because otherwise no one's right and property is secured. The reason why this cosmopolitan federation may not itself consider legislation and administration of justice for the members of this cosmopolitan society, and hence no cosmopolitan republic[a] may be established, is because mere outer freedom alone is the object[b] which they are justified in demanding, hence only the formal condition of all rights within a civil whole, although the matter of the power of choice, property, and what 23:353 belongs to it should also be attended to.

Each human being has a right to be in peace, and therefore a right to have others who will not leave us in peace to us to enter with us into a condition where we live with each other in peace, or to distance themselves from us.

Right or to have a right

The former means merely the authorization to act externally even without an outer object[c] being mine or yours, the latter means the possession of something outer namely the intellectual connection with my power of choice by which I preclude something outer from belonging to anyone, e.g. I do right if I make use of a thing which belongs to no one; but I have a right regarding the same if even prior to the possession of what is outer I am authorized to restrain others from it. In the first case both of them have exactly the same right and merely the priority in time makes the difference, in the second case the one excludes the other in accordance with time.

Loses Blatt E 16 [The first three pages of LB E 16 are included in the "contin- 23:241 *uous signed draft" within the section on Private Right. This final page of the final sheet of that continuous draft abruptly turns from the topic of property to the death penalty, a matter of Public Right. After this discussion Kant wrote a few paragraphs about morality, which are omitted.]*

[a] *dieser Weltbürgerlichen Societät . . . keine Cosmopolitische republik*
[b] *Object*　　　　　　　　　　　　　　[c] *Gegenstand*

[fourth page]

N.B. Of the death penalty. Each member of the commonwealth does not actually say, "I will that every murderer dies" (hence also myself in such a case) but rather "I consider it just that this happens." For if he said "I allow others to kill me in such a case," then without his permission it must be unjust, and this he cannot give. Furthermore it is then no law because law imposes punishment as necessary. If instead he said "I will and command that in such a case others kill me or all others" then he says more than **he** has in his authority. – Therefore it must already

23:242   be recognized in advance as right that the murderer suffers death prior to his agreeing. Hence this is hereby unnecessary especially since in accordance with reason the *publicum* can be given no other appropriate satisfaction.

It is absurd to say that one wills to be killed if one becomes a murderer. For then either one knows oneself as someone who could indeed become a murderer, in which case his assurance is untrue, or if one knows oneself to be otherwise then the case to which one commits oneself is impossible.

23:353   *Loses Blatt* E 23, after May 22, 1796.

[first page, in upper margin:] When the laws alone govern.

* *

Transition from doctrine of right to ethics.

Each transition from one order of things into another (μεταβασις εἰς αλλο γενος {change to another kind[15]}), thus also that from one science such as the doctrine of right to ethics, contains a phase at the instant, which is not a jump, an instant in which the science belongs neither to the one nor to the other of the two but instead is one whose step has each foot standing on its particular ground distinct from another (*styx interfusa coercet* {Styx imprisons with his circles[16]}) and is only superseded if the other foot stands fast.

The firmly established peace pertaining to expanded relations[a]

23:354   among human beings is the idea through which alone the transition from duties of right to duties of virtue is made possible, since if the laws outwardly secure freedom, those maxims can come to life to also govern oneself internally in accordance with laws, and conversely these maxims can in turn facilitate the influence of lawful coercion through their dispositions, so that peaceful behavior under public laws and peaceable dispositions (also to obviate the inner war between principles[b] and inclinations), hence legality and morality within the concept of freedom, coincide with the fulcrum supporting the transition from the doctrine of right to the doctrine of virtue.

However to achieve this peace secured by public laws (*status justificus* {condition providing justice}) does not first involve the transition from

[a] *Verkehr*   [b] *Grundsätzen*

the duties of virtue to the duties of right, but rather conversely (*si vis pacem, para bellum* {if you wish for peace, prepare for war}): to advance from the laws of right to the laws of virtue, hence not as meddlesome (know it all) clever ones[a] who would instruct monarchs in worldly wisdom (to which belongs the adage: that it would only be good for peoples if either monarchs philosophized or philosophers were monarchs).

[*third page*]

The virtue of the highest commander as such is justice. Beneficence can only be exercised at the expense of subjects. Of the idea of a justice that can be personified. A blood-guilt lies upon a country. In any event it must be removed by innocent successors etc.

Monarchs are, however, always in danger of using their supreme power to prosecute wars where they themselves are judges in their own case regarding whether their rights are infringed upon, and hence to destroy the world; this is something which republicanism does not do, instead it must involve the consent of the people.

IV. DRAFTS OF THE APPENDIX OF EXPLANATORY REMARKS

Loses Blatt F 22   23:357

[*first page*]

That there can be hereditary monarchs and indeed even in a good government is shown by experience – that there could be countless hereditary nobles and estates is more difficult. However a hereditary professorship cannot be instituted. Neither can there be perpetual religious privileges and rights. In all actions by which one human being makes use of another he also assumes duties without which he would not have the authorization.

The human reproductive capacity is the human capacity to bring forth a person into the world together with a human being of the opposite sex. The means for this, or the act by which this effect can occur, is the carnal union of the pair. Now a person is a being towards whom all other human beings have duties. Therefore this union (called begetting) is an action by which the person who allows this assumes commitment to possible duties. However these would be duties towards a child which could be generated from it and to whose sustenance both immediately obligate themselves in case this effect follows. And even if the pair of them may be unable to procreate due to the age or the fragility of one party, nevertheless the universal concept of personality suffices for a law which is grounded merely upon the idea of both sexes in accordance

---

[a] *vorwitzige (naseweise) Klüglinge*

with their **natural end** which is universal, and to agree with which (not to contest it) is a universal law.

This corresponds completely with my previous method of proof that regarding the carnal enjoyment of a person, the treatment of the same person as a thing would thus be a dishonor to humanity since the contract would not include any condition limiting it to duty, hence the personality of both parties would be negated.

23:358

The *jus instar realis personale* {personal right in the form of a real right} within the household proves the necessity of introducing it into the doctrine of right, also regarding the duty of servants not to be bound merely to determinate household services but rather also to protection against all evil on the part of the head of the household and children hence something belonging to the dominion of what is his. A coachman and footman belong solely to the servants in any event only outside the house.

[*second page*]

Of the possibility of acquiring a person distinct from me in accordance with laws of freedom, i.e. of a right to persons akin to a right to a thing.[a] This belongs to the household and the acquisition can hereby be none other than one person through the other reciprocally, so that one becomes the other's property and reciprocally. *quasi contractus: Do ut des* {quasi-contractually: I give that you may give} within the sexual community.

To give his body to another for the immediate satisfaction of his desire for the other, i.e. for enjoyment, is on the part of him who gives himself a violation of the **humanity** (of personality, i.e. of imputability) in him, and indeed in point of right in general. He who so gives himself makes himself into a thing which can be regarded as usable and even consumable[b] (*res fungibilis* {fungible thing}), as in the case of sexual union through which one party, through depletion of vitality, as well as the other, through pregnancy and unfortunate delivery, can be subject to death. Such an enjoyment is thus one and utterly the same with cannibalism in accordance with the **spirit** of the proscriptive law, whether he condemns another human being to death with his mouth or with other bodily members, whether intentionally or by concurring contingent causes, and no human being can give himself to another for this purpose for any price without by such a contract renouncing his personality and thus annihilating its validity. That this is a question of right (not one of ethics) requires no particular explication. Since an outer legisla-

23:359

tion for all outer mine and yours is possible, and the limitation of outer freedom to the condition of the agreement with everyone's freedom here grounds a concept of duty in accordance with outer laws by which shall

[a] *dem auf dingliche Art persönlichen Recht*   [b] *brauchbar und verbrauchbar*

be established whether the contract of sexual union grounds a right in things[a] or a merely personal right or both united in one and the same act. However the first as such contradicts itself since a human being is not a thing. The second is here not the case.

[*in margin:*] Someone can be wronged by another through a deed despite having given his consent to it. For since he should not have allowed the other to do this toward him, the **humanity** in his person would be wronged (because he has acted against a law that contains unconditioned universality). Humanity in one's person is the personality that ought not to be used merely as a thing, above all not enjoyed, which would be a *laesio enormis* {monstrous wrong}. From this arises the shame of humanity, unworthy *turpitudo naturalium* {natural shame}. A human being shames himself in his animality in begetting, he hides his *actus*, and can be an honorable human being only through a *pactum* {contract} of coalition in a moral person who has the same duties and rights reciprocally. Marriage is reciprocal use of the sexual organs.

* *
*

NOTES IN RESPONSE TO BOUTERWEK'S REVIEW OF THE DOCTRINE OF RIGHT

Selected passages from the review are quoted or summarized below prior to Kant's responses. Most of the review consists of a summary of the *Doctrine of Right*. Bouterwek presented his own objections to Kant's positions in parentheses to set them apart from the summary. Page references to the *Doctrine of Right* in Bouterwek's review have been converted to the pagination of *Kants gesammelte Schriften*.

[Bouterwek on equity:] *There are only two cases (6:234) that call for juridical decisions for which no such decision can be found. They ground equivocal right. Of these the first is that of **equity**. Whoever demands something on grounds of equity, e.g. because he did more than others within a Mascopey[17] in which all are to benefit equally, bases himself not merely upon the moral obligation of the others but rather upon a right, except that he lacks the necessary conditions on which a judge can base his judgment. (But how, if the member of the Mascopey can, e.g., reckon precisely at least in cash how much has been added?)* 20:447

[Kant:] this is because he demands it upon his strict right. 20:448

---

[a] *Sachenrecht*

[Bouterwek on wrong:] *Something is **rightfully mine** with which I am so*   20:44*connected that the use that another makes of it without my consent would wrong me. (But what is "**wrong**"? Doesn't the concept of juridical wrong presuppose the concept of mine and yours?)*

20:449   [Kant:] No; the formal principle of action, to proceed in accord with the law of freedom, precedes (*forma dat esse rei* {the form gives being to
20:450   the thing}) and belongs to the legislating **will**. What is mine and yours is the matter, the object[a] of the **power of choice**, so far as I have the object in my control, to use it without contradicting the law of freedom in outer relation (to others).

20:448   [Bouterwek on the right to a person akin to a right to a thing:] *Now follows (6:259 ff) the division of right into rights in things,[b] personal rights and – yet a third? Our jurists and philosophers will be surprised by this, but Mr. Kant contends there is actually a third, namely a **personal** right **as a thing**.[c] What this is, or is supposed to be, will surprise many even more than the new idea itself.*

[Bouterwek summarizes Kant's account of the right to a thing and contract right before returning to the third type of property right.]

20:449   **Of the right to a person akin to a right to a thing**[d] *(6:276 ff). This then is the new phenomenon in the juridical heavens. Here Mr. Kant has in mind what he calls the category of reciprocity. Here we find, completely unexpectedly, **marriage right, parental right**, and **household right**. (Relations of the head of household to his servants.) The husband acquires a wife, the pair acquire children, and the family (including the children?) acquire servants. This properly acquired right is not merely a personal right; since the husband can claim his wife who has fled as his, the father his child, the master his servant. (Is it possible that a first-rate thinker does not see the circularity of this argumentation? **If** it is true that the husband can to an extent claim his wife, etc., then the relation between the married couple, etc. is certainly more than personal. Now the*
20:450   *greater part of the juridical world, and among others also this reviewer, deny the hypothetical premise, and hence also the Kantian conclusion.) In the case of sexual relations one party gives itself to the other for enjoyment of the **thing**. (The reviewer would suppose, for reciprocal performance of service. The moral self can never become a thing nor ever be enjoyed. But corporeal performances of service, of whatever kind, belong to personal right.) Only monogamy is marriage in accord with right because neither can possess the other as thing except insofar as he would give himself to the other as thing. (But how so, if neither*

[a] *Object*   [b] *Sachenrecht*
[c] *ein persönlich dingliches Recht*
[d] *Von dem auf persönliche Art dinglichen Rechte*

party claims more than a performance of personal service? If a porter allows me to climb upon his shoulders so that I can climb over a wall (the wall of need), has the bearer thus become a thing?) For this reason, according also to natural law, left-handed marriage[18] *or concubinage is no true marriage. (Indeed not, according to Kantian ideas.) Hence even marriage prior to marital cohabitation is not to be regarded as consumated. Hence also by natural law impotence prior to marriage annuls the marriage contract, though not impotence consequent to marital cohabitation. (Hence just as the honorable Jus canonicum {canon law} will have it.) In order not to be too longwinded we pass over how on the basis of this theory parental right and the right of the head of the household are developed, which in any event are sensible enough. –*

[Kant's notes on this issue constitute the remainder of this draft:]   20:450

A right to a person akin to a right to a thing would be the right to have another person as one's own. Indeed not as her **proprietor**;[a] for that contradicts her personality (I cannot dispose of her possessions, I cannot lend, give or misuse her). Moreover I acquire another person neither by unilateral taking into possession (*facto* {by a deed}) since he is no thing nor by mere contract; for the other party (*pacto* {by contract}) cannot accept this offer, because it would be an impermissible contract (*pactum* 20:451 *turpe*) to give oneself as a thing into another's possession. Therefore if a human being is to be or to become one's own of another human being then this acquisition can occur only as the **lawful consequence** (*lege* {by law}) of the use which one makes of another's person, not merely of her powers (which would belong to personal right) since as *possessor* of this person I may dispose over her condition.

Of course the teacher of right[b] at least cannot simply dismiss the question whether among the relations of human beings in accordance with concepts of right, aside from rights in things and personal rights, a right to a person akin to a right to things could be thought, because otherwise the division (as trichotomy) within the system of concepts of right would 20:452 not be complete, hence he must beforehand make this third kind of right representable, at least problematically, before he rejects such a right as untenable. – Thus it has always been an error in the logical completeness of division that no one has ever designated the place for the concept of a personal right akin to a right to a thing in order thus at least to note that this concept falls aside as untenable. – Even were it also to be merely a falling star in the juridical heavens, yet it nonetheless would regularly settle in this position even though upon more attentive observation it always disappears; such a phenomenon which appears of its own accord could not be passed over in silence.

[a] *Eigentümer*   [b] *der Rechtslehrer*

20:453 Whether the concept of a right to have another person as one's own though indeed not as proprietor (able to loan, give, sell or destroy) but as possessor, – this concept requires a deduction and proof of its objective reality.*

[*Kant's footnote*] *The article of the Catechism: Thou shall not covet thy neighbor's **wife, child, bondsman** (maid) or anything which is his, is the formula of a personal right akin to a right to a thing (namely equally as house and home) and here the human being, although a person, is nevertheless at the same time counted among the things (house and home) belonging to the head of the household.

That the concept of a personal right akin to a right to a thing is not to be simply rejected out of hand but is rather first to be displayed within the doctrine of right as problematic in order to examine its possibility; in addition whether it were subsequently to be found dispensable lies in the logical apparatus of division according to synthetic principles, which in metaphysical tasks is not satisfied by dichotomy but rather requires a three-fold relation of concepts in accordance with the order of categories. – Admittedly the right to a thing and the right to a specific person exhaust all rightful objects,[a] although not (and this is the point at issue) all forms of right, specifically because a right against a person according 20:454 to her analogy with a thing can be thought (for conversely a right to a thing akin to a right regarding a person[b] cannot be thought).

Whether this new appearance in the juridical heavens be a new star or merely a falling star is now to be determined.

A right to a person akin to a right to a thing would be explained once and for all by the rightful possession of a person outside me; not that I am merely the holder[c] of another person but rather that I have her as mine, i.e. I am authorized to demand of her not only services as from a person but to bring her immediately and actively under my control, and to use her as a means to some of my ends, although not to any arbitrary end of mine (since then I would be the proprietor of a person which is a contradiction). However the subject who subjects himself to me for my immediate use thereby makes himself into a thing in that he becomes someone else's own.

[*inserted later:*] This right is a right grounded upon a person's consent to use her as a thing.*

[*Kant's footnote*] * The tenth commandment of the catechism (after enumerating the duties regarding rights to things and rights to persons) further indicates the right which issues from their unification: Thou shalt not covet thy neighbor's wife, child and bondsman (maid), and assigns these persons to that which is **his** and those of whom he can

---

[a] *Gegenstände*
[b] *gegen eine Sache gleich als einer Person*
[c] *Inhaber*

put himself into corporeal possession (according to substance), hence directly as things, in accordance with principles of right. – In this connection it may be remarked that the word **mine** used adjectivally does not have the significance which is thought of here namely of **what is mine**. If I say my father it is not thus understood that he would belong to what is mine, however well he may say this about his son so long as the latter is still a child. Hence **Luther** made the point in his translation of the bible with the expression "Father **of us**" (since in regard to God all human beings can be regarded as children) better than others with their "our Father"[a] –

The question is whether a human being could be **someone's** own: so that one can say that he is in merely rightful (intelligible) possession of the former, who belongs to his holdings be it the manipulation of it 20:455 (arbitrary alteration of his condition) or merely usufruct (*jus utendi fruendi* {the right to enjoy use}) though not as its **proprietor** (*jus disponendi* {the right to dispose} to alienate or intentionally to destroy him) since for a **person** as such to be the property of another is a contradiction. – Now if such a right of external mine and yours is **possibly** found, indeed due to physical relations among human beings such a title would have **necessarily** been found, within a complete system of right, then the concept of a **right to a person akin to a right to a thing** would be entered in the constellation of the juridical heavens no matter how gladly it would be counted by the previous system among the falling stars.*

[Kant's footnote,] *Conversely there is no right to a thing akin to 20:455 a right to a person,[b] i.e. no right regarding a thing equal to one to a person, since this contains a contradiction because there can be no duties towards things.

A right to a person akin to a right to a thing would be the authorization stemming from consent by another person to make use of her as a thing for usufruct (*jus utendi fruendi persona alteri* {the right to enjoy use of another person}) and thus to possess her as his own (as belonging to his goods, *bona*), though without being her **proprietor** since that (*jus disponendi de persona* {the right to dispose of a person}) is in contradiction with personality (one human being cannot lend, alienate, or use up another human being). – One can easily see that this rightful relation cannot be turned around to allow a right to a thing akin to a right to a person. For towards a thing there is no obligation like that towards a person. Personality is the highest condition of all rightful relation.

[a] *u.V.*, reading: *unser Vater* for "our Father." Earlier in the sentence is the normal German order in the prayer, *Vater unser*.
[b] *kein auf persönliche Art dingliches Recht*

But suppose more broadly that such a right were rejected as entirely inadmissible; nevertheless in a system of right the place for that concept cannot remain undesignated because here the division is not **logical** (since I abstract from the matter of knowledge and so divide analytically into *a* and non-*a*) and hence a dichotomy, but rather **metaphysical** and as a real relation synthetically and hence a trichotomy is required, and so that the division into "as to a thing"[a] and "as not to a thing" (the personal) is not yet sufficient; rather both must still be at least represented as united in a third relational concept (whether it be to accept or to reject it).

20:456

So much for what concerns the method of the division of right in general and now to determine whether the new phenomenon in the juridical heavens is a *stella mirabilis* {miraculous star} or a shooting star.

That a human being would count as another human being's **own**,[b,*] consequently, although a person, still could belong to another's goods and possessions and hence to whose use is bound an authorization (though indeed not use up because this possessor of a human being cannot indeed be his proprietor) in accordance with laws of freedom, is at first glance a paradoxical and repellent concept. – **For** a human being, who of course is a person and not a thing, would give his neighbor a right to use him **as a thing** which must be called **a right to a person akin to a right to a thing**, namely first of all a personal right because the **right** to use another human being [rests upon] the other's lawful consent (which at least must be ascribed to him as following from the nature of the case), second of course also concerning the **kind** of use the authorization by consent to allow another to use oneself as if one were a thing, which consists in the person who allows herself to be known to belong to what is another's own, and can be brought into the other's **corporeal possession**, i.e. into holding.[c]

20:457

20:456

[Kant's footnote] *Mine and yours taken **adjectivally**, e.g. **my** father **my** omission and the like, means rather less than what is **mine** understood **substantively**, which represents the object of possession itself whereas instead the former expression means only the relation of one or another object to the subject who represents it.

23:457

Now I say no one could have something outer (hence also not another person) as his own if he were not entitled to hold it, and hence would also have a right to the person as a thing whom he counts among what is his own, and conversely no one can through a contract consider himself to give his person over to another's holding for use.

[a] *Dingliche* [b] *dem Seinen*
[c] *Inhabung*

That someone could be another's own through holding according to an *a priori* principle yet without being property where the human being has the other in his possession just like a thing.

How can a human being become someone else's own? Not by obligation insofar as he is a person since then he belongs simply to himself, but rather insofar as another holds him, i.e. insofar as he is in the corporeal (bodily) possession of the other as a thing in accordance with the right of use of a thing, though a right by which the other makes use of him (as a person) is limited to the condition of personal right (of obligation).

Here is a relation of holding in community and indeed as an unequal society (whose members are subordinated to (not coordinated with) one another) since one belongs to another, the wife to the man, the child thereby produced to the parents, and servants to the household for their mutual preservation. – The bond (*copula*) in all of these relations is bodily   20:458 (*corporalis*), though in the first carnal (*copula carnalis*) for progeneration of the members of the household, in the second the bond between parent and child, etc.

Therefore it is necessary for the completeness of the rational system of all rights to ground a particular title of right beyond that of rights to things and personal rights: namely that of mine and yours in the authorization to be the holder of another person. The authorization of the use of another person (whether it is her substance or powers) can either presuppose possession as its condition or derive possession from it. In the latter case mine and yours is merely a personal right (*jus ad rem* {right to the thing}). The person does not become mine this way, rather she is merely necessitated to do something for me which through this deed becomes mine. However if I must previously become the possessor of a person before I can demand performances of her, if my holding without prior wrong to the other party is an authorization, then formally this right is a right in a thing regardless of whether materially, namely concerning the performance itself, it is merely personal as a right to a person akin to a right to a thing. – If, e.g., I offer myself as hostage (to secure the rights of another) this occurs according to a right to a person akin to a right to a thing which however is always grounded on a prior contract.

The right to a person akin to a right to a thing is the right of one human being to have as his own another honorable human being; not indeed as proprietor, since no honorable human being of his own accord can be that, also not a dishonorable human being, i.e. one who has forfeited his personality such as a criminal in chains. For if he can count this latter kind of corporeal being among what is his, then he is in pos-   20:459 session of the latter **as a thing** and the sign of this possession is **holding,**

347

namely that he is authorized if that man has fled or is kidnapped from him to bring that man back under his control, not merely to bind him through intelligible possession to fulfill what he has promised (which would be a personal right), but rather he can keep him in his custody unilaterally and make a use of him as a passive subject which is a right as to a thing[a] – since it is however a right against a person not to a thing[b] (*jus ad rem* {right to a thing} not *jus in re* {right in a thing}) – thus it can be called a right to a person akin to a right to a thing.

The connection of a human being with an object[c] of the power of choice regarding its use can be called **possession**. If it is an outer and corporeal object, then the possession is physical, i.e. holding, and the holding of another human being is bodily possession, (otherwise this possession is merely his right to the promise given him by another), an intelligible possession which also can be counted among one's goods.

If holding an outer person regarding his use is possible, then a right to a person akin to a right to a thing is also possible; since I can thus not only subject another's powers to coercible **performances** in accordance with personal right but subject him as a passive instrument of my will for the use of his person and treat him as my own, which treatment has the same formal conditions as the right to a thing although according to its matter, i.e. the object, it still constitutes a personal right. According to personal right [*breaks off*]

That teachers of right[d] can present as complete the division of rights into those to a thing (against any holder of a thing) and the **personal** 20:460 (against a particular person) insofar as they have proceeded just like logicians who abstract from all content of knowledge and provide the mere form of thought, and they have not been bothered because from a merely logical point of view all division is analytic and is thus always only dichotomy (right is to a thing or not to a thing, the latter, then, leaves only a personal right). – However insofar as he as metaphysician shall connect his division also to **objects** of right which are thinkable *a priori*, an attempt must at least be made to grasp them synthetically in accord with the order of the categories under the same function and as a trichotomy, which in addition to right to a thing and personal right also provides a right to a person akin to a right to a thing* (even if subsequently this should drop out as inadmissible) which cannot be utterly passed over in silence; instead at least a place must remain open for it as a problematic concept which one can fill out or, if it cannot be worked out, condemn.

---

[a] *ein dingliches Recht*   [b] *auf eine Sache*
[c] *Gegenstand* in this and the following paragraphs
[d] *Rechtslehrer*

[Kant's footnote] *The reversal of the order in this conditioned concept, e.g. to think of a right to a thing akin to a personal right, would be a contradiction.

Now whether that concept as a new **phenomenon in the juridical heavens** be a *stella mirabilis* (a newly appearing star that gradually disappears but promises to return in the same place) or merely a **falling star** shall be examined here.

"The right to a person akin to a right to a thing is the right of one human being to have as his own another human person." I say deliberately a **person**; since against someone who has forfeited his freedom (hence his personality) through crime (against slaves) an actual right to a thing can obtain not merely as a formally analogous right. What is here understood as his own is thus not that kind of property which a   20:461
human being can never have in his own person (to alienate himself to others or to destroy himself). – The above-named right is the right of possession, i.e. that connection of the subject with an object[a] by which his use of it becomes possible. – Now the possession of an outer thing can be either an intelligible (merely rightful) possession of a thing such as promise made, or a sensible possession (in space and time). The latter is **holding**. – The proper holding which one person has of another and the authorization to bring him back into his control by force if the other absconds, is the sole though sufficient sign that the latter is the former's own.

According to the above explanation of the concept of a right to a person akin to a right to a thing there can only be the question of the objective reality of this concept, i.e. whether and how it is possible that one human being has another human being (without prejudice to his personality) as his own, hence also whether and how he could acquire another human being (like a thing) in accordance with laws of freedom.

Possession is either **virtual** or corporeal (**bodily**), the community and the union is fleshly (*copula carnalis*). How is the kind of union possible in which one gives oneself to another in enjoyment. How is a person thereby acquired.

It is a personal right by contract (*jus ad rem* {right to a thing}) but how can a right in a thing against that human being (*jus in re* {right in a thing}) thereby result.

The first case of the acquisition of a person like a thing is the marriage contract.

The use which a husband makes of the sexual organs of a wife[b] for   20:462
satisfying his desire is the use of a human being by another person like

---

[a] *Gegenstand*   [b] *Mann . . . Weibes*

a thing (physical use), and if there is a right so to do then it is a right in a thing (*jus in re*), yet this right, because this use rests upon a contract of mutual consent, is at the same time a personal right (*jus ad rem*) owing to the role of personality; both kinds of right together, however, would result in a right to a person akin to a right to a thing. – The pleasure immediately associated with this commingling as motive for the use of the person is called **enjoyment** of her, which can always be called cannibalistic, even though it does not occur by mouth and teeth, whether or not the enjoying party is indifferent to any unfortunate result of this fleshly co-occupation (called commingling). – However, since this should not be indifferent to him, even with just the mere possibility that this could well be the consequence, it thus must be that sexual commingling, as an act of connecting the fate of the one party with that of the other (*copula carnalis* {bodily coupling}) is thought at the same time as the ground of a lawful connection like that among persons who mutually obligate each other (*copula legalis* {legal coupling}). Now this union is marriage.

This use (commingling with a person of the opposite sex) can be called **enjoyment** of this other person if he has immediate pleasure, not merely pleasure derived from the intended consequences, and can always be called cannibalistic, because that simply does not require that the other party also immediately finds pleasure in it, even though it does not occur directly by mouth and teeth, since here the object is handled as consumable (*res fungibilis* {fungible thing}) namely it is injected with impure juices or also (if it is the female party) by becoming pregnant [*breaks off*]

The right to a person akin to a right to a thing is the right to have another human person as one's own; hence not merely another human being (since he could have forfeited his personality by crime) but rather a human being who also has his rights, since then a human being who belongs to the corporeal possessions of another human being, i.e. to be held by the latter as a thing, hence akin to a thing, can have a duty.

To acquire this kind of right and an act in this manner would be impossible and a self-contradiction (because no human being can give herself in a rightful manner over to another's power of choice as a thing to allow her body to be used by the other according to his desires[a]) so that the contract with the passive person would have to be regarded as shameful (*pactum turpe* {an immoral contract}), since a human being would thereby humiliate herself before humanity if this contract were not

20:463

---

[a] "her" and "his" both refer back to the masculine *der Mensch* (rendered as the gender neutral "human being"). Since Kant considers homosexuality wrong, the translation using two genders better captures Kant's meaning.

connected to a prior one by which no human being can dismember herself (to leave a member to another's corporeal possession while retaining of proprietorship over the others) – whereby I say that the human being who gives himself over to another like a thing to be acquired does so only under the condition that this other is to be acquired reciprocally, and within this bodily community to be one moral person (as if having only one body), whereby the personality which would have been infringed upon by the unilateral act (as *jus in re*), is reconstituted by the reciprocal act (*jus ad rem*), and humanity in its integrity is maintained (in conformity with the concept of right).

That in light of the authorization of two persons of both sexes to commingle carnally, each of them, though especially the female party in the condition of nascent culture, would unavoidably feel shy about the considerable breach against the dignity of humanity which may be called shame, and hence something moral which even in marriage still demands seclusion, is sufficient proof that by this giving of his body to use as a thing the human being always does something which must shame him, because it is actually in itself beneath the dignity of humanity, though due to natural need and the propagation of the species it is not left to a choice by reason but instead it is entrusted to the animal instinct to become a permissive law.

20:464

Now if the manner of use which a human being makes of another's sexual organs **immediately for his pleasure** (not for other ends) is called enjoyment, then that is exactly the expression proper to the action and to the object[a] itself. Whoever would think of cannibalistic meals suited to gullet and gut in connection with the not uncommon though vulgar phrase "wanting to devour someone for love" (whereby the kiss is a kind of attempt so to do), sees that it is enough that the human being is authorized to serve another not according to her personality as a means to his aim but rather like a thing to directly serve his lust only if she subjects herself to the conditions under which, because she gives herself to another person as that person's own she of course reciprocally acquires that person and thereby also herself within the corporeal community, which is marriage.

That the marriage contract is elective and not necessitated by the presupposition of mutual cohabitation, i.e. that if two persons of the opposite sex will to enjoy each other carnally it may occur only through marriage, is contained in the foregoing. – But that and how by concluding such a contract one could acquire not merely a personal right to mutual dutiful performances (*mutuum adiutorium* {mutual assistance}) but rather a right to a person akin to a right to a thing, and the treatment of one party by the other of the relation of one person not merely towards

[a] *Gegenstand*

another person but also analogous to a right to a thing, must still be proven.

One party relates himself to the other party as one person to a not merely **usable** object[a] (means to his ends), but rather also as a **consumable** corporeal **thing** (*res fungibilis*) for the very reason that it is a bodily and not merely intelligible possession, as would be one in which a promise made to him is performed by providing something which falls entirely within personal right. – Since one party can demand from the other carnal cohabitation which contains an action whereby on the one hand one party's powers are exhausted by the other and on the other hand also the female half of this human body is by impregnation subject to birth pangs and even death and a person is thereby consumed, which exhibits a relation towards her akin to one towards a thing. The bilateral help they are to provide one another does not necessarily even belong to the establishment of a marriage. For one party can be raised above all remaining household burdens and can make use of others for this purpose, as is often the case for the wife if the husband is rich enough; this party together with the husband only enjoys the situation and is not to be troubled to assist with matters of domestic well-being.

20:465

The first kind of acquisition of a person was one in which a person who already existed yet now is brought into another's possession and so is made into what is his own. Now the second is that by which through a couple's physical act one human being brings forth another human being, who is made by these sources of this person's existence to belong to what is the couple's own. – This act of creation simultaneously introduces the obligation of the creators to preserve the child's life (*infantem tollere* {to raise the child}) hence also to support the successful continuation of his existence so long as the child cannot yet do so. This acquisition need not be judged as the creators' profit (*lucrum*): it may be that the child is a very unwelcome guest, so that the parents make no genuine acquisition, yet nevertheless the child belongs to what is the parents' own, and thus it is a duty towards a rational creature to preserve its existence and make it happy. Hence here again is a personal right akin to a right to a thing which parents have in a child they have produced, and whom they acquire in light of their duty. – What is odd about this is that here I have a right against a person like that in a thing.

20:466

Whether, as belonging to the father, a child could be circumcised, with this one act carried on his body, like a slave of his people. Whether he can allow this to be done to himself. The age of miracles (the Abrahamic), an immediate divine government, is not here at issue for they have ceased.

[a] *Gegenstand*

[*Two versions of the final two paragraphs are provided in the Academy edition. Both are included here. They are identical for the first few lines and then diverge. Version one:*] The third manner in which to have another person as one's own, i.e. akin to a thing, within the household is that of domestic service (*famulatus* {servants}).[a] Originally in accordance with what is naturally right,[a] there are those who remain as members of the household for their maintenance, even after attaining the age of majority, until they are released by the father of the house, and who prior to their release (*emancipatio*) belong to what is the head of the house's own according to a personal right akin to a right to a thing. Akin to a right to a thing because like household animals he feeds and protects them and hence 20:467 must be in possession of them as things, yet also according to personal right because clearly this obligation arises without requiring any particular contract. Upon reaching majority, however, it can be revoked by both parties as free human beings, and one who previously belonged to the house becomes his own master (*sui juris*) in accordance with natural law (*lege*) upon cessation of the cause of the obligations, just as before he was in another's possession. [*breaks off*]

The word **servant**, used for domestic service[b] (*famulatus domestica*), is not well suited to the concept of household **society** nor to the rights of its members toward each other: For society can only be thought among **equals** and the expression *societas inaequalis* contains a contradiction; while a **servant** is related to a master[c] as a relation of the head to the subordinates over whom he has control (*superioris et inferioris*): Master and servant constitute no society in connection with the household and such a relation is also not natural but instead requires particular justifying grounds of a contract of subjection. Household membership (*familia*) is that society [*breaks off*]

[*Version two:*]

The third manner in which to have another person as one's own, 20:466 i.e. akin to a thing, within the household is that of domestic service (*famulatus* {servants}).[d] Originally in accordance with the naturally right, there are those who remain as members of the household for their maintenance, even after attaining the age of majority, until they are released by the father of the house, ~~and could in any case be obligated to perform this service in a similar status[e], yet for a salary, and yet in a way so that they are obligated to protect and maintain the house~~

---

[a] Kant's one-sentence paragraph is broken up in the translation.
[a] *nach dem natürlichen Recht*
[b] *Das Wort Gesinde für die häusliche Dienerschaft*
[c] *Herrschaft* here and in the following sentence
[d] Kant's one-sentence paragraph is broken up in the translation.
[e] *in der ähnlichen Qualität*

(belongings and children) as something that would be theirs, at best for a wage. Serving in their lower status, in which they perform the labor that is possible merely mechanically and without use of their own judgment, they are called servants. Those who are hired only to perform specifically designated labor, and who are paid specifically for that, are not agents (*mandatarii* {given mandates}) like the former and do not belong to the household as members but are instead wage laborers (like footmen, oven stokers, etc. *mercenarii* {hired workers})

The members of the household stand in a society, indeed one of unequals (*superioris et inferioris*), which cannot really be called a society, because one party to the association is connected to the other party in accordance with right to a thing while the other is associated with the first in accordance with personal right. The husband possesses the wife, the father (or the mother) possesses the child, and the head of the household possesses the servants, not with the same degree of duties and rights but in accordance with the quality of the fate that both met with (*socii malorum* {associates in misfortune}), and the relation of the one party to the other is not mutual **possession**, which generally does not occur in a relation of one human being to another, but only the holding of the household, which can be mutual and yet unequal.

Drafts for *Conflict of the faculties*

Editor's introduction

Kant wrote to his friend Johann Heinrich Tieftrunk on Friday, October 13, 1797, with morbidity on his mind. After discussing Tieftrunk's proposal to publish a collection of Kant's minor writings, he writes,

> It is possible that death will overtake me before these matters are settled. If so, our Professor Gensichen will find two of my essays in my cabinet; one of them is complete, the other almost so, and they have lain there for more than two years. Professor Gensichen will then tell you how to make use of them. But keep this matter confidential, for possibly I shall still publish them myself while I live. (12:208)

Kant scholars have generally identified these two essays as the first and second parts of what later became the *Conflict of the Faculties*.[1] Prior to 1798, Kant had not yet conceived of the published work that united three essays on the relation between the philosophy faculty on the one hand and the theology, law, and medical faculties on the other, so he would have treated the first two parts as distinct essays. Other indications, however, suggest that Kant did not leave the essay, titled "An old question raised again: Is the human race constantly progressing?," in his cabinet drawer but had submitted the essay for publication earlier in the month. In a draft of this same letter Kant notes that "a treatise of mine for the *Berliner Blätter* has been sent off" (13:464), and the "old question" essay is clearly identified by that precise title as that treatise in another letter to Tieftrunk of April 5, 1798, when Kant complains that the censors had quickly and quietly rejected it for publication in the *Berliner Blätter* on October 23, 1797 (12:240). Whether Kant had a copy of this essay in his drawer or not, from these sources it is clear that any drafts of this essay would date prior to October 1797, possibly coinciding with work on the *Doctrine of Right* and probably not afterward.

A beginning date for work on this essay is more difficult to pinpoint. Since the essay prominently features the French Revolution as an anchor for the claim that humanity is progressing, it cannot be earlier than 1789. Kant's publication of *Theory and Practice* in 1793 suggests a later beginning point, given that the third part of that work concerns essentially

357

the same question, "are there in human nature predispositions from which one can gather that the race will always progress toward what is better and that the evil of present and past times will disappear in the good of future times?" (8:307).[2] He returned to the question in *Toward Perpetual Peace* with a section entitled "On the guarantee of perpetual peace." In both of these pieces Kant expresses confidence that nature will bring about progress and peace. Likely, then, Kant did not conceive of another essay on the topic until after the publication of *Toward Perpetual Peace* in 1795. Kant might have thought the matter settled, only after publication to be drawn back to the issue. The year 1795, then, appears to be the earliest date Kant would have conceived of a new essay on a similar topic. Since Kant himself was returning to the issue, the title "Erneuerten Frage: ob das menschliche Geschlecht im beständigen Fortschreiten zum Besseren sei?" might better be translated as "A question renewed" instead of "An old question raised again."

The fragments that have been identified as drafts for the progress essay have been dated from between fall 1795 and fall 1797. Some of these specific drafts certainly must stem from no earlier than 1795: one mentions the French Directory, which was not established until 1795. One can be dated to no earlier than very late September, 1797, showing that Kant was continuing to work through the material in the essay just before he submitted it for publication.

The material translated below includes the drafts that contain Kant's direct discussion of the French Revolution, the English constitution, the relation between a republican constitution and the likelihood of war, the means to attain a republican constitution, and other political topics. The more strictly historical material concerning the general manner of making predictions about the future course of the human species is not included here.[3]

Drafts for *Conflict of the faculties*

TRANSLATED BY FREDERICK RAUSCHER

Loses Blatt F1 (fall 1795–fall 1797)   23:459

Why has there never been a monarch who has risked declaring openly that he thinks nothing of the concept of right and takes it to be mere pedantry ~~and that the people must be satisfied with that and will be if they only conduct themselves passively under his governance and simply let him lead them and care for them as a shepherd does a herd of sheep, and thereby really feel themselves comfortable and well-off~~ and that his people are also completely satisfied under his governance, which is often the case: why does he consider himself required in each of his decrees to feign respect for the right of the people (although he has none) and why does he fear, not without reason, that such a naïve declaration should completely alienate the people from him. – The reason is not to be sought in a claim that the concept of right and its principle would be a concept that unites all natural aims of the people and its whole interest, so that the well-being of the people is made into a motivating ground of obedience for the people; instead in the eyes of the people right has for itself its unconditioned highest worth to which they pay homage, and the politician considers himself, against his will, constrained by the concept of right as to a point lying outside the sensible world but connected to it, like Archimedes placing his lever in order to move the world when he wants, because of the expected benefits and happiness; a state that is absolutely monarchical   23:460
and wisely ~~administered~~ governed but merely passive also really inclines to these benefits and happiness; more than a state in which is found the turbulence resulting from having been led around by the voices of the majority, which is a state that achieves nothing.

Loses Blatt E 77, four pages (dated after September 29, 1797, St. Michael's   23:461
Day)

[*second page*]

The first thing that nature wills for a multitude of human beings in a certain limited area is that they would all be free, that is, for each to live next to one another as each sees fit, *consensus singulorum* {an agreement of each} through which a multitude becomes a people; and here a compatibility produced through the conflict of all against all is the logical standard for comparison, which is analytic. The second is synthetic unity of ends in which all consent to a government to which each is subject and in which each limits his freedom through the freedom of others. – Thus here is a principle[a] for the form of living together and indeed an *a priori* principle in which either a whole or all together rule each individual (because that a few rule over the remainder, e.g. the nobles over the people, would yield *status in statu* {a status within a status}, which would again yield to a conflict of the multitude against a multitude). – There must therefore initially be agitation[b] as in the *status naturalis* {state of nature} because even if human beings were all good natured, the diversity of opinions would certainly bring them to violence.[c] Then someone will certainly say: "See what comes from our freedom and equality!" – Empirical principles of union thus fail completely. But somewhere now in a great city which contains the representatives of the mass of enlighteners from all classes, a deputation of and from them[d] conceives of an agreement for a union of departments, which is a union arising from necessity, a union still crude regarding the final end, meaning freedom and equality not of property but of wills and their unity; this agreement contains at the same time executive power[e] under the name of the *Directory*, composed of a few persons whose total must be an odd number, and from which transcendental unity (*a priori*) must emerge.[4] – The highest power cannot be thought as limited (*inferior*); but [*breaks off*]

23:462

Loses Blatt Krakau and R8077 (fall 1795–fall 1797)

These two sheets were found in two distinct locations at two different times but have been identified as belonging together as a draft for the second section of *Conflict of the Faculties*. *L.B.* Krakau has the title "*Erneuerte Frage: Ob das menschliche Geschlecht im beständigen Fortschreiten zum Besseren begriffen sey?*" and the letter "A" in the upper margin of page one, with a note "*vid b[ogen] B oben*" [see sheet B, top] at the bottom of page four. R8077 has the title "*Fortschritt B*" and note "*vid B[ogen] A, unten*" [see sheet A bottom] at the top of page one. The text of *L.B.* Krakau ends abruptly, but earlier in the fragment there is a sign Kant employed to show continuation on another sheet. Kant's thoughts at that point are clearly continued at the beginning of R8077. Generally speaking, the topics of *L.B.* Krakau conform to the earlier sections

---

[a] *Princip* in this paragraph   [b] *Ärger*
[c] *Gewalttätigkeit*
[d] *derselben* could refer to the representatives or the enlighteners
[e] *Gewalt*

of the Progress essay while the topics of R8077 conform more to the latter sections.[5] Some material in each fragment is not directly relevant to political philosophy and has not been included. Pagination for *Loses Blatt Krakau* is to page numbers in its published version in *Kantstudien* 51 (1959–60): 3–13.

[*Much material on first and second pages about history and moral progress of human beings omitted.*]

[*first page in margin:*] To accommodate politics to right is good and beneficial but the reverse is false and abhorrent. The most dangerous of all experiments is the violent alteration or even more transformation of the state constitution,[a] a conscientious person would also not want to take on the guilt stemming from this ill.

[*third page*]   KSt 6

KSt 4

PROBLEM

What is the most favorable occasion and when is the point in time that must arise, and will certainly be seized by humanity, when by means of a revolution in public principles a condition can be brought about from which time onward there will be constant irreversible progress toward the better in the course of the human species.

SOLUTION

KSt 7

Because of their natural propensity to evil and the resulting situation in which they use force on one another, human beings require a power that holds the ever-increasing mob under the constraint of public laws and thereby secures everyone his right, which cannot occur earlier than after they voluntarily perpetrate hostilities; this nonsense is called war, and improvements in culture are treated as means for it, and rulers use peoples who already have lawful systems, named states,[a] for their own ends, prosperity and population are only means to be used to wage a war in which the subjects are not being treated as citizens of a state (for then their agreement would be required for war) but as tools of destruction that are themselves also destructible.

Now in the most developed culture war becomes a greater evil that states inflict externally on one another and inwardly on everyone in the state (the people) not merely during wars but during the more and more pressing preparation for them in peacetime, and all progress toward the better, in which the promotion of the arts and sciences through education is seen as pragmatic means of progress toward the better, is always inhibited and interrupted through accursed war, and this is certainly a

---

[a] *die gewaltsame Veränderung oder vielmehr Umwandlung der Staatsverfassung*

Pandora's Box that one must examine to see whether it would sometime reveal a glimmer of hope.

The coercion by another to which human beings, as beings capable of rights, can be lawfully subjected is possible in no way other than by means of a lawgiving to which they have given their consent and so should obey, or even better laws that would be made only through the united will.[b] Now freedom and equality of rights, along with the unity of the will in accordance with these principles, are the inseparable conditions for the quality of a lawgiver, and human beings who have grasped these ideas and have taken to heart the dignity of humanity in their person could, given this quality, consider themselves no longer as mere tools that another can discard; but when situations appear under which they obtain the authority to participate in the lawgiving, through which they can better provide for their own happiness and what is more feel ennobled, they are eager to take on and keep this condition, and indeed on moral grounds because it is not just duty toward others but a still higher duty, namely duty toward oneself (humanity in one's person).

KSt 8   [*Some comments in the margin omitted. fourth page*]

Thus the key to this problem is use of the opportunity which an all-destroying war, which also cripples the power of the state's own government, presents to the people to unite themselves under a constitution[c] in which the people rule themselves through laws of freedom and equality. Under such a constitution[d] all desire for war must cease because otherwise everyone would vote at the cost of his own fortune and his own person since he simply can gain nothing for himself, and thus for himself he could bear no other than a defensive war, in which another state has little to fear from the first because it is not waged for conquests, and no other state will fear for the aim of expansion from such a state, above all when the threatened state possesses enough power for defense.

PROOF

That when the government is in the hands of a civil[e] people under this condition (of freedom and equality) and by this means the ills of war, which reverses and corrupts everything good, are averted, there can be perceived in the predispositions of humanity a propensity and direction which allows one to be able to conclude that there will be further progress of humanity toward perfection, although this cannot yet be confirmed through experience. But even less can it be contradicted by experience since even if the conditions which ought to bring it about are lacking, yet it is not impossible that they will someday appear and be

KSt 9

[a] *Staaten*
[c] *Constitution*
[e] *staatsbürgerlichen*

[b] *vereinigten Willen*
[d] *Verfassung*

strengthened since through culture reason had prepared many for it. – But *a priori* such an event (as a product of free choice) cannot be proven.

Even when politicians laugh over such sanguine hopes (as empiricists) they are still compelled, at least when they do not make a mockery out of all human predispositions to morality, to confess that there is enough of a basis to assume, from a practical point of view, that there would be continuous and never completely extinguished progress of the human species effected with all its powers.[a]

[*A sign in the margin indicates that the following is to be placed after the heading "proof," presumably as a second attempt at the proof:*]

That sometime an opportunity would and must appear, and the success of seizing it after many failed and damaging attempts is to be expected with the greatest probability, because the interest, so great and ineradicable, will and must be proclaimed by the soul of human beings universally and in the end publicly, that the opposition, which is not the enthusiasm of a savage mob but of an enlightened people, could be manifested as no more than growth toward an evolution (for revolution manifests itself in wild violence[b]) in ends and principles, long before nourished in people's minds.

But considering that those in power who are rational now already realize that it is unpreventable and also in accordance with right, one can predict that these rulers will voluntarily arrange it by themselves.

[*A sign shows that this text continues at the beginning of R8077 The version in Kantstudien continues here:*]

Admittedly it is a coincidence that this transformation of the state, already begun, has encountered a great people enlightened about its interests as well as its rights: but the cause of the event has still been prepared by nature.

[*these three sentences in margin:*] ~~Why is the French Revolution so~~ KSt 9
~~universally acclaimed by those who are not suffering, even up to~~
~~enthusiasm.~~[c]

~~Of the absurdity that there would be no progress toward the better.~~

~~It would of course be possible for a ruler to legislate monocratically~~
~~but to govern in a republican manner, e.g. in recruiting for positions.~~

The arts and sciences seemingly do not lead naturally to improvement in morality; however they still serve it in that they dispel barbarity and improve receptiveness for moral feelings. One cannot promise any direct support for the latter from the growth of the former; also concerning the former luxury is usually tied to the greatest moral ruin. Yet the arts and

[a] *Kräften*
[b] *ungestüme Gewalt*
[c] *Enthusiasm*

sciences could help to prevent any backsliding from the good already uncovered.

Another important question is whether human beings must already become better (through education, religious discipline, etc.) before one can hope for improvements in states, or must the work be done in the reverse direction (or must be provided by providence in an antagonistic way). The latter appears to be the case. For first the rulers have no money for schools, formation, and education (as Büsching complains[6]); they need all of it to prosecute war, an aim they attribute to each other, and this even, as things now stand, is a necessary aim even though not one favorable to progress in morality. Thus this progress toward the better must be provided by states and not by the people (from above and not from below). The inner form of the state must be reformed, of which the first and last is to form the state so that it is not always hatching wars, in part not to provoke others to war and in part also [*breaks off*]

19:604 **R8077**

[*first page, upper margin:*] Progress B
[*continued from page four of Loses Blatt Krakau at Kantstudien page 8:*]

Admittedly it is a coincidence that this transformation of the state, already begun, has encountered a great people enlightened about its interests, since a lesser people are open to counterrevolution and so the eventual yet inevitable transformation of things would be delayed.

General remark

What is it that the mere spectators of the revolution of a ~~state~~ people, previously ruled absolutely and who have now republicanized themselves amid the greatest internal and external difficulties, feel with such vivid participation and wishes for success for their undertaking: it is that the subjects themselves of a similarly governed state do not wish it for themselves even if it could happen without violent[a] revolution (in part because it goes tolerably well for them, but mostly because the situation of the state to which they belong among neighboring states allows no other constitution for them save the monarchical, without running the risk that the state be dissolved), that, I say, these mere spectators sympathize passionately with them. The *factum* {fact} is doubtless true and, in this crisis of the metamorphosis of the French state and irrespective of all evil and atrocities connected with it, can be observed unmistakably not merely in the base man who blathers about politics but also in the enlightened man desperate to know the situation with his impatient and ardent desire for newspapers as the raw material for highly interesting social conversations

---

[a] *gewaltsame*

(not at all like political clubs). – For this, and to arouse such enthusiasm generally, the spectator must have in mind a genuine or at least
well-intentioned interest in the entire human race, conceiving of an
epoch from which point on our species remains no longer tottering
back and forth from better to worse and back again* but will reach the   19:605
point of slow yet unbroken and continual progress toward the better. –
Pitt, who insists that things remain the same even for a neighboring
state, and who, if the state veers off course, insists on putting it back
on its old track, will be detested as an enemy of the human race, and
the name of him who brings the situation in France into the new order
is alone worthy of having a place in the temple of fame reserved for him
so that he will be revered in days to come.[7] – England, which despite
the fact that it could have been counted among the participants in the
improvement of humanity in the world because of its courageous support for its [*added*: illusory[a]] freedom, which is often under attack, has
now completely fallen from that rank after it had considered the proposed constitution in France, free in many basic ways, as a danger that
might disturb the stability of its own. – In order to gain insight into what
the genuine distinguishing characteristic of a state that can really boast
of the freedom of its people is, or to prove the opposite, I will take the
latter as an example.

[*Kant's footnote*:] *I place no special weight on the moral basis for a proof,
supposedly drawn from eternal wisdom (a *Deus ex machina*), that the
human species would not be allowed to transcend the absurdity of rolling
Sisyphus's stone up to a certain height and then letting it roll down again
in order only to begin this task anew.[8] It is a matter of freedom, something one cannot predict with certainty. It is also presumptuous to want
to determine what the most supreme power governing the world would
consider the proper procedure. Whether it is not the plan of that power
to allow the sheer multiplicity of the scenes of the human race, scenes
changing from within and consisting of an infinite variety of types, without human beings in any way being able to prove the honor of their own
persons. To us it is fitting only to look into what can be expected of the
future given the nature of human beings and their ways as we know them
and only as far as we can have insight into them. [*end of footnote*]

[*second page*]   19:606
A monarch who is so mighty he is able to declare "There shall be
war" and then there is war is an **unlimited** monarch and his people
are not free. – One, however, who must first make a public request of
the people whether they agree that there be war, and when they say,

[a] *scheinbaren*

365

"There shall be no war," then there is no war, is a **limited** monarch and his people are truly free. Now constitutionally the king of England has the first type of right, but the French republic only the second, for the Directory must ask the council representing the whole people.[9] Thus the head of state in England has absolute but in France only limited power, and the people in the former are not free but subjugated, for what burden can the British monarch not place on the shoulders of his subjects at will? Such an amount of power, pressing for an unforeseeable length of time, eventually perhaps overthrowing the entire state, directly undermining the morality of the people, cannot at all be thought compatible with the progress of the human species (a large part of it) toward the better, and although the flowering and growth of art can still stall the decay for a time, yet collapse will certainly come sooner or later.

It is an illusion by which one can fool only children that since the people through their representatives in Parliament must appropriate the costs of war (as well as approve the forced impressment of sailors) for the king, they are thus able to deny it and prohibit war. But apart from this nonsense the king declares war on another state and only then asks the people for the means to wage the war, which they can deny if they want, so the king must certainly know that the representatives of the people **will not have the will** to deny it even it this war would not be prudent or just. How can he know this for certain? Because he has the means at hand to control their will as he sees fit by his powerful influence on their self-interest: appointment to all the lucrative offices in the army, navy, civil courts, the church, not to mention sinecure. Now each and every one of the representatives of the people, even if he were selfless with regard to his own personal interests, has relatives and good friends to recommend for one or another of these posts and positions. The minister, who is required to protect his voting majority, does not lightly turn down those who are recommended to him, and we always find the majority of human beings succumbing to such influence in their conception of the common good. So even without assuming that these men are evil and base, the phenomenon of an undisturbed majority of votes declaring for the minister's side can be singled out as proof that the constitution of Great Britain is not that of a free people (since they do not have a veto) but is a political machine for carrying out the absolute will of the monarch. – That the laws protect each citizen in this country against the court seizing property, throwing individual persons into prison on a whim (the *Habeas Corpus Act*[10]), or otherwise being handled in an arbitrary fashion, and that instead the courts must be left to act without direction from the highest power, is something the English can boast of as a jewel of their constitution, but such a thing seldom occurs in an monarchical absolute state (as exemplified in the story of the miller

19:607

Arnold[11]) and is publicly criticized by the people, and like hail or a water-spout in good weather does nothing to mar it.

[*third page*]

Now if all absolute state constitutions have, owing to the ills of war through which each state threatens the others with dissolution, a natural tendency toward republicanism (so that even if they do not take on this form, the government still sees itself compelled to act in its spirit), should it not inevitably happen to a mighty people that, under the numerous changes of state, they ought at least once succeed in their quest for this end, and not merely through the frenzy of their egoistical claims to freedom but through the undeniable inspiration given by the idea of universally-valid human right in accordance with principles (which could not fail to appear in the advancement of culture), and finally to declare this republicanism, although by means of cruel acts   19:608 (which cannot fail to arise because spirited disagreement should precede passionate unanimity). – But from this point on and in this rebirth of a state, whose feverish inner movement did not result in utterly barbarous death of culture but has instead retained all the arts needed for it, from this state and its constitution, secured from external enemies, this is the point from which to date the condition[a] of the human species of future **constant progress toward the better**. [*in the margin:*] for the union of states would develop toward freedom.

[*several paragraphs omitted*]

[*in margin:*] It is only a concept of a completely pure state constitution,   19:609 namely the idea of a republic, where all those entitled to vote together have all power (either distributively in a democracy or conjunctively in a republic): *Respublica* {republic} *noumenon* oder *phaenomenon*. The latter   19:610 has three forms but *respublica noumenon* is only one and the same.

An absolute monarch can still govern in a republican manner without forfeiting his strength.

To me the concept of a limited state constitution appears to contain a contradiction: for then it would be only a part of the legislative power.[b]

[*several paragraphs at the end of R8077 omitted*]

---

[a] *Zustand*   [b] *Macht*

Glossary

Abbruch tun	infringe upon
abhalten	prevent, exclude
Absicht	aim, intention, purpose
Achtung	respect
Akt	act
allgemein	universal, general
allgemeine Gesetzgebung	giving universal law
Amt	office, public office
Anfangsgründe	first principles, foundations
angenehm	agreeable
Ankläger	prospector
Anlage	predisposition
Annehmung	assumption
Anordnung	arrangement
Anschauung	intuition
Anspruch	claim
Anständigkeit	appropriateness
Anwendung	application
Art	way, kind
Art und Grad	kind and extent
auffordern	require
Aufruhr	rebellion
Aufstand	sedition
ausführlich	exhaustive, complete
äusser	outer, external, express
Bedeutung	sense, significance
Bedingung	condition
Befehl	order
Befehlshaber	commander
Beförderung	promotion
Befugnis	authorization

368

Begierde	desire
Begnädigung	pardon
Begriff	concept
beharrlich	persisting, abiding
Beharrlichkeit	durability
Beherrscher	ruler
Beherrschung	sovereignty
Beleidigung	offense
Belieben (nach)	at (one's) discretion
beliebig	discretionary, arbitrary
Bemächtigung	taking control
Benutzung	utilization, use
berechtigen	justify, entitle
Bermerkung	observation
Beschaffenheit	property, charactistics, quality, nature
Besitz	possession
besitzen	possess
Besitznehmung	taking possession
bestanden	hold, exist
bestimmen	determine
Bestimmung	determination, vocation
bewahren	warrant
Bewegunggrund	motive
Bewohnen	dwell, inhabit
Bewußtsein	awareness
Beziehung	relation, reference
billig	equitable, fair
billigen	approve
Billigkeit	equity
bloß	mere, sheer, alone
Boden	land, piece of land, some land, ground
brauchbar	usable
Bürger	citizen
Bürgerbund	civil union
bürgerlich	civil
darlegen	establish
Darstellung	presentation
Dauer	duration
Ding	thing
dingliche Art persönlichen Recht	right to a person akin to a right to a thing
disponieren	dispose
dunkel	obscure
ehrlich	honest, honorable

eigen	one's own, proper
Eigennutz	self-interest
Eigentum	property, dominion
Eigentümer	owner, proprietor
einmütig	unanimous
einrichten	establish
Einrichtung	establishment
Einschränkung	limitation, restriction
Einstimmung	agreement
Einwilligung	consent
Endzweck	final end
entwickeln	develop
Erbe	heir
Erbschaft	inheritance, estate
Erfahrung	experience
ergreifen	take
erkennen	cognize, know, recognize
erklären	explain, declare
Erklärung	explanation, declaration
Erlaubnis	permission
Erlaubnisgesetz	permissive law
errichten	establish
Errichtung	founding
Erscheinung	appearance
erwerben	acquire
Erwerbung	acquisition
Erziehung	education
ewig	perpetual, in perpetuity
Folge	result, consequence
Fortschritt	progress
Frau	woman, wife
Freiheit	freedom
fremd	foreign, another
Fürst	ruler
Gattung	genus, race
Gebieter	commander
Gebot	command
Gebrauch	use
Gegenstand	object
Gehorsam	obedience
Gelehrte	scholar
gelten	be valid
Gemeinbesitz	common possession
Gemeinschaft	community

Gemeinschaftlich	communal
Gemeinwesen	commonwealth, community
gerecht	just
Gerechtigkeit	justice
Gerichtshof	court
Gesammtbesitz	collective possession
Gesellschaft	society
Gesetz	law
Gesetzgeber	legislator
Gesetzgebung	legislation, lawgiving
Gesetzmäßigkeit	lawfulness, conformity to law
Gesinde	servants
Gesinnung	disposition
Gewalt	power, authority, control, force, violence
Gewinn	profit, winnings
Gleichheit	equality
Glück	happiness, luck
glücklich	happy, lucky
Glückseligkeit	happiness
Grad	degree, extent
Grenze	boundary, limit
Grund	ground, basis
Grundbesitzer	possessor of land
Grundsatz	principle
Gültigkeit	validity
Handlung	action, act
Hausherr	head of the household
Herr	lord, master
Herrschaft	dominion, dominance
Herrscher	ruler
Herrschergewalt	sovereign authority
hervorbringen	produce
Hindernis	hindrance, obstruction
hinreichend	sufficient
Inhabung	holding, occupying
juridisch	juridical
Klugheit	prudence
Knecht	servant
körperlich	bodily, corporeal
Kraft	force
lädieren	wrong, injure
Land	country, land
Landesherr	lord of the land

371

Landrecht	law of the land
Läsion	wrong, injury
Legalität	legality
Lehre	doctrine
Leibeigener	bondsman
Leibeigenschaft	bondsmanship
leisten	perform, provide
Lust	pleasure
Macht	power
Mann	man, husband
Mannigfaltigkeit	manifold
Materie	matter
Mein, Dein, Sein	what is mine (yours, one's), my property, what belongs to me
Mensch	human being
Menschheit	humanity
menschlich	human
Moral	morals, morality
Moralität	morality
naturlich recht	right by nature
natürliches Recht	naturally right, natural right
Naturrecht	natural right
Naturzustand	state of nature
Neigung	inclination
Notfall	case of necessity
nötigen	necessitate
Nötigung	necessitation
Notwendigkeit	necessity
Nutzen	benefit, use, utility
Oberhaupt	head
Oberherrschaft	sovereignty, sovereign power
oberst	supreme
Object	object
Obrigkeit	authority
occupieren	take control
öffentlich	public
Pfand	security deposit
Pflicht	duty
pflichtmäßig	in conformity with duty
Prinzip	principle
provisorisch	provisional
publizieren	publicize, promulgate
Rache	vengeance
Recht	right

Rechtens	laid down as right
rechtlich	rightful, by right
rechtmäßig	in conformity with right, legitimate
rechtschaffen	righteous
rechtskräftig	having rightful force
Rechtszustand	rightful condition
Regent	ruler
Regierung	government, governing
Reich	kingdom
restellen	represent
Sache	thing
Satz	proposition, principle
schaden	harm
schätzen	value, estimate
Schranke	limit
Schuld	guilt, fault, debt
Schuldigkeit	obligation
Selbständigkeit	independence
Selbstrache	vendetta
Sennlichkeit	sensibility
Servitut	easement
Sicherheit	security
sichern	secure, assure, guarantee
Sinn	sense, meaning
Sitten	morals, morality
Sittlichkeit	morals, morality
Souverän	sovereign
Souveränität	sovereignty
Staatsrecht	right of a state
Stand	condition, status
stiften	establish, found
strafbar	punishable
Strafgesetz	penal law
strafwürdig	deserving of punishment
Streit	conflict
Tat	deed
Tätigkeit	activity
Titel	title (i.e. deed for property)
Trieb	drive, impulse
Triebfeder	incentive
Tugend	virtue
Übel	ill
übereinstimmen	agree
Übertretung	transgressing, overstepping

Unabhängigkeit	independence
unerlaubt	forbidden
ungerecht	unjust
ungereimt	absurd
unrecht	wrong
unterlassen	refrain from, omit
Unterlassung	omission
Unterschied	difference, distinction
Untertan	subject
Unterwerfen	subjection
Urheber	author
Ursache	cause
ursprünglich	original
verändern	alter, change
Veränderung	change
Veräusserung	alienation
Verbindlichkeit	obligation
Verbindung	combination, connection
Verbot	prohibition
verbrauchbar	consumable
verbrauchen	consume
Verbrechen	crime
Verein	union
Vereinigung	unification, uniting
Verfassung	constitution
vergeltend	retributive
Verhältnis	relation
Verkauf	sale
Verkehr	trade, commerce
Verknüpfung	connection
Verleihen	lending
Verletzung	violation
Vermögen	capacity, faculty, means
Vernunft	reason
vernünftelnd	rationalizing
Verpflichtung	obligation
Verstand	understanding
Verstellung	representation
Verteilung	distribution
Vertrag	contract
verüben	commit, perpetrate
Verwaltung	administration
Volk	the people, a people, nation
Völkerbund	league of nations

Völkerrecht	right of nations
vollkommen	perfect
vollständig	complete
vornehm	noble
Vorrecht	privilege
Vorschrift	precept
vorsetzlich	intentional
Vorstellung	representation
Vorteil	advantage
Vorzug	superiority
wählen	choose
wechselseitig	reciprocal
Weib	wife
weit	wide
weltbürgerlich	cosmopolitan
Wert	worth, value
Wesen	being, entity, essence
Widerstand	resistance
widerstehen	oppose
Widerstreit	opposition, conflict
Wilde	savage
Wille	will
Willkür	power of choice, choice
willkürlich	discretionary, voluntary, arbitrary, chosen
wirklich	actual
Wirkung	effect
Wohl	well-being
Wohlfahrt	welfare
Wohlgefallen	satisfaction
Wohltun	beneficence, benefit
Wohlwollen	benevolence
wollen	will
Wollen	volition
Würde	dignity
Zueignung	appropriation
zufällig	contingent
Zufriedenheit	satisfaction
zurechnen	impute
Zusammenhang	connection
zusammenstimmen	agree, harmonize
Zustand	condition, status, state (of nature)
Zwang	coercion, constraint
Zweck	end, purpose

Glossary

abiding	beharrlich
absurd	ungereimt
acquire	erwerben
acquisition	Erwerbung
act	Akt
action	Handlung
activity	Tatigkeit
actual	wirklich
administration	Verwaltung
advantage	Vorteil
agree	übereinstimmen, zusammenstimmen
agreeable	angenehm
agreement	Einstimmung
aim	Absicht
alienation	Veräusserung
alone	bloß
alter	verändern
annul	aufheben
another	fremd
appearance	Erscheinung
application	Anwendung
appropriateness	Anständigkeit
approve	billigen
arbitrary	willkürlich
arrangement	Anordnung
assumption	Annehmung
assure	sichern
at (one's) discretion	Belieben (nach)
author	Urheber
authority	Obrigkeit, Gewalt
authorization	Befugnis
aversion	Abscheu
awareness	Bewußtsein
basis	Grund
be valid	gelten
being	Wesen
beneficence	Wohltun
benefit	Nutzen, Wohltun
benevolence	Wohlwollen
bodily	körperlich
bondsman	Leibeigener

bondsmanship	Leibeigenschaft
boundary	Grenze
by right	rechtlich
capacity	Vermögen
case of necessity	Notfall
cause	Ursache
change	verändern, Veränderung
charactistics	Beschaffenheit
choice	Willkür
choose	wählen
chosen	willkürlich
citizen	Bürger
civil	bürgerlich
civil condition	Civilzustand
civil union	Bürgerbund
claim	Anspruch
coercion	Zwang
cognize	erkennen
collective possession	Gesammtbesitz
combination	Verbindung
command	Gebot
commander	Befehlshaber, Gebieter
commerce	Verkehr
commit	verüben
commonwealth	Gemeinwesen
communal	Gemeinschaftlich
community	Gemeinschaft, Gemeinwesen
complete	vollständig, ausführlich
concept	Begriff
condition	Bedingung, Stand, Zustand
conflict	Streit, Widerstreit
conformity to law	Gesetzmäßigkeit
connection	Verbindung, Verknüpfung, Zusammenhang
consent	Einwilligung
consequence	Folge
constitution	Constitution, Verfassung
constraint	Zwang
consumable	verbrauchbar
consume	verbrauchen
contingent	zufällig
contract	Vertrag, Contract
control	Gewalt
corporeal	körperlich

cosmopolitan	weltbürgerlich
country	Land
court	Gerichtshof
crime	Verbrechen
debt	Schuld
declaration	Erklärung
declare	erklären
deed	Tat (cf. title)
degree	Grad
deserving of punishment	strafwürdig
desire	Begierde
determination	Bestimmung
determine	bestimmen
develop	entwickeln
difference	Unterschied
dignity	Würde
discretionary	beliebig, willkürlich
dispose	disponieren
disposition	Gesinnung
distinction	Unterschied
distribution	Verteilung
doctrine	Lehre
dominance	Herrschaft
dominion	Herrschaft, Eigentum
drive	Trieb
durability	Beharrlichkeit
duration	Dauer
duty	Pflicht
dwell	Bewohnen
easement	Servitut
education	Erziehung
effect	Wirkung
end	Zweck
entitle	berechtigen
entity	Wesen
equality	Gleichheit
equitable	billig
equity	Billigkeit
essence	Wesen
establish	darlegen, einrichten, errichten, stiften
establishment	Einrichtung
estate	Erbschaft
estimate	schätzen

exclude	abhalten
exhaustive	ausführlich
exist	bestanden
experience	Erfahrung
explain	erklären
explanation	Erklärung
extent	Grad
external	äusser
faculty	Vermögen
fair	billig
fault	Schuld
federalism	Föderalism
federation	Bundesgenossenschaft
final end	Endzweck
first principles	Anfangsgründe
forbidden	unerlaubt
force	Kraft, Gewalt
foreign	fremd
found	stiften
foundations	Anfangsgründe
founding	Errichtung
freedom	Freiheit
general	allgemein
genus	Gattung
giving universal law	allgemeine Gesetzgebung
governing	Regierung
government	Regierung
ground	Grund, Boden
guarantee	sichern
guilt	Schuld
happiness	Glückseligkeit, Glück
happy	glücklich
harm	schaden
harmonize	zusammenstimmen
having rightful force	rechtskräftig
head	Oberhaupt
head of the household	Hausherr
heir	Erbe
hindrance	Hindernis
hold	bestanden
holding	Inhabung
honest	ehrlich
honorable	ehrlich
human	menschlich

human being	Mensch
humanity	Menschheit
husband	Mann
ill	Übel
impulse	Trieb
impute	zurechnen
in conformity with duty	pflichtmäßig
in conformity with right	rechtmäßig
in perpetuity	ewig
incentive	Triebfeder
inclination	Neigung
independence	Selbständigkeit, Unabhängigkeit
infringe upon	Abbruch tun
inhabit	Bewohnen
inheritance	Erbschaft
innate	angeboren
inner	inner
intention	Absicht
intentional	vorsetzlich
internal	inner
intuition	Anschauung
juridical	juridisch
just	gerecht
justice	Gerechtigkeit
justify	berechtigen
kind	Art
kind and extent	Art und Grad
kingdom	Reich
know	erkennen
laid down as right	Rechtens
land	Boden, Land
law	Gesetz
law of the land	Landrecht
lawfulness	Gesetzmäßigkeit
lawgiving	Gesetzgebung
league of nations	Völkerbund
legality	Legalität
legislation	Gesetzgebung
legislator	Gesetzgeber
legitimate	rechtmäßig
lending	Verleihen
limit	Grenze, Schranke
limitation	Einschränkung
lord	Herr

lord of the land	Landesherr
luck	Glück
lucky	glücklich
man	Mann
manifold	Mannigfaltigkeit
master	Herr
matter	Materie
meaning	Sinn
means	Mittel, Vermögen
mere	bloß
morality	moralität
morality	Moral, Sitten, Sittlichkeit
morals	Moral, Sitten, Sittlichkeit
motive	Bewegunggrund
nation	Volk
natural right, a natural right	Naturrecht, (ein) natürliches Recht
naturally right	natürliches Recht
nature	Beschaffenheit
necessitate	nötigen
necessitation	Nötigung
necessity	Notwendigkeit
noble	vornehm
obedience	Gehorsam
object	Gegenstand, Object
obligation	Verbindlichkeit, Schuldigkeit, Verpflichtung
obscure	dunkel
observation	Bermerkung
obstruction	Hindernis
occupy	Inhaber sein
offense	Beleidigung
office	Amt
omission	Unterlassung
omit	unterlassen
one's own	eigen
oppose	widerstehen
opposition	Widerstreit
order	Befehl
original	ursprünglich
outer	äusser
overstepping	Übertretung
owner	Eigentümer
pardon	Begnädigung

penal law	Strafgesetz
people	Volk
perfect	vollkommen
perform	leisten
permission	Erlaubnis
permissive law	Erlaubnisgesetz
perpetrate	verüben
perpetual	ewig
persisting	beharrlich
person	Person
pleasure	Lust
possess	besitzen
possession	Besitz
possessor of land	Grundbesitzer
power	Gewalt, Macht
power of choice	Willkür
precept	Vorschrift
predisposition	Anlage
presentation	Darstellung
prevent	abhalten
principle	Grundsatz, Prinzip, Satz
privilege	Vorrecht
produce	hervorbringen
profit	Gewinn
progress	Fortschritt
prohibition	Verbot
promotion	Beförderung
promulgate	publizieren
proper	eigen
property	Beschaffenheit, Eigentum, Mein, Dein, Sein
proprietor	Eigentümer
prospector	Ankläger
provide	leisten
provisional	provisorisch
prudence	Klugheit
public	öffentlich
publicize	publizieren
punishable	strafbar
purpose	Zweck, Absicht
quality	Beschaffenheit
race	Gattung
rationalizing	vernünftelnd
reason	Vernunft

rebellion	Aufruhr
reciprocal	wechselseitig
recognize	erkennen
reference	Beziehung
refrain from	unterlassen
relation	Verhältnis, Beziehung
represent	repräsentieren
representation	Vorstellung
representative	Repräsentant
require	auffordern
resistance	Widerstand
respect	Achtung
restriction	Einschränkung
result	Folge
retributive	vergeltend
right	Recht
right of nations	Völkerrecht
right by nature	naturlich recht
right of peace	Friedensrechts
right to a person akin to a right to a thing	dingliche Art persönlichen Recht
right of a state	Staatsrecht
right of war	Kriegsrechts
righteous	rechtschaffen
rightful	rechtlich
rightful condition	Rechtszustand
ruler	Beherrscher, Herrscher, Regent, Fürst
sale	Verkauf
satisfaction	Wohlgefallen, Zufriedenheit
savage	Wilde
scholar	Gelehrte
secure	sichern
security	Sicherheit
security deposit	Pfand
sedition	Aufstand
self-interest	Eigennutz
self-possession	der Besitz seiner selbst
sense	Sinn, Bedeutung
sensibility	Sennlichkeit
servants	Gesinde
sheer	bloß
significance	Bedeutung
society	Gesellschaft

sovereign	Souverän
sovereign power or authority	Herrschergewalt
sovereignty	Souveränität, Oberherrschaft, Beherrschung
state of nature	Naturzustand
status	Stand, Zustand
subject	Untertan
sufficient	hinreichend
superiority	Vorzug
supreme	oberst
take	ergreifen
take control	occupieren
taking control	Bemächtigung
taking possession	Besitznehmung
thing	Ding, Sache
title (i.e. deed for property)	Titel
trade	Verkehr
transgressing	Übertretung
unanimous	einmütig
understanding	Verstand
unification	Vereinigung
union	Verein
universal	allgemein
unjust	ungerecht
usable	brauchbar
use	Nutzen, Gebrauch, Benutzung
utility	Nutzen
utilization	Benutzung
validity	Gültigkeit
value	schätzen, Wert
vendetta	Selbstrache
vengeance	Rache
violation	Verletzung
violence	Gewalt, Gewalttätigkeit, Violenz
virtue	Tugend
vocation	Bestimmung
volition	Wollen
voluntary	willkürlich
warrant	bewahren
way	Art
welfare	Wohlfahrt
well-being	Wohl
what belongs to me	Mein, Dein, Sein
what is mine (yours, one's)	Mein, Dein, Sein

Glossary

wide	weit
wife	Weib, Frau
will	Wille, wollen
winnings	Gewinn
woman	Frau
worth	Wert
wrong	lädieren, Läsion, unrecht

Topical and chronological concordance

This chart correlates the topics in Gottfried Achenwall's *Jus Naturae* (1763) with the content of the *Feyerabend Natural Right* lecture notes (1784) and with various Reflections Kant wrote inside the Achenwall book and in other places.

The Achenwall book contents includes both the paragraph numbers (§§) and page numbers (J) of the original text, both reproduced in the Academy edition (19:325–442). The Reflections include reference to these page and paragraph numbers. Note that the paragraph numbers restart with the second volume, which is also the only volume Kant's copy of which survived to be included in the Academy edition.

The Feyerabend division headings are retained even when inaccurate; pages in that column refer to the Academy edition pagination. Kant skipped over some divisions in Achenwall in their entirety and sometimes discussed a single topic in more than one place. His introduction covers material not in the Achenwall text at all, such as the idea of human beings as ends in themselves and the absolute value of freedom. Still, for the most part Kant's discussion adheres to the outline provided by these headings.

The Reflections are presented in two columns: those directly written in Kant's copy of Achenwall's book or assigned by Adickes to the section of Reflections on Philosophy of Right are in the third column, while other Reflections included in this anthology are assigned by the editor to an appropriate topic in the fourth column. In many cases the content of the Reflection does not neatly fit into only one topic; readers are urged to use the index for the most thorough search on any specific topic. The Reflections identified in the Academy edition as "general" rather than correlated with particular sections in Achenwall are placed here with the "Introduction."

In this chart the Reflection numbers are printed with variations in italic, bold, and underlining in order to present their rough chronological order. This table provides only the *initial year* of what Adickes considered the most plausible period in his system; thus, a Reflection in the "1772–1774" category might have been written years later if the range indicated in the heading for that Reflection extends past 1774. Refer to particular Reflections to determine the range of the possible ending dates. Bold Reflections date after the Feyerabend course lecture. Although the French Revolution occurred in 1789, Adickes's dating classifications did not have a separate class of Reflections from 1789, so any Reflections dated 1788 or later and even a few earlier that might range over the entire 1780s could be responses to the French Revolution. There are only a handful of Reflections after 1790 because Kant no longer taught his Natural Right course and the notes that have survived are drafts for his published work in that decade.

Rough chronological order based on initial date given for each Reflection:

1764–1771
1772–1774
1775–1779
1780–1784
1785–1787
1788–1790
1791–1799

Achenwall *Jus Naturae* (1763)	Feyerabend Natural Right (1784)	Reflections from section on Philosophy of Right	Reflections from other sources
FIRST VOLUME Introduction to natural right §§ 1–6	Introduction 27:1319–29	General: 7701, 7919, *7920*, *8076*	1432, *1438*, *1443*, 6583, 6594, 6670, 6733, 6746, 6767, 7084, 7271, *7309*
Title I Of the rule for free actions and obligation in general §§ 7–19 Title II Of natural laws §§ 20–33 Title III Of perfect laws §§ 34–48 Title IV Of perfect laws as external laws §§ 49–60 Addition to the Introduction: Literary history of natural right §§ I–IX	Title 1: Of the rule for free actions and in general 27:1329–38 (includes the topics of the remaining Titles in the Introduction)		6667, 6896, 7078, *7275*
Book I. Natural right in the most narrow sense of the term §§ 61–62	**Book I. Natural right in the narrower sense of the term** 27:1338		
Section I Unconditional natural right §§ 63–108	Section I: Original natural right 27:1338–40 (includes the topics of the remaining Titles in the Section)		

(cont.)

389

Achenwall *Jus Naturae* (1763)	Feyerabend Natural Right (1784)	Reflections from section on Philosophy of Right	Reflections from other sources
Title V Of right to dispose of one's property §§ 156–64	Title V Of right to dispose of one's property 27:1348–49		
Title VI Of contract §§ 165–81	Title VI Of a rightful bilateral deed or contract 27:1349–53		
Title VII Of the effects of a contract §§ 182–97	Title VII Of effect 27:1353–56		
Title VIII Of price and money §§ 198–207	Title VIII 27:1356–57		3355
Title IX Of beneficial and onerous contracts §§ 208–23	[title missing but content is discussed] 27:1357–63		
Title X Of guarantee §§ 224–29	Title X Of guarantee 27:1363–64		
Title XI Of oaths §§ 230–35	Title XI Of oaths 27:1365–66		
Title XII Of succession §§ 236–40	Title XII Of succession to the goods of the deceased 27:1366–68		
[named but unnumbered] Of prescription § 241	Title XIII Of prescription 27:1368–69		
Title XIII Of the ways in which right and obligation having been contracted are removed from a contract §§ 242–57	Title XIII Of the ways in which right and obligation are removed 27:1369–71		

391

(*cont.*)

Achenwall *Jus Naturae* (1763)	Feyerabend **Natural Right** (1784)	**Reflections from section on Philosophy of Right**	**Reflections from other sources**
Title I Of marriage §§ 42–52 J 31–39	Title I Of marriage 27:1379–80	7568, 7572, 7580, 7587, 7591, 7599, 7602, 7880, 7881	
Title II Of parental society §§ 53–64 J 39–49	Title II Of parental society 27:1380	7608, 7702, 7704	
Title III Of the society of a master §§ 65–77 J 49–60	Title III Of the society of a master 27:1380–81	7633, 7638, 7895, 7897, 7930	
Title IV Of family §§ 78–84 J 61–64			
Book III Universal state right, in particular universal public right §§ 85–87 J 65–70	**Book III Universal state right in particular** 27:1381	7681, 7683, 7708, 7710, 7712, 7713, 7719, 7721, 7723, 7725, 7847, 7932, 7937, 7938	1464, 1468, 6855, 7075
Section I Universal public right in general §§ 88–111 J 71–95	Section I Public Right 27:1381–84	7430, 7432, 7439, 7540, 7644, 7646, 7647, 7651 7663, 7664, 7665, 7667, 7684, 7686, 7687, 7691, 7733, 7734, 7735, 7736, 7737, 7738, 7742, 7744, 7747, 7748, 7752, 7754, 7756, 7758, 7765, 7769, 7771, 7777, 7853, 7854, 7959, 7953, 7955, 7960, 7961, 7966, 7969, 7970, 7971, 7975, 7976, 7977, 7980	

(cont.)

Achenwall *Jus Naturae* (1763)	Feyerabend Natural Right (1784)	Reflections from section on Philosophy of Right	Reflections from other sources
Section III Conditional universal public right § 148 p. 141	Section III Conditional universal public right 27:1388–90		
Title I Of monarchy §§ 149–57 141–49	Title I Of monarchy 27:1388	8014, 8018, 8019	
Title II Of the ways of coming to have a sovereign monarch §§ 158–73 J 150–63	Title II Of the ways of coming to have a sovereign monarch 27:1388–89		
Title III Of the other forms of states §§ 174–90 J 164–76	Title III Of the other forms of states 27:1389–90	8023	
Section IV Of the way of prosecuting one's right in a state §§ 191–207 J 177–90	Title IV Of the way of prosecuting one's right in a state 27:1390–92	7680 *7695, 7810, 7812, 7814, 7815, 7912, 7913, 7914, 7915, 7916,* 8026, 8027, *8028,* **8031, 8033,** 8035, *8036, 8037,* **8041,** 8042, **8043, 8044, 8046,** 8047, **8048, 8049,** 8050, 8051, **8054, 8055**	*6681, 7192, 7287, 7289*
[named but unnumbered] Universal private right of isolation in natural right § 208 J 190–94	[omitted]		

Editorial notes

Reflections on the philosophy of right

1 Quoted from an account by Reinhold Jachmann in the collection *Immanuel Kant in Rede und Gespräch*, ed. Rudolf Malter (Hamburg: Felix Meiner, 1990), p. 217. Further material in this paragraph is from the same selection, pp. 217–22.

2 The catalogue of Kant's books by Arthur Warda mentions only the *Pars Posterior* of Achenwall's *Jus Naturae* (Warda, *Bücher*). But since this book is itself not included in the list stemming from the inventory of the estate of Johann Friedrich Gensichen, to whom Kant had bequeathed his books and manuscripts (see editor's main introduction), it might not reflect the actual set of books that Kant owned.

3 Here is a good place to note that for the material on right the table of contents in Academy edition Volume 19 gives incorrect Greek letters in some cases and leaves out an entire chapter. The correct number of chapters and their periods I give here are based on the text itself rather than the table of contents.

4 The practice of dueling to defend one's honor dated back to medieval times and was still widely practiced in Europe in the eighteenth century. Although outlawed in England in 1571 by Queen Elizabeth and through similar bans nearly everywhere, the practice continued and punishment was often lenient or nonexistent. It lingered in Germany longer than in England. Dueling declined during the Enlightenment and into the nineteenth and twentieth centuries, but whether the cause of its decline was an increase in enlightened attitudes, a decrease in the importance of the nobility, or even a rise of middle-class values amid industrialization is a subject of debate.

5 The Swiss Revolution Kant refers to is the war in 1499 between the Swiss confederation on the one hand and the Habsburg rulers of Germany and the Holy Roman Empire on the other. At the end of the war Emperor Maximilian I granted the Swiss Confederacy independence from the Empire. The Dutch Revolt of the second half of the sixteenth century saw the seven northern provinces throw off the rule of King Philip II of Spain and proclaim the Republic of the Seven United Netherlands. Kant's reference to the English Revolution of the mid-seventeenth century is probably to the Glorious Revolution of 1688 that replaced King James II of England with William III from Holland and his wife and James's daughter Mary II of England. That relatively bloodless conflict resulted in the promulgation of the Bill of Rights in 1689 and established the

modern limited monarchy in England. Kant could also, less likely, be referring to the English Civil War of the mid-seventeenth century which saw a struggle for power between the monarch King Charles I and supporters of Parliament. This bloodier conflict created the first English republic but also resulted in the arrest and execution of King Charles, an event that Kant describes as one "that strikes horror in a soul filled with the idea of human rights" in the *Doctrine of Right* (6:321). The establishment of Parliamentary rule was relatively shortlived as Oliver Cromwell soon dismissed Parliament and became "Lord Protector" of England. After his death the Royalists restored Charles II to the throne and treated Cromwell as a rebel, unearthing and hanging his body.

6 Kant's support of the American Revolution is illustrated by an anecdote told by his biographer Jachmann. One afternoon Kant was walking in the park with some friends when the subject of the British–American war arose. Kant took the side of the Americans and was complaining about British attitudes when a stranger who overheard the conversation approached Kant and told him that he was English, said that he was offended on behalf of his entire nation, and challenged Kant to a duel. Kant is said to have declined the duel and instead engaged the man in conversation about world-citizenship, patriotism, and the like. In this way Kant began his friendship with Joseph Green, an English merchant living in Königsberg. (Malter, *Rede und Gespräch*, pp. 134–35.) Manfred Kuehn casts doubt on the accuracy of this story, pointing out that Kant and Green met in the mid-1760s, about a decade before any military action between the two nations and that if there is any truth to the story it must involve an earlier, pre-Revolutionary dispute such as the tax on tea and the Boston Tea Party (Kuehn, *Kant: A Biography* (New York: Cambridge University Press, 2001) p. 155).

7 Mercury was the Roman god of merchants also associated with being a swift messenger. A variation of this passage was used by Kant in the "Idea for a Universal History with a Cosmopolitan Aim" in 1784 (8:23).

8 For example, in the Vigilantius lecture notes, Kant discusses material related to the doctrine of right from 27:587 to 27:600, translated in the Cambridge Edition volume *Lectures on Ethics*.

9 Kant is alluding to Jean-Jacques Rousseau's prize-winning *Discours qui a remporté le prix a l'academie de Dijon en l'année 1750 sur cette question proposée par la même Académie: si le rétablissement des sciences des Arts a contribué à épurer les moeurs* (Geneva: Barillot, 1750) {Discourse which won the prize of the academy of Dijon in the year 1750 on the question proposed by that academy: whether the restoration of the sciences and the arts contributed to the purification of mores}, commonly known as the Discourse on the Sciences and the Arts. Rousseau's answer was in short "no" as he indicted the modern arts and sciences for corrupting morals and weakening individual character, making people accept their degraded roles in modern society.

10 In *Leviathan* (London: Andrew Crooke, 1651) Thomas Hobbes (1588–1679) argued that the sovereign had virtually no limits on action and did not require the consent of the people for any laws, since the people contracted to give all their sovereign power to the government. See also endnote 26 to the Feyerabend lecture for information on Kant's access to Hobbes's writings.

11 The term *cadet* refers to the second and younger sons of royal or noble families who inherited less wealth according to the rules of primogeniture that gave dominion and title to the eldest son.

12 While most of Kant's uses of *Bürger* signify a citizen in general, in this instance he uses it to refer specifically to untitled city- and town-dwellers who are economically independent, thus neither on the one hand workers or servants nor on the other hand members of the nobility. Even his claims about citizens in general are qualified by a need for economic independence. The published *Theory and Practice* (8:294–96) as well as drafts for it in this volume (23:134–37) discuss these qualifications. Kant equates a citizen in general, *Staatsbürger*, with the French *citoyen* and the city- and town-dwellers, *Stadtsbürger*, with the French *bourgeois* (8:295).

13 Cesare Beccaria, the Italian advocate of penal reform, author of *On Crimes and Punishments* (*Dei delitti e delle pene*, Livorno: Coltellini, 1764), argued that a social contract would not allow for capital punishment because no individual could rationally agree to give up his own life. For more on Beccaria see endnote 42 to "Natural Right course lecture notes by Feyerabend."

14 Hobbes allows the sovereign to sell or give the right to govern to another in *Leviathan* Chapter 19. Regarding individuals he argued in Chapter 14 that some rights were inalienable and contracts transferring them were void because they surrender the right of security without providing any benefit; whether Hobbes intended a contract selling oneself to be among them is unclear.

15 The Physiocrat school of economics developed in France in the eighteenth century and is associated with François Quesnay (1694–1774) who coined the term *laissez-faire*. The Physiocrats argued against the dominant Mercantilist theory that agricultural productivity rather than accumulation of a national treasure was the basis of national wealth. They also held that lower taxes, a reduction or elimination of internal tolls, a reduction in tariffs, and deregulation would enhance the economy. No information is available about the term "physiopath" in economic terms.

16 "Declaration and Determination of the Rights of Man" was issued by the French National Assembly in August 1789. The aim of the declaration was to set forth the principles of government that would form the basis of a new constitution replacing the French absolute monarchy. Kant is objecting to the fourth and fifth articles. The fourth article specifies that "Liberty consists in the ability to do whatever does not harm another; hence the exercise of the natural rights of each man has no other limits than those which assure to other members of society the enjoyment of the same rights." The fifth article states that "The law only has the right to prohibit those actions which are injurious to society." (*The French Revolution and Human Rights: A Brief Documentary History*, trans. and ed. Lynn Hunt (New York: St. Martin's Press, 1996), pp. 77–78.)

Natural right course lecture notes by Feyerabend

1 This and the following paragraph reconstruct likely events related to the course. Information about Kant's lecturing activity is taken from Steve Naragon's exhaustive website *Kant in the Classroom*, www.manchester.edu/kant/Lectures/lecturesTableLectureSemester.htm, last accessed July 14, 2014, and the

material provided by Emil Arnoldt (Arnoldt, *Kritische Exkurse im Gebiete der Kant-Forschung*, 2 parts, reprinted in Arnoldt, *Gesammelte Schriften*, ed. Otto Schöndörffer, 10 vols., vols. 4 and 5 (Berlin: Bruno Cassirer, 1908–1909)). Naragon provides the course schedule and available meeting days for each semester that Kant taught, with more detailed information being available for the period after 1770 when Kant assumed the Chair of Logic and Metaphysics as an Ordinary Professor paid by the University and was obligated to teach a certain cycle of courses. The information Naragon provides shows the course meeting times and the number of registered students but there is no way of knowing whether all actual meeting times were used or how many students actually attended the lecture. Strictly speaking, each course meeting probably began fifteen minutes after the hour as is the custom in Germany and each of Kant's lectures would have lasted forty-five minutes.

2 It is possible but unlikely that Kant did teach Natural Right during the winter semester 1789–90 in the wake of the French Revolution. The University's published catalogue for that term, confirmed by a draft version, lists "Jus naturae ad Achenwallium h. VIII Prof. Kant" – a reference to Kant's lecture course on *Naturrecht* using Achenwall. No other source is available to confirm or deny that Kant followed through to present the course. The post-semester university report that would have listed the courses actually offered is missing. Emil Arnoldt (Arnoldt *Kritische Exkurse*, p. 313) and, following him, Steve Naragon (Naragon, 2014) doubt that the course was actually offered. For discussion of this possibility in relation to Kant's Reflections on the French Revolution in his copy of Achenwall, see Frederick Rauscher, "Did Kant Justify the French Revolution Ex-Post Facto?," in Robert Clewis, ed., *Reading Kant's Lectures* (Berlin: Walter de Gruyter 2015).

3 Friedrich von Gentz (1763–1832) matriculated at Königsberg University on April 26, 1783. His father sent Kant a letter dated April 16, 1783, telling Kant that he was hoping that Kant would help to "form him into a virtuous, wise, and useful human being" (10:314). As with Feyerabend, the only set of lecture notes associated with Gentz is for the course on Natural Right. Gentz's set is mentioned in Stargardt, KAT 234 (an autograph and antique manuscript and book house in Berlin), as being in private possession and is now unaccounted for. Information about the state of these manuscripts is from the resources provided by the Marburg Kant Archive in Werner Stark, *Online*.

4 In his lectures on Ethics Kant also discussed in general terms the difference between right and virtue, the purpose of the state, punishment, and other matters related to political philosophy. The Cambridge Edition of Kant's *Lectures on Ethics* contains translations of the main representative sets of lecture from the Academy edition. The Vigilantius lectures from the 1790s has more than the earlier lectures, and the material in the earlier lectures is scant, so they provide little information about Kant's earlier detailed views on natural right.

5 In his editor's notes about the *Metaphysic der Sitten* Natorp notes that the Feyerabend lecture is structured very similarly to the Achenwall text, and that the *Rechtslehre* differs from both (6:528–29).

6 Naragon offers some information about the manuscript (Naragon, *Classroom*) and further information is available in the editor's introductions to the *Kant Index* edition (Delfosse, *Feyerabend*).

7 Of the two numbering systems at least one and perhaps both were added by the library. The first numbering system starts with the first page of text and marks each page through page 15, after which 16 pages appear to have no page marking or to have had the pagination erased, after which the number 16 mysteriously appears and the count is continued through to the final page numbered 116, which is actually page 132. The second set of page numbers begins with the title page and refers to each set of facing pages as a single unit. This second set was clearly added later because the person responsible crossed out and sometimes wrote over the first set of numbers. This second set ends at 67 on the penultimate manuscript page.

8 Lehmann describes this process in his introduction to volume 27.2.2, 27:1052–55.

9 Gianluca Sadun Bordoni has published his translation of Feyerabend into Italian as *Lezioni sul diritto naturale. (Naturrecht Feyerabend)*, ed. Norbert Hinske and Gianluca Sadun Bordoni (Milan: Bompiani, 2016). That edition includes the complete *Kant Index* version of the German text alongside the Italian translation.

10 The original publication information is Gottfried Achenwall, *Jus Naturae*, 2 vols., 5th edition (Göttingen: Victor Bossiegel Verlag, 1763). The title is sometimes reported as *Jus Naturalis* or *Juris Naturalis*.

11 The original publication information is Gottfried Achenwall and Johann Stephan Pütter, *Elementa Juris Naturae* (Göttingen: Johann Wilhelm Schmidt Verlag, 1750).

12 Information about the development of Achenwall's text is in Byrd and Hruschka, *Kant's Doctrine of Right*, pp. 15–19. The original edition authored by Achenwall and Pütter has been translated into German by Jan Schröder, who also provides an overview of the development of the text and Achenwall's subsequent career (Achenwall and Pütter, *Anfangsgründe des Naturrechts*, ed. and trans. Jan Schröder (Main and Leipzig: Insel Verlag, 1995), pp. 331–51).

13 Kant's example of paying a mason for building a house likely comes from his experience renovating his newly purchased house around the time of this lecture. In a letter dated April 28, 1784, to Johann Friedrich Fetter, Kant describes some of the renovation work he had contracted for his new house and which he apparently left for Fetter to manage for him. In this letter Kant discusses the money he agreed to pay the workers "so that the workers too will be completely satisfied" (Letter to Johann Friedrich Fetter, April 28, 1784). This letter does not appear in the Academy edition but in Immanuel Kant, *Briefwechsel*, selected and annotated by Otto Schöndörffer, ed. Rudolf Malter, 3rd expanded edition (Hamburg: Felix Meiner Verlag, 1986), pp. 933–34.

14 Kant refers to *Essay on Man* by Alexander Pope (1688–1744) (London: Wilford, 1733–34), Epistle 3.1, lines 43–48:

> Know, Nature's children all divide her care;
> The fur that warms a monarch, warmed a bear.
> While man exclaims, "See all things for my use!"
> "See man for mine!" replies a pampered goose:
> And just as short of reason he must fall,
> Who thinks all made for one, not one for all.

A German translation by Barthold Heinrich Brockes, *Versuch vom Menschen* (Hamburg: Zinck, 1740), would have been available to Kant, who did not read English.

15 *The Life and Strange Surprizing Adventures of Robinson Crusoe, Of York, Mariner* (London: W.Taylor, 1719) by Daniel Defoe (1660–1731) was first translated into German as *Das Leben und die ganz ungemeine Begebenheiten des berühmten Engländers Mr. Robinson Crusoe* (Hamburg, 1720). Kant might have also been aware of a later, looser translation into German in 1779, *Robinson der Jüngere* ("The Young Robinson") by Joachim Heinrich von Campe. Campe was part of the Philanthropin school of educators who adopted Rousseau's suggestions regarding the aim of education as the cultivation of the natural goodness of children, and his loose translation of the novel reflected this approach. Kant supported the Philanthropin school near Königsberg and might have been interested in the novel because of its connections to the Philanthropin ideas. Kant also mentions Crusoe and the footprint in his Anthropology lectures; see 25:677.

16 Marc-Joseph Marion du Fresne (1724?–1772) was a French explorer who thought he had discovered New Zealand for the Europeans, unaware that the British Captain James Cook had already sailed the same bays. After a storm, his two ships needing repair, du Fresne and his crew landed near the Bay of Islands (near present-day Russell) and befriended the local Maori natives. Some weeks later the Maori suddenly attacked the French, killing du Fresne and some 25 others. The remaining French officers and crew killed over 100 Maori in retaliation before fleeing the area. The most likely explanation for the killings is that du Fresne and the others were fishing in a taboo area, thus inciting the wrath of the Maori for violating their sacred spaces. Maori cannibalized the bodies of enemies killed in battle, possibly in order to increase the humiliation of their enemies or to further a religious purpose. Kant's claim that the Maori killed the French sailors specifically in order to eat them is unlikely. Kant also mentions this event in his Anthropology lectures; see 15:1421–22.

17 Anders Erikson Sparrman (1748–1820) was a Swedish naturalist who traveled to the Cape of Good Hope and then served on a voyage under James Cook, writing of his experience in *Resa till Goda Hopps-Udden, södra Polkretsen och omkring Jordklotet, samt Till Hottentott- och Caffer-Landen Åren 1772–1776* (Stockholm, 1783). The book was translated by Christian Heinrich Groskurd as *Reise nach dem Vorgebirge der guten Hoffnung: den südlichen Polarländern und um die Welt, hauptsächlich aber in den Ländern der Hottentotten und Kaffern in den Jahren 1772 bis 1776* in 1784 (Berlin: Haude und Spener) calling Sparrman "Andreas Sparrmann." The Feyerabend text misidentifies it as *Reise auf dem Vorgebirge der guten Hofnung*.

18 Anthony Ashley Cooper, Third Earl of Shaftesbury (1671–1713), was one of the first of the British Moral Sense theorists. His *An Inquiry Concerning Virtue, or Merit*, originally published in an unauthorized version by John Toland (1699), was later updated and incorporated by Shaftesbury into his arrangement of his essays and books, *Characteristicks of Men, Manners, Opinions, Times* (London: Darby, 1711, revised edition 1714). Shaftesbury wrote against Hobbes's basing morality on self-interest by suggesting that a distinct moral goodness not connected to self-interest but still able to motivate human beings is possible. Our

moral sense provides us with awareness of this goodness in the same way that our aesthetic responses provide awareness of beauty. Happiness is thus not the basis of morality.

19 Francis Hutcheson (1694–1745) provided a more systematic philosophical argument for moral sense theory in Shaftesbury's wake. He was one of the first major modern philosophers to be a university professor. His *An Inquiry into the Original of Our Ideas of Beauty and Virtue* (London: Darby, 1725) and *An Essay on the Nature and Conduct of the Passions and Affections, with Illustrations on the Moral Sense* (London: Darby and Browne, 1728) argued that we have an inner sense of beauty and a distinct inner moral sense, the latter of which produces a feeling of approbation in response to benevolent actions. This feeling is moral and not equated with the natural good of pleasure, and the moral goodness of the action is valued independently of any natural pleasure that might arise. Kant owned translations of these works into German: *Untersuchung unsrer Begriffe von Schönheit und Tugend in zwo Abhandlungen* (Frankfurt and Leipzig, 1762) and *Abhandlungen über die Natur und Beherrschung der Leidenschaften und Neigungen und über das moralische Gefühl insonderheit* (Leipzig, 1760). For information on the books Kant owned, see Warda, *Bücher*.

20 This is the first reference to the author of the textbook, Gottfried Achenwall. This particular reference is to Achenwall's *Prolegomena Juris Naturalis* (Göttingen: Victorini Bossiegel, 1758), a distinct book from the *Jus Naturalis* that Kant used for his lectures. The *Prolegomena*, a work only about one-sixth as long as the *Jus Naturalis*, was written by Achenwall alone and published in five editions (1758, 1763, 1767, 1774, and 1781). It contains general discussions of moral imputation and obligation rather than specific details about natural right. Kant refers to Achenwall's *Prolegomena* only here and in the remainder of Kant's "Introduction."

21 Kant used Alexander Baumgarten's *Initia philosophiae practicae primae* (Halle: Carl Hermann Hemmerde, 1760) as the textbook for his lectures on ethics. The full text is reprinted in *Kants gesammelte Schriften*, 19:7–91. The particular reference here is to §54 (19:58).

22 Kant's reference to *linea recta*, Latin for straight line, makes an analogy to geometry. English does not capture the precise linguistic connections Kant refers to here. The link between the German "*recht*" (straight, also right) and Latin "*recta*" (straight, also upright) is not captured in the English word "straight." There is also a different connection between German "*lineal*" (straight edge or ruler) and Latin "*linea*" (line). Kant is thus exemplifying his claim that something is called right if it agrees with a rule by invoking the mathematical example of a right (straight) line being called a rule. I thank Daniel Sutherland for this explanation.

23 The passage from Marcus Tullius Cicero (106–43 BC) that Kant is likely citing reads: "si, quid rectissimum sit, quaerimus, perspicuum est, si, quid maxime expediat, obscurum; sin ii sumus, qui profecto esse debemus, ut nihil arbitremur expedire, nisi quod rectum honestumque sit, non potest esse dubium, quid faciendum nobis sit.", which is translated as "If we ask which is the most clearly right, the answer is obvious. If we ask which is the most expedient, it is doubtful. But if we are the men we surely should be and judge nothing to be expedient except what

is right and honorable, there can be no question how we ought to act" (Cicero, *Letters to Friends*, vol. II, ed. D. R. Shackleton Bailey (Cambridge, MA: Harvard University Press, 2001)), IV (ii). An alternative source is V (xix) "quid rectum sit apparet, quid expediat obscurum est," "what is right is clear, what is expedient is obscure."

24 David Hume (1711–76) argued that a "sensible knave" would want to make exceptions to the rules: "A sensible knave, in particular incidents, may think, that an act of iniquity or infidelity will make a considerable addition to his fortune, without causing any considerable breach in the social union and confederacy. That honesty is the best policy, may be a good general rule; but is liable to many exceptions: And he, it may, perhaps, be thought, conducts himself with most wisdom, who observes the general rule, and takes advantage of all the exceptions" (*Enquiry Concerning the Principles of Morals* (London: A. Millar, 1751)), IX.22. Kant owned the German translation *Sittenlehre der Gesellschaft* (1756) as the third volume of Hume, *Vermischte Schriften*, 4 vols. (Hamburg and Leipzig: Grund und Holle, 1754–56).

25 Domitius Ulpianus, known as Ulpian (*c*.170–228), was a Roman jurist and official serving various emperors. He wrote extensively about the law, and his works provide about one-third of the content of the Emperor Justinian's *Digest*. In the *Digest* (1.1.10.1) Ulpian is said to say: "Juris praecepta sunt haec: honeste vivere, alterum non laedere, suum cuique tribuere," "These are the precepts of the law: live honestly, do not wrong anyone, give to each what is his."

26 Thomas Hobbes (1588–1679) in *Leviathan* argues that the two fundamental laws of nature are that all persons should seek peace or in its absence use all means of defense, and that all should surrender their right to use all means of defense to a sovereign. Jean-Jacques Rousseau (1712–78) views the move from a state of nature to civil society as a necessary development given the progression of human society toward greater complexity, in particular the emergence of property and social classes, in the *Discourse on the Origin and Foundation of Inequality Among Men* (*Discours sur l'origine et les fondements de l'inégalité parmi les homes* (Amsterdam: Marc Michel Rey, 1755)). The move to a civil society is protective, as in Hobbes, but not based on any objective law of nature. In *On the Social Contract or Principles of Political Right* (*Du contrat social ou Principes du droit politique* (Amsterdam: Marc Michel Rey, 1862)) Rousseau presents the systematic position that a civil society provides the only conditions for genuine freedom by limiting individuals to conformity to the general will. Kant was able to read French but not English. Kant's direct knowledge of Hobbes may have come through his Latin writings, in particular *De Cive* (*On the Citizen*) (Paris, 1642) since the *Leviathan* was not translated into German until 1794 as *Des engländers Thomas Hobbes Leviathan, oder der kirchliche und bürgerliche Staat* (Halle: J. C. Hendels Verlag, 1794–95).

27 Kant here presents the relation between right and virtue on the one hand and form and matter on the other hand in precisely the reverse way than that presented in his published works. While here in "Feyerabend" he correlates right with matter and virtue with form, in both the *Doctrine of Right* and the *Doctrine of Virtue* he correlates right with the mere form of the action

and virtue with its matter (6:230, 6:380). Kant appears to be referring to different aspects of the right/virtue distinction: the action itself and the conditions for freedom. In the Feyerabend lecture his claim is that right does not consider the form of the action itself, that is, the structure of an action considered in moral psychology, but only identifies the actions that accord with freedom, in which case the matter can be associated with the content of a list of right actions. Virtue includes in addition the formal structure of a moral action, under which Kant would include the proper incentive. In the *Doctrine of Right* the formal condition is that of a relation between individual decisions, namely that their choices be free. No account of the matter of the choices, i.e. the end to be attained by the actors, is included in the merely formal relationship among powers of choice. In the *Doctrine of Virtue*, the formal condition of freedom is identified as the consistency of the laws when made universal and the material condition of freedom is the matter, an end that is also a duty. These statements about form and matter in "Feyerabend" and in the published works, then, are not contradictory to one another, since in the published works the matter is understood as the end of an action, whereas in "Feyerabend" the matter is the action itself but not the formal structure that would make an action moral.

28 Kant draws this example from David Crantz, *Historie von Grönland* (Leipzig: Heinrich Detlef Ebers, 1765), p. 234. He relied on this book for anecdotes for his Anthropology lectures as well.

29 Hugo Grotius (1583–1645) was a Dutch humanist and natural law theorist famous for his three-volume *De jure belli ac pacis*, "The Law of War and Peace" (Paris: Nicolaus Buon, 1625) in which he held that property is derived from an original common property (Book II, Ch. 2). Samuel Pufendorf (1632–94), was a German philosopher and jurist who presented a secularized natural law theory inspired in part by Grotius. In *De jure naturae et gentium*, "On the Law of Nature and of Nations" (1672) and a shorter summary *De officio hominis et civis juxta legem naturalem*, "On the Duty of Man and Citizen According to Natural Law" (1673), Pufendorf similarly held that property is possible only if there is prior common possession.

30 Núñez Balboa (1475?–1519) was a Spanish explorer who was the first European to see the Pacific Ocean in the Americas. His expedition to the South Seas lasted from 1513 to 1514.

31 It was said of the Roman Emperor Augustus (63 BC–14 AD) that "He always shrank from the title of Lord [*dominus*] as reproachful and insulting," among other signs of modesty (Suetonius, *The Lives of the Twelve Caesars*, trans. J. C. Rolfe (Cambridge, MA: Harvard University Press, 1913), pp. 206–07). Kant is suggesting that Augustus refused the title because it meant "owner" as well as "lord."

32 The Romans called this kind of promise a "stipulation" for unknown reasons. One conjecture that Kant here endorses is provided by Isidore of Seville in *The Etymologies* (v.xxiv.30): "A stipulation is a promise or a pledge, whence stipulators are also called promissors. And stipulation (*stipulatio*) is so called from straw (*stipula*), for the ancients, when they would promise each other something, would break a straw that they were holding; in joining this straw together again

they would acknowledge their pledge. (Or is it because people would have called something firm *stipulus*, according to Paulus the jurist.)" (Isidore of Seville, *The Etymologies*, trans. Stephen Barney, W. J. Lewis, J. A. Beach, and Oliver Berghof (New York: Cambridge University Press, 2006) p. 121).

33 Adam Smith (1723–90), Scottish economist, took grain (using the British term "corn") to be the most accurate cross-temporal and cross-cultural measure of value because he takes the amount of labor used in producing corn to be roughly the same across different grains and different production methods (Adam Smith, *An Inquiry into the Nature and Causes of the Wealth of Nations* (London: Strahan and Cadell, 1776), 1.xi.e.29). Kant misunderstands Smith's theory by overlooking the role of labor: "Labour, then, is the real measure of the exchangeable value of all commodities" (Smith, 1.v.1).

34 Plutarch (46–120) argues that atheism is superior to superstition in *De superstitione*, but does not make the precise point about forgiveness that Kant attributes to him. He does say "The atheist thinks there are no gods; the superstitious man wishes there were none, but believes in them against his will; for he is afraid not to believe" (Plutarch, *Moralia*, Vol. ii, trans. Frank Cole Babbitt (Cambridge, MA: Harvard University Press: 1928) p. 491).

35 Matthew 5:36. In the Luther Bible the passage reads: "Auch sollst du nicht bei deinem Haupt schwören; denn du vermagst nicht ein einziges Haar weiß oder schwarz zu machen," which translates as "And you ought not swear by your head for you cannot make a single hair white or black."

36 The source of Kant's claim about the Tungusi, a Siberian tribe, is unclear. He makes a similar claim about "the Negroes of Guinea" in the *Doctrine of Right* (6:304) as well as the *Physical Geography* (9:415–16) and the Geography lectures (26:278); the material is drawn from travelers' accounts collected in Johann Joachim Schwabe, ed., *Allgemeine Historie der Reisen zu Wasser und zu Lande*, 21 vols. (Leipzig, 1747–74), the third and fourth volumes of which included the relevant material.

37 Kant mentions this oath in his Logic lectures in 1782 as well. After a discussion of the way in which Aristotle was followed "slavishly" and his philosophy revered as almost holy during the "desert of scholastic philosophy," he says, "The Königsberg University had the same, when, because a new Magister had ridiculed Aristotle, he was emphatically prohibited from ever again ridiculing Aristotle in his lectures" (*Logik Hechsel*, p. 24, in Immanuel Kant, *Logik-Vorlesung Unveröffentlichte Nachschriften II*, ed. Tillmann Pinder (Hamburg: Felix Meiner Verlag, 1998), pp. 300–01). Magister is the degree that allowed one to teach private lessons through the university. I thank Werner Stark for the reference.

38 The Thirty-Nine Articles constitute the doctrinal statement of the Church of England. They were codified and approved by Parliament in 1571 after the restoration of Protestant rule with the accession of Queen Elizabeth to the throne.

39 Eviction is not merely expulsion from a property but also, more broadly, the recovery of anything one owns by legal proceeding. In the remainder of this paragraph Kant uses the term in this broader sense.

40 See note 26 above in this section on Hobbes and leaving the state of nature.

41 The Greek Amphictyonic League was a league of confederated Greek cities created to protect sacred places and temples. The cities in the league sent deputies to a council to determine administrative matters for a central shrine and did not discuss political disputes, although member cities pledged not to harm one another.

42 Italian jurist and politician Cesare Beccaria (1738–94) was noted as the major force for penal reform in the European Enlightenment. In his *On Crimes and Punishments* he argued that individuals could not rationally agree in a social contract to surrender their lives because they would be giving up life itself, the greatest of goods, the preservation of which is the main reason individuals would enter a social contract. Further, he claims, individuals have no moral right to dispose of their own lives so they could not have a right to transfer that authority to the state. His book was translated into German as *Abhandlung von den Verbrechen und Strafen* by Albrecht Wittenberg (Hamburg: Bock, 1766), followed quickly by two other translations.

43 Rousseau, *On the Social Contract*, book II, Ch. 5. See note 26 above in this section.

44 Niccolò Machiavelli (1469–1527) was an Italian politician and writer whose *The Prince* (*Il Principe*, published posthumously in Florence in 1532) has been treated as the epitome of power politics in lieu of justice or morality. Like most of those who see Machiavelli in terms of raw unprincipled power politics, Kant was probably unfamiliar with Machiavelli's republicanism and his hope that a prince would use political power in order to found a republic. These views are expressed in the posthumously published *Discourses on Livy* (*Discorsi sopra la prima deca di Tito Livio* (Florence, 1531)).

45 The Monarchomachs were a group of political theorists supporting the right of violence, including tyrannicide, against a ruler thought to be ruling unjustly. Those primarily identified as Monarchomachs were French Calvinists such as Francois Hotman (1524–90) and Theodore Beza (1519–1605), but others have been identified with this approach as well, including the English writer John Milton (1608–74).

46 Kant refers his students to the German translation of a book on the right of nations, Emerich de Vattel, *Le droit des gens, ou Principes de la loi naturelle*, 1758, 2 vols. Vattel (1714–67) was a Swiss intellectual who defended Leibnizian principles. This work, his most famous, essentially popularized the work of Christian Wolff on this topic in Latin, *Jus Gentium* (Halle in Magdeburg, 1749). The specific edition Kant cites and owned is the translation into German by Johann Philip Schulin, *Völkerrecht, oder gründliche Answeisung wie die Grundsäze des natürlichen Rechts auf das Betragen und auf die Angelegenheiten der Nationen und Souveräne angewendet werden müsen* (Frankfurt and Leipzig: 1760) in 3 vols.

47 Kant is using the term *Bürger* to refer to town-dwellers with independent livelihoods. See endnote 12 to "Reflections on the philosophy of right."

Drafts for published works

1 Kuehn, *Kant*, p. 222.
2 As related by Kant's early biographer Wasianski, quoted in Malter, *Rede und Gespräch*, p. 361.

3   In the end Volume 20 came to include Kant's marginal notes in his own copy
     of his early *Observations on the Feeling of the Beautiful and Sublime* (translation
     included in *Notes and Fragments*); his "First Introduction" to the *Critique of the
     Power of Judgment* (translation included in *Critique of the Power of Judgment*); the
     many drafts and final form of his unpublished essay "What Real Progress has
     Metaphysics Made in Germany Since the Time of Leibniz and Wolff?" (trans-
     lation included in *Theoretical Philosophy after 1781*); and a collection of shorter
     material, including drafts of his work against Eberhard (translation included in
     Theoretical Philosophy after 1781), two draft Prefaces for *Religion within the Bound-
     aries of Mere Reason* (not translated in the Cambridge Edition), and Kant's drafts
     of a reply to an early review of his *Doctrine of Right* (translation included in this
     volume).

4   See Stark, *Nachforschungen*, pp. 186–87, 279–319. These tables were essential for
     the identification of the drafts translated in this volume since many were not
     included in the Academy edition.

5   Quoted from Kuehn, *Kant*, p. 240, who draws the quotation from Borowski's
     biography of Kant.

Drafts for Theory and practice

1   The Feyerabend lectures of 1784 note that the people in a civil condition have no
     right to question the legitimacy of the sovereign (27:1383). Earlier Reflections
     show that Kant held this view in the 1770s (see R7812, R7815, R7847).

2   The professor of mathematics is not named in Kant's draft; however the
     Academy edition editor Lehmann, citing Rinke, suggests that he is the mathe-
     matician and all-round critic Abraham Gotthelf Kästner of Göttingen, author of
     the book *Gedanken über das Unvermögen der Schriftsteller Empörungen zu bewirken*
     (Göttingen, 1793) {*Thoughts on the Inability of Writers to Cause an Uprising*}, which
     contains the passage mentioned in the text. The full passage reads "Many Ger-
     man writers wanted to improve the condition of their fatherland and deemed it
     to be too unyielding for them. Some thought this not really evil, as befitting the
     age, and wrote, as was the fashion, of pedagogy, enlightenment, critical philoso-
     phy, human rights; they rolled their empty barrels, but not exactly like Diogenes,
     for whom it was satire, for they believed they were serious." See 23:525, the quo-
     tation is from Kästner, *Gedanken*, pp. 24f.

3   For discussion of Rehberg, see Frederick C. Beiser, *Enlightenment, Revo-
     lution, and Romanticism* (Cambridge, MA: Harvard University Press, 1992),
     pp. 302–09. His claim that metaphysics caused the French Revolution is in his
     collection of essays on the French Revolution: August Wilhelm Rehberg, *Unter-
     suchungen über die Französische Revolution* (Hanover: Christian Ritscher, 1793).

4   Kant does not name his opponent; however, it has been suggested that he is
     responding to claims made by August Wilhelm Rehberg as noted in the editor's
     introduction to this section. See previous endnote.

5   It is not clear which three principles Kant is referring to here.

6   Thomas Hobbes argued that to escape the state of nature, individuals must sur-
     render their "Right of Nature" to the sovereign. He takes "the Right of Nature"
     to be a right to do anything at all that one judges to contribute to preserving one's

life (*Leviathan*, Ch. 14). It is this right that individuals surrender. Hobbes does allow that the right of immediate self-defense cannot be surrendered. See also endnote 26 to "Natural Right course lecture notes by Feyerabend" and endnote 10 to the "Reflections on the philosophy of right."

7 Kant associated Hobbes with Machiavellianism in that he thinks that both allow the sovereign to do anything without any restrictions stemming from morality or right. For more on Machiavelli, see endnote 44 to the "Natural Right course lecture notes by Feyerabend."

8 The number "III" is not preceded by any other numbers but instead corresponds to section III of *Theory and Practice*.

9 Aeon is an alternative name for the Greek god Chronos, a personification of time. The name can also be associated with being or life, and is the root of the English word "æon" or "eon." Here Kant presumably means great beings. See a similar discussion in *Perpetual Peace*, 8:350 note.

Drafts for Toward perpetual peace

1 Information about Kant's work for *Toward Perpetual Peace* is taken from Heiner Klemme's Introduction to his edition of Immanuel Kant, *Über den Gemeinspruch: Das mag in der Theorie richtig sein, taugt aber nicht für die Praxis [und] Zum ewigen Frieden*, ed. Heiner Klemme (Hamburg: Meiner, 1992), pp. x–xii.

2 See, for example, Heinrich Meier in his Introduction to the Academy edition of *Toward Perpetual Peace* (8:506) who considers it "probable" that the Peace of Basel was an influence on Kant's decision. Klemme is rightfully skeptical of this claim, noting that the coincidence of these events is no argument (Klemme, *Frieden*, p. xi).

3 Charles-Irénée Castel, the Abbé St. Pierre (1658–1743), published his *Projet pour rendre la paix perpétuelle en Europe* {Project for Establishing Perpetual Peace in Europe} (Utrecht: A. Schouten, 1713). Kant mentions St. Pierre as early as 1755 when claming that "practicing the rules of Christianity" was "in connection with the Abbe Pierre's proposal, impossible" (R2116, 16:241) in a note for his lectures on Logic regarding the meaning of possibility and impossibility.

4 Stark, *Nachforschungen*.

5 James Harrington (1611–77), a political theorist advocating republicanism, was most famous for *The Commonwealth of Oceana* (London: J. Streater, 1656) in which he presented a utopian society where political authority rested with the landed gentry. Harrington advocated particular reforms, such as an end to primogeniture, a limit to individual ownership of land, a written constitution, and rotation of officeholders. Oliver Cromwell seized copies of *Oceana* during its initial printing but was soon convinced to allow its publication; the published work subsequently included a dedication to Cromwell. Harrington influenced William Penn, who founded the colony of Pennsylvania partly on Harrington's ideals, and others including Montesquieu and the fashioners of the Constitution of the United States.

6 The Graf von Windischgrätz, Joseph Niklas, (1744–1802), was a philosopher, politician, and treasurer of the household of Austrian Duchess Marie Antoinette, later Queen of the French. In 1785 he established a prize competition to

determine a way in which contracts could be written to avoid ambiguity of interpretation. Since of course none of the proposed solutions were plausible, no prize money was awarded.

7 No source connecting this saying to La Mettrie has been found. Rudolf Reicke, the original transcriber of these drafts for his collection *Lose Blätter aus Kants Nachlass* (Königsberg: F. Beyer, 1889–98), read the name as "Lemarti" but after finding no anatomist by that name conjectured (and printed) the name of the anatomist "La Mettrie" (reported by Lehmann, 23:526).

8 Kant elaborates on this reference in the published version, where he has a Bulgarian prince respond to a Greek emperor's challenge to a duel by saying "A smith who has tongs will not lift the glowing iron from the coals with his own hands" (8:354), essentially meaning that the people not the rulers must shed blood in international conflicts. Lehmann identified the Bulgarian Prince as Michael Schischman (Mikhail III) (1280–1330) after contacting the Bulgarian Academy of Sciences (23:526).

9 The quotation comes from Virgil, *Aeneid* 1.294–6, and reads in full: "furor impius intus saeva sedens super arma et centum vinctus aenis post tergum nodis fremet horridus ore cruento" {within, impious Rage, sitting on savage arms, his hands fast bound behind with a hundred brazen knots, shall roar in the ghastliness of blood-stained lips} (Virgil, *Eclogues, Georgics, Aeneid I–VI*, revised edition, trans. H. Rushton Fairclough, rev. G. P. Goold (Cambridge, MA: Harvard University Press, 1999). The English translation in Mary Gregor's edition of *Perpetual Peace* in *Practical Philosophy* at 8:357 reads "within, impious rage – shall roar savagely with bloody mouth."

10 See Kant's discussion of Samoyeds and Finns (Lapps) in the published version at 8:364–65. In a footnote Kant identifies the blood prohibition as addressed to Noah (Genesis 9:4–6) (8:364).

11 Kant discusses the Bedouin Arabs in an even less flattering light in the published version when he says that they claim to have a right to plunder any nomadic tribes that may approach (8:358).

12 In the published version Kant uses the inhabitants of the Barbary Coast as an example of the inhospitality of some coastal peoples, also referencing both robbery and slavery (8:358).

13 Horace, *Ars Poetica*, line 163, speaking of youth (Horace, *Satires, Epistles, and Ars Poetica*, trans. H. Rushton Fairclough (Cambridge, MA: Harvard University Press, 1926)).

14 Friedrich Schlegel's review of *Perpetual Peace* appeared in the journal *Deutschland* 3 (1796) and was reprinted in *Deutschland: eine Zeitschrift*, ed. J. F. Reichardt (Leipzig, 1989), p. 180.

Drafts for the Metaphysics of morals

1 The story of Kant's various descriptions of this project in letters to friends as well as the relation to his work on other publications can be found in detail in Bernd Ludwig, "Einleitung," in Immanuel Kant, *Metaphysische Anfangsgründe der Rechtslehre*, ed. Bernd Ludwig (Hamburg: Felix Meiner Verlag, 1986), pp. xiii–xxiv.

2 In addition to material in his edition of the *Rechtslehre* cited in the previous endote, Ludwig argues the case in detail for the corrupt nature of the text sent to the printer and for his own reconstruction of the text in Bernd Ludwig, *Kants Rechtslehre*, in the series *Kant Forschungen* Band 2, hrsg Reinhard Brandt and Werner Stark (Hamburg: Felix Meiner Verlag, 1988) and through one example in English in Bernd Ludwig, "'The Right of a State' in Immanuel Kant's *Doctrine of Right*," *Journal of the History of Philosophy* 28 (1990): 403–15.

3 In Ludwig, *Anfangsgründe der Rechtslehre*, pp. 201–06.

4 I cite the Cambridge pagination rather than the Academy edition pagination because in at least some editions the correct Academy editions pages are missing from the margins of the Cambridge Edition. The deleted material included in Gregor's footnote begins on 6:250 and continues (as properly marked) through 6:251. This footnote material could be considered a draft. The material in the main text beginning with "Postulate of practical reason with regard to rights" had been moved by Ludwig. It appears in the Academy edition at 6:246 and continues (as properly marked) through 6:247.

5 The deceptive title page is at 20:441. For reproductions of both Kant's handwritten sketch and the deceptive title page as well as a discussion of this particular facet of Lehmann's work, see Stark, *Nachforschungen*, pp. 204–205.

6 Kant had earlier praised Bouterwek for his understanding of Kant's critical philosophy as expressed in material Bouterwek sent Kant summarizing his plans to lecture on Kant's philosophy at the University in Göttingen. In a letter to Bouterwek in May 1793, Kant called it a "well-thought out plan" and added "I always wished but dared not hope for a poetic mind that would have the intellectual power to explain the pure concepts of the understanding and make these principles more readily communicable; for to be able to unite scholastic precision in determining concepts with the popularizing of a flowering imagination is a talent too rare to count on meeting up with very easily" (11:431–32) and in the published response to Bouterwek Kant praised the reviewer for "insight and rigor" (6:356).

7 As noted in the journal of the theologian Johann Friedrich Abegg from Würzburg, who visited his brother the Königsberg merchant Georg Philipp Abegg from May through July 1798 and dined with Kant on June 1 (Malter, *Rede und Gespräch*, p. 444).

8 Although the second edition is dated 1798, it was apparently released in 1799 at the Easter book fair, a traditional time for release of new books (Ludwig, *Anfangsgründe der Rechtslehre*, xxiii).

9 Westphal has translated not only Bouterwek's original review but also his follow-up review of Kant's "Explanatory Remarks." They are published as "Friedrich Bouterwek's reviews of Kant's *Metaphysical Foundations of the Doctrine of Right*," trans. Kenneth R. Westphal, *Kant Studies Online* (2014): 240–61, posted October 1, 2014 at www.kantstudiesonline.net.

10 The parallelism in this sentence suggests that a German word corresponding to the Latin *acquisitio* is missing: Kant equates *Besitznehmung* with *apprehensio*, *Zueignung* with *appropriatio*, and then simply provides *acquisitio* alone. The German term Kant generally uses for acquisition is *Erwerbung*.

11 Kant's reference to Schiller indicates his concern with a "monkish" (*Cartheuser*) morality. Schiller made his famous objection to Kant's moral philosophy in "Über Anmut und Würde," *Neue Thalia* (1793) (On Grace and Dignity), claiming that Kant's morality appears to offer a "gloomy and monkish asceticism." Kant seeks to disavow and avoid this kind of "monkish morality," as he explains in his reply to Schiller in a footnote in the *Religion within the Boundaries of Mere Reason* (6:24 note, cf. 23:98). The Carthusian order of monks and nuns, founded in 1084 by Saint Bruno, lived in quiet solitude isolated from the outside world.

12 Kant refers obliquely to Gotthold Ephraim Lessing (1729–81), who published fragments of a critique of biblical narratives by Hermann Samuel Reimarus (1694–1768), who himself had not published them. Lessing found them in the Wolfenbüttel library in Braunschweig and published them without attribution to Reimarus while replying with his own defense of Christian beliefs. See Kant's reference in the *Religion* (6:81, footnote).

13 Theodor Schmalz (1760–1831) was a professor of law at the university in Rinteln when called to Königsberg in 1788. In the 1790s he also assumed various government posts. He applied Kant's critical ethics to matters of right in his book *Das reine Naturrecht* (Königsberg: F. Nicolovius, 1792), treating the exposition of right as a matter of analysing the concept of freedom.

14 Aristotle's category "ἔχειν" ("habere," to have) is the tenth of Aristotle's categories to receive full treatment (in *Categories* 15) although the eighth on his initial list (*Categories* 4). As typical in Aristotle, he claims that ἔχειν is "said in many ways," one of which is "as a possession (for we are said to have a house and a field)" (*Categories* 15b26–27). In Greek, "to possess" is the most common meaning of ἔχειν. Kant refers to Aristotle's category again at 23:327. I am grateful to Emily Katz for explanations of Aristotle and Greek terminology.

15 μεταβασις εἰς αλλο γενος {change to another kind} is drawn from Aristotle's *Posterior Analytics*, 75a38, where he uses the phrase in noting that one cannot use a method of proof applicable in one area in another area, giving the example of geometry and arithmetic. In his *On the Heavens*, 268b1, he uses the phrase when denying that one can move from body to some further kind as one had been able to move from a line to a surface and from a surface to a three-dimensional body. Kant uses the phrase in the remark on the thesis in the fourth antinomy when arguing that one cannot jump from an empirical regress to a supersensible ground independent of that regress (A458/B486).

16 Virgil, *Aeneid* 6.439. The full sentence is "*Fata obstant, tristique palus inamabilis unda Alligat, et novies Styx interfusa coercet*" (VI, lines 438–39), "Fate withstands; the unlovely mere with its dreary water enchains them, and Styx imprisons with his ninefold circles" (Virgil, *Eclogues, Georgics, Aeneid I–VI*, revised edition, trans. H. Rushton Fairclough, rev. G. P. Goold (Cambridge, MA: Harvard University Press, 1999)). The legendary river Styx wrapped around Hades nine times, making its basin difficult to traverse. Kant uses the simile as a warning against classificatory confusion.

17 A mascopey is a commercial society founded to provide equal benefits.

18 Left-handed marriage is an informal term for morganatic marriage, from the Latin *matrimonium morganaticum*. In Prussia it designated marriage between

partners of different social standing (*Preußisches Allgemeines Landrecht von 1794*, 2:1, §§835–944), which often included a man's marriage to his mistress, cases of pregnancy out of wedlock, and also for love.

Drafts for Conflict of the faculties

1 Arnulf Zweig, translator and editor of Kant's *Correspondence* in the Cambridge Edition of the Works of Immanuel Kant, follows most others in his notes to the letter when identifying the two essays referred to by Kant as those destined to become the first and second parts of *Conflict*. Another commentator who held this view was Arthur Warda, "Der Streit um den *Streit der Fakultäten*," *Kant-Studien* 23 (1919): 385–405. For an argument that Kant was not referring to the Progress essay in this letter, see Reinhard Brandt, "Zum Streit der Fakultäten," in Reinhard Brandt and Werner Stark, eds., *Neue Autographen und Dokumente zu Kants Leben, Schriften, und Vorlesungen*, Kant Forschungen Band 1 (Hamburg: Felix Meiner Verlag, 1987), 31–78, pp. 65–66. Brandt identifies the two essays as the first part of *Conflict*, on the relation between the philosophy and theology faculties, and his unpublished draft for an essay competition"What real progress has metaphysics made in Germany since the time of Leibniz and Wolff?" An excellent source for the development of the Progress essay is Piero Giordanetti's editor's introduction to Immanuel Kant, *Streit der Fakultäten* (Hamburg: Felix Meiner Verlag, 2004).

2 Further, a contemporaneous reprint of the third part of *Theory and Practice* in a journal in 1795 used the title "Is humanity progressing toward the better?" The reprint is "Schreitet die Menschheit zum Bessern fort? von Kant" in *Beiträge zur Beruhigung und Aufklärung über diejenigen Dinge, die dem Menschen unangenehm sind oder sein können, und zur nähern Kenntniß der leidenden Menschheit* 4 (1794): 3–15. This journal, edited by J. S. Fest, was published in Leipzig from 1788 to 1797. See Brandt, "Zum Streit," p. 45.

3 Among the material not included here is a passage from the *Opus Postumum* (22:619–24, the first sheet of the thirteenth convolute). The first two pages of that sheet are a Reinschrift for 7:91–94. The third and fourth pages of the sheet are draft material for a conclusion to the essay substantially different than the published conclusion. This draft conclusion returns to the questions raised in the early sections of the essay about the confirmation of progress and are not directly related to political matters. *Loses Blatt* Kullmann (23:455–59) is also not included because it concerns similar questions about the nature of history and lacks direct relevance to political issues. R1471a (15:650–51) (1790–1804, most likely 1796–98) is identified by Adickes as likely draft for *Conflict* as well, a claim echoed by Lehmann at 23:513. Its content is likewise about history in general rather than political matters.

4 The Directory was the executive institution of the French government from 1795 to 1799, after the Thermidorian Reaction suppressed the radical elements of the French Revolution in 1794–95. A new convention promulgated in August 1795 gave executive power to five directors whose rotating terms were to last five years, while legislative power was assigned to a bicameral legislature. The Directory was given powers to ensure the internal and external safety of the

nation but was still dependent upon the legislature for taxation, declarations of war, and of course designation of the laws. In 1799 Napoleon Bonaparte and others overthrew the Directory and established the Consulate, also made up of an odd number of individuals, presumably for the same transcendental purpose Kant mentions.

5 For an explanation of *Loses Blatt Krakau* and its relation to R8077, see Werner Stark, "Krótkie wyjasnienie historyczne odnoscie Fragmentu krakowskiego" ("Short historical commentary on the 'Krakauer Fragment'"), in: Immanuel Kant, *Spór Fakultetów* (Polish translation of the *Conflict of the Faculties*), ed. and trans. Mirosław Żelazny (Toruń / Lubicz 2003), 169–86. The text of *Loses Blatt Krakau* has been published in *Kantstudien*: Klaus Weyand, "Ein Reinschriftfragment zu Kants Streit der Fakultäten," *Kantschriften* 51 (1959–60): 3–13.

6 Anton Friedrich Büsching (1724–93) was a geographer, minister, and educator. He was superintendent of the Grauen Kloster Gymnasium in Berlin and an advocate for education, although he is most famous for his writings on geography.

7 William Pitt the Younger (1759–1806) was Prime Minister of Britain when the French Revolution broke out and throughout its progress in the 1790s. He had already secured an anti-French alliance even before 1789 and worked to contain the revolutionary fervor to France in part by restricting radicals at home. He defended Britain and British interests when the French declared war in 1793 but did not attempt to overturn the revolution or restore the French monarchy. As the war progressed and the French increasingly threatened Britain, Pitt changed his policy to support restoration.

8 According to Greek legend, Sisyphus displeased the gods and was condemned to roll a large stone up a hill, only to have the stone roll down from the top, forcing Sisyphus to repeat his task eternally.

9 For information about the French Directory, see endnote 4 for this section. In Britain war-making powers reside entirely with the monarch or the ministry acting in the name of the monarch through a royal prerogative, although as Kant goes on to discuss, funding to pay for a war has to be approved by Parliament.

10 The Habeas Corpus Act, enacted by the English Parliament in 1679, codified the practice of requiring courts to have a lawful reason for jailing a person. Although this practice had been in use for centuries, the Parliament's Act was the first to enact a law requiring due process in detaining individuals as a means to check potential arbitrary arrests.

11 In 1773, Christian and Rosine Arnold, who operated a watermill on land belonging to the Landrat von Gersdorff, were unable to make their annual payment to the lord. The lord had them brought before a court in which he himself was the judge and ordered the mill to be auctioned off to raise the money. A higher court upheld the ruling. The Arnolds petitioned King Frederick II (the Great), who considered the process unjust, intervened to reverse the ruling, and had the judges of the higher court removed. Although it appears that the king had acted to right an injustice, this case has generally been regarded as a landmark example of the misuse of executive power in interference with judicial proceedings. See David M. Luebke, "Frederick the Great and the Celebrated Case of the Millers Arnold (1770–1779): A Reappraisal," *Central European History* 32 (1999): 379–408.

Index

a priori conditions, 264–65, 319
a priori principles, 190, 213, 237, 263,
    347, 360
abandonment, 118, 145–46, 193
abeyance, thing in, 63, 117, 122, 125,
    127, 144–45
absolute value, 90, 386
Academy edition, xviii–xix, xxiii–xxvi,
    xxxiii, xxxiv, 3, 5, 76–77, 79,
    183–85, 190–92, 223, 386
    pagination, 5, 77, 185–86, 386
acceptans, 122, 126, 129, 134–35, 148, *see
    also* accepter
acceptatio, 122, 124, 129, 132
accepter, 122–23, 124–25, 127
accession, 116–17, 121, 257, 389
accessories, 116–18
accessory conventions, 139
Achenwall, Gottfried, xvi, xvii,
    xxvii–xxviii, 3–4, 5–6, 11, 21, 75,
    78–79, 94, 386–88
acquirability, 252, 257, 260
acquirable objects, 260, 310
acquisition, 111, 116–18, 149–50, 199,
    257–59, 265–66, 302–03, 310,
    312–13, 314–15, 322–23, 352
    first, 199, 250, 275, 312–13, 319
    of land, 314
    manner of, 208–09
    original, 121, 250, 260
    outer, 259, 310, 312
    right of, 258, 259, 261, 285
    rightful, 121, 257, 259, 271, 273, 302,
        336
    of rights, xxviii, 33, 250
    unilateral, 285, 318
action, equality of, 101
actions
    determinate, 248

free, 15, 45, 93, 98, 109, 238, 388
    moral, 88, 89, 94
acts, 12–14, 85–86, 91–92, 100–01,
    138–39, 235–37, 242–46, 263–64,
    313–14, 315–19, 329–32, 335–37
    juridical, 111, 199–200, 318
    of possession (*actus possessorii*), 112,
        114, 127–28
    rightful, 24, 290, 308–10, 312–17,
        318–19, 323
    unilateral, 257, 259, 260, 276, 322, 351
Adickes, Erich, xix–xxv, 3–5, 183–84,
    186, 191, 386
administration, 21, 28, 32, 36, 43, 52, 56,
    62, 148–49, 165, 167, 374–76
    external, 170, 393
    of justice, 8, 21, 337
affirmative obligation, 96, 107
age of majority, 353
agents, 97, 138, 329, 354
agreement, 90–92, 98–99, 158, 235–36,
    257–58, 273–74, 280, 283–84,
    296–97, 312–13, 325–26, 360
    of powers of choice, 254, 321
alienation, 25, 26, 29, 115, 119, 120, 122,
    131, 135–36, 345, 349, 374–76
analytic law, 237, 280
analytic(al) principles, 212, 244, 271,
    295, 297–98
anarchy, 10, 220, 329–30
anthropology, iii, xxi, xxvi, 4–7, 207
antinomy, xxxii, 250, 261, 263, 266–67,
    269, 272, 274, 276, 284, 321, 329
antithesis, 261, 268, 320–22, 325, 329
appearance, xxv, 224, 252–53, 269–70,
    271, 285–86, 309, 320, 370, 376
apprehensio, xxxii, 110–11, 238, 256, 305,
    311, 314–15, *see also* taking
    possession

414

Index

Index

loose sheets, xvi–xxiii, xxv–xxvii, 9, 72,
183–89, 197–98, 216–17, 230–35,
238–41, 284–86, 337–39, 359–61
lords, 22, 27, 28, 32, 39–40, 45, 49, 177,
180, 201, 209, 371
supreme, 50, 52–53, 62, 64
loses Blatt, see loose sheets
loss, 42, 47, 59, 133, 148, 151, 154,
223

Machiavelli, Niccolò, 177
magistrates, 40, 56–59, 167, 210
maintenance, 26, 34, 168, 322, 353
majesty, 35, 44, 54, 167, 226, 336
right of, 334–35
majority, age of, 353
mala fide possessor, see bad faith
possession
mandat (commission), 138, 179
mandatarius (delegate), 138, 179, 354
manner of acquisition, 208–09
manuscripts, xii, xviii, xxvi, 75–78, 79,
185–86, 205, 223, 230
marriage, xxvii–xxviii, xxxii, 24–25, 26,
45, 102, 105, 159, 160–61,
341–43, 350–52, 392
contracts, 26, 161, 343, 349, 351
masters, 9, 106, 160, 162–63, 176, 236,
259, 276, 353, 371, 381, 392
material, xv–xvi, xvii–xxii, xxv–xxvi,
xxviii–xxx, xxxv, 7, 72, 76–78,
183–86, 190–91, 229–31, 234,
358
deleted, 230
draft, xxiii, 183, 229
quantity of surviving draft arguments
for, xxviii, 184
matrimonium, 24, 159, 160–61, *see also*
marriage
maxims, 42–43, 224–25, 236–37, 238,
241–45, 246–48, 299, 300–02,
306, 309, 333, 338
of actions, 233, 242, 245
good, 68, 243
members, 22–23, 38, 39–40, 54, 159–60,
191, 197–98, 200–01, 294–95,
337–38, 347, 353–54
mendacium, 108, *see also* deceit
merit, 39, 198, 220–21
metaphysics, xxi–xxii, 4, 5, 7, 184, 190,
192, 196–97, 207, 229, 237,
240–41

Metaphysics of Morals, vii, xxii,
xxvii–xxviii, xxx, xxxii–xxxiii, 71,
76, 77, 184, 186, 227–33
military government, 53
mine and yours
distinction of, 251, 253, 266, 271, 303
possession of, 280, 295
mixed types of government, 166, 173
mob rule, 63, 195, 211, 220
modality, 256, 275, 279, 300, 302
modus acquirendi (means of acquisition),
57, 111, 116, 118, 121, 122,
161–62
monarchs, 33, 36, 41–42, 53, 55, 58–59,
65, 166–67, 171–73, 177, 339,
365–66
hereditary, 172, 287, 339
monarchy, xvi, 78, 166, 171–73, 177,
211, 216, 226, 234, 329–30, 394
universal, 67, 219, 240
money, 47, 81, 84, 92, 115, 119, 130–31,
132–33, 136–37, 139–41, 168,
364
moral actions, 88, 89, 94
moral concept, 249, 331
moral disposition, 234, 239, 250
moral laws, 30, 88–89, 196, 220, 224,
234, 328, 331
moral necessitation, 89, 95, 248
moral persons, 45, 194, 226, 341, 351
moral philosophy, 14, 76
moral principles, 88, 107, 142, 190, 198,
224, 241
morality, 14, 16, 90–91, 102–03, 192–93,
212–13, 225, 226, 242–43,
337–38, 363–64, 372
morals, 76, 83, 88–89, 98, 99, 107, 229,
231, 241, 248, 372–73, 381
doctrine of, 236, 246
motives, 68, 95, 242, 245, 350, 369, 381
Mrongovius metaphysics lectures, 76
murderers, 46–47, 60, 176, 336, 338
mutual relations, 273, 280, 297

nations, xxxiii, 64, 67–68, 69, 174,
178–79, 217, 219, 222–23, 374,
381, 395
league of, 67–69, 174, 178, 337, 374,
380
right of, 42, 62, 67, 177–78, 196–97,
208, 214, 217–20, 223, 375, 383,
394–95